THE INTERNATIONAL COURT OF JUSTICE AND SELF-DEFENCE IN INTERNATIONAL LAW

The legal rules governing the use of force between states is one of the most fundamental, and the most controversial, aspects of international law. An essential part of this subject is the question of when and to what extent a state may lawfully use force against another in self-defence. The parameters of this inherent right remain obscure, despite the best efforts of scholars and, notably, the International Court of Justice.

This book examines the burgeoning relationship between the ICJ and the right of self-defence. Since 2003 there have been three major decisions of the ICJ that have dealt directly with the law governing self-defence actions, in contrast to only two such cases in the preceding fifty years. This, then, is an opportune moment to reconsider the jurisprudence of the Court on this issue. This book is the first of its kind to comprehensively draw together and then assess the merits of this jurisprudence. It argues that the contribution of the ICJ has been confused and unhelpful, and compounds inadequacies in existing customary international law. The ICJ's fundamental conception of a primary criterion of 'armed attack' as constituting a qualitatively grave use of force is brought into question. The book then goes on to examine the underlying causes of the problems that have emerged in the jurisprudence on this crucial issue.

Studies in International Law: Volume 25

Studies in International Law

Volume 1: Between Light and Shadow: The World Bank, the International Monetary Fund and International Human Rights Law
Mac Darrow

Volume 2: Toxics and Transnational Law: International and European Regulation of Toxic Substances as Legal Symbolism
Marc Pallemaerts

Volume 3: The Chapter VII Powers of the United Nations Security Council
Erika de Wet

Volume 4: Enforcing International Law Norms Against Terrorism
Edited by Andrea Bianchi

Volume 5: The Permanent International Criminal Court
Edited by Dominic McGoldrick, Peter Rowe and Eric Donnelly.

Volume 6: Regional Organisations and the Development of Collective Security *Ademola Abass*

Volume 7: Islamic State Practices, International Law and the Threat from Terrorism: A Critique of the 'Clash of Civilisations' in the New World Order
Javaid Rehman

Volume 8: Predictablity and Flexibility in the Law of Maritime Delimitation
Yoshifumi Tanaka

Volume 9: Biotechnology and International Law
Edited by Francesco Francioni and Tullio Scovazzi

Volume 10: The Development of Human Rights Law by the Judges of the International Court of Justice
Shiv Bedi

Volume 11: The Environmental Accountability of the World Bank to Third-Party Non-state Actors
Alix Gowlland-Gualtieri

Volume 12: Transnational Corporations and Human Rights
Edited by Olivier De Schutter

Volume 13: Biotechnologies and International Human Rights
Edited by Francesco Francioni

Volume 14: Human Security and International Law: Prospects and Problems
Barbara Von Tigerstrom

Volume 15: The Arms Trade and International Law
Zeray Yihdego

Volume 16: Africa: Mapping New Boundaries in International Law
Edited by Jeremy Levitt

Volume 17: Forced Migration, Human Rights and Security
Edited by Jane McAdam

Volume 18: The Use of Nuclear Weapons and the Protection of the Environment during International Armed Conflict
Erik Koppe

Volume 19: The Shifting Allocation of Authority in International Law: Considering Sovereignty, Supremacy and Subsidiarity
Edited by Tomer Broude and Yuval Shany

Volume 20: Counterterrorism: Democracy's Challenge
Edited by Andrea Bianchi and Alexis Keller

Volume 21: Amnesty, Human Rights and Political Transitions
Louise Mallinder

Volume 22: Property Rights and Natural Resources
Richard Barnes

Volume 23: Human Dignity and the Foundations of International Law
Patrick Capps

Volume 24: Sovereignty and the Stateless Nation: Gibraltar in the Modern Legal Context
Keith Azopardi

The International Court of Justice and Self-Defence in International Law

James A Green

• HART •
PUBLISHING

OXFORD AND PORTLAND, OREGON
2009

Published in North America (US and Canada) by
Hart Publishing
c/o International Specialized Book Services
920 NE 58th Avenue, Suite 300
Portland, OR 97213-3786
USA
Tel: +1-503-287-3093 or toll-free: 1-800-944-6190
Fax: +1-503-280-8832
E-mail: orders@isbs.com
Website: www.isbs.com

Hart Publishing Ltd, 16C Worcester Place, Oxford, OX1 2JW
Telephone: +44 (0)1865 517530 Fax: +44 (0)1865 510710
E-mail: mail@hartpub.co.uk
Website: www.hartpub.co.uk

British Library Cataloguing in Publication Data
Data Available

ISBN: 978-1-84113-876-3

Typeset by Hope Services, Abingdon, Oxon
Printed and bound in Great Britain by
CPI Antony Rowe Ltd, Chippenham, Wiltshire

Preface

I was just about to embark on my doctoral studies in the autumn of 2003 when the International Court of Justice produced its merits decision in the *Case Concerning Oil Platforms*. That decision—with its implications for and place in the development of the jurisprudence of the Court on self-defence—helped to shape a research agenda that ran for the next five years. This work therefore began life as a PhD thesis, which was ultimately submitted at the University of Nottingham in the autumn of 2007.

During the writing of that thesis and its subsequent morphing in to this monograph form, I benefited from the help and support of numerous people. The most important amongst them are my PhD supervisors, Dino Kritsiotis (University of Nottingham) and Robert McCorquodale (University of Nottingham and now also Director of the British Institute of International and Comparative Law), to whom I express my deepest gratitude for all of their advice and encouragement. I also would like to acknowledge the support offered more generally by the University of Nottingham (particularly the School of Law) during my time there and to thank staff and friends at the University. I would similarly like to thank friends and colleagues at the University of Reading and other academic colleagues throughout the United Kingdom and beyond. I would especially like to highlight the contributions of Sandy Ghandhi (University of Reading) and Christopher Waters (University of Windsor) in terms of their support and guidance over recent years. I also want to express my gratitude to my PhD examiners, Christine Gray (University of Cambridge) and Colin Warbrick (University of Birmingham), whose comments on and criticisms of my thesis were invaluable contributions to its development into this final form.

I wish to acknowledge the financial assistance of the Arts and Humanities Research Council. The production of my doctoral thesis—and therefore this monograph—would have not been possible were it not for the support generously provided by that body between 2003 and 2006. This work benefited greatly from the time I spent conducting research at the University of Michigan in 2005. I would like to thank the University for awarding me a research scholarship and for all the support I received from staff and fellow researchers whilst I was in Ann Arbor. This research visit was also sponsored by the Arts and Humanities Research Council, which I again would like to acknowledge.

Finally, I want to thank my parents for their unwavering love and support in all of my endeavours, academic or otherwise, and Lia, for making me happy.

It is my intention that, so far as possible, the material herein is current as of 1 December 2008. Any errors in this work, be they small or not so small, are mine and mine alone.

James A Green
University of Reading
December 2008

Contents

Table of Cases

Table of International Treaties and Conventions

Introduction

The conditions for the exercise of self-defence are well settled.

International Court of Justice, *Case Concerning Oil Platforms* (2003)[1]

Self-defence is still largely obscure from a legal point of view.

HE Judge Pieter Kooijmans, International Court of Justice (1997–2006)[2]

I. THE INTERNATIONAL COURT OF JUSTICE AND SELF DEFENCE

INTERNATIONAL EVENTS SINCE the turn of the century have had a significant impact on the perception, academic and public, of the international law on the use of force (the *jus ad bellum*).[3] More specifically, it is certainly arguable that the attacks of 11 September 2001, the subsequent intervention of coalition forces in Afghanistan (2001) and Iraq (2003) and the emergence of a contentious doctrine of pre-emption (the so-called 'Bush Doctrine')[4] have influenced the content of this area of international law.[5]

An essential aspect of the *jus ad bellum* is the inherent right of self-defence. Indeed, it represents one of only two universally accepted exceptions to the legal prohibition on the use of military force and is the only indisputable basis under which a state may resort to force unilaterally. Given the current potential for paradigmatic shifts in the law on the use of force, it is crucial that the rules governing actions taken in self-defence be

[1] *Case Concerning Oil Platforms (Islamic Republic of Iran v United States of America)* merits (2003) ICJ Reports 161, para 76.

[2] P Kooijmans, 'The International Court of Justice in the Twenty-First Century: What Lies Ahead?' British Institute of International and Comparative Law Annual Lecture, 12 December 2006. A version of this lecture has since appeared in print, although the quoted passage is absent: P Kooijmans, 'The ICJ in the 21st Century: Judicial Restraint, Judicial Activism, or Proactive Judicial Policy' (2007) 53 *International and Comparative Law Quarterly* 741.

[3] As Gray has put this, 11 September 'led to a fundamental reappraisal of the law on self-defence'. C Gray, *International Law and the Use of Force*, 3rd edn (Oxford, Oxford University Press, 2008) 193.

[4] First articulated by the United States in 2002. See, eg, the National Security Strategy of the United States of America, September 2002, available at www.whitehouse.gov/nsc/nss.pdf. We will return to this document in ch 2, section VI-A.

[5] Eg, it has been argued that 11 September and the forcible responses to it 'represent a new paradigm in the international law relating to the use of force'. D Brown, 'Use of Force against Terrorism after September 11th: State Responsibility, Self-Defence and Other Responses' (2003–04) 11 *Cardozo Journal of International and Comparative Law* 1, 2.

carefully scrutinised. Running parallel to this increased scrutiny and influence of the law in this area has been a greatly increased jurisprudential contribution from the International Court of Justice (ICJ) with regard to the specific circumstances under which force may be lawfully used in self-defence; there have been a succession of post-millennial decisions of the Court that relate to this issue. This book focuses on the law of self-defence through an examination of the relationship between the ICJ and the legal rules in this fundamental area of international law.

No state would deny that a right of unilateral self-defence exists in international law.[6] The existence of the right in the period following the inception of the United Nations (UN) is confirmed by Article 51 of the UN Charter. That Article provides a codification of the right of self-defence, both individual and collective:

> Nothing in the present Charter shall impair the inherent right of individual or collective self-defence if an armed attack occurs against a Member of the United Nations, until the Security Council has taken measures necessary to maintain international peace and security. Measures taken by Members in the exercise of this right of self-defence shall be immediately reported to the Security Council and shall not in any way affect the authority and responsibility of the Security Council under the present Charter to take at any time such action as it deems necessary in order to maintain or restore international peace and security.

Article 51 therefore sets out the basic UN-era rules on self-defence. However, it is also undeniable that the right of self-defence is, at least to some extent, governed by customary international law. There are crucial and universally accepted legal criteria that appear in customary international law but are not set out in Article 51 at all, most notably the requirements of necessity and proportionality. The relationship between Article 51 and the customary rules on self-defence will be a central theme of this work, and the question of how treaty law and custom interrelate in this area will be returned to.[7] For the present, however, it is simply necessary to keep in mind that self-defence derives from two different 'sources' of international law.[8]

[6] Here 'unilateral' is used to indicate the lack of authorisation by the United Nations Security Council, and not necessarily that the defensive action was taken by a single state; action in self-defence can be collective.

[7] See especially ch 3.

[8] The traditional reference point for the 'sources' of international law in the UN era is Art 38 of the Statute of the ICJ:

> 1. The Court, whose function is to decide in accordance with international law such disputes as are submitted to it, shall apply:
>   a. international conventions, whether general or particular, establishing rules expressly recognized by the contesting states;
>   b. international custom, as evidence of a general practice accepted as law;
>   c. the general principles of law recognized by civilized nations;

cont. over/

The ongoing importance of the right of self-defence can be seen from the fact that in the UN era, states have justified international uses of force (as opposed to wholly 'internal' conflicts) as being lawful instances of self-defence on a consistent and regular basis. In 1961, Rosalyn Higgins stated, 'The plea of self-defence is perhaps the most frequently heard justification for a particular use of force.'[9] In the intervening years since then, little has changed in terms of the regularity of the invocation of the right. As Christine Gray put it more recently, 'States using force against another state *almost invariably* invoke self-defence' (emphasis added).[10]

It is impossible to quantify conclusively the number of international disputes involving the use of force since 1945, let alone to specify with any certainty the number of such instances in which a legal claim of self-defence was made. What may be said is that in the majority of disputes involving the use of force, at least one claim is made under the right of self-defence. Writing in 1987, Oscar Schachter contended that the number of use of force disputes since 1945 was 'surely in the hundreds'.[11] Even a cursory glace at this plethora of state practice clearly demonstrates the regularity and consistency of self-defence claims in the UN era.[12]

In contrast to the numerous invocations of self-defence by states in the UN era, the ICJ has produced only a handful of merits decisions in contentious cases that substantially deal with this area of the law. Given the regularity of self-defence claims made by states, this discrepancy is

d. subject to the provisions of Art 59, judicial decisions and the teachings of the most highly qualified publicists of the various nations, as subsidiary means for the determination of rules of law.

2. This provision shall not prejudice the power of the Court to decide a case *ex aequo et bono*, if the parties agree thereto.

[9] R Higgins, 'The Legal Limits to the Use of Force by Sovereign States: United Nations Practice' (1961) 37 *British Yearbook of International Law* 269, 297. Similarly, Schachter has said: 'When [states] have used force, they have nearly always claimed self-defence as their legal justification. Governments disputing that claim have usually asserted that the legal conditions of self-defence were not met in the particular case.' O Schachter, 'Self-Defence and the Rule of Law' (1989) 83 *American Journal of International Law* 259, 259.

[10] Gray, *International Law and the Use of Force* (n 3) 114.

[11] O Schachter, 'Disputes Involving the Use of Force' in LF Damrosch (ed), *The International Court of Justice at a Crossroads* (New York, Transnational, 1987) 223. In 1997, Weisburd asserted that in the period between the end of the Second World War and the Iraqi invasion of Kuwait in 1990, there were over 110 distinct instances in which force was used in an international context. AM Weisburd, *Use of Force: The Practice of States Since World War II* (University Park, Pennsylvania State University Press, 1997) 308. The current author would argue that this estimate is somewhat conservative. More recently, Gray has contended that 'over a hundred *major* conflicts [have occurred] since 1945' (emphasis added). C Gray, 'The Use of Force and the International Legal Order' in MD Evans (ed), *International Law*, 2nd edn (Oxford, Oxford University Press, 2006) 589, 589.

[12] This is not to say that in all cases in which a claim of self-defence could be advanced, such a claim has in fact been put forward. Eg, one may reference the somewhat mysterious Israeli raid into the Tall al-Abyad region of Syria in 2007: Israel simply did not set out any legal justification for the action. See JA Green, 'An Unusual Silence' (2007) 157 *New Law Journal* 1478. However, such incidents are notable by reason of their comparative uniqueness.

particularly notable. The ICJ is 'the principal judicial organ of the United Nations',[13] and as the UN itself is the closest thing that international relations has to a central organisational structure, the ICJ therefore represents the primary organ for inter-state adjudication.[14] The position of the Court regarding self-defence, or indeed any issue of international law, is of great importance to the application and development of that law. As has been pointed out:

> Although in principle the Court's judgments are binding only with respect to the particular case and the parties involved, their impact and influence in state practice and judicial and arbitral decisions are well known, so any statement made by the Court could become a landmark in the current debate on self-defence.[15]

However, in the context of self-defence the involvement of the Court has traditionally been limited.[16] Before 1986, the view of the ICJ on the law governing self-defence was almost nonexistent. Because of this, Bhupinder Singh Chimni stated in 1986 that 'in the past 40 years the International Court has not played a very significant role in containing major conflicts which have affected international society'.[17]

On 27 June of that same year, the ICJ delivered its merits judgment in the case of *Military and Paramilitary Activities in and against Nicaragua* (hereafter *Nicaragua*).[18] In that decision, the Court did—for the first time—tackle much of the law of self-defence head on, delivering an extensive decision that undoubtedly provides a conception of the law in this area. The *Nicaragua* decision is therefore crucial for our analysis, still representing, as it does, the Court's first and most complete assessment of self-defence. Moreover, the *Nicaragua* decision had the effect of beginning a

[13] UN Charter, Art 92; Statute of the International Court of Justice 1945, Art 1. The ICJ was established by the UN Charter and is the successor to the Permanent Court of International Justice. The statute under which it functions is based upon the Permanent Court's Statute (UN Charter, Art 92).

[14] ND White, *The United Nations System: Towards International Justice* (London, Lynne Rienner, 2002) 111–14 and 117–19.

[15] N Ochoa-Ruiz and E Salamanca-Aguado, 'Exploring the Limits of International Law Relating to the Use of Force in Self-Defence' (2005) 16 *European Journal of International Law* 499, 501.

[16] Of course, it may be said that the number of cases heard by the ICJ relating to *any* area of international law is but a small percentage of the total number of disputes that have arisen between states since the Court's inception. On this basis, it has been argued that once a dispute has been identified, there is a 'presumption against' states turning to the ICJ as a settlement mechanism. See MW Janis, 'The International Court' in MW Janis (ed), *International Courts for the Twenty-First Century* (Dordrecht, Martinus Nijhoff, 1992) 19–20. However, it would seem that this discrepancy is particularly pronounced in relation to disputes concerning the use of force, such as those relating to self-defence.

[17] BS Chimni, 'The International Court and the Maintenance of Peace and Security: The *Nicaragua* Decision and the United States Response' (1986) 35 *International and Comparative Law Quarterly* 960, 969.

[18] *Military and Paramilitary Activities in and against Nicaragua* (*Nicaragua v United States of America*) merits (1986) ICJ Reports 14.

relationship between the law on the use of force and the ICJ that had previously not existed.

Since *Nicaragua*, there has been a notable increase in the number of applications to the Court that relate in some measure to aspects of the *jus ad bellum*. There have been twenty-six contentious applications on matters related to a use of force by at least one state party since 1986.[19] This is almost double the number of such applications filed with the Court's Registry in the forty-year period between the ICJ's inception and 1986.[20]

[19] These were: *Border and Transborder Armed Actions* (*Nicaragua v Costa Rica*) application instituting proceedings (1986) ICJ Pleadings 3; *Aerial Incident of 3 July 1988* (*Iran v United States*) application instituting proceedings (1989) ICJ Pleadings vol I, 3; *Border and Transborder Armed Actions* (*Nicaragua v Honduras*) jurisdiction of the court and admissibility of the application (1988) ICJ Reports 69; *Territorial Dispute* (*Libya/Chad*) merits (1994) ICJ Reports 6 (though this decision at no point *directly* referred to the use of force); *Fisheries Jurisdiction* (*Spain v Canada*) jurisdiction of the court (1998) ICJ Reports 430; *Application of the Convention on the Prevention and Punishment of the Crime of Genocide* (*Croatia v Yugoslavia*) application instituting proceedings (1999) www.icj-cij.org/docket/files/118/7125.pdf; *Maritime Delimitation between Nicaragua and Honduras in the Caribbean Sea* (*Nicaragua v Honduras*) application instituting proceedings (1999) www.icj-cij.org/docket/files/120/7083.pdf; *Legality of Use of Force* (*Yugoslavia v Spain*) provisional measures order (1999) ICJ Reports 761; *Legality of Use of Force* (*Yugoslavia v United States*) provisional measures order (1999) ICJ Reports 915; *Aerial Incident of 10 August 1999* (*Pakistan v India*) jurisdiction of the court (2000) ICJ Reports 10; *Armed Activities on the Territory of the Congo* (*DRC v Rwanda*) application instituting proceedings (1999) www.icj-cij.org/docket/files/117/7071.pdf; *Armed Activities on the Territory of the Congo* (*DRC v Burundi*) application instituting proceedings (1999) www.icj-cij.org/docket/files/115/7127.pdf; *Land and Maritime Boundary between Cameroon and Nigeria* (*Cameroon v Nigeria: Equatorial Guinea intervening*) merits (2002) ICJ Reports 9; *Oil Platforms* merits (n 1); Eight more *Legality of Use of Force* cases (*Serbia and Montenegro v Belgium; Canada; France; Germany; Italy; Netherlands; Portugal* and the *United Kingdom*) all preliminary objections (2004) all available from www.icj-cij.org/docket/index.php?p1=3&p2=3; *Armed Activities on the Territory of the Congo* (*Democratic Republic of the Congo v Uganda*) merits (2005) www.icj-cij.org/docket/files/116/10455.pdf; *Armed Activities on the Territory of the Congo* (*New Application: 2002*) (*DRC v Rwanda*) jurisdiction of the court and admissibility of the application (2006) www.icj-cij.org/docket/files/126/7070.pdf; *Application of the Convention on the Prevention and Punishment of the Crime of Genocide* (*Bosnia Herzegovina v Serbia and Montenegro* merits (2007) www.icj-cij.org/docket/files/91/13685.pdf (though the initial request contained in the Application of Bosnia-Herzegovina that the Court adjudge and declare on use of force aspects of the dispute was ultimately dropped from the submissions of that State); and *Application of the International Convention on the Elimination of All Forms of Racial Discrimination* (*Georgia v Russian Federation*) provisional measures order (2008) www.icj-cij.org/docket/files/140/14801.pdf (though, whilst Georgia raised various issues relating to the use of force in its pleadings, the sole base of the Court's jurisdiction is the International Convention on the Elimination of All Forms of Racial Discrimination of 1965. As such, the Court is not directly able to examine use of force issues).

[20] Fourteen such applications were filed between 1945 and 1986. Of these, only four resulted in merits decisions: *Corfu Channel* (*United Kingdom v Albania*) merits (1949) ICJ Reports 4; *United States Diplomatic and Consular Staff in Tehran* (*United States v Iran*) merits (1980) ICJ Reports 3; *Frontier Dispute* (*Burkina Faso/Mali*) merits (1986) ICJ Reports 554; and *Nicaragua* merits (n 18) itself. The remaining ten applications were either dismissed or discontinued. These were: *Treatment in Hungary of Aircraft and Crew of the United States of America* (*United States v Soviet Union*) (1954) ICJ Reports 99; *Treatment in Hungary of Aircraft and Crew of the United States of America* (*United States v Hungary*) (1954) ICJ Reports 103; *Aerial Incident of 7 October 1952* (*United States v Soviet Union*) order (1956) ICJ Reports 9; *Aerial Incident of 10 March 1953* (*United States v Czechoslovakia*) order (1956) ICJ Reports 4; *Aerial Incident of 7 November 1954* (*United States v Soviet Union*) order (1959) ICJ Reports 276; *Aerial Incident*

Further, it is evident that in many instances, these pre-1986 cases were only indirectly related to a use of force, or in the event resulted in little examination by the Court of the relevant substantive law.[21] In contrast, the applications since the *Nicaragua* judgment have for the most part explicitly requested a finding that a state party has used force unlawfully. Therefore, it can be seen that the ICJ is not only being called upon more regularly to resolve disputes that relate to the use of force but also to determine whether force has been used by one or more state party and whether that force amounts to a lawful or an unlawful action.

This increase is arguably symptomatic of a growing perception that the Court has an important role to play in the cessation of violent conflicts and the maintenance of international peace and security, or at least a growing willingness on the part of states to turn to the Court in such circumstances. Indeed, it is very telling that during her speech to the General Assembly regarding the annual report of the ICJ in October 2006, the Court's President, Judge Higgins, stated: 'Another category of cases which is *frequently* referred to the Court concerns the use of force' (emphasis added).[22] It is unthinkable that such a statement would have been made when Judge Higgins first came to the Court in 1995.

It would be reasonable to assume that the increased reliance on the Court in the context of the use of force, and specifically with regard to self-defence claims, may lead to a corresponding increase in the contribution made by the Court in this area of international law. Indeed, this has certainly been the case, although it was a further ten years on from *Nicaragua* before the Court again dealt substantively with self-defence. This was in its advisory opinion on the *Legality of the Threat or Use of Nuclear Weapons* (hereafter *Nuclear Weapons*).[23] Moreover, it was not until 2003 that the Court again decided a contentious case on the merits by way of reference to the law governing self-defence, in the *Case Concerning Oil Platforms* (hereafter *Oil Platforms*).[24]

Notably, since the turn of the century there have been three decisions in which the Court has contributed to its jurisprudence on the issue of self-defence: *Oil Platforms* (2003), *Legal Consequences of the Construction of a Wall*

of 4 September 1954 (*United States v Soviet Union*) (1958) ICJ Reports 158; *Aerial Incident of 27 July 1955* (*United Kingdom v Bulgaria*) order (1959) ICJ Reports 264; *Aerial Incident of 27 July 1955* (*United States v Bulgaria*) order (1960) ICJ Reports 146; *Aerial Incident of 27 July 1955* (*Israel v Bulgaria*) preliminary objections (1959) ICJ Reports 127; and *Trial of Pakistani Prisoners of War* (*Pakistan v India*) (1973) ICJ Reports 328. In addition, obiter remarks relating to the law on the use of force have been made in other cases, eg, the *Fisheries Jurisdiction* (*United Kingdom v Iceland*) jurisdiction of the court (1973) ICJ Reports 3, 14.

21 Schachter, 'Disputes Involving the Use of Force' (n 11) 223–27.

22 Speech by HE Judge Rosalyn Higgins, President of the International Court of Justice, to the General Assembly of the United Nations, 26 October 2006, http://www.icj-cij.org/presscom/index.php?pr=1874&p1=6&p2=1&search=%22higgins+speech+2006%22.

23 *Legality of the Threat or Use of Nuclear Weapons* advisory opinion (1996) ICJ Reports 226.

24 *Oil Platforms* merits (n 1).

in the Occupied Palestinian Territory (2004) (hereafter *Israeli Wall*)[25] and *Armed Activities on the Territory of the Congo* (*Democratic Republic of the Congo v Uganda*) (2005) (hereafter *DRC v Uganda*).[26] In contrast, only two cases (*Nicaragua* and *Nuclear Weapons*) appeared in the preceding *fifty-eight years* of the Court's existence. Whilst the *Nicaragua* case was examined by scholars to a certain extent when it emerged, a comprehensive assessment of the relationship between the ICJ and the international law governing forcible responses taken in self-defence—taking into account recent decisions—has not as yet been produced, and a number of factors make it more desirable than ever that this is done. These include the unprecedented emergence of three judgments that deal substantively with self-defence in a three-year period; the corresponding increase of applications to the Court relating to the use of force since the *Nicaragua* case; and the general scrutiny of forcible intervention and the international legal system's (in)ability to restrain it following 11 September 2001.

This work aims to clarify the position taken by the Court with regard to the law governing self-defence and to test the validity and coherence of that position. Its purpose is not to provide a comprehensive study of the law governing self-defence. Nor does this book offer a general examination of the ICJ as an institution of the UN. Instead, the following represents an attempt to identify the crucial aspects of the jurisprudence of the Court governing self-defence and to analyse the picture that emerges through an assessment of both the law and the ICJ.

Albeit through a limited number of decisions, the Court has clearly contributed a conception of the right of self-defence to international law. Whilst this conception is not always consistent, it is certainly evident that, for the Court, the fundamental aspect of the law on self-defence is the criterion of an 'armed attack', which is seen as having a particular normative content. As such, chapter one does not begin with an exhaustive overview of the Court's pronouncements with regard to self-defence but instead focuses upon the criterion of an armed attack and its content, as expressed by the ICJ across the relevant decisions. The chapter draws together and critiques this conception of the criterion.

Chapter two then moves to an assessment of the criteria of necessity and proportionality. As these criteria are not present in Article 51 of the UN Charter or in other treaties that deal with self-defence, this involves an assessment of customary international law, through an examination of state practice and *opinio juris sive necessitatis*. It is worth noting at the outset that when examining the content of customary international law in chapter two and beyond, this work predominantly takes an 'incident-based' approach to assessing the content of customary international law.

[25] *Legal Consequences of the Construction of a Wall in the Occupied Palestinian Territory* advisory opinion (2004) ICJ Reports 135.

[26] *DRC v Uganda* merits (n 19).

This is to say that the analysis focuses on incidents of state practice, coupled with the corresponding legal claims made by states, as well as the responses of other states to such legal claims (the *opinio juris* element). The current author takes the view that an examination of actual instances of the use of force 'in action' and the legal consequences of such incidents provides a stronger indication of the state of customary law than a reliance on, for example, more abstract debates over declarations relating to the use of force adopted by the General Assembly.[27] The position taken here is that, as has been noted by Ruth Wedgwood, 'incidents' have a 'central importance' in the formation of customary international law, particularly in the area of self-defence.[28]

The downside of this incident-based approach is that it is difficult to be comprehensive. As has already been noted, there have been literally hundreds of incidents involving military force since 1945. A full study of the practice relevant to the development and current state of the customary international law governing self-defence would represent an entire book in itself, or more.[29] One of the aims of this book, however, is to use the customary international law position to highlight, reflect and contrast the position taken by the ICJ. Therefore, where reference is made to the customary international law governing self-defence, what is actually being referred to must be seen as a 'sketch' of self-defence in practice and of the *opinio juris* of states with regard to this practice.[30] The claims being made herein with regard to the content of customary international law are not set forward as being necessarily authoritative: they are better viewed as *interpretations* of the state practice.

[27] Though this is not to say that debates of this kind have been wholly ignored, and they do feature in the analysis in this work on occasion.

[28] R Wedgwood, 'The ICJ Advisory Opinion on the Israeli Security Fence and the Limits of Self-Defence' (2005) 99 *American Journal of International Law* 52, 52.

[29] Compare the study on the customary aspects of the *jus in bello* prepared for the International Committee of the Red Cross, J-M Henckaerts and L Doswald Beck (eds), *Customary International Humanitarian Law: Vol I, Vol II (Parts 1 and 2)*, ICRC Study (Cambridge, Cambridge University Press, 2005). That study had more than two hundred contributors and comprised two volumes that together ran to over five thousand pages of text.

[30] As such, a number of particular incidents of state practice have been chosen and focused upon. It is acknowledged that selecting any particular incident for legal analysis whilst declining to examine others in the same way, runs the risk of orchestrated selection, representing the bias of the scholar (a fact noted by AR Willard, 'Incidents: An Essay in Method' (1984–85) 10 *Yale Journal of International Law* 21, 21–23; and WM Reisman, 'International Incidents: Introduction to a New Genre in the Study of International Law' (1984–85) 10 *Yale Journal of International Law* 1, 13). To attempt to limit this risk somewhat, the specific incidents selected have been chosen so as to provide as diverse a view as possible of the practice of states, for the most part since the inception of the UN system in 1945. Thus, the incidents selected relate to different aspects of the law on self-defence and in general cover a temporal range from 1945 to the present. Equally, they have been chosen to represent geographically disparate practice, involving states from every continent and major legal system. From this, a number of 'threads' highlighting the development and current status of the customary international law on self-defence have been identified.

Based on such interpretations of customary international law, it is argued in chapter two that, at least in custom, the primary aspect of a self-defence claim is not in fact the criterion of an armed attack at all but rather the dual requirements of necessity and proportionality. Chapter two is designed to highlight both the discrepancy between the importance of the criteria in practice and their marginal treatment by the ICJ, and an alternative conception of self-defence against which the Court's own conception, as set out in chapter one, may be contrasted.

Having examined the law as it would seem to be applied in practice, chapters three, four and five expand upon the problems with the Court's conception of self-defence. In chapter three, these problems are discussed in more detail through further examination of the *lex lata* of self-defence. This expands upon chapters one and two and indicates that the notion of two competing 'conceptions' of self-defence is too simplistic: in actuality these conceptions interrelate. It is contended that the law *in itself* is unclear and contradictory. Thus the view is put forward that, whilst the jurisprudence of the Court regarding self-defence has compounded these problems, the ICJ is far from solely responsible for them. Chapter three sets out the argument that many of the difficulties inherent in the law of self-defence stem from the development of 'armed attack' as constituting a particularly grave use of force. Following on from this, chapter four is prescriptive in nature: it suggests possible reform to attempt to improve upon some of the deficiencies in the law of self-defence that the ICJ has faced when making its decisions, through a reinterpretation of the concept of 'armed attack'.

Coupled with the problems inherent in the *law*, is the argument, set out in chapter five, that many of the difficulties with the Court's position regarding self-defence stem from the inherent nature of the ICJ and the various internal limitations that the Court faces, particularly with regard to disputes involving the use of force. The tension between the political aspects of the Court and the purely legal conception of the ICJ is explored, as are issues such as the Court's jurisdictional and evidential restraints.

The ultimate goal of this work is to contribute a clearer understanding of the law governing uses of force in self-defence and of the position that has been, and should be, taken by the ICJ with regard to it.

II. FACTS AND RULINGS OF THE PRIMARY CASES

Before we move to chapter one and the Court's conception of an 'armed attack', it is useful at this introductory stage—given that this book is examining the jurisprudence of the ICJ on self-defence—to briefly set out the factual background to and the ruling made in each of the key cases. This will underpin all subsequent discussion.

It was noted in the previous section that there have been five decisions of the Court that have dealt directly with the rules governing self-defence: three merits decisions (*Nicaragua, Oil Platforms* and *DRC v Uganda*) and two advisory opinions (*Nuclear Weapons* and *Israeli Wall*). A summary of each of these decisions is set out below. However, it is also worth noting that, in addition, there are a number of other judgments of the Court in contentious cases that relate to self-defence issues in some limited manner. The classic example of such a decision is *Corfu Channel* (*United Kingdom v Albania*),[31] in which the United Kingdom asserted that it had been acting under a right of 'self-help'.[32] Whilst the decision does not strictly deal with a claim of self-defence in the contemporary sense, there are a number of parallels between that right and the UK claim of self-help—certainly the fact that the case dealt directly with issues concerning the use of force means that it has some bearing on this book. A more recent example is the *Case Concerning the Land and Maritime Boundary between Cameroon and Nigeria*.[33] In that case, both parties accused the other of breaching principles of the *jus ad bellum*,[34] and Nigeria explicitly claimed to have been acting in self-defence.[35] Ultimately, the ICJ did not examine the use of force aspects of the dispute on the merits—nonetheless, the decision is still of some use to us.

For the most part, however, the analysis herein is based upon the five key pronouncements of the Court, the main features of which will now be set out in turn.

A. The *Nicaragua* Case

The case came before the ICJ following an application made on 9 April 1984 by Nicaragua,[36] alleging that the United States had supported and was continuing to support military and paramilitary actions of 'contra' forces opposing the Nicaraguan government. Nicaragua asserted that this support amounted to a sustained use of force on the part of the United

[31] *Corfu Channel* merits (n 20).

[32] *Corfu Channel* reply of the United Kingdom (1948) ICJ Pleadings vol II 241, 284.

[33] *Cameroon v Nigeria* merits (n 19).

[34] Eg, Cameroon asked the Court to adjudge and declare, inter alia, 'that by using force against the Republic of Cameroon, the Federal Republic of Nigeria has violated and is violating its obligations under international treaty law and customary law'. *Cameroon v Nigeria* application instituting proceedings (1994) www.icj-cij.org/docket/files/94/7201.pdf, para 20. For the corresponding counterclaims of Nigeria, see *Cameroon v Nigeria* counter-memorial submitted by Nigeria (1999) www.icj-cij.org/docket/files/94/8602.pdf, Part VI.

[35] *Cameroon v Nigeria* counter-memorial of Nigeria (*ibid*) Part V, para 24.49. See also *Cameroon v Nigeria*, CR 2002/14, www.icj-cij.org/docket/files/94/5029.pdf, para 41 and CR 2002/18, www.icj-cij.org/docket/files/94/5045.pdf, para 68.

[36] *Nicaragua* application instituting proceedings (1984) ICJ Pleadings vol I, 3–26.

States, contrary to international law.[37] Further, Nicaragua alleged that the United States had used force in a more direct manner against it by way of attacks, such as the mining of ports and aerial incursions into Nicaraguan territory, 'carried out by persons in the pay of the United States government, and under the direct command of United States personnel, who also participated to some extent in the operations'.[38] These actions took place against the background of revolutionary change in Nicaragua. In 1979 the Sandinista regime had toppled the previous government, which had been headed by President Anastasio Somoza. The new government was threatened by the 'contras'—irregular military forces comprised largely of the former National Guard and other supporters of the deposed Somoza government. Relations between the United States and the new Sandinista Government had soured by 1981, and by the end of that year the United States had begun to aid the contra forces.[39]

Once the Court had ruled that it could entertain the dispute,[40] the United States made it clear that it would participate no further in the case.[41] Thus, it filed no pleadings on the merits, nor was it represented at the oral proceedings of 12–20 September 1985.[42] However, before its abstention from the proceedings, the United States indicated in its counter-memorial on jurisdictional issues that its actions with regard to Nicaragua, while uses of force, were lawful actions of collective self-defence. This was claimed to be in response to uses of force by Nicaragua against neighbouring states. It was alleged, for example, that Nicaragua had provided support to the armed opposition in El Salvador.[43] The Court concluded that there had been a certain amount of aid from Nicaraguan territory to the Salvadorian rebels up to early 1981.[44] However, the scale of

[37] Specifically contrary to Art 2(4) of the UN Charter; Arts 18 and 20 of the Charter of the Organisation of American States; Art 8 of the Convention on the Rights and Duties of States; and Art I, Third, of the Convention Concerning the Duties and Rights of States in the Event of Civil Strife.

[38] *Nicaragua* merits (n 18) para 20.

[39] *Ibid*, paras 18–19. For an exploration of the factual background to the *Nicaragua* case, see C Dickey, *With the Contras: A Reporter in the Wilds of Nicaragua* (New York, Touchstone, 1987); R Kagan, *A Twilight Struggle: American Power and Nicaragua, 1977–1990* (New York, Free Press, 1996); and Z Modabbler, 'Collective Self-Defence: *Nicaragua v United States*' (1988) 10 *Loyola of Los Angeles International & Comparative Law Review* 449, 451–53.

[40] The Court held that it had jurisdiction to entertain the dispute on two grounds: based on declarations of the parties accepting the jurisdiction of the Court under Art 36(2) of the Statute of the ICJ, and based upon Art XXIV of the Treaty of Friendship, Commerce and Navigation (with Protocol) between the United States of America and Nicaragua, signed in Managua on 24 April 1956, which came into force 24 May 1958. See *Nicaragua* jurisdiction of the court and admissibility of the application (1984) ICJ Reports 392, especially the operative part of the judgment, para 113.

[41] *Nicaragua* merits (n 18) para 10.

[42] *Ibid*, para 17.

[43] *Nicaragua* counter-memorial of the United States (1984) ICJ Pleadings vol II, Part II, esp 57–59.

[44] *Nicaragua* merits (n 18) para 152.

this was viewed as minimal, and evidence for continued aid after the initial months of 1981 was insufficient for the Court to accept its existence.[45] In addition to its claims concerning indirect support, the United States also indicated that Honduras and Costa Rica had been the victims of *direct* armed intervention by Nicaraguan agents.[46] The Court found that these trans-border incursions were imputable to the Nicaraguan government.[47]

A notable aspect of the *Nicaragua* decision was the effect of a reservation entered by the United States when it declared its acceptance of the ICJ's jurisdiction under Article 36(2) of the Court's Statute. In its declaration of 26 August 1946, the United States in general accepted the jurisdiction of the ICJ but made a number of reservations to this acceptance.[48] One of these was that it did not recognise the jurisdiction of the Court over 'disputes arising under a multilateral treaty, unless . . . all parties to the dispute affected by the decision are also parties to the case before the Court'.[49] The ICJ took the view that a decision on the merits would necessarily 'affect' El Salvador,[50] in that this would reflect upon any measures El Salvador had taken in individual self-defence against Nicaragua.[51] As such, the ICJ concluded that the United States reservation essentially precluded it from applying multilateral treaty law in the case.[52] Therefore, in effect, the law that the Court was able to apply to the dispute was customary international law alone,[53] at least with regard to the aspects of the case relevant to our discussions.[54]

The Court therefore outlined and applied the customary international law on self-defence, specifically collective self-defence. It concluded that it was not satisfactorily established that the requirements for a lawful exercise of self-defence in customary international law had been met. Therefore, the justification supplied by the United States that it had been

[45] *Nicaragua* merits (n 18) para 160.

[46] *Nicaragua* counter-memorial of the United States (n 43) Part II, 60–61.

[47] *Nicaragua* merits (n 18) paras 163–64.

[48] For the US declaration, see S Rosenne, *Documents on the International Court of Justice*, 2nd edn (Alphen aan den Rejn, Sijthoff & Noordhoof, 1979) 415.

[49] *Ibid.*

[50] Indeed, the United States argued that a decision by the Court would affect not only El Salvador but also Costa Rica and Honduras: *Nicaragua* counter-memorial of the United States (n 43) Part III, 86–89. The ICJ reached a conclusion on this question only regarding El Salvador. However, the Court made it clear that this was because it was unnecessary to examine the possible effect of a merits decision upon the other states, as its conclusion regarding El Salvador was enough in itself to mean that the US reservation was applicable: *Nicaragua* merits (n 18) para 48.

[51] *Nicaragua* merits (n 18) paras 42–56, esp para 51.

[52] This meant, eg, that the Court could not apply either the UN Charter or the Charter of the Organisation of American States. *Ibid*, paras 42–56.

[53] It was the contention of the United States that the reservation precluded the Court from examining the dispute *at all*. *Nicaragua* counter-memorial of the United States (n 43) Part III, 91–97.

[54] The Court could, of course, apply bilateral treaties between the parties, such as the 1956 Friendship, Commerce and Navigation Treaty. *Nicaragua* merits (n 18) para 271.

acting in collective self-defence was rejected. The Court found that by supporting the contra forces, the United States had violated the principle of non-intervention and in some circumstances the prohibition on the use of force. It was further held that the 'direct' incursions by people controlled by the United States constituted unlawful uses of force.[55]

B. The *Oil Platforms* Case

As with *Nicaragua*, the *Oil Platforms* case also had the United States as its respondent party. The case involved military action taken by the US Navy against offshore Iranian oil production complexes, which were situated in the Persian Gulf.[56] The first set of attacks against Iranian oil platforms occurred on 19 October 1987. US destroyers attacked the Iranian Reshadat complex, completely demolishing one platform of that installation and severely damaging another. Further, these attacks caused damage to a second complex, the Resalat. Neither complex was producing oil at the time of the attacks, due to previous damage done to them by Iraqi forces.[57] Naval forces of the United States took military action against Iranian oil installations again on 18 April 1988. This second set of attacks led to the almost total destruction of two further installations, the Salman and the Nasr.[58] The attacks on the Salman and the Nasr formed part of a wider US operation codenamed 'Operation Preying Mantis'.[59] However, the question of the legality of the wider aspects of the operation was not examined by the Court.[60]

These incidents led to Iran instituting proceeding against the United States before the ICJ on 2 November 1992,[61] alleging that they amounted to a violation of provisions of the 1955 Treaty of Amity, Economic

[55] *Ibid*, para 292. However, the Court did find that the breaches of human rights and humanitarian law by the contra forces were not imputable to the United States.

[56] These incidents occurred in the context of the Iran–Iraq conflict of 1980–88. For background to this conflict, see C Gray, 'The British Position in Regard to the Gulf Conflict' (1988) 37 *International and Comparative Law Quarterly* 420; R Leckow, 'The Iran–Iraq Conflict in the Gulf: The Law of War Zones' (1988) 37 *International and Comparative Law Quarterly* 629; HHG Post, 'Border Conflicts Between Iran and Iraq: Review and Legal Reflections' in IF Dekker and HHG Post (eds), *The Gulf War of 1980–1988: The Iran–Iraq War in International Legal Perspective* (Dordrecht, Martinus Nijhoff, 1992) 7–38. For useful factual reports from the relevant period, see *Newsweek*, 2 May 1988, 11; and *Time*, 2 May 1988, 22–23.

[57] The earlier damage occurred between October 1986 and August 1987. *Oil Platforms* merits (n 1) para 46.

[58] In consequence, oil production from these complexes was interrupted for a number of years. *Ibid*, paras 65 and 66.

[59] *Ibid*, para 68. This operation not only involved the destruction of the Nasr and Salman complexes but also included attacks on Iranian naval vessels and aircraft.

[60] As this was not at issue before the Court. *Ibid*, para 77.

[61] *Oil Platforms*, application instituting proceedings, www.icj-cij.org/docket/files/90/7211.pdf.

Relations, and Consular Rights between the United States and Iran.[62] The pertinent question before the ICJ on the merits was whether there had been a breach by the United States of Article X(1) of the 1955 Treaty.[63] That Article provided

> Between the territories of the two High Contracting Parties there shall be freedom of commerce and navigation.

The Court first examined whether Article XX(1)(d)—providing that nothing in the Treaty precluded the application by either state of measures 'necessary to protect its essential security interests'—could constitute a sufficient defence for the attacks on the oil installations. In interpreting the scope of the Article, the Court concluded that if the actions of the United States could be justified as acts of self-defence under international law, then they equally would amount to measures necessary to ensure its essential security interests.[64]

Following the first set of attacks on 19 October 1987, the United States reported to the Security Council that its actions were justified as self-defence under Article 51 of the Charter. It claimed that a Kuwaiti-owned US flag vessel, *Sea Isle City*, had been struck by a 'Silkworm' missile on 16 October 1987[65] and that this attack was attributable to Iran. It stressed that this was an 'armed attack' and further contended that the *Sea Isle City* incident was the latest in a series of armed attacks against US vessels instigated by Iran.[66] In front of the ICJ, the United States maintained its position that the attacks were a lawful response in self-defence.[67] Yet, it should be noted that at final submissions stage, the United States made it clear that this was not a question which it felt the Court had jurisdiction to examine,[68] and, as Judge Higgins rightly pointed out, self-defence was invoked 'as a final submission in the *alternative*, arising only should the Court find its other arguments do not avail' (emphasis added).[69]

[62] Signed in Tehran on 15 August 1955 and entered into force on 16 June 1957. The United States instituted a corresponding counterclaim based on the same treaty. *Oil Platforms* counter-memorial and counterclaim submitted by the United States (1997) www.icj-cij.org/docket/files/90/8632.pdf, Part VI, esp paras 6.01–6.02. It was the position of the United States that Iran's actions during the conflict had caused 'significant' damage to US commercial and military vessels and had generally created 'extremely dangerous conditions for shipping' in the Persian Gulf. On this basis it was claimed that Iran was in breach of provisions of the Treaty of 1955.

[63] Due to the US counterclaim, the Court also had to assess whether Iran was in breach of the same provision of the 1955 Treaty.

[64] *Oil Platforms* merits (n 1) para 43.

[65] 'Silkworm' missiles are land-launched HY-2 cruise missiles, in this case of Chinese manufacture. *Ibid*, para 53.

[66] UN Doc S/19219. For details of the additional incidents that the United States attributed to Iran before the Court, see *Oil Platforms* counter-memorial and counterclaim of the United States (n 62) Part VI, para 6.08.

[67] *Oil Platforms* counter-memorial and counterclaim of the United States, *ibid*, Part IV.

[68] See, eg, *Oil Platforms* CR 2003/11, www.icj-cij.org/docket/files/90/5153.pdf, 11–15.

[69] *Oil Platforms* merits (n 1) separate opinion of Judge Higgins, para 50.

However, the Court determined that while the evidence presented by the United States was 'indicative' of Iranian responsibility, it was 'not sufficient to support the contentions of the United States'. On the basis of the evidence, it had not been established that the missile attack of 16 October 1987 was imputable to Iran.[70]

In relation to the second set of attacks, the United States contended, again before both the Security Council[71] and then before the Court, that these were lawful responses—both in self-defence and under Article XX(1)(d)—to the mining of the USS *Samuel B Roberts*, a US warship, which occurred on 14 April 1988, being the latest in a series of Iranian attacks against US vessels. The main evidence supporting the view that this mine was laid by Iran was that mines were found in the same area bearing Iranian serial numbers. However, as both parties in the Iran–Iraq conflict were laying mines at this time, this evidence was viewed by the ICJ as 'highly suggestive, but not conclusive'.[72] Again, the inadequacy of the evidence attributing the attack on the USS *Samuel B Roberts* to Iran meant that, in the view of the ICJ, the United States had not discharged its burden of proof that it had been the victim of an act giving rise to the right of self-defence.[73]

On this basis, the Court determined that the oil platform attacks could not be justified as measures taken in self-defence and, as such, could not be justified under Article XX(1)(d) of the 1955 Treaty of Amity. However, notably, the United States was not explicitly found to be in breach of Article 2(4) of the UN Charter. Ultimately, the Court concluded that there was no actual direct commerce between the parties at the time of either set of US attacks, and therefore the United States was not in breach of Article X(1) of the Treaty in any event.[74]

C. *DRC v Uganda*

The *DRC v Uganda* case related to aspects of an extremely complex conflict that took place in central Africa—one that is, to some extent, still

[70] *Oil Platforms* merits (n 1) para 61.

[71] UN Doc S/19791.

[72] *Oil Platforms* merits (n 1) para 71.

[73] *Ibid*, para 72.

[74] *Ibid*, paras 92 and 97. For more on this, see JA Green, 'The *Oil Platforms* Case: An Error in Judgment?' (2004) 9 *Journal of Conflict and Security Law* 357, 364–70. Regarding the US counterclaim, the Court examined the question of whether acts attributable to Iran had impaired the freedom of either commerce or navigation between the two parties. None of the vessels that the United States alleged had been attacked by Iran were, in the view of the Court, engaged in commerce or navigation between the two parties at the time of any of the incidents (*Oil Platforms* merits (n 1) paras 119–21). Therefore continued trade between the parties during the conflict and the lack of specific evidence of actual impediment to that commercial activity attributable to Iran meant that the counterclaim of the United States was dismissed.

ongoing.[75] On 2 August 1998, troops of Uganda, Rwanda and Burundi entered the territory of the Democratic Republic of the Congo (DRC).[76] These forces joined with troops from those states that were already present in the DRC, initially with the consent of the DRC government.[77] The forces of Uganda, Rwanda and Burundi acted in support of a number of rebel groups, comprised largely of Banyamulenge Tutsis[78] who opposed the dictatorship of President Laurent Kabila.[79] Fifteen months before, these same states had aided Kabila's rise to power and the overthrow of the previous totalitarian President, Mobutu Sese Seko.[80] Yet once he was in power, Kabila began to pursue a more independent policy. This fact, coupled with the increase in actions from various militant rebel groups operating from within the DRC against neighbouring states,[81] was perceived to constitute a threat to the territories of these states, particularly Uganda and Rwanda. The former allies of the DRC's President thus began aiding those in the Congo who sought to remove the new government. Following the intervention of Uganda, Rwanda and Burundi, a number of other foreign states initiated military action in support of the Kabila government, adding to the scale of the conflict.[82]

On 23 June 1999 the DRC filed three linked applications in the registry of the ICJ, initiating proceedings against Uganda, Burundi and Rwanda.[83] In these applications it was alleged that the three states involved in the conflict on the side of the rebels had each committed an 'armed aggression' against the territory of the DRC 'in flagrant violation' of the United Nations Charter and the Charter of the Organisation of African Unity[84] and that their forces had committed various breaches of international humanitarian law.[85] The applications initiating cases against Burundi and

[75] For background and the general development of the Congo conflict, see *The Economist*, 6 July 2002, 55; and *Power and Interest News*, 5 August 2003. On the legal issues arising from the conflict specifically, see PA Kasaija, 'International Law and Uganda's Involvement in the Democratic Republic of Congo' (2001–02) 10 *Miami International and Comparative Law Review* 75.

[76] UN Doc A/53/232 and *DRC v Uganda* application instituting proceedings (1999) www.icj-cij.org/docket/files/116/7151.pdf, 5. It should be noted that the DRC was called Zaire between 1971 and 1997.

[77] Consent that had been withdrawn in July 1998. *DRC v Uganda* merits (n 19) para 49.

[78] Most prominently, the Rassemblement Congolais pour la Démocratie (RCD) and the Mouvement de Libération du Congo (MLC).

[79] *The Financial Times*, 4 August 1998, 18.

[80] *The Guardian*, 30 May 1997, 16; and *The Financial Times*, 26 May 1997, 21.

[81] *The Financial Times*, 4 August 1998, 18.

[82] These states were Zimbabwe, Angola, Namibia and Chad. news.bbc.co.uk/1/hi/world/africa/country_profiles/1072684.stm.

[83] *DRC v Uganda* application instituting proceedings (n 76); *DRC v Rwanda* application instituting proceedings (n 19); and *DRC v Burundi* application instituting proceedings (n 19).

[84] *DRC v Uganda* application instituting proceedings (n76) esp 5.

[85] *Ibid*, 5, 7–9 and 15–17. These aspects of the decision—Uganda's belligerent occupation of areas of eastern Congo, issues concerning alleged human rights violations and claims regarding the appropriation of the DRC's mineral wealth—will not be discussed here, as they do not have a bearing on this work. For the Court's findings on these issues, see *DRC v Uganda* merits (n 19) paras 167–250.

Rwanda were later withdrawn by the DRC.[86] More recently, the DRC also filed a second application initiating proceedings against Rwanda in relation to the conflict. However, in 2006 the Court found that it did not have the jurisdiction to hear the case on the merits.[87] As such, the *DRC v Uganda* case was the only dispute arising from the conflict to reach the merits phase of proceedings.[88]

For its part, Uganda claimed that, at the very least from when Kabila came to power (in May 1997) to 11 September 1998, it had the consent of the DRC to have forces on its territory[89] and, in any event, that it did not participate in many of the activities alleged by the DRC.[90] Further, Uganda argued in counterclaim that there had been a resumption of attacks by anti-Ugandan militant groups, particularly the Allied Democratic Forces (ADF), emanating from the DRC against the territory of Uganda.[91] Thus, Uganda additionally claimed that, following 11 September 1998, it had been acting in self-defence in intervening in the DRC and supporting rebel groups acting against the government.[92] The DRC responded to this by arguing that it was not responsible for the attacks of any militant groups against the territory of Uganda.[93] In the alternative, the DRC additionally claimed that it was entitled to respond in self-defence in any event due to the Ugandan intervention.[94] Thus, *both parties* claimed to have been acting in self-defence.

The Court found that Uganda was responsible for the majority of the actions attributed to it by the DRC[95] and that the consent of the DRC could

[86] *DRC v Rwanda* order (2001) ICJ Reports 6; and *DRC v Burundi* order (2001) ICJ Reports 3. It may be speculated that this was because the basis of jurisdiction was much weaker in relation to the DRC's claims against these states as opposed to its case against Uganda. See C Gray, 'The Use and Abuse of the International Court of Justice: Cases Concerning the Use of Force since *Nicaragua*' (2003) 14 *European Journal of International Law* 867, 869.

[87] *DRC v Rwanda* (New Application: 2002) jurisdiction of the court and admissibility of the application (n 19) esp the *dispositif*, para 128.

[88] Prior to its decision on the merits in *DRC v Uganda*, the Court issued an order indicating provisional measures. This required *both parties* to 1) refrain from military action; 2) comply with their obligations under international law; and 3) respect fundamental human rights in the 'zone of conflict'. *DRC v Uganda* provisional measures order (2000) ICJ Reports 110, esp para 47. See D Kritsiotis, 'Armed Activities on the Territory of the Congo (*Democratic Republic of Congo v Uganda*): Provisional Measures' (2001) 50 *International and Comparative Law Quarterly* 662.

[89] *DRC v Uganda* rejoinder submitted by Uganda (2002) www.icj-cij.org/docket/files/116/8314.pdf, paras 89–105.

[90] *Ibid*, paras 106–60 and 551–95.

[91] *DRC v Uganda* counter-memorial submitted by Uganda (2001) www.icj-cij.org/docket/files/116/8320.pdf, paras 11–47. Such attacks had occurred prior to Kabila's ascendance to power, and Uganda argued that in a strategic shift, the DRC's government again began to support groups such as the ADF, as Zaire had done before.

[92] Eg, see *DRC v Uganda* counter-memorial of Uganda (*ibid*) paras 52–54.

[93] See, eg, *DRC v Uganda* CR/2005/16, http://www.icj-cij.org/docket/files/116/4343.pdf, 3–18.

[94] *DRC v Uganda* CR 2005/11, www.icj-cij.org/docket/files/116/4321.pdf, 24–30

[95] Although the Court held that it was not established that Uganda participated in the attack on Kitona on 4 August 1998. *DRC v Uganda* merits (n 19) paras 62–71.

not act as justification for any of the Ugandan actions that occurred after 8 August 1998 at the latest.[96] The Court therefore turned to Uganda's self-defence claim. It concluded that no satisfactory proof had been advanced to indicate that the DRC had any involvement in the attacks perpetrated by the ADF against Uganda prior to Uganda's intervention in the DRC.[97] Due to this lack of involvement the ICJ held that Uganda could not have been exercising its right of self-defence against the DRC,[98] and therefore it was in breach of Article 2(4) of the UN Charter.[99]

The ICJ also dismissed Uganda's counterclaim, which argued that in supporting the ADF and other groups, the DRC had itself violated Article 2(4). The Court reiterated that it had not been established that the DRC (or Zaire before it) had supported anti-Ugandan groups acting from within its territory.[100] Indeed, the Court found that following the fall of Mobutu, the DRC had attempted to act *against* such rebels, although this was difficult due to the nature of the terrain of its eastern border.[101] As such, the DRC was not in breach of Article 2(4). Further, the ICJ held that any prima facie breach by the DRC of Article 2(4) following 2 August 1998 could be justified as an action of self-defence taken in response to Uganda's own violation of that Article,[102] though the Court again stressed that no such prima facie breach had been established.[103]

D. The *Nuclear Weapons* Advisory Opinion

The *Legality of the Threat or Use of Nuclear Weapons* advisory opinion was delivered on 8 July 1996, following a request made by the UN General Assembly in December 1994.[104] The General Assembly asked that the ICJ render an advisory opinion in reference to the question: 'Is the threat or use of nuclear weapons in any circumstance permitted under international law?'[105] A number of states made submissions, both written and oral, prior to the Court's deliberations on the question.[106]

[96] The Court held that any consent from the DRC as to the presence of Ugandan forces on its territory was terminated by 8 August 1998, and potentially even before this date, though it was not necessary to decide conclusively on this point. Therefore 'invitation' could not offer a justification for the actions of Uganda after this period. *Ibid*, paras 42–54, esp para 53.
[97] *Ibid*, paras 133–47.
[98] *Ibid*, para 147.
[99] *Ibid*, paras 148–65.
[100] *Ibid*, paras 297–301.
[101] *Ibid*, para 303.
[102] *Ibid*, para 304.
[103] *Ibid*.
[104] GA Res 49/75[K].
[105] *Ibid*.
[106] *Nuclear Weapons* advisory opinion (n 23) paras 5–6. These submissions are all available at www.icj-cij.org/docket/index.php?p1=3&p2=4&k=e1&case=95&code=unan&p3=1.

Having concluded that it had jurisdiction to deliver an opinion on this issue,[107] the Court examined a number of areas of international law in the context of nuclear weapons. Following a discussion of international human rights standards,[108] the prohibition of genocide[109] and international environmental law,[110] the Court found that 'the most directly relevant applicable law governing the question . . . is that relating to the use of force . . . and the law applicable in armed conflict which regulates the conduct of hostilities', along with any specific treaties on nuclear armaments.[111] For our purposes the first of these is obviously the most relevant.

In relation to the prohibition of the threat or use of force, the Court noted that neither Article 2(4) of the UN Charter nor customary international law specifically prohibited the use of nuclear weapons as such.[112] It implied that the threat or use of nuclear weapons would constitute a violation of Article 2(4) prima facie.[113] However, the Court also applied the law of self-defence in this context. It concluded that the threat or use of nuclear weapons could potentially constitute a lawful action in self-defence. However, the Court made it clear that this would be the case only if such a threat or use of nuclear armaments met *the relevant criteria for any self-defence action*, and it stressed that meeting these criteria would be particularly difficult in such circumstances.[114]

The Court additionally held:

> A threat or use of force should also be compatible with the requirements of international law applicable in armed conflict, particularly those of the principles and rules of international humanitarian law, as well as with specific obligations under treaties and other undertakings which expressly deal with nuclear weapons.[115]

Thus it was concluded that the threat or use of nuclear weapons 'would generally be contrary to the rules of international law,' but the Court could

[107] It was found in this regard that: a) the General Assembly was authorised to make such a request of the ICJ by virtue of Art 96 of the Charter; b) the political elements of the question did not bar the Court from making a legal response; c) the 'vague' nature of the question similarly was not 'a compelling reason [for the Court] to decline to exercise its jurisdiction'; and finally d) there were sufficient relevant rules on the matter in international law for the Court to avoid 'legislating' upon the issue in a manner beyond its competence. See *Nuclear Weapons* advisory opinion (n 23) paras 10–22.

[108] The Court here concluded that the applicability of the International Covenant on Civil and Political Rights 1966 could only be discerned by reference to the relevant rules of the *jus in bello*. See *Nuclear Weapons* advisory opinion (n 23) paras 24–25.

[109] It was held that the use of nuclear weapons may indeed amount to a breach of the 1948 Convention on the Prevention and Punishment if the Crime of Genocide, if the relevant intent was present in this context. *Nuclear Weapons* advisory opinion (n 23) para 26.

[110] *Nuclear Weapons* advisory opinion (n 23) paras 27–33.

[111] *Ibid*, para 34.

[112] *Ibid*, paras 39 and 105.

[113] *Ibid*, paras 37–39 and 105.

[114] *Ibid*, paras 43 and 105.

[115] *Ibid*, para 105.

not exclude the possibility that such threat or use may be lawful in extreme circumstances.[116]

E. The *Israeli Wall* Advisory Opinion

The *Legal Consequences of the Construction of a Wall in the Occupied Palestinian Territory* advisory opinion was delivered on 9 July 2004. It concerned the construction by Israel of a barrier in the West Bank, which was planned to stretch some 720 kilometres.[117] This was avowedly designed to protect Israel against the infiltration of Palestinian suicide bombers.[118] Work began on the barrier in June 2002, and it is today around 50 per cent complete.[119]

As with *Nuclear Weapons*, the *Israeli Wall* advisory opinion was delivered at the request of the General Assembly, in a resolution of its Tenth Emergency Special Session.[120] The question posed by the General Assembly was:

> What are the legal consequences arising from the construction of the wall being built by Israel, the occupying power, in the Occupied Palestinian Territory, including in and around East Jerusalem, as described in the report of the Secretary-General, considering the rules and principles of international law, including the Fourth Geneva Convention of 1949, and relevant Security Council and General Assembly resolutions?[121]

The ICJ first assessed whether it had jurisdiction to deliver an opinion on the question posed. Despite the contentions of some states,[122] the Court concluded that it had jurisdiction to pronounce upon this question[123] and

[116] *Nuclear Weapons* advisory opinion (n 23) para 105.

[117] UN Doc A/ES-10/248, 3.

[118] Website for the Israeli Ministry of Defence, www.securityfence.mod.gov.il/Pages/ENG/purpose.htm.

[119] For more detail on the factual background to the *Israeli Wall* advisory opinion, see www.vtjp.org/background/Separation_Wall_Report.htm; and BBC News Online, especially news.bbc.co.uk/1/hi/world/middle_east/2930785.stm and news.bbc.co.uk/1/hi/world/middle_east/3506907.stm. In addition, M Sorkin (ed), *Against the Wall* (New York, New Press, 2005) provides excellent geopolitical, social, cultural, architectural and philosophical analysis of the wall and its background. For the ICJ advisory opinion, see in that volume S Koury, 'Why this Wall?' 48–65. However, *Against the Wall* must be treated with care, as it is a self-confessed 'polemical' work ('Introduction', vi), something its very title indicates.

[120] GA Res ES-10/14.

[121] *Ibid*.

[122] See, eg, the written submission of the United States (2004) www.icj-cij.org/docket/files/95/8700.pdf, Part III.

[123] This was on the basis that: a) the General Assembly had competence to make such a request under Art 96 of the Charter, and the Tenth Emergency Session of the General Assembly, at which the resolution requesting the opinion was adopted, was properly convened and the resolution correctly constituted; b) the question posed was a 'legal' one, with any ambiguity as to its meaning being capable of interpretation by the Court; and c) the political elements to the question did not act as a bar to jurisdiction. *Israeli Wall* advisory opinion (n 25) paras 14–42.

further that it was proper for the Court to in fact exercise this jurisdiction.[124]

It was concluded by the Court, in the substance of its opinion, that the acquisition of territory in consequence of a breach of Article 2(4) of the UN Charter was unlawful[125] and that the occupation by Israel of the territory in question fell into this category. The ICJ affirmed that the principle of self-determination was relevant to the Occupied Palestinian Territory[126] and held that the barrier under construction 'severely impede[ed] the exercise by the Palestinian people of its rights to self-determination, and [was] therefore a breach of Israel's obligation to respect this right'.[127] The Court further applied a number of aspects of both international humanitarian law and human rights law to the situation.[128]

The most important section of the opinion for our purposes is the Court's application of the law on the use of force—and particularly the *lex lata* on self-defence—to the question posed by the General Assembly. This was actually dealt with in a limited manner by the ICJ.[129]

Israel had argued, inter alia, that construction of the wall was lawful on the basis that it constituted an action of self-defence consistent with Article 51.[130] In response to this claim, the Court held:

> Article 51 of the Charter . . . recognises the existence of an inherent right of self-defence in the case of armed attack by one state against another state. However, Israel does not claim that the attacks against it are imputable to a foreign state . . . Israel exercises control in the Occupied Palestinian Territory and that, as Israel itself states, the threat which it regards as justifying the construction of the wall originates within, and not outside, that territory. The situation is thus different from that contemplated by Security Council resolutions 1368 (2001) and 1373 (2001), and therefore Israel could not in any event invoke those resolutions

124 Under Art 65(1) of the Court's Statute, it has the discretion to decline to exercise its jurisdiction in relation to a request for an advisory opinion. The Court concluded that there were no 'compelling reasons' for it to do so in this instance. *Ibid*, paras 43–65.

125 Under both the Declaration on Principles of International Law Concerning Friendly Relations and Cooperation Among States in accordance with the Charter of the United Nations 1970, GA Res 2625 and general customary international law. See *Ibid*, para 87.

126 *Ibid*, para 88.

127 *Ibid*, para 122.

128 The Court first assessed whether these norms (deriving primarily from Fourth Geneva Convention of 1949, the International Covenant on Civil and Political Rights 1966, the International Covenant on Economic Social and Cultural Rights 1966 and the Convention of the Rights of the Child 1989) were *applicable* to the situation (*ibid*, paras 89–113). Having determined that they were so applicable, the Court went on to in fact apply them (paras 123–37).

129 Reference to self-defence constitutes a mere two paragraphs of the opinion. *Ibid*, paras 138–39.

130 This argument was made in the General Assembly. See UN Doc A/ES-10/PV.21, 6. However, Israel did not put this argument forward with quite the vociferousness implied by the ICJ; self-defence would seem to be in the nature of a *secondary* argument on the part of Israel. The Court, in para 138, cited the Report of the Secretary-General (UN Doc A/ES-10/248) as additional evidence of an Israeli claim of self-defence, but all that the Report does in fact is to itself refer to UN Doc A/ES 10/PV.21, 6.

> in support of its claim to be exercising a right of self-defence. . . Consequently, the Court concludes that Article 51 of the Charter has no relevance in this case.[131]

Thus the Court brusquely dismissed this argument as put forward by Israel on the basis that the attacks it alleged were not imputable to a foreign state but rather originated from within Israeli-controlled territory. Nonetheless, even such a brief application of the law of self-defence offers an insight into the conception of self-defence as held by the Court, as we will see.

[131] *Israeli Wall* advisory opinion (n 25) para 138.

1

The Criterion of an Armed Attack in the Jurisprudence of the International Court of Justice

THIS CHAPTER BEGINS the substantive analysis of the jurisprudence of the International Court of Justice (ICJ) concerning self-defence in international law.[1] The aim here is not to examine self-defence in its entirety or even to highlight the totality of what the Court has said on the issue,[2] but rather to focus upon the *primary* aspect of the Court's conception of the law in this area: the criterion of an armed attack. Equally, this chapter focuses upon the *ICJ's* conception of an armed attack. We will return to the concept of armed attack as it appears in state practice (and elsewhere) in chapter three.

[1] It must be acknowledged that the structure and methodology of some of this chapter, most notably sections III–VI, is in part adapted from that employed in D Kritsiotis, 'Rules on Self-Defence in International Law', memorandum for the Royal Institute of International Affairs, London Chatham House International Law Programme, 8 December 2004 (unpublished), section IV, 6–13.

[2] Eg, this chapter does not examine the criteria of necessity and proportionality, which are discussed in ch 2. Moreover, this work does not discuss the Court's examination of the 'reporting requirement' contained in Art 51. See *Military and Paramilitary Activities in and Against Nicaragua* (*Nicaragua v United States of America*) merits (1986) ICJ Reports 14, para 200; *Legality of the Threat or Use of Nuclear Weapons* advisory opinion (1996) ICJ Reports 226, para 44; and *Armed Activities on the Territory of the Congo* (*Democratic Republic of the Congo v Uganda*) merits (2005) www.icj-cij.org/docket/files/116/10455.pdf, para 145. This is because the Court's position on this aspect of self-defence is largely uncontroversial (see J Macdonald, 'The *Nicaragua* Case: New Answers to Old Questions' (1986) 24 *Canadian Yearbook of International Law* 127, 153), and it has little bearing upon the issues raised herein. Equally, there is not an examination of the question of whether self-defence can be extended to protect nationals abroad: this work only touches upon this notion superficially. Such a claim has been made by a number of states in the UN era, though such claims remain controversial. For discussion, see RJ Zedalis, 'Protection of Nationals Abroad: Is Consent the Basis of Legal Obligation?' (1990) 25 *Texas International Law Journal* 209, especially 235–48; and TC Wingfield, 'Forcible Protection of Nationals Abroad' (1999–2000) 104 *Dickinson Law Review* 447. This is currently a topical issue with regard to self-defence, in that Russia supported its intervention in Georgia in August 2008 by reference to self-defence by way of the protection of nationals abroad (UN Doc S/545). However, as the notion of the protection of nationals abroad as an aspect of self-defence is not examined by the ICJ, any further discussion of this question is beyond the scope of this work.

I. ASSESSING THE JURISPRUDENCE OF THE COURT

When considering the jurisprudence of the ICJ as set out in this and subsequent chapters, there is a need for a degree of caution, for a number of reasons. It is important that these be briefly set out here. First, reference is often made herein to the 'view' or 'position' of the Court. The question of whether the ICJ can be seen as a single entity and the issue of whether it can in actuality have a 'view' is examined in chapter five.[3] For the present, it is important to note that terms such as the 'view' or 'position' of the Court are employed as shorthand to indicate the decision of the *majority* in any given judgment, though this has in many instances been augmented and elucidated upon by separate and even dissenting opinions, as indicated.

Second, in *Military and Paramilitary Activities in and against Nicaragua* (hereafter *Nicaragua*), the Court stressed that it does not possess 'authority to ascribe to states legal views which they do not themselves advance'.[4] This statement is useful at this juncture, as it can be seen as being applicable not only to the Court's assessment of the legal conclusions or positions of states, but equally to the assessment by academics *of the positions taken by the Court*. It is important, when determining the law as presented by the ICJ, that one does not ascribe legal conclusions to the Court that it did not itself advance. However, particularly given the somewhat ambiguous nature of much of what the Court has pronounced in regard to self-defence, in attempting to understand the jurisprudence in this area a level of interpretation and presumption that goes beyond what the Court has explicitly held is inevitable. Thus, care has been taken throughout this chapter (and those that follow) to indicate when the position presented regarding the jurisprudence of the ICJ is a *possible reading* of the decisions and as such may not be conclusive.

Third, it must be kept in mind that court decisions, including those of the ICJ, necessarily represent the law (as perceived by the relevant court) at the time that the case was decided. This point is fairly self-evident; nonetheless, caution must be exercised when referencing a judgment of the ICJ as an expression of the law, as it may no longer be representative in this way. In the context of self-defence, it is essential to recall that the

[3] See ch 5, section III-A.

[4] *Nicaragua* merits (n 2) para 207. This is an expression of the so called *non ultra petita* rule, which aims to preserve the consensual nature of the Court's jurisdiction and provides that the ICJ cannot examine aspects of a dispute not raised by the parties. See *Asylum* case (*Colombia/Peru*) merits (1950) ICJ Reports 266, 402; *Case Concerning Certain German Interests in Polish Silesia* merits (1926) PCIJ Reports, Series A 7, 35; and *Nicaragua* merits (n 2) para 207. See also IFI Shihata, *The Power of the International Court to Determine its Own Jurisdiction* (The Hague, Martinus Nijhoff, 1965) 219–21.

crucial *Nicaragua* judgment is over twenty years old.[5] Of course, *interpretations* of a judgment can (and do) alter over time, and jurisprudence can evolve as new cases on comparable issues are decided. However, there exists a danger for states and scholars in perceiving judgments as an expression of international law, when in fact any judgment represents at best a 'freeze-frame' of that law.[6] This problem is obviously not something the Court can do anything about; it can only ever pronounce upon the law as it is (or at least as it appears to the Court to be) at the time the dispute is heard. Therefore, it may be unfair to criticise the Court for an earlier decision that is no longer in conformity with the law. Equally, in the study of international law and, more importantly, in *practice*, ICJ decisions must be treated with ever more caution as to their status as pronouncements of 'the law' as the amount of time that has elapsed since they were delivered increases.

With these cautionary remarks in mind, we can now move to an examination of what the Court has pronounced regarding self-defence, starting, in this chapter, with the concept of an armed attack.

II. ARMED ATTACK AS THE CONDITION *SINE QUA NON* FOR SELF-DEFENCE

A. The Requirement of an Armed Attack

Article 51 of the United Nations (UN) Charter holds that 'Nothing in the present Charter shall impair the inherent right of individual or collective self-defence *if an armed attack occurs* against a Member of the United Nations' (emphasis added). Therefore, it is undeniable that the Charter provides that it is a requirement for the lawful exercise of the right of self-defence that an armed attack has occurred against a UN member.

The jurisprudence of the ICJ certainly takes the position that an armed attack is a prerequisite for the lawful exercise of self-defence. A cursory examination of the decisions of the Court that relate to self-defence show that the ICJ has invariably turned to the question of whether there is a need

[5] Having said this, as we will see, the *Nicaragua* decision is still continually referenced by scholars. Moreover, in the more recent *Oil Platforms* and *DRC v Uganda* cases, the Court itself has relied heavily upon aspects of *Nicaragua*.

[6] In relation to the somewhat analogous assessment of how far 'codifying' treaties may be seen to reflect customary international law, Baxter has utilised the metaphor of a photograph. Such treaties 'photograph' the relevant aspect of customary international law as it is perceived at the point the treaty is drafted, but this does not necessarily mean that a codifying treaty will accurately represent the state of customary international law years later. RR Baxter, 'Multilateral Treaties as Evidence of Customary International Law' (1965–66) 41 *British Yearbook of International Law* 275, 299. The same may be said for judicial decisions.

for an armed attack, and if so, what constitutes such an attack, before examining any other potential requirements.[7]

In the *Nicaragua* judgment, the majority asserted conclusively and repeatedly that an armed attack is required before the right of self-defence can be activated. In paragraph 195, the Court stated:

> In the case of individual self-defence, the exercise of this right is subject to the state concerned having been the victim of an armed attack. Reliance on collective self-defence of course does not remove the need for this.[8]

Accordingly, the Court held that an armed attack is the most important criterion required to trigger the right of self-defence in cases when it is exercised by the victim state *and* in cases where the right is exercised by other states collectively on behalf of the victim state: specifically, it concluded that the United States '*must* first find that Nicaragua engaged in an armed attack against El Salvador, Honduras or Costa Rica' (emphasis added).[9] The finding that an armed attack is a prerequisite for self-defence is reinforced by the Court throughout the *Nicaragua* decision.[10] Indeed, notably, the Court labelled the armed attack requirement 'the condition *sine qua non* for the exercise of the right of collective self-defence'.[11]

Reaffirming this proposition from *Nicaragua*, the Court has also stressed the fundamental requirement of an armed attack elsewhere. For example, in the *Case Concerning Oil Platforms* (hereafter *Oil Platforms*), it was held that

> in order to establish that it was legally justified in attacking the Iranian platforms in exercise of the right of self-defence, the United States *has to show* that attacks had been made upon it for which Iran was responsible; and that those attacks were of such a nature as to be qualified as 'armed attacks' within the meaning of that expression in Article 51 of the United Nations Charter, and as understood in customary international law on the use of force (emphasis added).[12]

As the actions taken by the United States against Iran in *Oil Platforms* were purportedly an exercise of the right of self-defence taken individually, as opposed to the collective measures taken in *Nicaragua*, the ruling in *Oil Platforms* strengthens the view expressed in the earlier judgment

[7] This is with the exception of *Nuclear Weapons*, in which the Court started by affirming the conditions of necessity and proportionality and only mentioned armed attack in a quoted passage from *Nicaragua*. See *Nuclear Weapons* advisory opinion (n 2) para 41.

[8] *Nicaragua* merits (n 2) para 195.

[9] *Ibid*, para 229.

[10] The Court indicated the need for an armed attack throughout the *Nicaragua* judgment, although some of these indications were merely implicit: see *Nicaragua* merits (n 2) paras 35, 127, 191, 210, 211 and 237.

[11] *Ibid*, para 237.

[12] *Case Concerning Oil Platforms* (*Islamic Republic of Iran v United States of America*) merits (2003) ICJ Reports 161, para 51. See also para 71.

that the requirement for an armed attack applies equally to either manifestation of the right. The advisory opinion in *Legal Consequences of the Construction of a Wall in the Occupied Palestinian Territory* (hereafter *Israeli Wall*) confirms this position: 'Article 51 of the Charter thus recognises the existence of an inherent right of self-defence *in the case of armed attack*' (emphasis added).[13] Finally, in *Armed Activities on the Territory of the Congo* (*Democratic Republic of the Congo v Uganda*) (hereafter *DRC v Uganda*), the notion of an armed attack was referred to as if it were a self-evident requirement of the contemporary law governing self-defence actions, without the Court ever specifically stating that an armed attack is needed or outlining what the term means.[14]

Clearly then, the ICJ has affirmed the armed attack requirement with a degree of consistency across its case law on the question.[15] This is uncontroversial, given that the criterion appears clearly in Article 51. What is perhaps more interesting is that the Court has taken the view that the occurrence of an armed attack is the primary criterion for self-defence—the condition *sine qua non*. Again, this conclusion does not appear to be contrary to Article 51, which after all remains silent on some of the other potential requirements for a lawful exercise of self-defence, whilst being explicit regarding the need for an armed attack. It is therefore certainly a possible reading of the Article to hold that the armed attack requirement is of a special importance. Having said this, it is also important to note that the ICJ has held not only that an action taken under Article 51 must be in response to an armed attack (above all else), but that this also holds true in customary international law.[16]

[13] *Legal Consequences of the Construction of a Wall in the Occupied Palestinian Territory* advisory opinion (2004) ICJ Reports 135, para 139.

[14] See, eg, *DRC v Uganda* merits (n 2) paras 143, 146. Indeed, in accepting the DRC's claim to have been acting in self-defence in response to Uganda's counterclaim, the Court apparently saw the need for an armed attack as so self-evident that it did not mention the criterion at all. See para 304.

[15] This is not to say that this position has been wholly accepted by all members of the Court in any given decision. Eg, in his dissenting opinion to *Nicaragua*, Judge Schwebel indicated that the issue of whether a response could be taken in self-defence to something other than an armed attack was not at issue in the case, as the parties agreed that the actions complained of by the United States would constitute armed attacks if proved. *Nicaragua* merits (n 2) dissenting opinion of Judge Schwebel, paras 172–73.

[16] This is evident from the fact that the Court applied customary international law exclusively in *Nicaragua* (n 2), given the US multilateral treaty reservation. See specifically, para 176; and also *Oil Platforms* merits (n 12) para 51, where the Court stated that for lawful self-defence the attacks being responded to must be 'of such a nature as to qualify as "armed attacks" within the meaning of that expression in Article 51 of the United Nations Charter, and *as understood in customary international law on the use of force*' (emphasis added).

B. Armed Attack in the Context of Preventative Action

The possible exception to the need for an armed attack that can be found in the Court's jurisprudence is the notion of self-defence taken as a preventative measure: self-defence in response to the *threat* of attack, rather than an actual attack. As Christine Gray has pointed out, the terminology with regard to this alleged manifestation of self-defence is somewhat confused in the literature, with the terms 'interceptive', 'preventative', 'anticipatory' and 'pre-emptive' self-defence all having been employed (at some times synonymously and at others to express different meanings).[17] Therefore, it is worth being clear at this juncture as to the terminology that will be used in this book. The current author employs the following terminology, treating the phrases used as terms of art: 'anticipatory self-defence' is employed to refer to action taken in response to an *imminent* threat; 'pre-emptive self-defence' is used to denote action taken in response to a perceived threat that is more temporally remote.[18] Finally, the term 'preventative self-defence' is used to refer to *any* self-defence claim made in relation to a threat rather than an actual attack. (In other words, this concept covers both of the first two terms.)

The lawfulness of any form of preventative self-defence is something that the Court has as yet refused to pronounce upon. In *Nicaragua*, for example, the Court stated that it 'expresses no view on the issue [of preventative self-defence]'.[19] This statement was referred to and the same stance taken in *DRC v Uganda*.[20] In *Oil Platforms*, the notion of preventative self-defence was not even referenced by the Court. Certainly, then, the ICJ has not ruled out the possibility that such action could be lawful. Therefore, the notion of self-defence taken in response to the threat of force remains open for the Court.

Although the Court has refused to endorse the use of force in preventative self-defence, it would seem that even in this context, the Court takes an 'armed attack' to be the relevant standard. As was pointed out in *Legality of the Threat or Use of Nuclear Weapons* (hereafter *Nuclear Weapons*),

[17] C Gray, *International Law and the Use of Force*, 3rd edn (Oxford, Oxford University Press, 2008) 211–12.

[18] This particular terminological distinction is employed by both C Antonopoulos, 'Force by Armed Groups as Armed Attack and the Broadening of Self-Defence' (2008) 55 *Netherlands International Law Review* 159, 172 and N Shah, 'Self-Defence, Anticipatory Self-Defence and Pre-Emption: International Law's Response to Terrorism' (2007) 12 *Journal of Conflict and Security Law* 95, 111.

[19] *Nicaragua* merits (n 2) para 194.

[20] *DRC v Uganda* merits (n 2) para 143. Having said this, at para 148, the majority did state: 'Article 51 of the Charter may justify a use of force in self-defence only within the strict confines there laid down. It does not allow the use of force by a state to protect perceived security interests beyond these parameters.' Potentially, this could be seen as going against a notion of preventative self-defence, but this would depend on how one perceives the 'parameters' of Art 51, which are not 'laid down' particularly clearly.

a threat to use force is as much a violation of Article 2(4) of the UN Charter as an actual use of force.[21] Yet in the context of preventative self-defence, the issue that the Court has identified—and then decided that it is unable to pronounce upon—is not the threat of *force* but rather the threat of an *armed attack*. Thus at paragraph 35 of *Nicaragua*, the Court said:

> [I]n the circumstances of the dispute now before the Court, what is at issue is the purported exercise by the United States of a right of collective self-defence in response to an armed attack on another state. The possible lawfulness of a response to the imminent threat of an *armed attack* which has not yet taken place has not been raised (emphasis added).[22]

Then, again, at paragraph 194:

> In view of the circumstances in which the dispute has arisen, reliance is placed by the Parties only on the right of self-defence in the case of an armed attack which has already occurred, and the issue of the lawfulness of a response to the imminent threat of an *armed attack* has not been raised (emphasis added).[23]

In neither passage does the Court affirm the lawfulness of preventative self-defence. However, the implication is clearly that if such action *is* lawful, it is lawful *only* in the case of a threatened *armed attack*.

The lawful use of force in response to a threatened armed attack would appear somewhat contrary to the Court's conclusion that 'the exercise of this right [of self-defence] is subject to the state concerned *having been the victim* of an armed attack' (emphasis added).[24] It can be asked: how can a state show that an armed attack 'had been made upon it'[25] if there has not yet been an attack at all?[26] However, it is possible to see that such pronouncements of the Court were made in relation to the arguments presented before it in each case. Preventative self-defence was not explicitly claimed by the parties in *Nicaragua, Oil Platforms* or *DRC v Uganda*.[27] This fact may have contributed to the Court presenting its view of self-defence

[21] *Nuclear Weapons* advisory opinion (n 2) para 47. See also N Stürchler, *The Threat of Force in International Law* (Cambridge, Cambridge University Press, 2007) esp 38–43; R Sadurska, 'Threats of Force' (1988) 82 *American Journal of International Law* 239; and A Randelzhofer, 'Article 2(4)' in B Simma (ed), *The Charter of the United Nations: A Commentary, Volume I*, 2nd edn (Oxford, Oxford University Press, 2002) 112, 124–25.

[22] *Nicaragua* merits (n 2) para 35.

[23] *Ibid*, para 194.

[24] *Ibid*.

[25] To use the Court's phrase. *Oil Platforms* merits (n 12) para 51.

[26] JM Ruda, 'Some of the Contributions of the International Court of Justice to the Development of International Law' (1991–92) 24 *New York University Journal of International Law and Politics* 35, 40.

[27] Having said this, it may be argued that some *implicit* preventative argumentation has been presented to the Court. In *Oil Platforms*, the United States referred not only to the need to respond to the attacks it had suffered but also, in a limited manner, to the need to *secure against future threats*. *Oil Platforms* counter-memorial and counterclaim submitted by the United States (1997) www.icj-cij.org/docket/files/90/8632.pdf, Part IV, paras 4.27–4.30. Similarly, in *DRC v Uganda*, the Court noted that the Ugandan High Command document much relied on by Uganda to support its self-defence claim referred in detail to Uganda's

in response to an actual attack only. In such cases, the 'victim' state must have been the victim of an armed attack.

In any event, it does appear that even in the controversial situation of an preventative response to the threat of an attack, the Court has seen 'armed attack' to be the relevant standard for assessing the lawfulness of self-defence claims, assuming such claims are valid at all. One interpretation of the Court's position, then, is that an armed attack is required; the question is merely whether the armed attack was actual or potential. However, it must be concluded that, as the Court itself has maintained, the jurisprudence of the ICJ is inconclusive with regard to the lawfulness of preventative military action. As such, a detailed examination of this question would go beyond the scope of this work: an assessment of the lawfulness of preventative action would represent another monograph in itself. This is an extremely important issue but one that must be tackled elsewhere.[28] Thus, whilst this book will at times touch upon the notion of preventative action,[29] it is important to keep in mind that no conclusion is made herein as to lawfulness or unlawfulness of military force employed in response to a *threat* rather than an actual attack.

What is crucial to this analysis is that the ICJ has seen armed attack as the standard, and insofar as it refused to reject the lawfulness of preventative action, it did so with regard to preventative response to a threatened armed attack. Thus, the merits judgment in *Nicaragua* has led Terry Douglas Gill to state, following his examination of that decision: 'There can be no doubt that an armed attack, or at any rate the threat of an armed attack, is an absolute precondition for the exercise of the right of self-defence.'[30] The existence of an armed attack is—for the ICJ—the condition *sine qua non* for lawful self-defence.

need to secure against future attacks. The Court stated that such reference to future security amounted to a claim that was 'essentially preventative'. *DRC v Uganda* merits (n 2) para 143. Yet, as the decision also noted, *before the Court*, Uganda was clear that its self-defence action was taken only *as a response* to actual attacks. See *DRC v Uganda* merits (n 2) para 144 and, eg, *DRC v Uganda* counter-memorial submitted by Uganda (2001) www.icj-cij.org/docket/files/116/8320.pdf, para 6.

[28] The notion of preventative self-defence has generated a vast amount of literature since the adoption of the UN Charter, and academic writing on the subject has increased since 11 September 2001 (particularly with regard to responses to terrorist activity). Maogoto gives a useful overview of the main arguments concerning this issue and provides a survey of the literature: JN Maogoto, *Battling Terrorism: Legal Perspectives on the Use of Force and the War on Terror* (Aldershot, Ashgate, 2005) 111–49. See also M Sapiro, 'Iraq: The Shifting Sands of Pre-Emptive Self-Defence' (2003) 97 *American Journal of International Law* 599; C Greenwood, 'International Law and the Pre-Emptive Use of Force: Afghanistan, Al-Qaida, and Iraq' (2003) 4 *San Diego International Law Journal* 7; AD Sofaer, 'On the Necessity of Pre-Emption' (2003) 14 *European Journal of International Law* 209; and C Gray, 'The US National Security Strategy and the New "Bush Doctrine" on Pre-Emptive Self-Defence' (2002) 1 *Chinese Journal of International Law* 437.

[29] Most notably in ch 2, section VI-A.

[30] TD Gill, 'The Law of Armed Attack in the Context of the *Nicaragua* Case' (1988) 1 *Hague Yearbook of International Law* 30, 35.

III. IDENTIFYING AN ARMED ATTACK: A QUESTION OF GRAVITY

Once it is seen that the ICJ has perceived the criterion of an armed attack in this way, the next question must necessarily be: what, then, is an armed attack?[31] Without a clear view of what an armed attack actually constitutes, the law on self-defence as conceived by the ICJ cannot be applied in any real sense; it becomes impossible to test the legal validity of invocations of the right. Article 51 itself offers no guidance in the regard: the text of the Article simply states that an armed attack must have occurred. Therefore, having set down the fundamental criterion for lawful self-defence, the Court has further attempted to outline its content. In the ICJ's jurisprudence, the issue of defining an armed attack has been most extensively examined in the *Nicaragua* case, although *Oil Platforms* also offers some important insights.

A. Relating Armed Attack, Use of Force and Non-intervention

The starting point for examining the Court's conception of armed attack is the view that it has taken on the relationship between such attacks and other uses of force. In determining whether any measures taken amount to a lawful exercise of the right of self-defence, the Court has viewed it as 'necessary to distinguish the most grave forms of the use of force (those constituting an armed attack) from other less grave forms'.[32] Thus it would seem that a 'grave' forcible action will amount to an armed attack, whilst 'less grave' forcible action will not. This statement therefore posits the notion of 'gravity' in the determination of an armed attack.

Although it appears obvious that the Court is here making a distinction between uses of force of different levels of gravity, it should be noted that the Court's presentation of this distinction is far from helpful. The above quoted phrase as it appears in the judgment is nonsensical. It distinguishes the 'most grave' uses of force from 'other less grave forms'. By using the phrase '*other* less grave forms', the Court seems to imply that the 'most grave' forms are themselves in some manner 'less grave', which is simply illogical. It must be assumed that the Court meant either that 'most grave' uses of force were to be distinguished from 'less grave' uses of force, or instead intended to differentiate between grave uses and 'other uses' that are less grave.[33] The Court compounds this by repeating the phrase in *Oil*

[31] J Allain, 'The True Challenge to the United Nations System of the Use of Force: The Failures of Kosovo and Iraq and the Emergence of the African Union' (2004) 8 *Max Planck Yearbook of United Nations Law* 237, 242.

[32] *Nicaragua* merits (n 2) para 191.

[33] This point was raised during a seminar on the *jus ad bellum* taught by Dino Kritsiotis at the University of Michigan, 9 March 2005.

Platforms without alteration or comment.[34] This criticism may seem minor, given that what the Court *intends* to express appears relatively clear. However, this linguistic mistake is symptomatic of the Court's inadequate presentation of many of its legal conclusions with regard its conception of self-defence, as we will see.

Notwithstanding this, it is apparent that the suggestion made by the Court here is not merely that the gravity of an incident affects its status as an armed attack, but that this is the *primary* distinguishing feature of an armed attack. In itself, this provides little clarity as to the scope of an armed attack. It may be asked, 'how grave is grave?' Yet, while not providing much guidance as to how 'grave' a use of force must be to qualify as an armed attack, this statement of the Court does confirm that an armed attack must amount to a grave *use of force*, meaning that it must in itself be contrary to Article 2(4) of the UN Charter.[35] Of course, this is largely self-evident, particularly given the label of *armed* attack, but confirmation by the Court of the inherently forcible nature of such attacks is conceptually valuable nonetheless.

In fact, the Court goes further by highlighting the relationship between the concept of an armed attack and the principle of non-intervention.[36] An unlawful use of force is a breach of Article 2(4) of the Charter. Yet the ICJ has made it clear that an unlawful use of force also constitutes a breach of the principle of non-intervention.[37] From this it can be understood that in the Court's conception, a use of force amounts to a breach of the principle of non-intervention involving force, and an armed attack amounts to a particularly grave breach of this kind. As such, all armed attacks amount to both uses of force *and* interventions. In contrast, not all unlawful interventions, or indeed unlawful uses of force, amount to armed attacks. The framework the Court employs can thus be represented by Figure 1.1, with armed attack at the core.

An understanding of this relationship becomes particularly useful when the question of what amounts to an armed attack is examined in more detail.

[34] *Oil Platforms* merits (n 12) para 51.

[35] On the same basis, it would seem that (if one were to assume that the Court accepted the lawfulness of preventative self-defence) only the threat of *force*—which is equally a breach of Art 2(4)—would allow a forcible response. Indeed, perhaps only the threat of an armed attack (that is to say, *the threat of a grave use of force*) would give rise to this right. See above, section II-B. However, this essentially amounts to speculation and is not made explicit by the ICJ.

[36] The principle of non-intervention essentially requires states to refrain from coercion or interference in relation to the sovereign rights of other states. See the Declaration on the Admissibility of Intervention in the Domestic Affairs of States and the Protection of their Independence and Sovereignty 1965, GA Res 2131; and the Declaration on Principles of International Law Concerning Friendly Relations and Cooperation among States in accordance with the Charter of the United Nations 1970, GA Res 2625.

[37] *Nicaragua* merits (n 2) paras 205 and 247.

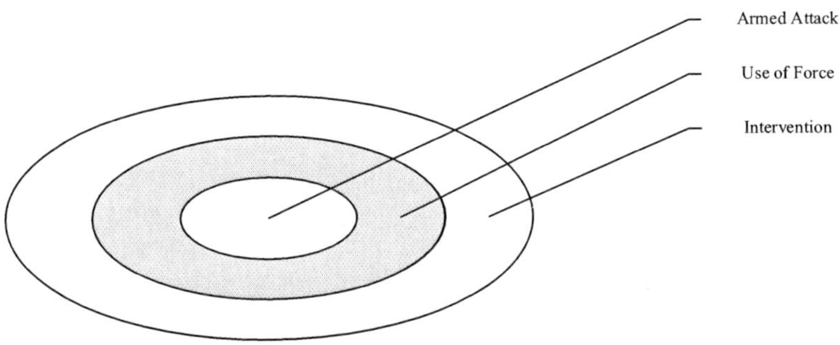

Figure 1.1 The Relationship between the ICJ Concepts of 'Armed Attack', 'Use of Force' and 'Intervention'

B. Specific Actions

In defining the 'most grave form of the use of force' the majority in *Nicaragua* claimed that there was a 'general agreement' as to situations that could be regarded as armed attacks.[38] To elucidate upon this 'general agreement', the Court turned for guidance to the Definition of Aggression adopted by the General Assembly in 1974,[39] which the *Nicaragua* judgment cited as reflecting customary international law.[40] Based on this, the Court outlined the 'nature of the acts which could be treated as constituting armed attacks' in paragraph 195 of the *Nicaragua* decision:

> [I]t may be considered to be agreed that an armed attack must be understood as including not merely action by regular armed forces across an international border, but also 'the sending by or on behalf of a state of armed bands, groups, irregulars or mercenaries, which carry out acts of armed force against another State of such gravity as to amount to' (inter alia) an actual armed attack conducted by regular forces, 'or its substantial involvement therein'. . . [I]n customary law, the prohibition of armed attacks may apply to the sending by a State of armed bands to the territory of another state, if such an operation, because of its scale and effects, would have been classified as an armed attack rather than a mere frontier incident had it been carried out by regular armed forces. But the Court does not believe that the concept of 'armed attack' includes not only acts by armed bands where such acts occur on a significant scale but also assistance to rebels in the form of the provision of weapons or logistical or other support.[41]

[38] *Ibid*, para 195.

[39] Definition of Aggression annexed to GA Res 3314. The Court particularly relied on Art 3(g).

[40] *Nicaragua* merits (n 2) para 195.

[41] *Ibid*. Quoted passages are derived from the Definition of Aggression annexed to GA Res 3314.

Despite the somewhat contorted wording of the passage, it is evident that the Court identified a number of 'acts' that may be attributable to states and then went on to determine whether these would amount to armed attacks. The first of these is 'action by regular armed forces across an international border'. This amounts to a 'classic' forcible intervention[42] and is included within the scope of an 'armed attack' under paragraph 195. The second situation is the sending of 'irregulars' and the like 'by or on behalf of' a state. This too the Court defined as amounting to an armed attack. However, it placed a limit upon this: not all actions by irregulars qualify as armed attacks, only those operations that by reason of their 'scale and effects' would not amount to a 'mere frontier incident' (as opposed to an armed attack) had they been conducted by regular forces. Thus only actions with sufficient 'scale and effects' by irregulars amount to armed attacks.

Whether the Court intended for this qualification to be seen as applying equally to the actions of regular armed forces is debatable. It was 'non-committal' as to the issue of what constituted a 'frontier incident' and how this was relevant to the finding of an armed attack.[43] If the term 'mere frontier incidents' is taken as another allusion to 'scale and effects' then it would seem that the Court was indicating that 'low-level' attacks by *either* regular or irregular forces are not armed attacks: the actions of regular armed forces must equally be sufficiently grave.

Alternatively, the phrase 'mere frontier incidents' could be taken to mean something different to 'scale and effects'; it could be seen as referring to the territorial integrity of the state concerned. Taking this interpretation of the jurisprudence, the actions of regular armed forces would constitute armed attacks *whatever the scale and effects of such actions*, unless they did not intervene across the border of the defending state or at least did not significantly intervene across that border. In such a case, the action of said regular forces could be seen as a mere frontier incident, even if that action was of a significant scale.

Yet a third interpretation of the phrase 'mere frontier incidents' could be that the Court was referring to such incidents as situations that may be about 'policing' rather than strictly constituting instances of military conflict, particularly in cases where border forces act without authority.[44] It may be that the Court was referring to the *nature* of incidents along the border of states, rather than the *gravity* of such actions as such. Under such

[42] H McCoubrey and ND White, *International Law and Armed Conflict* (Aldershot, Dartmouth Publishing Company Ltd, 1992) 48, in reference to the Definition of Aggression annexed to GA Res 3314.

[43] Gray (n 17) 178. See also C Greenwood, 'The International Court of Justice and the Use of Force' in V Lowe and M Fitzmaurice (eds), *Fifty Years of the International Court of Justice: Essays in Honour of Sir Robert Jennings* (Cambridge, Cambridge University Press, 1996) 373, 381.

[44] WH Taft IV, 'Self-Defence and the *Oil Platforms* Decision' (2004) 29 *Yale Journal of International Law* 295, 302.

an interpretation a 'frontier incident' refers to states policing their own territory, rather than initiating an attack on their neighbours. As such, the question of an armed attack would not arise as such an action would not constitute an international use of force.

In the view of this author, the first of these three interpretations of the phrase 'mere frontier incidents' is most logical: the question of whether the actions of 'regular armed forces' amount to an armed attack is for the Court dependent upon the scale and effects of those actions, as with irregular forces. This interpretation is taken for two reasons. First, the use of the word 'mere' indicates that the term 'frontier incidents' is used in relation to a notion of gravity, not simply to territorial integrity, or the nature of such incidents.[45] Second, reading the phrase to include the notion of gravity corresponds with the Court's position on the actions of irregular forces. As Gray argues, 'it is clear from the context of the Court's pronouncement that the difference envisaged [between an armed attack and a frontier incident] is one of degree rather than of kind.'[46] However, whilst the present author supports this position, it is not conclusive. For example, Ruth Wedgwood has taken the view that in *Nicaragua* the ICJ identified a gravity criterion for armed attack with regard to the actions of irregular forces *only*. In her view, the Court held that in the case of attacks by *regular* forces 'armed attack' is established per se.[47]

Wedgwood goes on, quite correctly, to indicate that by applying the gravity criterion to the facts in the *Oil Platforms* decision, the ICJ clearly indicated that a degree of gravity is required for an armed attack, irrespective of whether the incidents relied upon emanate from regular or irregular forces.[48] For Wedgwood, this was an addition by the Court to its earlier *Nicaragua* formulation; for this author it was merely a confirmation of it. In any event, it is clear that, following *Oil Platforms*, the Court conceives the need for an armed attack to constitute a qualitatively grave use of force, whether conducted by 'regular' or 'irregular' forces. Nonetheless, when examining the *Nicaragua* decision itself, it is evident that the Court was far from conclusive as to whether the 'armed attack as a grave use of force' criterion applied to both regular and irregular uses of force. This again highlights the difficulty in understanding the Court's conception of self-defence due to the manner in which that conception is presented.

[45] Having said this, of course, the fact that an incident takes place at a frontier does not necessarily reflect upon its gravity. See Y Dinstein, *War, Aggression and Self-Defence*, 4th edn (Cambridge, Cambridge University Press, 2005) 195. Indeed, this point was first made nearly sixty years ago by Fitzmaurice, acting as the UK representative to the Sixth Committee of the General Assembly: GG Fitzmaurice, 'Definition of Aggression (Speech)' (1952) 1 *International and Comparative Law Quarterly* 137, 139.

[46] Gray (n 17) 177–84, quoted at 178.

[47] R Wedgwood, 'The ICJ Advisory Opinion on the Israeli Security Fence and the Limits of Self-Defence' (2005) 99 *American Journal of International Law* 52, 57.

[48] *Ibid*. See *Oil Platforms* merits (n 12) generally, but especially at para 51.

Additionally, it should be noted that the Court also pointed out in paragraph 195 of the *Nicaragua* decision that the 'provision of weapons or logistical or other support' to rebels cannot be sufficient to qualify as an armed attack, although the Court held that it may amount to an unlawful use of force or a breach of the principle of non-intervention (or perhaps both). However, it was indicated later in the judgment that the 'mere supply of funds' to the contras by the United States could not amount to a threat or use of force against Nicaragua.[49] As such, based on the Court's earlier reasoning, it might be concluded that the *funding* of rebels (as opposed to the 'provision of weapons or logistical or other support') is neither an armed attack nor a use of force, although it may still amount to a breach of the principle of non-intervention.

Although it may not be concluded with absolute certainty, it is argued here that the ICJ intended to set out a 'gravity threshold' for armed attack applicable to attacks from both regular and irregular forces. In *Nicaragua*, the Court employed a variety of terms to describe the gravity threshold for an armed attack; it referred to 'most grave' uses of force, 'scale and effects', 'significant scale' and 'mere frontier incidents'. Do these phrases all amount to the same thing—namely a dividing line between 'armed attacks' and all other activities? Or do they relate to specific types of activity? For example, does a small scale intervention by a 'regular armed force' that takes place well within the territory of the 'victim' state amount to an armed attack? Such an incident would be hard to describe as a 'mere frontier incident'—the terminology that the Court specifically employed in relation to actions by the regular armed forces—yet it would nonetheless have nominal gravity. As noted above, the meaning of the term 'mere frontier incident' is rather unclear, but it is herein suggested that, in the context of the judgment, the term was intended by the Court to mean simply 'lacking in gravity'. Ultimately, it would seem that, despite the diverse terminology used, the Court essentially employed a test in *Nicaragua* that is based on *gravity*. However, the essential question remains: how grave is grave?[50]

Leaving aside this question as to where exactly the 'gravity threshold' lies, it is apparent that *Nicaragua* provides a framework for the determination of an armed attack and indeed for the use of force below the level of an armed attack. This is essentially based upon the gravity of the incident in question. On first appraisal, this framework has the appearance of being largely comprehensive in scope.

[49] *Nicaragua* merits (n 2) para 228. See also para 242, where the Court reaffirmed that the US funding of the contras amounted to a breach of the principle of non-intervention.

[50] As Reisman puts it, the Court sets out an 'unspecified threshold' of gravity: WM Reisman, 'Allocating Competences to Use Coercion in the Post-Cold War World: Practices, Conditions and Prospects' in LF Damrosch and DJ Scheffer (eds), *Law and Force in the New International Order* (Boulder, Westview Press, 1991) 26, 38.

Table 1.1 ICJ Framework for the Determination of an Armed Attack

Action	ICJ Classification
Sending of 'regular forces' with 'sufficient gravity'	Armed attack, use of force, intervention
Sending of 'irregular forces' with 'sufficient gravity'	Armed attack, use of force, intervention
'Frontier incidents'/sending of 'regular' or 'irregular' forces with insufficient gravity	Use of force, intervention
Provision of weapons/logistical support	Use of force, intervention
Funding of rebels	Intervention

The first two acts in Table 1.1 are above the required 'gravity threshold' to amount to an armed attack, whilst the other acts fall below this level. It has been argued that the various acts outlined by the Court and derived from the Definition of Aggression were employed in *Nicaragua* to act as a helpful list of possible uses of force, which—depending upon the gravity of a specific incident—may or may not qualify as an armed attack.[51] Thus, any act can be tested with regard to its scale and effects, and those of a certain level qualify as armed attacks.[52]

This is broadly true; however, the situation is slightly more complex than this. Whilst it appears that the Court applied a gravity criterion to actions of both regular and irregular forces, with regard to the provision of logistical or weapons support, the majority held that this *cannot* constitute an armed attack. This position was taken apparently regardless of the scale of the support.[53] It may be that the Court took the view that such material support is insufficiently qualitatively grave, by its very nature, to constitute an armed attack. However, this would mean that material support even on a vast scale would not be grave enough to give rise to the right of self-defence.

The particular problem of the provision of logistical or weapons support aside, in general it is clear is that whilst the Court has taken pains to label certain activities as armed attacks and others not so, the critical distinction is clearly the gravity or scale of the incident (and not the 'category' that the

[51] A Constantinou, *The Right of Self-Defence under Customary International Law and Article 51 of the UN Charter* (Brussels, Bruylant, 2000) 66.

[52] *Ibid.*

[53] Reisman (n 50) 39.

action falls into). It remains the case that, in determining whether an incident amounts to an armed attack in the view of the ICJ, 'the key is the scale of the activity.'[54]

Following *Nicaragua*, the issue remains as to where the line lies between 'the most grave form of the use of force' and 'less grave forms'. This issue was subsequently clouded further by the *Oil Platforms* judgment of 2003. In that decision, the two primary incidents that the United States referred to as triggering the right of self-defence were a missile attack on 16 October 1987 upon a single US flag vessel, the Kuwaiti tanker *Sea Isle City*, and the mining on 14 April 1988 of a single US warship, the USS *Samuel B Roberts*. In determining whether these incidents amounted to armed attacks, the Court turned to its previous incantation in the *Nicaragua* judgment that armed attacks were defined as 'the most grave forms of the use of force' and that, conversely, 'less grave forms' did not constitute such attacks.[55]

The issue of whether the specific instances cited by the United States amounted to armed attacks was ultimately not determinative for the decision, as the Court found that it had not been established that either were attributable to Iran.[56] However, the Court did make obiter statements in this regard.

In relation to the missile attack on the *Sea Isle City*, taken in conjunction with the other incidents cited by the United States as adding to the gravity of the *Sea Isle City* attack and potentially amounting to armed attacks in themselves, the Court stated that 'these incidents do not seem to the Court to constitute an armed attack on the United States.'[57] Therefore the majority held that even if it had been attributable to Iran, the attack on the *Sea Isle City* was not, in itself or as part of a wider pattern of forcible action, an armed attack. On initial inspection, the most obvious reason for this is that the Court concluded that an attack against a single vessel was not a sufficiently grave use of force to cross the 'gravity threshold' and thus to trigger the right of self-defence. This is logical: based upon the *Nicaragua* schema this action would—as an attack on just one individual vessel and thus being of a comparatively minor gravity—constitute something akin to 'a mere frontier incident'.

However, regarding the attack of 14 April 1988 on the USS *Samuel B Roberts*, it was held: 'The Court does not exclude the possibility that the mining of a single military vessel *may be sufficient* to bring into play the inherent right of self-defence' (emphasis added).[58] Here, then, the Court

[54] R Higgins, *Problems and Process: International Law and How We Use It* (Oxford, Oxford University Press, 1994) 250.
[55] *Oil Platforms* merits (n 12) para 51.
[56] *Ibid*, paras 61 and 72.
[57] *Ibid*, para 64.
[58] *Ibid*, para 72.

was saying that while the mining could not be satisfactorily attributed to Iran in the present case, in principle the USS *Samuel B Roberts* incident (or at least, an incident of a similar kind) could amount to an armed attack. Based on this it can be contended that an attack on a single vessel may in fact constitute a use of force of sufficient 'scale and effects' to qualify as an armed attack. This somewhat confuses the notion of gravity as detailed in *Nicaragua,* as it is arguable that the destruction of one vessel falls short of being one of the 'most grave forms of the use of force'. Certainly, this conclusion appears to widen the scope of armed attack—and therefore the ICJ's conception of self-defence—beyond the restrictive *Nicaragua* position.

As noted, the Court was clear that the *Sea Isle City* incident, even if taken in conjunction with other incidents, could not amount to an armed attack. Based simply on the question of gravity, it is very hard to distinguish between the *Sea Isle City* incident and 'the mining of a single military vessel'. Both amount to an attack on a single vessel. Yet there are factual differences between the *Sea Isle City* incident and the USS *Samuel B Roberts* incident. The Court did not elucidate which of these factual differences legally distinguishes the two incidents in terms of the armed attack requirement.

First, the *Sea Isle City* was a *merchant* vessel owned by Kuwait, although flagged by the United States. In contrast, the USS *Samuel B Roberts* was a *military* vessel of the US Navy. If the Court distinguished the two incidents based upon a distinction between military and non-military vessels, it could be argued that this distinction was similar to the one advanced in *Nicaragua* between armed attacks and 'mere frontier incidents', if one were to take the view that with the phrase 'frontier incidents' the Court was referring to domestic 'policing' actions along a state's own border, rather than using the term to imply the application of a gravity threshold. Force used against a merchant vessel could potentially be a 'policing' exercise, whilst force against a military vessel could never be. However, it has already been argued that a more contextually logical view of the distinction between 'frontier incidents' and armed attack in *Nicaragua* is based upon a question of gravity and not the nature of such incidents as such.

Maintaining the view that *Nicaragua* essentially set out a requirement of gravity for armed attack, it is difficult to identify a distinction between an attack on a merchant vessel as being any less grave than an attack on a military vessel. Both actions constitute attacks on single vessels. Even if one accepts, as the ICJ appeared to in *Oil Platforms,* that an attack on a single vessel meets the gravity test set down in *Nicaragua* (something that may certainly be questioned), can it be argued that an attack on a military vessel is qualitatively more grave than an attack on a merchant vessel?

So far in the discussion, we have viewed 'gravity' as a single criterion based on the scale of the activity. However, in one formulation employed by the Court at least, the general notion of 'gravity' has two aspects. It could be argued that an attack on a single military vessel, while not amounting to a use of force of a more significant *scale* than the use of force against a merchant vessel, may in fact produce more detrimental *effects* for the responding state. This could be detrimental to the national security and defence of the state concerned in a way that an attack on a merchant vessel—or even on the nationals of that state—could never be. Admittedly, the Court does not refer to the idea of 'effects' as being specifically relevant to this aspect of the *Oil Platforms* case. Nonetheless, this idea offers a plausible explanation of the distinction made in the *Oil Platforms* case between the two incidents, based upon the notion of gravity: an attack on a single military vessel may be seen as having more grave effects than an attack on a single merchant vessel. Ultimately, though, this amounts to conjecture, and the application on the armed attack requirement by the Court here is, again, far from clear.

The Court's distinction between the *Sea Isle City* incident (which it concluded would not have amounted to an armed attack even if it had been imputable to Iran) and the mining of the USS *Samuel B Roberts* (which it saw as having the potential to have amounted to an armed attack) would certainly suggest that the military nature of a target is significant as to whether an attack constitutes an 'armed attack' where that attack occurs outside of the territory of the victim state. However, there were other factors that may have influenced the Court's distinction between the *Sea Isle City* and the USS *Samuel B Roberts*.

For example, whilst the *Sea Isle City* flew the flag of the United States, it was a Kuwaiti-owned vessel, again unlike the USS *Samuel B Roberts*. Thus the Court may have held that only an attack against a vessel owned by the state (military or otherwise) may constitute an armed attack. However a more detailed examination of the case would suggest that attacks on commercial vessels can constitute armed attacks, as long as the vessel in question was *flying the flag* of the responding state.[59] This was implied when the Court concluded:

> The *Texaco Caribbean* [a merchant vessel of US ownership], whatever its ownership, was not flying the United States flag, so that an attack on the vessel is not in itself to be equated with an attack on that State.[60]

As this statement was made in the context of the question whether the United States had suffered an armed attack, it could be taken to imply that

[59] N Ochoa-Ruiz and E Salamanca-Aguado, 'Exploring the Limits of International Law Relating to the Use of Force in Self-Defence' (2005) 16 *European Journal of International Law* 499, 513.

[60] *Oil Platforms* merits (n 12) para 64. The mining of the *Texaco Caribbean* on 10 August 1987 was one of the series of attacks, along with the *Sea Isle City* incident, cited by the United States as justifying its response of 17 October 1987. *Oil Platforms* preliminary objection submitted by the United States of America (1993) www.icj-cij.org/docket/files/90/8624.pdf, annex, para A1.15.

an attack on a merchant vessel might not only be 'an attack on a state' but an *armed* attack on a state (if the vessel attacked was flying that state's flag).[61] However, again this cannot be said with certainty.

Perhaps the best reading of the *Oil Platforms* judgment is that a distinction was drawn between military vessels and non-military vessels, the former reaching the gravity threshold for an armed attack, given the different effects of such an attack. This interpretation is supported by the Definition of Aggression, which explicitly provides that '[a]n attack . . . on the land, sea or air forces, or marine or air fleets' would qualify as an act of aggression,[62] whilst other forms of non-territorial 'aggression' are not mentioned. Given the Court's reliance on the Definition in determining the scope of armed attack, this acts to strengthen the proposition that the ICJ has accepted only *military* non-territorial targets as being capable of constituting armed attacks.[63] As with so much of the jurisprudence of the ICJ on the issue, however, this cannot be said with any certainty.

C. A Variable Standard

It is arguable that the 'gravity threshold' set out by the Court with regard to self-defence may itself be a variable standard. By this it is meant that, in the ICJ's conception of self-defence, there is not an objective criterion against which actions can be tested to ascertain whether or not they are armed attacks. Instead, the gravity threshold may be different in every case, depending on the facts of the situation. In other words, it may not be merely the case that the scale of the activity must be considered in *conjunction* with contextual factors, but that other factors actually *determine* the gravity threshold necessary to trigger self-defence: in other words, 'gravity' is context specific.[64] Thus, not only is the occurrence of an armed

[61] Ochoa-Ruiz and Salamanca-Aguado (n 59) 513.

[62] Definition of Aggression annexed to GA Res 3314, Art 3(d).

[63] Having said this, it must be kept in mind that the acts set out in the Definition were never intended to be an exhaustive list of activities qualifying as acts of aggression. See Art 4.

[64] See the view taken by Gray in the context of the Eritrea/Ethiopia Claims Commission's decision on the *jus ad bellum* aspects of that dispute. In that decision, the Claims Commission emphatically stated: 'Localised border encounters between small infantry units, even those involving the loss of life, *do not* constitute an armed attack for the purposes of the Charter' (emphasis added). Eritrea/Ethiopia Claims Commission Partial Award, *Jus ad Bellum* (Ethiopia claims 1–8) http://www.pca-cpa.org/upload/files/FINAL%20ET%20JAB.pdf, para 11. Gray has argued first that the Claims Commission should have elaborated upon what an armed attack did in fact entail (not merely upon what did *not* equate to an armed attack) and second, that the Claim Commission's view that frontier incidents can *never* constitute armed attacks may be erroneous. Instead, she takes the position that the jurisprudence of the ICJ in cases such as *Nicaragua* and *Oil Platforms* should be taken in the context of those cases (collective self-defence and third-state intervention during an ongoing conflict respectively). Thus, *in the right context*, a border incident may be sufficiently grave to constitute an armed attack. C Gray, 'The Eritrea/Ethiopia Claims Commission Oversteps its Boundaries: A Partial Award?' (2006) 17 *European Journal of International Law* 699, esp 717–20.

attack a question of fact (whether there has in fact been a grave unlawful use of force), but the *threshold* for the legal assessment of what constitutes an armed attack may also be dependant upon the factual circumstances of each dispute.

This would certainly explain why the Court has not stated definitively the gravity threshold between armed attacks and other uses of force: that threshold is different in relation to each dispute. This in many ways makes sense, as any rigid threshold would be difficult to apply in practice.[65] However, once again, the Court does not make its position clear in this regard; this 'context-specific gravity threshold' theory amounts to an inferred hypothesis of the Court's position following, particularly, the conclusion in *Oil Platforms* regarding the mining of a single military vessel. Given the fundamental nature of an armed attack as the condition *sine qua non* for the lawful exercise of self-defence, there appears to be little in the ICJ's jurisprudence to effectively guide states as to where the 'gravity threshold' lies or, if it is subjective, what factors may affect it in any given situation.

IV. ARMED ATTACK AS AN ACCUMULATION OF EVENTS

Whether the ICJ's view is that the 'gravity threshold' required for an armed attack is a fixed or variable standard, the Court appears to have held, albeit implicitly, that the requisite level can be achieved through the accrual of a number of uses of force against the responding state that in themselves fall below the level of an armed attack. In principle at least, the Court has accepted the theory that a number a small-scale uses of force falling below the level of an armed attack can collectively amount to such an attack. This is the so-called 'accumulation of events' theory.[66]

The position of the Court in this regard is best illustrated by paragraph 64 of the *Oil Platforms* decision. In relation to the initial claim of the United States that the attack on the *Sea Isle City* was not the sole ground for its actions against the first set of platforms, the Court took the view that the question before it was 'whether that attack [on the *Sea Isle City*], either in itself *or in combination* with the rest of the "series . . . of attacks" cited by the United States can be categorised as an "armed attack" on the United

[65] Gill (n 30) 36.

[66] On the accumulation of events theory generally, see NM Feder, 'Reading the UN Charter Connotatively: Towards a New Definition of Armed Attack' (1987) 19 *New York University Journal of International Law and Politics* 395, 415–18; DW Bowett, 'Reprisals Involving Recourse to Armed Force' (1972) 66 *American Journal of International Law* 1, 5; RJ Erickson, *Legitimate Use of Military Force Against State Sponsored International Terrorism* (Maxwell Air Force Base, Air University Press, 1989) 143–44; TJ Farer, 'Law and War' in CE Black and RA Falk (eds), *The Future of International Order* (*Vol III: Conflict Management*) (Princeton, Princeton University Press, 1971), 64–67; and Gray (n 17) 155–56.

States' (emphasis added).[67] In responding to that question, the Court concluded in the same paragraph that '*even taken cumulatively* . . . these incidents do not seem to the Court to constitute an armed attack on the United States' (emphasis added).[68] Therefore, while the Court rejected the view that the United States had been the victim of an armed attack by accrual on the facts of the case, it clearly accepted that this was possible in principle.

The theory was also implicitly accepted in *Nicaragua*, where it was stated that due to a lack of evidence, it was difficult for the Court to determine whether certain incursions into the territories of Honduras and Costa Rica could be treated 'as amounting, singly or collectively, to an armed attack'.[69] In *DRC v Uganda*, the Court similarly appeared to accept the notion that an accumulation of smaller attacks could constitute an armed attack. However, this acceptance was again merely implicit. In relation to a number of attacks perpetrated by the Allied Democratic Forces (ADF), the ICJ held that 'on the evidence before it, even if this series of deplorable attacks could be regarded as cumulative in character, they still remained non-attributable to the DRC.'[70]

It should be noted that in all three contentious cases, this apparent acceptance was not directly relevant to the Court's conclusion on the facts. Nonetheless, the Court has repeatedly accepted the theory prima facie, even though this acceptance has equally repeatedly been of an obiter nature. Further, in *Cameroon v Nigeria*, the ICJ was asked to rule by Cameroon upon a number of frontier incidents purportedly committed by Nigeria, as a single collective action giving rise to Nigerian responsibility.[71] The Court felt that neither party had produced sufficient evidence to show that such incidents had or had not occurred and thus refused to pronounce upon the question.[72] As such, it did not reject the idea that a number of comparatively minor attacks could be treated as a single grave attack in principle. This has been viewed as a further implicit acceptance by the ICJ of the accumulation of events theory in relation to armed attacks.[73] Whilst this is possible, such an interpretation may perhaps amount to reading a little too much into the Court's decision in *Cameroon v Nigeria*. Unlike in *Nicaragua*, *Oil Platforms* or *DRC v Uganda*, the Court did not imply an acceptance of the theory in its reasoning; it simply refused to

[67] *Oil Platforms* merits (n 12) para 64.

[68] *Ibid.*

[69] *Nicaragua* merits (n 2) para 231.

[70] *DRC v Uganda* merits (n 2) para 146.

[71] Eg, see *Cameroon v Nigeria* replique de la Republique du Cameroun (2000) www.icj-cij.org/docket/files/94/8603.pdf, Part III, para 11.168 [translated for the author by N Peregrine].

[72] *Land and Maritime Boundary between Cameroon and Nigeria* (*Cameroon v Nigeria: Equatorial Guinea intervening*) merits (2002) ICJ Reports 9, paras 323–24.

[73] Gray (n 17) 156.

pronounce upon it at all. Equally, Cameroon did not claim to have been acting in self-defence explicitly[74] and as such did not equate an accumulation of events to the notion of an armed attack as such but rather argued that the assessment of the lawfulness of Nigerian actions should be made by reference to the alleged incidents collectively.[75]

In any event, taken together, the decisions of the Court would appear to indicate a provisional acceptance on the part of the ICJ of the accumulation of events theory. In addition, Judges Nagendra Singh[76] and Jennings[77] implicitly accepted the possibility that an armed attack could occur through an accumulation of events in their opinions attached to *Nicaragua*, and Judge Schwebel similarly stated that the actions of Nicaragua were 'cumulatively tantamount to an armed attack upon El Salvador'.[78] In contrast, Judge Simma rejected this view in his *Oil Platforms* separate opinion:

> Also, there is in the international law on the use of force no 'qualitative jump' from iterative activities remaining below the threshold of Article 51 of the Charter to the type of 'armed attack' envisaged here.[79]

Judge Simma's position aside, there has been general acceptance of the accumulation of events theory by the Court, and this can be seen to pose further problems in attempting to determine the lawfulness of any given action ostensibly taken in self-defence. For example, how many 'minor' attacks are required to constitute an armed attack?[80] This problem is essentially the same as the 'gravity threshold' problem prevalent in the Court's conception of 'singular' armed attacks. Where does the line lie? Yet the lack of certainty is compounded in relation to cumulative armed attacks in that the varying gravity of a number of incidents must be taken into account. Therefore, not only must the gravity of an incident be assessed and tested against an uncertain standard, but a 'net gravity' must be calculated and tested against an uncertain standard.

V. THE LEVEL OF STATE INVOLVEMENT IN AN ATTACK

The next question that arises regarding the determination of an armed attack is the identity of the perpetrator. The issue here is whether the insti-

[74] In contrast to Nigeria, see *Cameroon v Nigeria* counter-memorial submitted by Nigeria (1999) www.icj-cij.org/docket/files/94/8602.pdf, Part V, para 24.49. See also *Cameroon v Nigeria*, CR 2002/14, www.icj-cij.org/docket/files/94/5029.pdf, para 41 and CR 2002/18, www.icj-cij.org/docket/files/94/5045.pdf, para 68.

[75] *Cameroon v Nigeria* replique de la Republique du Cameroun (n 71) para 11.168.

[76] *Nicaragua* merits (n 2) separate opinion of President Nagendra Singh, para 154.

[77] *Ibid*, dissenting opinion of Judge Jennings, para 543.

[78] *Ibid*, dissenting opinion of Judge Schwebel, para 6.

[79] *Oil Platforms* merits (n 12) separate opinion of Judge Simma, para 14.

[80] A Laursen, 'The Judgment by the International Court of Justice in the *Oil Platforms* Case' (2004) 73 *Nordic Journal of International Law* 135, 155.

gator of an armed attack must be a state or whether a state that has suffered an attack perpetrated by non-state actors may use force in response. This question has particular resonance with regard to responses against terrorist activity, in that terrorists groups are not state actors (though they may of course have a strong connection to a state entity). As such, it is notably topical, in the context of the so-called 'war on terror'.

In terms of the gravity criterion alone, it is clear that attacks from terrorists can reach the threshold to be considered armed attacks.[81] The best example of this is the attacks of 11 September 2001, which were considered by many to be grave enough to constitute an armed attack or armed attacks.[82] Perhaps somewhat obviously, a large-scale attack by a terrorist group can be as much an armed attack in terms of 'scale and effects' as an attack by regular forces. However, a response in self-defence is invariably going to be directed at a state; where terrorist forces emanate from a 'host' state that has no control over them (and potentially no means of stopping their activity), the question of whether the law does—or should—allow for a response becomes a problematic one.

Turning once again to the jurisprudence of the ICJ, a statement in the *Israeli Wall* opinion of 2004 appears to indicate that, for the Court at least, the correct view is that an armed attack must come from a state: 'Article 51 of the Charter thus recognises the existence of an inherent right of self-defence in the case of an armed attack by one state against another state'.[83] Thus, it seems that the Court requires the author of the armed attack to have been a state.[84]

Indeed, taking this passage from *Israeli Wall* at face value, it would seem to indicate that only *direct* action by a state (to use *Nicaragua* terminology: the sending of 'regular armed forces') can constitute an armed attack. However, as we have seen, in *Nicaragua*, the ICJ accepted that forms of indirect action, such as the sending of irregulars and the like, could amount to an armed attack. This clearly goes beyond a classic 'one state attacking another' situation, and thus one would assume that the Court in

[81] Shah (n 18) 105; and M Byers, 'Terrorism, the Use of Force and International Law After 11 September' (2002) 51 *International and Comparative Law Quarterly* 401, 412.

[82] See SD Murphy, 'Terrorism and the Concept of Armed Attack in Article 51 of the UN Charter' (2002) 43 *Harvard International Law Journal* 41, esp 45–51; Antonopoulos (n 18) 169; and APV Rogers, 'Terrorism and the Law of War: September 11 and Its Aftermath', Crimes of War Project, 2001, www.crimesofwar.org/expert/attack-apv.html. By recognising the right of self-defence in the aftermath of 11 September 2001, the Security Council appeared to imply that this attack could be viewed as an armed attack in SC Res 1368. However, this was not explicit in the resolution.

[83] *Israeli Wall* advisory opinion (n 13) para 139.

[84] This is the interpretation of the jurisprudence taken, eg, by Antonopoulos (n 18) 165. Having said this, the wording of this passage is once again somewhat ambiguous. As has been pointed out, the Court did not state that self-defence must be taken *only* in response to an attack by one state against another state. SD Murphy, 'Self-Defence and the *Israeli Wall* Advisory Opinion: An *Ipse Dixit* from the ICJ?' (2005) 99 *American Journal of International Law* 62, 63.

Israeli Wall was indicating the need for an 'armed attack [be it direct or indirect] by one state against another state'.

Nonetheless, it will also be recalled that the Court in *Nicaragua* held that it was only action by irregulars or other 'non-state' actors *that were sent* 'by or on behalf of a state' that amounted to an armed attack.[85] The implication here is that the actions of actors having no connection to or direction from a state do not qualify as armed attacks.[86] This is strengthened by another passage from the *Israeli Wall* advisory opinion. Here, mention is made of the fact that Israel did 'not claim that the attacks against it [were] *imputable* to a foreign state' (emphasis added), which meant for the Court that Israel's actions were beyond the scope of self-defence.[87] Most recently, in *DRC v Uganda*, the Court stated:

> [W]hile Uganda claimed to have acted in self-defence, it did not ever claim that it had been subjected to an armed attack by the armed forces of the DRC. The 'armed attacks' to which reference was made came rather from the ADF . . . [and] there is no satisfactory proof of the involvement in these attacks, direct or indirect, by the government of the DRC. The attacks did not emanate from armed bands or irregulars sent by the DRC or on behalf of the DRC.[88]

As the attacks were seemingly not directly attributable to the DRC, in spite of the fact that they emanated from the territory of that state, the ICJ felt Uganda had no basis for a response in self-defence against the DRC.

It would seem, then, that whilst the Court has accepted that indirect attacks may constitute armed attacks, a state that is merely unable to stop attacks of this kind occurring will not have committed an armed attack, and thus self-defence action cannot be taken. Yet the requirement for a degree of state involvement has caused controversy in the Court. A number of judges have expressed their disapproval over this general acceptance by the majority of a requirement for an action giving rise to self-defence to have been perpetrated by a state. For example, Judge Higgins argued in her separate opinion to *Israeli Wall*:

> There is, with respect, nothing in the text of Article 51 that thus stipulates that self-defence is available only when an armed attack is made by a state. That qualification is rather a result of the Court so determining in [*Nicaragua*].[89]

[85] *Nicaragua* merits (n 2) para 195.

[86] Gray (n 17) 132. However, the Court did not hold conclusively in *Nicaragua* that an armed attack *could not occur* if irregulars were sent by or on behalf of a *non-state* entity. This point was made by Christopher Greenwood at a lecture at University College London, 10 November 2004. For a contrary view—that *Nicaragua* confirmed that states could not respond in self-defence against states 'harbouring' but not directing or controlling terrorist groups—see M Byers, 'Geopolitical Change and International Law' in D Armstrong, T Farrell and B Maiguashca (eds), *Force and Legitimacy in World Politics* (Cambridge, Cambridge University Press, 2005) 51, 56.

[87] *Israeli Wall* advisory opinion (n 13) para 139.

[88] *DRC v Uganda* merits (n 2) para 146.

[89] *Israeli Wall* advisory opinion (n 13) separate opinion of Judge Higgins, para 33. A similar point is made by Shah (n 18) 97.

Similar positions were taken in *Israeli Wall* by Judges Kooijmans[90] and Buergenthal,[91] and in *DRC v Uganda* by Judges Simma,[92] Koroma[93] and Kooijmans (once again),[94] with the last of these stating:

> If armed attacks are carried out by irregular bands . . . against a neighbouring state, they are still armed attacks even if they cannot be attributed to the territorial state [from which they originate].[95]

From one perspective, a requirement of state involvement in an attack would appear fairly logical, prima facie, as it is states against which actions of self-defence are taken. However, when one examines the notion more thoroughly, a number of problems emerge beyond the mere fact that a 'state author' requirement cannot be identified from Article 51. First, it can be suggested that such a requirement may not be consistent with state practice, particularly following the atrocities of 11 September 2001. Thus, if indeed it was ever the case that the law required state involvement before self-defence could be invoked, it has been argued by a number of writers that contemporary customary international law has developed to allow for self-defence against actors that have little or no relationship to or with their 'host' state whatsoever.[96] Given this, it is striking that the ICJ should apparently put forward a 'state author' requirement in 2004 at a time when non-state terrorism had such a prevalent influence on international politics and the use of force.[97]

More importantly, the requirement of attribution to a state is problematic in itself in terms of application. Under such a criterion, it is possible to argue that a state could 'host' terrorists that launch an attack against another state on a truly massive scale, but this would not qualify as an armed attack (despite being particularly grave), due to an insufficient

[90] *Israeli Wall* advisory opinion (n 13) separate opinion of Judge Kooijmans, para 35.

[91] *Ibid*, declaration of Judge Buergenthal, para 6.

[92] *DRC v Uganda* merits (n 2) separate opinion of Judge Simma, paras 4–15.

[93] *Ibid*, declaration of Judge Koroma, para 9.

[94] *Ibid*, separate opinion of Judge Kooijmans, paras 19–30.

[95] *Ibid*, para 30.

[96] This is not the place to discuss such arguments in detail. For more, see below, ch 4, section IV. See also KN Trapp, 'Back to Basics: Necessity, Proportionality and the Right of Self-Defence Against Non-State Terrorist Actors' (2007) 56 *International and Comparative Law Quarterly* 141, esp 147–55; TM Franck, 'Terrorism and the Right of Self-Defence' (2001) 95 *American Journal of International Law* 839, 840; R Wedgwood, 'Responding to Terrorism: Strikes Against bin Laden' (1999) 24 *Yale Journal of International Law* 559, esp 564; Wedgwood (n 47) 57–59; and Murphy (n 84) 63–70. However, it is true that other scholars writing post-11 September have taken a position more closely aligned to that of the ICJ, seeing at least some level of state involvement as being a prerequisite for a response in self-defence. See I Scobbie, 'Words My Mother Never Taught Me: In Defence of the International Court' (2005) 99 *American Journal of International Law* 76, 80–81; and T Gazzini, *The Changing Rules on the Use of Force in International Law* (Manchester, Manchester University Press, 2005) 184–91.

[97] I Scobbie, 'Smoke, Mirrors and Killer Whales: the International Court of Justice's Opinion on the Israeli Barrier Wall' (2004) 5 *German Law Journal* 1107, 1127.

degree of complicity on the part of the 'hosts'.[98] This potentially offers terrorist organisations a degree of impunity against potential military responses, in a world where traditional 'one state against another' style conflict is no longer the norm.

Despite the reservations expressed both from within the Court and outside of it, the majority decisions of the ICJ certainly support the view that there needs to be some level of involvement between a state and the physical perpetrators of an action before that action can qualify as an armed attack. Indeed, the main issue that emerges from the jurisprudence here is not whether the ICJ has held that there needs to be a degree of state involvement: this is fairly clear. The question is rather *what* level of involvement is required by the Court.

The level of involvement of a host state with a terrorist group or other form of non-state actor operating from its territory can vary greatly. It may be that a state tolerates the activities of the group (meaning it fails to take steps within its power to stop the activities of the group or to remove the threat posed from within its territory to other states). It may be that the non-state actors are encouraged by the 'host' state or provided with logistical and other support. Indeed, it may be that the group is directly controlled by the state. Equally, it is possible that a state is not at fault, in that it is doing everything within its power to stop the operations of the group but is simply unable—due to resources, for example—to do so effectively. What degree of involvement on the part of the 'host' state does the ICJ require before the grave attack of a non-state actor can be responded to?

Nicaragua indicates that the attack must have been 'by or on behalf of' the 'attacking' state, which suggests an element of direction: the irregulars must be under the control of the state. In the alternative, Judge Schwebel argued that the majority should have employed a less strict test, given its reliance upon Article 3(g) of the Definition of Aggression. That Article does not employ the phrase 'by or on behalf of' with regard to irregulars but instead uses the term 'substantial involvement therein'. Based upon this test, then, any substantial involvement by a state would be enough for the actions of irregulars to constitute an armed attack:

> To be entitled to [respond in self-defence, a state] is not required to show that the irregulars operating on its territory act as the agents of the foreign state or states which support them. It is enough to show that those states are 'substantially involved' in the sending of those irregulars onto its territory.[99]

Yet even this slightly widened test of 'substantial involvement' requires a degree of culpability—what Farer terms 'a level of collaboration'[100]—on the part of a state entity.

[98] Murphy (n 84) 66.
[99] *Nicaragua* merits (n 2) dissenting opinion of Judge Schwebel, para 167.
[100] TJ Farer, 'Drawing the Right Line' (1987) 81 *American Journal of International Law* 112, 113.

It is worth noting here that an interpretation of the Court's jurisprudence on this issue has been advanced that makes a distinction between, on the one hand, a response taken by the victim state against a host state when only the non-state actors operating within that state are targeted and, on the other hand, actions in self-defence when the government or forces of the host state itself are additionally targeted.[101] It has been argued that in *Nicaragua*, *Israeli Wall* and *DRC v Uganda*, the Court has held that there must be a level of collaboration on the part of the host state in the latter situation but not in the former. In cases in which the response is directed solely at, say, a terrorist military base, all that is required is that the 'host' state was unable or unwilling to act.[102]

This has a degree of both practical and conceptual appeal. However, there is no basis for identifying such a distinction in the jurisprudence of the ICJ. It appears fairly clear, given the use of the phrases 'by or on behalf of' (in *Nicaragua* and *DRC v Uganda*) and 'imputable' (in *Israeli Wall*) that the ICJ requires a degree of collaboration on the part of a host state in all cases in which self-defence is invoked. The ICJ has required more than a mere unwillingness or inability to act. The next issue, then, is how one determines the level of 'culpability' or state involvement required to trigger the right of self-defence.

One possible means of assessing this is to base the 'involvement test' upon state *responsibility*. In other words, if a state is legally responsible for the actions of the irregulars, then the actions of said irregulars may amount to an armed attack. A state is 'responsible' in international law if it is established that a violation of an international legal obligation, attributable to that state, has occurred.[103] Yet establishing international legal responsibility is notoriously difficult, due to the very nature of employing necessarily general rules to determine whether any particular action amounts to a breach of an international obligation.[104]

Nicaragua itself does provide some guidance as to the specific question of determining state responsibility in international law for the actions of armed irregulars, and this is essentially based upon 'effective control':

[101] Trapp (n 96) 142–45.

[102] *Ibid*.

[103] Articles on the *Responsibility of States for Internationally Wrongful Acts*, adopted by the International Law Commission (ILC) at its fifty-third session, November 2001, Chapter I.

[104] D Bodansky and JR Crook, 'Symposium: The ILC's State Responsibility Articles: Introduction and Overview' (2002) 96 *American Journal of International Law* 773, 773–74. The inherent problems involved in finding workable general rules for establishing state responsibility is well evidenced by the forty-eight years taken by the ILC to produce its articles on the subject (n 103). The emergence of the ILC Articles does clarify the position somewhat: R Rosenstock, 'The ILC and State Responsibility' (2002) 96 *American Journal of International Law* 792, 796–97. However, there remains much controversy over the ILC's work on this issue and the determination of the legal responsibility of states for their actions generally: P Allott, 'State Responsibility and the Unmaking of International Law' (1998) 29 *Harvard International Law Journal* 1, esp 12.

> For this conduct [of the contra forces] to give rise to legal responsibility of the United States, it would in principle have to be proved that that state had effective control of the military and paramilitary operations in the course of which the alleged violations [of human rights and humanitarian law] were committed.[105]

A similar effective control test is now embodied in Article 8 of the International Law Commission (ILC) Articles on the Responsibility of States for Internationally Wrongful Acts,[106] in relation to state responsibility for the actions of 'agents' of the state, as opposed to organs of the government of the state. In *Corfu Channel* (*United Kingdom v Albania*) (hereafter *Corfu Channel*), the Court held that a state is under an obligation 'not to allow knowingly its territory to be used contrary to the rights of other states'.[107] These cases therefore suggest tests based upon *control* or *knowledge* respectively. As such, it has been argued that the jurisprudence of the ICJ indicates that 'if self-defence is invoked against action by armed groups it must be attributed to another state in the sense of proving the existence of substantial or effective control by that state of the armed group.'[108]

However, the statements in both *Nicaragua* and *Corfu Channel* were made with regard to 'state responsibility'—a term of art meaning the responsibility of a state for *a breach of international law*[109]—not with regard to the level of state involvement necessary for an armed attack giving rise to the right of self-defence. These are conceptually different things. Under the Court's view of self-defence, an armed attack is obviously a breach of international law, but then so is a use of force below the level of an armed attack, and indeed a breach of the principle of non-intervention *simpliciter* below that. As such, the level of involvement required for a state to have committed an armed attack and the level of involvement for it to be responsible in international law for the actions of irregular forces operating from within its territory cannot necessarily be treated synonymously.

In any event, whilst a test based upon the wider notion of state responsibility would appear in many ways logical, there is nothing in the Court's jurisprudence to suggest that it has envisaged employing such a test with regard to state involvement in an armed attack.[110] Indeed, in his declara-

[105] *Nicaragua* merits (n 2) para 115. It should be noted that this finding was limited to the specific question of whether the United States was responsible for violations of humanitarian law and human rights committed by the contra forces.

[106] See n 103.

[107] *Corfu Channel* (*United Kingdom v Albania*) merits (1949) ICJ Reports 4, 22.

[108] Antonopoulos (n 18) 168.

[109] Higgins has defined state responsibility in its most basic form as being 'about accountability for a violation of international law': Higgins (n 54) 147. See also the Articles on the *Responsibility of States* (n 103) Chapter I.

[110] Irrespective of academic contention to the contrary. See Shah (n 18) 108–11, who uncritically assumes that the 'effective control' test and the question of state involvement in an armed attack are treated by the ICJ as being synonymous. See also Antonopoulos (n 18) 168.

tion attached to *DRC v Uganda*, Judge Koroma made it clear that he saw international responsibility for the actions of irregular forces and the level of state involvement of the degree necessary for an attack of such irregulars to constitute an armed attack as different things. He argued that 'a state [that] is powerless to put an end to the armed activities of rebel groups despite the fact that it opposes them'[111] has not committed an armed attack. However, he nonetheless took the view that the inability to prevent such an attack by irregulars 'would engage the international responsibility of the state concerned'.[112]

The fact that there is a conceptual distinction between a state incurring international responsibility for the acts of irregulars and the question of whether it has been sufficiently 'involved' with such irregulars to allow a state that has suffered a grave use of force against it perpetrated by such irregular forces is also supported by some analogous reasoning from the *DRC v Uganda* merits judgment. In that decision, with regard to the first counterclaim of Uganda, the Court was clear that the responsibility of a state in international law for a breach of a duty of vigilance with regard to the actions of irregulars—for example by 'acquiescing' to the presence of terrorist organisations on its territory, contrary to the Declaration on Friendly Relations[113]—was different from active support of an irregular group, which could of itself constitute a breach of the principle of non-intervention or a use of force (and therefore implicitly an armed attack).[114] In any event, even if state responsibility was viewed as the correct test in this context, the imprecise nature of determining state responsibility in the first instance would mean that such a test would far from solve the problem of determining what level of state involvement in an armed attack is necessary for self-defence to be invoked against it.

VI. ARMED ATTACK IN COLLECTIVE SELF-DEFENCE

As has been noted, the ICJ has been clear that the fundamental criterion of an armed attack is required in collective self-defence in the same way as in individual self-defence.[115] Indeed, all of the above analysis of the Court's

[111] *DRC v Uganda* merits (n 2) declaration of Judge Koroma, para 9.

[112] *Ibid.*

[113] Declaration on Principles of International Law Concerning Friendly Relations (n 36), which provides: 'Every state has the duty to refrain from organizing, instigating, assisting or participating in acts of civil strife or terrorist acts in another state or acquiescing in organized activities within its territory directed towards the commission of such acts, when the acts referred to in the present paragraph involve a threat or use of force.'

[114] *DRC v Uganda* merits (n 2) paras 276–305, esp para 300. It should be noted that the Court did not in fact find the DRC to be in breach of a duty of vigilance, nor did the ICJ hold it responsible for a breach of the principle of non-intervention in this context.

[115] See above, section II-A.

conception of the armed attack requirement can be seen as applying equally to individual and collective self-defence.

However, the ICJ also made clear in *Nicaragua* that it is not enough for a state using force in collective self-defence to identify that an armed attack has occurred against the state it claims to be acting on behalf of. It is not for the state invoking self-defence collectively to determine when an armed attack has taken place. Instead it is entirely up to the 'attacked' state to decide whether it has been the victim of an armed attack. Indeed, the ICJ has indicated that the victim state must not only form but also '*declare* the view that it has been so attacked'.[116] The Court stated:

> There is no rule in customary international law permitting another state to exercise the right of collective self-defence on the basis of its own assessment of the situation. Where collective self-defence is invoked, it is to be expected that the state for whose benefit this right is used will have declared itself to be the victim of an armed attack.[117]

More than simply requiring the victim state to have declared that it is or has been the target of an armed attack, the Court also made it plain in *Nicaragua* that the victim state must *request* the aid of a collective defender (be it one other state or a number of states) in responding to an armed attack. This request must be explicit and cannot be inferred from a declaration that the victim has suffered an armed attack:

> At all events, the Court finds that in customary international law, whether of a general kind or that particular to the inter-American system, there is no rule permitting the exercise of collective self-defence in the absence of a request by the State which regards itself as the victim of an armed attack. The Court concludes that the requirement of a request by the State which is the victim of the alleged attack is additional to the requirement that such a State should have declared itself to have been attacked.[118]

Despite contentions to the contrary,[119] this would certainly seem to indicate that the Court has required that a victim state requests aid before collective self-defence may be viewed as lawful. This is reinforced, albeit implicitly, by *DRC v Uganda*, in which the Court endorsed the right of collective self-defence by holding that 'a state may invite another state to assist it in using force in self-defence.'[120]

What is not clear from the paragraph quoted from *Nicaragua* is whether a victim state must request the aid of the state (or states) that actually respond to that request, or whether a general request for aid is acceptable. For example, was it required of El Salvador in the *Nicaragua* dispute that it

116 *Nicaragua* merits (n 2) para 195.
117 *Ibid.*
118 *Ibid*, para 199. See also para 165.
119 Gray (n 17) 186.
120 *DRC v Uganda* merits (n 2) para 128.

requested the aid of the United States? Or would it have been enough (assuming other criteria were met) for it to have simply made an open request of the international community at large? An earlier paragraph of the decision seems to provide an indication as to this. When it first turned to the issue of the request of the victim state, the Court stated:

> The question remains whether the lawfulness of the use of collective self-defence by the third state for the benefit of the attacked state . . . depends on a request addressed by that state *to the third state* (emphasis added).[121]

From this statement it can be inferred that the Court took the view that a request for aid must be directed at the state that in fact provides that aid. However, this is not clear: the Court sets out the question of requests in collective self-defence in this way, but in answering this question it does not refer again to the issue of to whom the request must be made.

These requirements of a declaration and a request by the victim state clearly place additional burdens upon states invoking collective self-defence. The identification of an armed attack is, as it were, 'out of their hands'. In his dissenting opinion to *Nicaragua*, Judge Jennings indicated that while the intention behind these requirements was commendable, expecting states to provide formal declarations and requests may be unrealistic in practice. Judge Jennings saw the requirements of declaration and request as potentially impairing the 'inherent' right of states to act in collective self-defence.[122]

A further issue is the implications of a failure to meet these additional requirements for collective self-defence. The question here is whether these criteria are what may be termed *determinative as to lawfulness*, meaning that a collective action that met all the other elements of lawful self-defence would be rendered unlawful by virtue of a failure to request aid by the victim. The language used by the Court in one instance appears to indicate that the criteria of declaration and request are legally determinative in this way: 'the *requirement* of a request by the state which is the victim of the alleged attack is additional to the *requirement* that such a state should have declared itself to have been attacked' (emphasis added).[123]

Similarly, Judge Ruda appears to have interpreted these conditions as requirements for collective self-defence, though this was not made explicit.[124] However, it has been argued that it is unlikely that the Court saw these aspects of collective self-defence as quite so fundamental but instead viewed them as evidentially beneficial in determining the lawfulness of a

[121] *Nicaragua* merits (n 2) para 196.

[122] *Ibid*, dissenting opinion of Judge Jennings, para 545. This point was also made by Judge Schwebel in his dissenting opinion, para 191.

[123] *Nicaragua* merits (n 2) para 199.

[124] *Ibid*, separate opinion of Judge Ruda, para 175. It should be noted that Judge Ruda saw the discussion of these aspects of collective self-defence in *Nicaragua* as unnecessary, given that the Court had already concluded that there was no armed attack upon El Salvador et al.

collective self-defence action.[125] This view is supported, at least in relation to the issue of a declaration by the victim state, by another pronouncement of the Court: 'it is *to be expected* that the State for whose benefit this right is used will have declared itself to be the victim of an armed attack' (emphasis added).[126] It is clear that these additional elements were stressed by the Court as aspects of collective self-defence. However, the actual consequences of the absence of a declaration of an armed attack and a request for aid to repel it on the part of the victim state are, as with so many of the issues discussed in this chapter, far from clear based upon the Court's jurisprudence.

VII. THE CONCEPT OF FORCIBLE COUNTERMEASURES

Given that the Court has placed such emphasis on the concept of an armed attack and, still further, has defined this as constituting something more than a mere use of force, it would seem that forcible action cannot be taken in response to a use of force that falls below the standard of an armed attack—in other words, a 'less grave' use of force. This would obviously mean that a state can only respond to a comparatively minor use of force against it with non-forcible measures.

However, an obiter statement made in *Nicaragua* appears to suggest otherwise. In paragraph 249 of that judgment, the Court indicated that in such a situation the victim state may be entitled to initiate 'proportionate countermeasures'.[127] Admittedly, the Court did not explicitly hold that these countermeasures could be forcible in nature. Indeed, it did not pronounce on the nature of the countermeasures it alluded to in paragraph 249 at all.[128] Nonetheless, it may be argued that the statements of the Court can be read as amounting to an acceptance of *forcible* countermeasures. Certainly this was the interpretation of this passage from the Court's 1986 judgment taken by Judge Simma in his 2003 separate opinion to *Oil Platforms*: 'by such proportionate countermeasures the Court cannot have understood mere pacific reprisals.'[129]

Judge Simma took this view because a pacific response to a use of force would in many instances be largely worthless to a defending state; if such responses are not forcible, this leaves states without the means to respond to a use of force against them. This position—that the 'armed attack as a grave use of force' requirement leaves a large 'gap' between forcible

[125] DW Greig, 'Self-Defence and the Security Council: What Does Article 51 Require?' (1991) 40 *International and Comparative Law Quarterly* 366, 376–78.

[126] *Nicaragua* merits (n 2) para 195.

[127] *Ibid*, para 249.

[128] Though it does refer to this notion elsewhere in the judgment. *Ibid*, para 210.

[129] *Oil Platforms* merits (n 12) separate opinion of Judge Simma, para 12.

attacks suffered and the forcible responses that may be taken—will be discussed in more detail in chapter three.[130] For the present it is simply enough to note that it has been seen as a factor that strengthens the interpretation that the Court intended to refer to *forcible* countermeasures. In addition to this, it can be argued that the Court's reference to the concept of 'proportional countermeasures' as being 'analogous' to self-defence[131] is a further indication that the Court saw these measures as entailing the use of force.

Although it can be argued that in *Nicaragua* the Court approved the lawfulness of forcible countermeasures, not all writers have drawn this conclusion. For example, Yoram Dinstein has indicated that the countermeasures mentioned by the Court 'cannot entail the use of force—however analogous to self-defence—in the absence of an armed attack'.[132] The notion of forcible countermeasures as a response to a low-level use of force has not appeared in the other relevant decisions of the ICJ. It has been suggested that the fact that the Court did not endorse the concept of forcible countermeasures in *Oil Platforms* in particular is evidence that the ICJ does not accept such action as lawful.[133]

However, the silence of the Court in *Oil Platforms* on this issue cannot be taken as a rejection of the idea of forcible countermeasures. The fact that the Court did not refer to forcible countermeasures in the judgment was understandable given that, on the evidence before the Court, it concluded that the attacks against the *Sea Isle City* and the USS *Samuel B Roberts* could not be attributed to Iran. Therefore the question of whether the response of the United States amounted to 'self-defence' or 'countermeasures' would be irrelevant, as it was not proved that Iran had in fact attacked these vessels. Nonetheless, as noted above, in his separate opinion to *Oil Platforms*, Judge Simma expressed his discontent that the Court in that decision failed to stress the legal validity of countermeasures that would prima facie breach Article 2(4) of the UN Charter.[134]

Thus, the less than emphatic way in which forcible countermeasures were put forward in *Nicaragua* remains the only judicial authority for such action. Perhaps the best way of looking at the issue is that in *Nicaragua* '[t]he Court *strongly suggested* . . . that the victim state's "proportionate countermeasures" *might* themselves include the use of force' (emphasis added).[135] The majority judgment in *Oil Platforms* neither supports nor weakens this conclusion.[136]

130 See especially ch 3, section VI.
131 *Nicaragua* merits (n 2) para 210.
132 Dinstein (n 45) 194.
133 Ochoa-Ruiz and Salamanca-Aguado (n 59) 509–10.
134 *Oil Platforms* merits (n 12) separate opinion of Judge Simma, para 12.
135 JL Hargrove, 'The *Nicaragua* Judgment and the Future of the Law of Force and Self-Defence' (1987) 81 *American Journal of International Law* 135, 138.
136 *Oil Platforms* merits (n 12) separate opinion of Judge Higgins, para 43.

If forcible countermeasures are accepted as lawful, despite constituting in themselves a use of force, such countermeasures would not amount to an action in *self-defence* as such, under the Court's conception. This is due to the obvious fact that there would have been no occurrence of an armed attack. However, the lawfulness of forcible countermeasures would mean that a use of force below the level of an armed attack, such as the provision of weapons or logistical support by State A against State B, could give State B the right to respond with force.

This *Nicaragua* idea of forcible countermeasures has been tentatively equated with the notion of armed reprisals.[137] The traditional notion of armed reprisals, as distinct from self-defence, is that they constitute a use of force either aimed at securing compliance with an obligation under international law or taken in punitive response to the breach of such an obligation.[138] As such, they are not conceptually *defensive* in nature.

However, it would seem unlikely that the ICJ was alluding to the lawfulness of armed reprisals when it referred to 'proportionate countermeasures' in *Nicaragua*, for a number of reasons. First, since the adoption of the UN Charter—and specifically due to Article 2(4)—armed reprisals have generally been condemned as being unlawful.[139] It would be anomalous for the Court to suddenly, albeit equivocally, affirm their lawfulness. Second, conceptually, the distinction between self-defence and reprisals is based upon the nature of the action taken in response,[140] not the gravity of what is being responded to. A response to a use of force taken a number of years after the event would still be deemed as an armed reprisal, however grave the initial attack was. This is because the action would clearly have been punitive.[141]

[137] Gazzini (n 96) 138–39.

[138] J Combacau, 'The Exception of Self-Defence in UN Practice' in A Cassese (ed), *The Current Legal Regulation of the Use of Force* (Dordrecht, Martinus Nijhoff, 1986) 9, 27–28.

[139] Eg, The Declaration on Principles of International Law Concerning Friendly Relations (n 36) states: 'States have a duty to refrain from acts of reprisal involving the use of force.' Similarly, the Security Council decreed, in relation to British aerial attacks against Yemen in 1964, that 'reprisals [are] *incompatible* with the principles and purposes of the UN' (emphasis added). See SC Res 188.

[140] RW Tucker, 'Reprisals and Self-Defence: the Customary Law' (1972) 66 *American Journal of International Law* 586, 589–90. However, Bowett has pointed out that this conceptual difference is actually difficult to establish in practice. This is partly because it is largely impossible to identify the punitive *intent* of a state and partly because the issue becomes clouded in the case of a conflict involving numerous uses of force on both sides. Here, an individual incident may appear to be an unlawful reprisal, but it may well be arguable that it constitutes self-defence in the overall context of the conflict. Bowett (n 66) 2–10. See also JA Green, 'Self-Defence: A State of Mind for States?' (2008) 55 *Netherlands International Law Review* 181, 188–201.

[141] However, the 'punitive' nature of an armed reprisal must be assessed not with regard to illusory notions of intent (as is traditionally done) but on the basis of a failure to meet the criteria of necessity and proportionality. See Green, *ibid*.

Having said this, it has been argued that armed reprisals may be divided into two classes, one being lawful and the other unlawful.[142] Thus, Cassese has suggested that whilst the traditional punitive conception of armed reprisals should be viewed as unlawful, it should be distinguished from armed reprisals that constitute 'an immediate armed reaction to a minor use of force'.[143] This second 'class' of armed reprisals would appear to reflect the ICJ's 'proportionate countermeasures',[144] so far as such a concept can be identified from the Court's obiter statement. Seen from this perspective, it may be possible to conclude that the ICJ was affirming the lawfulness of a particular form of armed reprisal. However, one may argue that this distinction between two types of armed reprisal is unhelpful: the term 'armed reprisal' has connotations that are distinct from what the Court has tentatively appeared to have considered as a lawful response to a comparatively minor use of force. The Court certainly cannot be said to have affirmed the lawfulness of punitive military sanctions or interstate retaliation involving force. To say that a certain type of armed reprisal is lawful implies that other 'types' may also be. It is then perhaps more helpful, in stressing this distinction, to refer to forcible countermeasures as opposed to a confusing notion of 'second-tier' armed reprisals.

In any event, whatever terminology is applied with regard to a forcible response to a 'less grave' attack, it becomes evident that, taken together, self-defence as set out by the ICJ and forcible countermeasures as suggested by it, would theoretically provide a means of responding to *any* unlawful use of force against a state. This conclusion somewhat undermines the Court's repeated focus upon the need for and the nature of an armed attack. Forcible countermeasures—if such action were in fact

[142] See, eg, A Cassese, *International Law*, 2nd edn (Oxford, Oxford University Press, 2005) 371–73; Bowett (n 66) esp 26–32; and Dinstein (n 45) 221–31.

[143] Cassese, *ibid*, 372.

[144] Though Cassese has not related the Court's notion of countermeasures to his secondary form of armed reprisals. *Ibid*, 371–73. Cassese is not the only scholar to make a distinction between reprisals that are 'lawful' and those that may be seen as 'unlawful'. Eg, both Dinstein and Bowett have identified what they see to be lawful 'types' of reprisal. However, these conceptions are both different from that advanced by Cassese and are indeed also different from each other. Dinstein holds that what he terms 'defensive armed reprisals' constitute actions of *self-defence* (meaning that they have been taken in response to a grave 'armed attack'), where the response has occurred 'at a time and a place different from those of the original armed attack': Dinstein (n 45) 221–31, quoted at 222. This conception of 'defensive armed reprisals' cannot be seen as being related to the ICJ's notion of forcible countermeasures, because the lawfulness of 'defensive armed reprisals' derives from the fact that they would fall under the rubric of self-defence. For Bowett, reprisals may be seen as lawful when they meet a standard of 'reasonableness'. He sets out criteria to establish this and refers to state practice—primarily from the Middle East—to support this notion: Bowett (n 66) esp 26–32. However, as with Dinstein's conception of lawful reprisals, this is unlikely to be linked to the ICJ's notion of 'forcible countermeasures'. In this case, it is because Bowett, unlike Cassese, retains the punitive element in his notion of 'second-tier' lawful reprisals, something which has clearly been rejected by both the Security Council and the General Assembly (above, n 139).

accepted as lawful by the ICJ—appear distinctly similar to an action in self-defence: both would constitute a forcible response to an unlawful use of force. The only difference between a 'forcible countermeasure' and an action taken in self-defence is that the use of force has not qualified as an armed attack (an already somewhat illusory standard). What, then, for the Court, is the difference between an action in self-defence and the use of lawful forcible countermeasures, other than semantics?

The answer is to be found in the situation of a collective action. Whilst it appears that the Court may have accepted the notion that a victim state may respond with either forcible countermeasures in the event of a use of force against it that falls below the level of an armed attack, or self-defence in the case of an actual armed attack, the Court has repeatedly concluded that third-party states can only forcibly come to the aid of the victim state if that state has suffered an armed attack. So, for example, the Court has stated:

> The acts of which Nicaragua is accused, even assuming them to have been established and imputable to that state, could only have justified proportionate countermeasures involving the use of force on the part of the state which had been the victim of these acts, namely El Salvador, Honduras or Costa Rica. *They could not justify countermeasures taken by a third state*, the United States, *and particularly could not justify intervention involving the use of force* (emphasis added).[145]

Thus, whilst it is arguable whether individual forcible countermeasures have been accepted by the ICJ, it appears clear that collective action can *only* be taken in response to an armed attack. In other words, the notion of individual forcible countermeasures may have been accepted by the Court as lawful, but collective forcible countermeasures have been ruled unlawful.

Ultimately, on this question, we are left with two possibilities that emerge from the jurisprudence of the Court, neither of which being particularly helpful. The first possibility is that the ICJ did not in fact intend to advocate forcible responses at all with regard to 'minor' uses of force, and reference to 'countermeasures' was to a non-forcible variety. Any suggestion to the contrary would therefore merely be symptomatic of the lack of clarity employed by the Court throughout *Nicaragua* and the other cases concerning self-defence. Under this interpretation of the jurisprudence, the only possible forcible response that can be taken by a state (other than one authorised under Chapter VII of the UN Charter) would be self-defence in response to a qualitatively grave use of force. In such a situation, of course, a victim state would be left with no recourse to defend itself against a forcible attack if that attack failed to reach the required (though largely undefined) level of gravity. This problem will be returned to in chapter three.[146]

[145] *Nicaragua* merits (n 2) para 249. See also paras 211 and 252.
[146] See especially ch 3, section VI.

We will turn for the present to the second possible interpretation of references to 'countermeasures' in *Nicaragua*. This is that the 'countermeasures' referred to in that decision amount to lawful military responses to attacks against a state that breach the prohibition on the use of force but do not reach the level of gravity to constitute an armed attack; the response must, however, come from the victim state itself and not from a third state acting collectively. Taking this interpretation, 'countermeasures' can be seen as individual self-defence by another name: 'low grade' individual self-defence, if you will. Under such a distinction, the Court could form a restrictive interpretation of armed attack whilst still allowing states to use force in response to forcible action against them that fell below that standard. Based on this analysis, it seems possible that the Court's restrictive conception of an armed attack criterion and its reliance on the notion of gravity may have been intended to restrict *third-party responses* in collective self-defence.[147] The Court's restrictive view of armed attack theoretically limits large conflicts, in that third-party states will not be lawfully empowered to respond forcibly in instances involving uses of force of a comparatively minor nature. As such, claims of collective self-defence and 'counter' collective self-defence are restricted, ensuring that disputes of lesser gravity do not lead to a large number of states all using force lawfully, or at least with a potential pretext of lawfulness.

Despite the benefits evident in this approach, there remain difficulties with the Court's position regarding the relationship between armed attacks and countermeasures. This aspect of the *Nicaragua* jurisprudence was criticised passionately by Judge Schwebel in his dissenting opinion to the case. He objected on the basis that weak states that have suffered a less grave attack have no means of defence under this position. This is because a weak state may well not possess the military capability to repel even a 'minor' attack, yet it would nonetheless be barred from requesting outside aid.[148] Indeed, the majority itself noted that only powerful states are likely to be able to use force internationally.[149]

The Court's apparent presentation of a notion of forcible countermeasures has also been criticised on the basis that it creates a new category of lawful uses of force not found in state practice—one that is 'open-ended

[147] See Gray (n 17) 180–81; MacDonald (n 2) 149; Farer (n 100) 114; and JN Moore, 'The *Nicaragua* Case and the Deterioration of World Order' (1987) 81 *American Journal of International Law* 151, 152.

[148] *Nicaragua* merits (n 2) dissenting opinion of Judge Schwebel, para 177. See also *Nicaragua* merits (n 2) dissenting opinion of Judge Jennings, para 543; TM Franck, 'Some Observations on the ICJ's Procedural and Substantive Innovations' (1987) 81 *American Journal of International Law* 116, 120; Moore, *ibid*, 155; and LB Sohn, 'The International Court of Justice and the Scope of the Right of Self-Defence and the Duty of Non-intervention' in Y Dinstein and M Tabory (eds), *International Law at a Time of Perplexity: Essays in Honour of Shabtai Rosenne* (Dordrecht, Martinus Nijhoff, 1989) 869, 877–78.

[149] *Nicaragua* merits (n 2) para 202, quoting *Corfu Channel* merits (n 107) 35.

and . . . unknown in content and limit'.[150] For example, one might presume that forcible countermeasures are regulated by the criteria of necessity and proportionality in the same way as self-defence actions. However, whilst the Court does explicitly refer to such countermeasures as being 'proportionate',[151] it does not elucidate upon this and does not touch upon the notion of necessity at all in this context.[152] The novel nature of forcible countermeasures means that there is not a legal framework for their operation, and the ICJ does not provide one. Thus, poorly defined, they are open to abuse.

VIII. CONCLUSION

Ultimately, the picture that emerges from the relevant decisions of the ICJ is that armed attack forms the heart of the Court's conception of the law of self-defence. This is not to say that the Court did not identify other aspects of the law governing the right. However, the Court clearly saw other criteria as being secondary in nature. The vast majority of the Court's jurisprudence on self-defence involves an analysis of the armed attack criterion: it identifies this requirement and then attempts to define what constitutes such an attack.

It is evident from the above analysis that to attempt any kind of definition of 'armed attack' based upon the Court's jurisprudence is difficult. Of course, it can be argued that a rigid definition would be counterproductive and impossible to apply to the realities of international disputes involving force.[153] However, some attempt must be made to collate the Court's view of armed attack, as it is essential that there is a level of clarity as to the existence of such attacks, given that they are claimed to be the condition *sine qua non* for the lawful exercise of self-defence.

For the Court, there are a number of factors that are relevant to the question of whether any particular action constitutes an armed attack. Amongst these factors, gravity forms the main basis of the armed attack criteria. Expanding upon Table 1.1 above, we can see the general relationships that the Court outlines in *Nicaragua* between certain types of action and the consequent legal responses available to the recipient or 'victim' state, including whether that state can seek collective aid from a foreign power.

[150] Hargrove (n 135) 142.

[151] *Nicaragua* merits (n 2) para 249. Additionally, it was also held in *Gabcikovo-Nagymaros* that countermeasures must be proportionate, though this was in relation to non-forcible countermeasures. *Case Concerning the Gabcikovo-Nagymaros Project* (*Hungary v Slokakia*) merits (1997) ICJ Reports 3, para 85.

[152] Having said this, the need for necessity was implicit in the Court's brief discussion of countermeasures. *Nicaragua* merits (n 2) para 210.

[153] SA Alexandrov, *Self-Defence against the Use of Force in International Law* (The Hague, Kluwer Law International, 1996) 97–98.

Table 1.2 Expanded ICJ Framework for the Determination of an Armed Attack

Action	ICJ Classification	Legally Valid Response	Who Can Respond?
Sending of 'regular forces' with 'sufficient gravity'	Armed attack, use of force, intervention	Self-defence	Victim state, others at the request of the victim state (individual or collective)
Sending of 'irregular forces' with 'sufficient gravity'	Armed attack, use of force, intervention	Self-defence	Victim state, others at the request of the victim state (individual or collective)
'Frontier incidents'/ sending of 'regular' or 'irregular' forces with insufficient gravity	Use of force, intervention	Forcible countermeasures*	Victim state (individual only)
Provision of weapons/logistical support	Use of force, intervention	Forcible countermeasures*	Victim state (individual only)
Funding of rebels	Intervention	Non-forcible countermeasures (counter-intervention)	Victim state (individual only)

* This cannot be said with certainty, as the forcible nature of individual countermeasures is implied but not explicit in the pronouncements of the Court.

Table 1.2 gives some guidance as to the Court's position regarding responses that a state can take to various attacks against it. However, as we have seen, not all state actions fit neatly into one of the 'types' in the left-hand column. The factual circumstances of *Oil Platforms* demonstrated this: the case did not involve the crossing of a frontier by regular or irregular forces, or indeed 'forces' at all, in the context of the *Nicaragua* formulation.

There are many questions that remain regarding the Court's conception of the armed attack requirement. For example: can attacks on merchant vessels constitute armed attacks? Does an armed attack need to emanate from a state, and if so, what level of state involvement in the attack is required? In the case of collective self-defence, does the Court require a victim state to determine for itself that an armed attack has occurred, declare this determination and then request aid in repelling it? Finally, and perhaps fundamentally, in regard to armed attack, we can still return to that most troublesome of questions: how grave is 'grave'? A lack of clarity regarding the lawfulness of preventative self-defence in response to a threatened armed attack and the lawfulness of forcible countermeasures further adds to this uncertainty.

Moreover, the problems with the jurisprudence are not merely substantive. The very presentation of the ICJ's position is consistently unhelpful, with much of what the Court has held being unclear. To attempt to understand the Court's conception, much must be inferred. Indeed, the pronouncements of the Court regarding self-defence have to be carefully 'unpicked' to determine the view taken in the decisions. The crucial paragraph 195 of *Nicaragua* illustrates this problem well; the Court had a certain conception of the armed attack criterion in mind, but this conception is hardly evident from a single reading of the contorted wording of the paragraph. Similarly, illogical phrases, such as 'it will be necessary to distinguish the most grave forms of the use of force . . . from other less grave forms', cloud an already complicated picture. All of which runs somewhat counter to the Court's claim in the *Oil Platforms* decision that '[t]he conditions for the exercise of self-defence are well settled'[154] and equally to the assertion of Judge Lachs that the main task of the Court is to 'ascertain the law, and *to leave no doubt as to its meaning*' (emphasis added).[155]

The lack of clarity provided by the Court on the determination of an armed attack is undeniably problematic for both states and scholars attempting to apply the criterion to specific uses of force avowedly taken in self-defence. A perhaps more pertinent problem with the position taken by the Court, though, is that an examination of the actual practice of states reveals a startling contrast with the jurisprudence: it would appear that an armed attack is not the fundamental criterion for self-defence in customary international law at all.

[154] *Oil Platforms* merits (n 12) para 76.
[155] *Nicaragua* merits (n 2) separate opinion of Judge Lachs, para 168.

2

The Criteria of Necessity and Proportionality

IN CHAPTER ONE, we saw that the ICJ has perceived an armed attack as the fundamental criterion for the exercise of a lawful self-defence action, and examined how the Court has interpreted this requirement. Despite the confusion involved in much of what the Court has held regarding self-defence, particularly in *Military and Paramilitary Activities in and against Nicaragua* (hereafter *Nicaragua*),[1] it is evident that the Court has had a reasonably consistent conception of self-defence across its jurisprudence. This conception has been presented as applying to both conventional and customary international law: the ICJ has been very clear that the armed attack requirement is the fundamental aspect of a self-defence action not merely under Article 51 of the United Nations Charter but also in *custom*.

In contrast, the traditional academic view of the customary international law governing actions taken in self-defence is based largely on the correspondence exchanged between the United Kingdom and the United States in relation to the dispute over the sinking of the *Caroline* in 1837.[2] This incident occurred long before the phrase 'armed attack' appeared in the international legal vernacular. In broad terms, the diplomatic correspondence following the *Caroline* incident outlined a requirement that an action taken in self-defence must be both 'necessary' and 'proportional'. Today, it is undeniable that criteria of necessity and proportionality govern actions taken in self-defence.[3] This '*Caroline* conception' of the customary

[1] *Military and Paramilitary Activities in and against Nicaragua* (*Nicaragua v United States of America*) merits (1986) ICJ Reports 14.

[2] An examination of this incident will follow in section I below. For a general discussion of this scholarly trend, see T Kearley, 'Raising the *Caroline*' (1999) 17 *Wisconsin International Law Journal* 325, esp 331.

[3] This claim will be supported by the state practice and *opinio juris* discussed throughout this chapter, though it is additionally supported by the writings of scholars. See J Gardam, *Necessity, Proportionality and the Use of Force by States* (Cambridge, Cambridge University Press, 2004) esp 6 and 11; O Schachter, 'Implementing Limitations on the Use of Force: The Doctrine of Proportionality and Necessity: Remarks' (1992) 86 *American Society of International Law Proceedings* 39; SA Alexandrov, *Self-Defence against the Use of Force in International Law* (The Hague, Kluwer Law International, 1996) 20; CHM Waldock, 'The Regulation of the Use of Force by Individual States in International Law' (1998) 81 *Recueil Des*

law on self-defence, assessed by reference to criteria of necessity and proportionality, can therefore be seen as contrasting with the Court's conception of customary international law, which focuses upon Article 51's armed attack requirement.[4]

Although the vast majority of the jurisprudence of the ICJ on the issue of self-defence has dealt with a conception of the armed attack criterion, the Court has also been consistent in requiring the restrictions of necessity and proportionality across its relevant decisions. Explicit reference was made to criteria of necessity and proportionality in *Nicaragua*,[5] the *Case Concerning Oil Platforms* (*Islamic Republic of Iran v United States of America*) (hereafter *Oil Platforms*),[6] *Armed Activities on the Territory of the Congo* (*Democratic Republic of the Congo v Uganda*) (hereafter *DRC v Uganda*)[7] and *Legality of the Threat or Use of Nuclear Weapons* (hereafter *Nuclear Weapons*).[8] For example, in the *Nuclear Weapons* advisory opinion, the Court categorically pronounced: 'The submission of the exercise of the right of self-defence to the conditions of necessity and proportionality is a rule of customary law.'[9]

To understand the Court's position and the scope of the current law governing self-defence, it is essential to examine the nature of the criteria of necessity and proportionality in contemporary international law. Given that these criteria are not present in Article 51 or in other treaties that deal with the issue, this involves an assessment of customary international law, through an examination of state practice and *opinio juris*. The views of the Court are then introduced where relevant.

Our starting point is to revisit the sinking of the *Caroline*. Given the importance of this incident in the academic assessment of the customary international law on self-defence, it will be examined here in some detail.

I. THE *CAROLINE* INCIDENT: FACTS AND LEGAL CLAIMS

In 1837, the United Kingdom was facing a rebellion in Canada, which at that time was still under British control. It was in the context of this

Cours 455, 463–64 (in respect of proportionality only); and C Gray, *International Law and the Use of Force*, 3rd edn (Oxford, Oxford University Press, 2008) 148.

[4] Though, as we will see in chapter three, in reality an image of two competing 'conceptions' of self-defence is overly simplistic.

[5] *Nicaragua v United States of America* merits (n 1) esp paras 176, 194 and 237.

[6] *Case Concerning Oil Platforms* (*Islamic Republic of Iran v United States of America*) merits (2003) ICJ Reports 161, esp paras 51 and 76.

[7] *Armed Activities on the Territory of the Congo* (*Democratic Republic of the Congo v Uganda*) merits (2005) www.icj-cij.org/docket/files/116/10455.pdf, paras 147 and 304.

[8] *Legality of the Threat or Use of Nuclear Weapons* advisory opinion (1996) ICJ Reports 226, para 41.

[9] *Ibid.*

rebellion that British forces attacked a privately owned US steamer, the *Caroline*. A number of rebel forces acting in support of the Canadian rebellion were stationed on Navy Island, in British territory. They were supplied with munitions and personnel by the *Caroline*.[10] On 29 December, whilst the *Caroline* was docked at Schlosser, in US territory, it was attacked by British-Canadian forces, which set fire to the steamer and towed it over Niagara Falls.[11] In the process at least one US citizen was killed.[12]

The territorial violation involved in the incident, as well as the death of an American national, caused uproar in the United States.[13] Yet the diplomatic response to these rising tensions between Britain and the United States was fairly muted from both parties.[14] It constituted a brief exchange of letters between the US Secretary of State, John Forsyth, and the British Minister in Washington, Henry S Fox,[15] during which Forsyth demanded 'redress' on behalf of the United States. In response, Fox argued that 'the necessity of self-defence and self-preservation, under which Her Majesty's subjects acted in destroying [the *Caroline*], would seem to be sufficiently established.'[16] In addition, Andrew Stevenson, the American Minister to Britain, sent a letter regarding the incident to Lord Palmerston, the UK Foreign Secretary, in which he argued that, as there was no imminent danger to UK forces, Britain could not claim to have acted in self-defence.[17]

Tensions over the *Caroline* had calmed somewhat by 1839, only for them to be reignited following the arrest in New York of Alexander McLeod in November 1840. McLeod, a British-Canadian, was apprehended due to his alleged part in the incident.[18] The UK responded to the arrest by stating that the attack was an official action, and thus McLeod could not be held

[10] H Jones, *To the Webster-Ashburton Treaty: A Study in Anglo–American Relations, 1783–1843* (Chapel Hill, University of North Carolina Press, 1977) 23.

[11] RY Jennings, 'The *Caroline* and *McLeod* Cases' (1938) 32 *American Journal of International Law* 82, 84.

[12] See the sworn affidavit of Gilman Appleby, Commander of the *Caroline*, as supported by nine other crew members, *British and Foreign State Papers*, vol XXVI (1837–1838) 1373–75. It should be noted that some more recent accounts additionally refer to the death of the ship's cabin boy (eg, JB Moore, *A Digest of International Law, Vol II* (Washington, Government Printing Office, 1906) section 217, 409; W Meng, 'The *Caroline*' in R Bernhardt (ed), *Encyclopaedia of Public International Law, Vol 3: Use of Force, War and Neutrality Peace Treaties (A–M)* (Amsterdam, North-Holland Publishing Company, 1982) 81, 81; and Jennings (n 11) 84). However, this may be brought into question, as this death was not mentioned in the various testimonies of the crew.

[13] Jones (n 10) 26.

[14] KR Stevens, *Border Diplomacy: The* Caroline *and McLeod Affairs in Anglo–American–Canadian Relations, 1837–1842* (Tuscaloosa, University of Alabama Press, 1989) 19.

[15] FO Docs 5/321–23; and *British and Foreign State Papers*, vol XXVI (1837–1838) 1376.

[16] Letter dated 6 February 1838 from Henry S Fox to John Forsyth, FO Doc 5/322.

[17] Letter dated 22 May 1838 from Andrew Stevenson to Lord Palmerston, FO Doc 5/327. It took Palmerston more than three years to respond to this letter: letter dated 18 September 1841 from Lord Palmerston to Andrew Stevenson, extract in Stevens (n 14) 126–27.

[18] Jones (n 10) esp 48–49.

personally responsible.[19] McLeod was eventually found to be not guilty on the evidence.[20]

Correspondence concerning the *Caroline* incident, and particularly that which followed McLeod's arrest and trial, between the new US Secretary of State, Daniel Webster, and the UK special representative to the United States, Lord Ashburton, gave birth to the so called '*Caroline* formula'. Embodied in this formula are concepts of necessity and proportionality that still govern the lawfulness of self-defence actions today.

The most important extract of these various exchanges came from a letter sent from Webster to Ashburton, dated 27 July 1842, in which Webster quoted a correspondence he had sent to Henry S Fox in April 1841:

> [I]t will be for Her Majesty's Government to show, upon what state of facts, and what rules of national law, the destruction of the *Caroline* is to be defended. It will be for that Government *to show a necessity of self-defence, instant, overwhelming, leaving no choice of means, and no moment for deliberation.* It will be for it to show, also, that the local authorities of Canada, even supposing the necessity of the moment authorized them to enter the territories of the United States at all, did nothing unreasonable or *excessive*; since the act justified by the necessity of self-defence must be limited by that necessity, and kept clearly within it. It must be shown that admonition or remonstrance to the persons on board the *Caroline* was impracticable, or would have been unavailing; it must be shown that daylight could not be waited for; that there could be no attempt at discrimination, between the innocent and the guilty; that it would not have been enough to seize and detain the vessel; but that there was a necessity, present and inevitable, for attacking her, in the darkness of the night, while moored to the shore, and while unarmed men were asleep on board, killing some, and wounding others, and then drawing her into the current, above the cataract, setting her on fire, and, careless to know whether there might not be in her the innocent with the guilty, or the living with the dead, committing her to a fate, which fills the imagination with horror. A necessity for this, the Government of the United States cannot believe to have existed (emphasis added).[21]

The United States and the United Kingdom disagreed as to whether the British actions met these requirements as Webster set them out. From the above passage, we can see that Webster clearly asserted: 'A necessity for this, the Government of the United States cannot believe to have existed.' In contrast, Lord Ashburton responded on 28 July with:

[19] See, eg, letter dated 12 March 1841 from Henry S Fox to Daniel Webster, *British and Foreign State Papers*, vol XXIX (1840–1841) 1127. Moore (n 12) s 179, 24; and Jennings (n 11) 93.

[20] AB Corey, *The Crisis of 1830–1842 in Canadian–American Relations* (New Haven, Yale University Press, 1941) 144–45; and Jones (n 10) 65.

[21] Letter dated 27 July 1842 from Daniel Webster to Lord Ashburton, *British and Foreign State Papers*, vol (1841–1842) 193–94, extract taken from Webster's earlier letter to Henry S Fox dated 24 April 1841, *British and Foreign State Papers*, vol XXIX (1840–1841) 1137–38.

> I would appeal to you Sir, to say whether the facts which you say would alone justify the act . . . were not applicable to this case in as high a degree as they ever were to any case of a similar description in the history of nations.[22]

Yet Lord Ashburton also stated that 'we are perfectly agreed as to the general principles of international law applicable to this unfortunate case'.[23] Indeed, he repeated Webster's terminology (specifically that states must show 'a necessity of self-defence, instant, overwhelming, leaving no choice of means') on more than one occasion in the correspondence.[24] Thus it would seem that while there was disagreement between the parties as to the factual nature of the episode, they were in agreement as to Webster's statement of the law.[25]

II. THE APPLICABILITY OF THE *CAROLINE* FORMULA

A. A Mythical Authority

In the *Caroline* exchange, many writers since the time of the League of Nations have found the basis for the customary international law concerning self-defence. Robert Jennings referred to the incident as the *locus classicus* of the law of self-defence.[26] This view has, in the majority, continued into the UN era.[27] Indeed, Christine Gray rightly refers to the incident as having obtained a 'mythical authority'.[28] The general academic position on the *Caroline* incident during the UN era may be summarised by the following:

> The *Caroline* doctrine asserts that use of force by one nation against another is permissible as a self-defence action only if force is both necessary and proportionate

[22] Letter dated 28 July 1842 from Lord Ashburton to Daniel Webster, *British and Foreign State Papers*, vol (1841–1842) 198.

[23] *Ibid*, 195.

[24] *Ibid*, 196 and 198.

[25] Meng (n 12) 81; Jennings (n 11) 92; and Moore (n 12) s 217, 411. However, this conclusion has been criticised on the basis that Lord Ashburton agreed with Webster's formulation only as a diplomatic concession and not as a matter of law: MB Occelli, 'Sinking the *Caroline*: Why the Caroline Doctrine's Restrictions on Self-Defence Should not be Regarded as Customary International Law' (2003) 4 *San Diego International Law Journal* 467, 475–79.

[26] Jennings (n 11) 92.

[27] JL Brierly, *The Law of Nations: An Introduction to the International Law of Peace*, 6th edn (Oxford, Clarendon Press, 1963) 405–6; O Schachter, 'The Right of States to Use Armed Force' (1983–84) 82 *Michigan Law Review* 1620, 1635; RY Jennings and A Watts (eds), *Oppenheim's International Law, Vol I*, 9th edn (Harlow, Longman, 1992) 420; SD Murphy, 'Self-Defence and the *Israeli Wall* Advisory Opinion: An *Ipse Dixit* from the ICJ?' (2005) 99 *American Journal of International Law* 62, 65; and R Higgins, 'The Legal Limits to the Use of Force by Sovereign States: United Nations Practice' (1961) 37 *British Yearbook of International Law* 269, 298.

[28] Gray, *International Law and the Use of Force* (n 3) 149.

> . . . [The correspondence relating to the incident] effectively defined the limits of self-defence.[29]

The *Caroline* is still consistently referred to by scholars today as embodying the customary international law on self-defence. Michael Byers, for example, states that from the *Caroline* incident 'the modern law of self-defence was born'.[30] He then applies the formula to Operation Enduring Freedom.[31] Recent reference to the *Caroline* is similarly well evidenced by a document prepared by the Chatham House International Law Programme in 2005, following the consultation of thirteen eminent international legal scholars in the United Kingdom, entitled 'Principles of International Law on the Use of Force by States in Self-Defence'.[32] It is notable that the *Caroline* exchange is referred to throughout this document as representing the applicable customary international law standard in this context.[33]

Such large-scale scholarly reverence for the *Caroline* formula is not, in some respects, unmerited. As we will see, an investigation of the requirements of necessity and proportionality in contemporary customary international law produces a picture of criteria that have a remarkable resemblance to the conception of self-defence set out in the *Caroline* correspondence. Having said this, reference to the *Caroline* correspondence alone is not an adequate substitute for such an investigation. The *Caroline* is an invaluable tool in aiding any understanding of the contemporary criteria, due to its similarities to and influence upon them. For this very reason, it will be used throughout this chapter to shed light on the state practice examined. Yet care must be taken when the *Caroline* is employed in this context, for a number of reasons. It is important that we discuss these reasons before turning to the content of the contemporary criteria of necessity and proportionality.

B. Limited Applicability to Certain Types of Self-Defence

First, it has been argued that the factual circumstances of the *Caroline* incident limit the application of the formula enunciated by Webster to a

[29] MA Rogoff and E Collins Jr, 'The *Caroline* Incident and the Development of International Law' (1990) 16 *Brooklyn Journal of International Law* 493, 498.

[30] M Byers, 'Terrorism, the Use of Force and International Law after 11 September' (2002) 51 *International and Comparative Law Quarterly* 401, 159.

[31] *Ibid*.

[32] 'The Chatham House Principles of International Law on the Use of Force by States in Self-Defence'(2006) 55 *International and Comparative Law Quarterly* 963 (originally published on the internet: Chatham House International Law Programme, 'Principles of International Law on the Use of Force by States in Self-Defence', Royal Institute of International Affairs, October 2005 ILP WP 05/01, http://www.chathamhouse.org.uk/files/3278_ilpforce.doc).

[33] *Ibid*, 965, 967, 969 and 970.

specific 'type' of self-defence claim.[34] The contention here is that Webster intended to articulate the legal structure applicable to the facts of the *Caroline* incident itself and not to other claims of 'self-defence'. For example, it has been argued that the *Caroline* formula is relevant only to actions of preventative self-defence, as the incident can be viewed as being of this character.[35] The rebels on Navy Island had not yet launched an attack against British territory.[36]

Alternatively, as the actions of the *Caroline* and its crew were not imputable to the US government, it has been claimed that the *Caroline* formula is only relevant to self-defence actions against non-state actors and not action taken in self-defence by one state against another.[37] Expanding on this, Timothy Kearley takes the view that the *Caroline* exchange was limited to the very specific situation of 'extra-territorial uses of force by a state in peacetime against another state which is unable or unwilling to prevent its territory from being used as a base of operations for hostile activities against the state taking action'.[38]

This view is supported by the fact that Webster indicated that when an action taken avowedly in self-defence 'has led to the commission of hostile acts *within the territory of a power at peace*, nothing less than a clear and absolute necessity can afford a ground of justification' (emphasis added).[39] Kearley argues that this indicates that Webster felt that in different circumstances, self-defence may be justified based upon criteria other than those that he was expounding.[40] However, this seems a tenuous inference: Webster's intention with regard to the scope of the formula he was articulating can only be guessed.[41] Certainly though, his focus was

[34] See Gardam (n 3) 41–42.

[35] Indeed, Judge Schwebel stated in his *Nicaragua* dissent, 'It should be recalled that the narrow criteria of the *Caroline* case concerned anticipatory self-defence, not response to an armed attack or to actions tantamount to an armed attack.' *Nicaragua* merits (n 1) dissenting opinion of Judge Schwebel, para 200. See also O Schachter, *International Law in Theory and Practice* (Dordrecht, Martinus Nijhoff, 1991) 151–52.

[36] Though some commentators take the view that it is a misconception to see the incident as an anticipatory action: at no point in the correspondence is the idea of 'anticipatory self-defence' expressed, and factually it could be argued that the supply of the rebels by the *Caroline* was already underway. See JJ Paust, 'Post-9/11 Overreaction and Fallacies regarding War and Defence, Guantanamo, the Status of Persons, Treatment, Judicial Review of Detention, and Due Process in Military Commissions' (2003–04) 79 *Notre Dame Law Review* 1335, 1345–46.

[37] This argument has been put forward by M Stein in postings (30 October 2004) on the internet forum of the American Society of International Law, www.asil.org/forum.htm.

[38] Kearley (n 2) 325.

[39] Letter of 27 July 1842 (n 21) 1133.

[40] Kearley (n 2) 329.

[41] Eg, Dinstein points out that there is a 'lack of evidence that Webster had in mind any means of self-defence other than extra-territorial law enforcement.' Y Dinstein, *War, Aggression and Self-Defence*, 4th edn (Cambridge, Cambridge University Press, 2005) 249. Whilst this is correct, it is equally true to say that there is little evidence to suggest that Webster had *only* such means in mind.

understandably upon the specific incident of the *Caroline* and the circumstances relevant to that incident: 'Under these circumstances, and under those immediately connected with the transaction itself, it will be for Her Majesty's Government to show upon what state of facts, and what rules of national law, the destruction of the *Caroline* is to be defended.'[42]

Notwithstanding the possible intentions of Daniel Webster in setting forward his formula, it is evident from even a cursory glance at state practice in the UN era that the criteria of necessity and proportionality are not restricted to specific 'types' of self-defence in this way. For example, they are not restricted to actions taken in preventative self-defence[43] (assuming, of course, that such actions are permissible under the Charter system at all).[44] Nor do they apply only to actions against non-state actors (again assuming that such actions are permissible today).[45] Therefore, even if it is accepted that the *Caroline* formula was originally intended to apply only to certain categories of state self-help, such as a response against non-state actors, the criteria of necessity and proportionality have since been applied more widely, to the point that it can now be said that *all* actions of self-defence are limited by these requirements.

C. Customary International Law in 1837

Despite the apparent agreement between Ashburton and Webster as to the law covering the *Caroline* incident (if not the application of that law to the particular facts), it is arguable that Webster's formula was not representative of the customary international law in 1837. The formula set out by Webster was not in conformity with much of the practice of states, which in general employed a wider and more 'vague' right of 'self-preservation' at the time.[46]

[42] Letter of 27 July 1842 (n 21) 1137.

[43] This will be demonstrated by the following examination of these criteria, but for the present, an example would be that the United Kingdom was careful to stay within the bounds of proportionality during the Falklands conflict, a situation that was clearly *not one* of anticipatory self-defence. See *Hansard* HC 21 vol 535 col 1045 (7 July 1982); and especially the statement of Prime Minister Margaret Thatcher, *Hansard* HC 22 vol 504 cols 980–81 (29 April 1982).

[44] It will be recalled that the ICJ took no position on this issue, and neither does this work: see ch 1, section II-B.

[45] One of many examples supporting this is that Tunisia consistently stressed that the actions it took *within its own territory* against French troops in 1958 were necessary. See inter alia UN Doc S/PV.819, 9 and 12.

[46] I Brownlie, *International Law and the Use of Force by States* (Oxford, Oxford University Press, 1963) 261. Further, although Webster generally adopted the term 'self-defence' throughout the correspondence, it has been argued that it cannot be said with certainty whether his famous formula was pronounced in relation to 'self-defence', 'self-preservation' or 'necessity'. DW Bowett, *Self-Defence in International Law* (Manchester, Manchester University Press, 1958) 59–60; T Gazzini, *The Changing Rules on the Use of Force in International Law* (Manchester, Manchester University Press, 2005) 130–31; and Kearley (n 2) 332–33. Eg,

Certainly it would seem that the *Caroline* formula was not employed by either the United Kingdom or the United States in relation to other incidents of that time. For example, one can reference the British action against the Copenhagen naval fleet in 1807 in response to the supposed threat of Napoleon launching an attack from Denmark. The UK government claimed the action was 'necessary for the nation's preservation.'[47] However, based upon the *Caroline* formula, the action would have to be considered disproportionate (or to use Webster's terminology, 'excessive'), particularly given the bombardment of Copenhagen proper.[48] A similar view can be taken of two incursions by the United States into Spanish territory in 1817: the occupation of Amelia Island and the invasion of Spanish-held Florida. In both cases, the United States claimed it was acting in 'self-defence',[49] but it seems unlikely that either instance would have met the standards of the *Caroline* formula.[50]

Acknowledging that the formula set out by Webster was unlikely to have been an expression of customary international law as it was at the time, Jennings stated in his famous 1938 article, 'It was in the *Caroline* case that self-defence was changed from a political to a legal doctrine.'[51] In his view, the exchange of letters following the sinking of the *Caroline* created new customary international law.[52]

whilst Webster spoke of 'self-defence', Lord Palmerston clearly saw the British action as one of 'necessity'. See letter dated 18 September 1841 from Lord Palmerston to Andrew Stevenson, extract in Jones (n 10) 29. This view of the legal argumentation employed has been adopted by the ILC, which has twice referred to the *Caroline* formula (in the context of its examination of the law of state responsibility) as representing a plea of 'necessity' rather than one of self-defence. See *Report of the International Law Commission on the Work of its Thirty-Second Session*, 1980, Chapter III, State Responsibility, commentary on Art 33, para 24 (footnote 155) untreaty.un.org/ilc/documentation/english/A_35_10.pdf; and *Report of the International Law Commission on the Work of its Fifty-Third Session*, 2001, Chapter IV, State Responsibility, commentary on Art 25, note 5, untreaty.un.org/ilc/reports/2001/2001report.htm

47 Stevens (n 14) 25.

48 Indeed, the action was criticised on this basis in the UK Parliament. *Ibid*, 25–26.

49 *Ibid*, 26.

50 In the context of Amelia Island, the intervention was avowedly undertaken to suppress privateers and freebooters operating from the island. However, it seems unlikely that there was an 'instant' or 'overwhelming' necessity for this suppression, and further, the intervention led to an occupation of the island, which would seem in this instance to be 'excessive'. Similarly, in an epitome of disproportionality, the invasion of Florida involved the full-blown occupation of two Spanish towns in response to the killing of two Englishmen in the province by Seminole Indians. *Ibid*, 25–26; and Occelli (n 25) 481. Some writers nonetheless defended these actions as lawful following the *Caroline*. Eg, Garner argued that both incidents (along with the *Caroline* itself) were lawful 'acts of necessity'. JW Garner, 'Some Questions of International Law in the European War' (1915) 9 *American Journal of International Law* 72, 78.

51 Jennings (n 11) 82.

52 *Ibid*, 92. See also Stevens (n 14) x.

D. Adoption of the *Caroline* Formula since 1842

Leaving aside the question of whether the incident in itself could have 'created' customary international law,[53] it is evident that in the period following the *Caroline* incident, Webster's formulation did not figure prominently in the practice of states. This lack of application of the *Caroline* criteria in the pre-UN period is evidenced, inter alia, by the Corfu incident. In 1923, Italy responded to the assassination of an Italian national by bombing and occupying Corfu. Whilst it did not explicitly invoke 'self-defence', Mussolini's government stressed that its intervention in Corfu was a lawful and 'pacific' response to the assassination.[54] This action was clearly disproportionate based on any reasonable calculation, yet the League of Nations Council of Ambassadors that dealt with the dispute failed to condemn the actions of the Italian government, and the proportionality criterion was left unconsidered.[55] Indeed, the Council held that the occupation was lawful.[56] Such incidents led Ian Brownlie to conclude in 1963:

> The formula used by Webster has proved valuable in recent years but the correspondence made no difference to the legal doctrine, such as it was, of the time.[57]

Yet when one begins to examine state *opinio juris* from the UN period, it is not altogether clear that the *Caroline* formula can been seen as an aspect of contemporary customary international law either. It is true that on occasion, states do refer to the *Caroline* incident in relation to their own self-defence claims or those of others. For example, Iraq invoked the *Caroline* incident and Webster's formula in regard to its conflict with Iran in the 1980s.[58] Similarly, Israel referred to the *Caroline* explicitly in relation to its invocation of self-defence to protect its nationals at Entebbe Airport,

[53] It seems highly problematic to conclude that an exchange of letters between two states could create a legal obligation binding upon all. Today it is generally accepted that for customary international law to form there must be a level of 'constant and uniform practice', to use a statement employed in a classic pronouncement by the ICJ in the *Asylum* case (*Colombia/Peru*) merits (1950) ICJ Reports 266, 276–77. Nonetheless, a single incident can *in the long term* form the basis of customary law, if it is later applied in practice and supported by additional *opinio juris*. However, it would be the cumulative effect of any subsequent acceptance of the principles stemming from the incident that would give such principles their normative value, not the individual incident itself.

[54] Brownlie (n 46) 220–21.

[55] JH Wigmore, 'The Case of Italy v Greece under International Law and the Pact of Nations' (1923–24) 18 *Illinois Law Review* 131, 142–47. Wigmore also concluded that the actions of Italy were unnecessary as Italy had not given Greece any opportunity to offer reparations for the assassination (see 133).

[56] *Ibid*, 145.

[57] Brownlie (n 46) 43.

[58] Specifically in 1980, UN Doc S/PV.2250, 23–25.

Uganda, in 1976.[59] In defending its aerial strike against the Iraqi Osiraq nuclear reactor in 1981, Israel again pointed to the *Caroline*, though this was to indicate that it was inapplicable to the facts of the case,[60] whilst Uganda referred to the *Caroline* in the context of condemning the same action.[61] However, despite the claims of some writers,[62] such invocation is rare, certainly in the UN era. This in itself does not mean that the *Caroline* formula is not part of contemporary customary international law; the mere fact that states do not use the term 'the *Caroline*' is not determinative in this respect.

More importantly, it is also true that states rarely refer to Webster's *formula*. Thus the view that the formula itself is a rule of international law is hard to maintain when it is so rarely invoked. Of course, there is practice contrary to this, a well known example being the fact that the representative of Ghana referred to Webster's formula (though not the *Caroline* incident) when addressing the Security Council with regard to the Cuban Missile Crisis in 1962.[63] Sierra Leone similarly cited Webster's formula as constituting an aspect of customary international law without referring to the *Caroline* itself in relation to the Osiraq incident.[64] However, as with explicit invocation of the *Caroline* incident, such practice is exceptional.

It is oft repeated that the International Military Tribunal at Nuremburg referred to Webster's formulation explicitly.[65] However, it is worth noting

[59] UN Doc S/PV.1939, 57.

[60] UN Doc S/PV.2288, 32. It is interesting that in this instance, Israel did not quote Webster's formula, nor did it provide much indication as to what it saw the content of 'the *Caroline*' as amounting to.

[61] UN Doc S/PV.2282, 6–7.

[62] Eg, Gray, *International Law and the Use of Force* (n 3, 149), who refers to United Arab Emirates and the German Democratic Republic as invoking *Caroline* in UN Doc S/PV.2616 and UN Doc S/PV.2677 respectively, when in fact neither state does so explicitly. In another example, Reisman indicates that in relation to its bombings of Sudan and Afghanistan in 1998, the United States invoked the *Caroline* formula in UN Doc S/1998/780: WM Reisman, 'International Legal Responses to Terrorism' (1999) 22 *Houston Journal of International Law* 3, 48–49. In fact, the United States did not invoke the *Caroline* in this case, though it did of course make general claims regarding necessity and proportionality. More generally, see Rogoff and Collins (n 29) 509, who make the erroneous claim that state invocation of the *Caroline* is 'common practice'.

[63] UN Doc S/PV.1024, 19.

[64] UN Doc S/PV.2283, 56.

[65] 'Judicial Decisions Involving Questions of International Law: *International Military Tribunal* (*Nuremburg*) Judgment and Sentences' (1947) 41 *American Journal of International Law* 172, 205. This was in specific reference to the lawfulness of anticipatory self-defence (what the tribunal referred to as 'preventative action'). See, eg, Brownlie (n 46) 252–53; RN Gardner, 'Neither Bush nor the Jurisprudes (Agora: Future implications of the Iraq Conflict)' (2003) 97 *American Journal of International Law* 585, 587; Bowett (n 46) 33; and Rogoff and Collins (n 29) 504–5. It is also sometimes said that the International Military Tribunal for the Far East (Tokyo) applied the *Caroline* formula. See, eg, C Greenwood, 'International Law and the Pre-emptive Use of Force: Afghanistan, Al-Qaida, and Iraq' (2003) 4 *San Diego International Law Journal* 7, 13; and G Schwarzenberger and ED Brown, *A Manual of International Law*, 6th edn (Abingdon, Professional Books, 1976) 150. However, it should be noted that, unlike in the Nuremburg judgment, this was not with explicit reference to the *Caroline*. Here, the Tribunal

here that in contrast to this, the ICJ has at no point referred to the *Caroline* incident in any of its cases relating to self-defence.[66] This is true in relation both to reference to the *Caroline* itself and to Webster's formula more generally. The reason for this is wholly unclear. It might be that the Court has viewed Webster's formula as being relevant to claims of preventative self-defence only and therefore not relevant to the various decisions before it. Perhaps the Court has taken the view that the *Caroline* formula has no place in contemporary customary international law. In any event, the fact that the Court has not invoked the *Caroline* is further circumstantial support for the view that it does not form an aspect of the law governing self-defence in the UN era.

E. Aspects of the *Caroline* Formula within Customary International Law

Despite the lack of frequent explicit state invocation of the *Caroline* formula, states do invariably refer to the criteria of necessity and proportionality in assessing the lawfulness of avowed self-defence actions, and the content of these contemporary criteria certainly suggests that the *Caroline* has in some measure contributed to that law. Therefore, it is not suggested here that the *Caroline* has had no impact upon customary international law: on the contrary, the *Caroline* formula is invaluable in understanding that law. Rather, what is argued is that the *Caroline* formula *in itself* does not represent the criteria of necessity and proportionality as they are today.[67]

As we will see in subsequent sections, the customary international law criteria of necessity and proportionality of today differ in some respects from the traditional *Caroline* formulation, though most of these alterations are admittedly subtle. Due to this fact, there has been criticism of the majority of scholars for referring to 'the *Caroline*' while actually applying an altered version of the formula.[68] It is true that many writers invoke *Caroline*, while they in fact apply it only selectively. This is obviously unhelpful: 'While it is perfectly acceptable to suggest that a doctrine has outlived its usefulness, it is not sound practice to alter its meaning without

concluded that the Netherlands had lawfully declared war in self-defence against Japan before it was attacked or had war declared upon it, due to the demonstrable imminence of an attack by Japan. 'The Tokyo War Crimes Trial, November 1948 (*International Military Tribunal for the Far East*)' reproduced in L Friedman (ed), *The Law of War: A Documentary History, Vol II* (New York, Random House, 1972) 1029, 1044–47.

[66] Although it should be noted that Judge Schwebel did make mention of the *Caroline* in relation to anticipatory self-defence. *Nicaragua* merits (n 1) dissenting opinion of Judge Schwebel, para 200.

[67] This point is argued more fully in JA Green, 'Docking the *Caroline*: Understanding the Relevance of the Formula in Contemporary Customary International Law Concerning Self-Defence' (2006) 14 *Cardozo Journal of International and Comparative Law* 429.

[68] Occelli (n 25) 482; and Kearley (n 2) 345.

clearly flagging the change.'[69] More importantly, the *Caroline* formula is too simplistic to be used as a label for the varied and complex application of necessity and proportionality that has occurred since 1837. As such, a distinction should be made between the *Caroline* formula itself and the contemporary criteria of necessity and proportionality. The former must be viewed as a guide to understanding the UN-era state practice and *opinio juris* on self-defence that is the basis of the latter, not as a substitute for it.[70] Therefore, the *Caroline* formula emerges both as an extremely valuable aid in understanding the contemporary criteria of necessity and proportionality, and as an erroneous form of shorthand employed by some scholars to refer to the criteria of necessity and proportionality as they are today. Such criteria clearly exist in customary international law, and they are certainly linked to the *Caroline*. Nonetheless, care must be taken in applying the *Caroline* formula directly to events occurring more than a hundred and sixty years after the incident itself took place.

III. THE CONTEMPORARY CONTENT OF THE *CAROLINE* CRITERIA

However much weight one places upon the *Caroline* incident today, it is largely uncontroversial that the criteria of necessity and proportionality still form part of the law of self-defence in some measure.[71] As Gray has put it:

> [I]rrespective of the status of the *Caroline* as a precedent, necessity and proportionality have played a crucial role in state justification of the use of force in self-defence and in international response.[72]

The problem for the international lawyer, then, is not whether the criteria form part of international law but rather the *content* of these accepted criteria. As Oscar Schachter has stated, 'The devil is in the details.'[73]

To be able to identify the 'details' that constitute the content of the criteria of necessity and proportionality, one must undertake an in-depth examination of the practice and *opinio juris* of states. In addition to the natural starting point of the *Caroline*, there is a wealth of state practice regarding the criteria of necessity and proportionality, much of which is from the UN era. Through this practice the development of the criteria may be traced and their contemporary content ascertained.

However, this is not an easy task, largely because the application of the criteria of necessity and proportionality to any given claim of self-defence

[69] Kearley (n 2) 345.
[70] Green (n 67) esp 473–80; and BQ Clemmons and GD Brown, 'Rethinking International Self-Defence: The United Nations' Emerging Role' (1998) 45 *Naval Law Review* 217, 221.
[71] See above, n 3.
[72] Gray, *International Law and the Use of Force* (n 3) 149.
[73] Schachter, 'Implementing Limitations on the Use of Force' (n 3) 39.

is wholly dependent upon the factual circumstances of that case. What is necessary or proportional in one situation may not be so in another.[74] This leads to uncertainty over the *general* content of the notions of necessity and proportionality. This uncertainty, which is inherent in the very nature of the criteria, is compounded by the fact that states themselves are in general unwilling to provide detailed content to them in the abstract. Flexibility in the law of self-defence is understandably appealing to states.[75] Thus, *opinio juris* pertinent to necessity and proportionality tends to relate specifically to the incident with regard to which the relevant statements are being made. It has been said on this basis:

> Vague as they may be, the boundaries of legitimate self-defence are inherent in the concept itself, and have been traditionally reduced to 'necessity and proportionality'. It is a matter of judgement in concrete instances what level and mode of response are proportionate to the assault, and all attempts to standardise the guidelines have proved unsuccessful because, as in the case of any other general principle of legal conduct, so much resides in the contingencies of a situation.[76]

It is therefore difficult to find general content in the criteria so that a degree of certainty can be developed as to whether (in application) any given forcible response will be viewed as necessary and proportional. Nonetheless, a detailed picture of the content of these requirements of customary international law can be built up through an examination of practice.

IV. NECESSITY

A. Necessity as 'Last Resort'

In attempting to understand the contemporary criterion of necessity in relation to claims of self-defence, it is useful to begin with reference to the *Caroline* incident. Webster's formulation indicates that the need to respond in self-defence must be 'overwhelming'. It has been argued that this indicates that the action being responded to must be of a nature as to threaten fundamentally the survival of, or at least the vital interests of, a state.[77]

[74] RR Baxter, 'The Legal Consequences of the Unlawful Use of Force under the Charter' (1968) 62 *American Society of International Law Proceedings* 68, 74; and Gardam (n 3) 21.

[75] E Cannizzaro and P Palchetti, 'Introduction' in E Cannizzaro and P Palchetti (eds), *Customary International Law on the Use of Force: A Methodological Approach* (Leiden, Martinus Nijhoff, 2005) 4.

[76] DP O'Connell, *The Influence of Law on Sea Power* (Manchester, Manchester University Press, 1975) 64. It is interesting that Daniel Webster made this point with regard to his conception of self-defence when he argued that 'the extent of this right [self-defence] is a question to be judged of by the circumstances of each particular case.' Letter of 27 July 1842 (n 21) 1113.

[77] G Schwarzenberger, 'The Fundamental Principles of International Law' (1955) 87 *Recueil Des Cours* 9, 97.

This would mean attacks that have a detrimental effect upon a state would not necessitate a response unless they impinge upon the *continued existence* of the state. In the *Nuclear Weapons* opinion, the ICJ stated that 'the Court cannot lose sight of the fundamental right of every state to survival, and thus its right to resort to self-defence . . . when its survival is at stake.'[78]

Therefore it could be argued that the Court has adopted this view that a response in self-defence can be necessary only in instances when the very survival of the state is threatened.[79] Based upon this statement of the Court alone, this would seem to be the case. Yet, this position appears limited to the context of the *Nuclear Weapons* opinion: the use of nuclear armaments in self-defence.[80] Upon examining the application of the necessity criterion in *Nicaragua* and *Oil Platforms*, there is no evidence to suggest that the Court saw the concept as restricted to extreme cases of national survival. Indeed, it could perhaps be argued that the survival of El Salvador *was* at stake in the *Nicaragua* dispute, yet the Court nonetheless found the actions of the United States to be unnecessary.[81]

It is true that states sometimes refer to a particular use of force in self-defence as being necessary to protect 'vital interests' or something similar. For example, this was the position taken by El Salvador with regard to its conflict with Honduras in 1969.[82] However, such cases are not the only circumstances in which self-defence is claimed and accepted. In practice, nothing so devastating as 'survival' is required before a response can be seen as legally necessary:

> The reality of self-defence in inter-state relations is much more prosaic: it transcends life-or-death existential crises and impinges on a host of commonplace situations involving the use of counter-force.[83]

A good example is the Falklands conflict of 1982. Here, the military response of the United Kingdom was generally accepted as a lawful self-defence action.[84] However, it could hardly be claimed that the occupation

[78] *Nuclear Weapons* advisory opinion (n 8) para 96.

[79] Dinstein, *War, Aggression and Self-Defence* (n 41) 175.

[80] Later in the opinion, eg, the Court stated that it could not 'conclude definitively whether the threat or use of nuclear weapons would be lawful or unlawful in an extreme circumstance of self-defence, in which the very survival of a state would be at stake'. *Nuclear Weapons* advisory opinion (n 8) para 105. See also the separate opinion of Judge Fleischhauer, para 5.

[81] *Nicaragua* merits (n 1) para 237.

[82] UN Doc S/9330.

[83] Dinstein, *War, Aggression and Self-Defence* (n 41) 175.

[84] The Security Council determined that the Argentine invasion was a 'breach of the peace'; SC Res 502, which only Panama voted against. (This resolution was reaffirmed by SC Res 505.) For the views of a number of states, see *The Times*, 27 April 1982, 4; and on the general acceptance by third-party states of the legality of the actions of the United Kingdom in relation to the Falklands, see MJ Levitin, 'The Law of Force and the Force of Law: Grenada, the Falklands, and Humanitarian Intervention' (1986) 27 *Harvard International Law Journal* 621, 638. However, support for the position of the United Kingdom was not unanimous, as can be seen from the reaction of Cuba. See *The Times*, 27 April 1982, 4.

of the Falklands posed a significant threat to the infrastructure or survival of the United Kingdom.

Therefore, it would seem that the criterion of 'necessity' in customary international law is not to be viewed as a requirement of 'absolute necessity' or 'do-or-die'. Nonetheless, it may still be said that necessity is established only if the action can be considered a 'last resort':[85] a state can use force in self-defence only if there is no other option open for it to defend itself (though this need not be to defend itself from total destruction). This idea can obviously be seen to correlate to the phrase 'no choice of means', as employed by Webster in the *Caroline* correspondence.

The view of necessity as a last resort is borne out in the practice of states. An early example of the UN era is the position taken by the Tunisian government in relation to its attempts to expel French troops from its territory in 1958. In stressing the necessity of its action, Tunisia claimed that 'it did everything in its power to avoid aggravating the situation'[86] and that as a sign of good faith, it had released thirteen French prisoners following the French bombing of Sakiet-Sidi-Youssef.[87] Further, Tunisia stressed that it had attempted to negotiate the withdrawal of French troops for over two years before it resorted to self-defence.[88] All this clearly indicates that Tunisia's actions were taken as a 'last resort', at least in the view of that state.[89] Similarly, during the Six Day War, Israel stressed before the Security Council that, despite the mounting threats it perceived that it was facing, and despite the alleged terrorist attacks against it from external sources, it refrained from responding with force in the hope of securing a peaceful settlement.[90] Israel claimed it was only when the crisis reached a point where no alternative other than the use of force existed that it responded in self-defence.[91]

[85] J Quigley, 'The Afghanistan War and Self-Defence' (2002–03) 37 *Valparaiso University Law Review* 541, 546; R Ago, *Addendum to the Eighth Report on State Responsibility*, UN Doc A/CN.4/318, Add 5–7, *Yearbook of the International Law Commission* (1980) I.1, 65–66; Jennings and Watts (eds) (n 27) 422; and the statement made by the Attorney General of the United Kingdom to the House of Lords in 2004, at least in relation to anticipatory self-defence *Hansard* HL vol DCLX col 370 (21 April 2004).

[86] UN Doc S/PV.819, 6.

[87] *Ibid.*

[88] *Ibid*, 11.

[89] Though it should be pointed out that it is uncertain as to whether Tunisia saw itself as *bound* to do so.

[90] UN Doc S/PV.1348, 71–75.

[91] However, it should be noted that some states criticised the Israeli action on the basis that the Security Council was seized of the matter, though they did not say this precluded a response in self-defence as such. Further, it is unclear whether this criticism was made due to the fact that Security Council involvement indicated that other—non-forcible—alternatives were being pursued (thus meaning the response was not a 'last resort') or due to the limitation in Art 51 that the right of self-defence exists only 'until the Security Council has taken measures necessary to maintain international peace and security'. See, eg, the positions taken by the Soviet Union (UN Doc S/PV.1348, 22–25) and Iraq (UN Doc S/PV.1348, 51).

Returning to the 1982 Falklands conflict, the United Kingdom stressed that its action in responding to the Argentine intervention was necessary because Argentina had failed to comply with the will of the Security Council in withdrawing from the islands:

> [The United Kingdom's use of force and particularly its imposition of a maritime exclusion zone] has been made necessary by the refusal of Argentina to comply with paragraph 2 of resolution 502.[92]

As such, the United Kingdom indicated that its response was taken as a last resort.[93]

Following the South African interventions in Zambia, Zimbabwe and Botswana in 1986, South Africa was heavily condemned. One of the reasons continually cited by other states when demonstrating the unlawfulness of the South African actions was that they occurred during negotiations directed by the Commonwealth Group, aimed at facilitating a peaceful resolution between the African National Congress (ANC), South Africa and the 'frontline states'.[94] As such, South Africa not only failed to act as a last resort by not following this process through, but equally, detrimentally affected the chance of peaceful measures resolving many of the problems of the region in the future. From the South African perspective, it saw the attacks as necessary, as demonstrated by the fact that it had repeatedly warned Zambia, Zimbabwe and Botswana that they would be attacked if they continued to aid ANC insurgents,[95] and it had also put forward an offer to set up a permanent 'joint mechanism' body to negotiate an end to ANC cross-border incursions, which was rejected.[96] Therefore, whilst there was disagreement as to what in fact was evidence of the attacks constituting a 'last resort', it was seemingly agreed that this was the required test.

The above practice suggests that the interpretation of the necessity criterion as requiring that forcible action in self-defence may be taken only as a 'last resort' is correct. It would also appear that in its limited application of the requirement, the ICJ has taken a similar position. In *Nicaragua*, the Court held that one of the reasons that the actions of the United States were not necessary in that case was because 'it was possible to eliminate the main danger to the Salvadorian Government without the United States

[92] UN Doc S/15025.

[93] Third-party state reaction in general confirmed the action of the United Kingdom as one of lawful self-defence. See above, n 84.

[94] See, eg, the statement of the representative of Australia to the Security Council (UN Doc S/PV.2685, 4–6); E Kwakwa, 'South Africa's May 1986 Military Incursions into Neighbouring African States' (1987) 12 *Yale Journal of International Law* 421, 432 and 440; and *New York Times*, 20 May 1986, A1.

[95] UN Doc S/PV.2684, 22.

[96] As was stressed by President Botha of South Africa in an address to the South African Parliament, 31 January 1986, reproduced in UN Doc S/PV.2684, 26.

embarking on activities in and against Nicaragua.'[97] Thus the Court implied that as the action was not a 'last resort', it was unnecessary.

It would seem, then, that the Court and state practice both indicate that action in self-defence must be taken as a 'last resort' for it to be necessary. However, the idea of 'last resort' has two distinct interpretations. One of these is procedural, whilst the other is more abstract. These are often not distinguished in the literature and are certainly not explicitly distinguished in state practice. This leads to confusion as to what is required of states when the criterion is applied to particular incidents. First, it is concluded by some writers that necessity requires an exhaustion of procedural means: 'the action must be by way of a last resort after all peaceful means have failed.'[98] Second, it could be argued that a state must show *either* that it resorted to peaceful measures before using force *or* that it was not reasonable or 'feasible'[99] to turn to peaceful measures at all. This is a more abstract, subjective notion.

B. Procedural Exhaustion of Non-forcible Measures

Taking the first interpretation of 'last resort', a state would have to demonstrate that it has actively sought peaceful resolution prior to using force. This would imbue the necessity criterion with a procedural or administrative element,[100] akin to the oft used compromissory clause in a treaty providing the ICJ with jurisdiction over a dispute only after diplomatic negotiations have failed.[101]

[97] *Nicaragua* merits (n 1) para 237.

[98] Gardam (n 3) 5 (though it must be noted that later in this book, Gardam presents a far more nuanced approach to the necessity criterion than this quote from the introduction suggests, see 148–55). The view that force should not be employed before an exhaustion of other possible measures can be traced back to a period in which the concept of necessity had little or no legal content at all in international relations. Eg, the idea appeared in the writings of Vattel, though he saw this as desirable, or what he termed 'voluntary law'. E de Vattel, *Le Droit des Gens, ou Principes de la Loi Naturelle, appliqués a la Conduite et aux Affaires des Nations et des Souverains, Vol III*, CG Fenwick (trans), in JB Scott (ed), *The Classics of International Law* (Washington, DC, Carnegie Institution, 1916) 305. For more recent support, see Dinstein, *War, Aggression and Self-Defence* (n 41) 225; Kearley (n 2) 326; Rogoff and Collins (n 29) 498; and TM Franck, *Recourse to Force: State Action against Threats and Armed Attacks* (Cambridge, Cambridge University Press, 2002) 132. (Here Franck indicates that this view can be taken of necessity, though he does not explicitly subscribe to it himself.)

[99] Y Dinstein, 'Implementing Limitations on the Use of Force: The Doctrine of Proportionality and Necessity: Remarks' (1992) 86 *American Society of International Law Proceedings* 54, 57.

[100] D Kritsiotis, 'Rules on Self-Defence in International Law' Memorandum for the Royal Institute of International Affairs, London Chatham House International Law Programme, 8 December 2004 (unpublished) 15.

[101] See, eg, Art XXI, para 2 of the 1955 Treaty of Amity, Economic Relations, and Consular Rights between the United States and Iran, which provided the ICJ with the basis for jurisdiction in *Oil Platforms*.

The jurisprudence of the Court would seem to support this interpretation. The majority in *Oil Platforms* did not find the actions of the United States to be necessary in that case, and one of the reasons it gave for this was that the United States had not complained to Iran regarding the alleged military activities of the platforms.[102] From this it can be inferred that there might need to be some prior negotiation—or at least complaint—for a response to become necessary. However, this conclusion was certainly not made explicit by the Court. Similarly, in his dissent to *Nicaragua*, Judge Schwebel concluded that the majority in that case found that an action in self-defence could be necessary *only* if all peaceful means of resolving the situation had been exhausted.[103] It must be said, though, that there appears to be little in the majority decision in *Nicaragua* to support this conclusion.

As we have seen, states do at times refer to failed attempts to negotiate when stressing that the actions that they have taken are necessary; conversely, states are sometimes condemned for not having exhausted peaceful means prior to acting in self-defence.[104] On initial inspection, such practice would suggest that a peaceful means of resolution *must* first be sought before force can be lawfully employed. However, upon closer examination, it is clear that such attempts are not always taken, and a failure to negotiate does not automatically lead to an action being condemned as unnecessary by third-party states.[105]

Further, when states refer to the fact that they have attempted to resolve disputes through negotiation prior to using force, they do not indicate that they were legally bound to do so. For example, in relation to the 2001 intervention in Afghanistan, the United States made a number of demands of the Taliban regime prior to the use of force, offering ultimatums if these were not met. The Taliban rejected these demands.[106] Yet, there was no indication that the United States felt itself required to seek to resolve the matter without resorting to the use of force or that it saw these ultimatums as anything other than politically or strategically relevant. Indeed, it can be argued that the United States had a number of possible non-forcible options open to it with regard to Afghanistan.[107] States in general nonetheless accepted Operation Enduring Freedom as constituting a lawful self-defence action.[108]

[102] *Oil Platforms* merits (n 6) para 76.

[103] *Nicaragua* merits (n 1) dissenting opinion of Judge Schwebel, para 201.

[104] Eg, a number of states criticised Israel's action in Uganda in 1976 on the basis that negotiations for the release of the hostages were underway and making progress. See the statement of the Libyan representative in the Security Council, UN Doc S/PV.1943, 3.

[105] As can be seen from the examples that follow below.

[106] *Washington Post*, 19 September 2001, A1; and *Washington Post*, 22 September 2001, A1.

[107] Quigley (n 85) 546–48.

[108] Eg, explicit condonation was advanced by Russia, China, Pakistan, Japan, the United Arab Emerites and Saudi Arabia, as well as by nineteen NATO states. Offers of direct military assistance to the United States came from the United Kingdom, Australia, Canada, Singapore, Spain, Turkey, Ukraine, Romania, Portugal, New Zealand, the Netherlands,

A trend can be seen in the practice of states as to when negotiation is more commonly employed. In cases in which the attack to which the state is responding has occurred on or against the territory of the invoking state, it is less common for that state to turn to peaceful measures before resorting to the use of force. Conversely, in the case of responses to extra-territorial attacks, states are much more inclined to seek first a peaceful solution and, importantly, to stress this when arguing that force was legally necessary if such solutions fail. This is also true in situations in which the invoking state is acting in collective self-defence and thus similarly responding to an attack that did not occur on that state's territory.

A good example of the former situation—an attack against the territory of the defending state—is the action of the Seychelles in repelling mercenaries from its territory in 1981. Here, the sole international airport in the Seychelles was attacked by a small group of mercenaries following the discovery of their weapons at customs.[109] Their presence in the Seychelles was to attempt a coup, apparently directed by South Africa.[110] The response of the Seychelles People's Defence Force, in repelling the mercenaries through force, was commended by all members of the Security Council, without any question being raised as to whether such a response was necessary.[111] This was despite the fact that no means other than forcible action were employed or seemingly even considered.[112]

The contrast between responses to attacks against the territory of a state, such as occurred in the Seychelles incident, and responses to *extraterritorial* attacks can be seen by the 1975 crisis over the *Mayaguez*. Here, Cambodian

Germany, Italy, Jordan, Belgium, Denmark, France and South Korea (collated by the US Department of State, www.state.gov/s/ct/rls/fs/2001/5194.htm and the United Kingdom Parliament, www.parliament.uk/commons/lib/research/rp2001/rp01-081.pdf, 31). In the General Assembly in November 2001, a representative of the European Union expressly stated that that organisation took the view that the coalition action constituted a lawful response in self-defence to the attacks of 11 September 2001, and this view was also taken at that time by Brazil and Chile. See UN Doc A/56.PV44, 37, 3–4 and 27 respectively. It is also notable that in two resolutions of the Security Council immediately following 11 September, that organ explicitly reaffirmed the right of self-defence in the context of those attacks: SC Res 1368 and SC Res 1373. For a more detailed examination of state practice with regard to Operation Enduring Freedom, see SD Murphy (ed), 'Contemporary Practice of the United States Relating to International Law' (2002) 96 *American Journal of International Law* 237, esp 248; MJ Kelly, 'Understanding September 11th: An International Legal Perspective on the War in Afghanistan' (2001–02) 35 *Creighton Law Review* 283, 285–86; and Gazzini (n 46) 76–77. However, whilst there was widespread state support for the action, it was not universal. See EPJ Myjer and N White, 'The Twin Towers Attack: An Unlimited Right to Self-Defence?' (2002) 7 *Journal of Conflict and Security Law* 5, 6–11. Similarly, it has also been argued that the acceptance of the Afghanistan intervention by other states was political, not legal. See Quigley (n 85) 554.

109 UN Doc S/PV.2314, 4–5.

110 South African involvement was never established as a certainty (1981 *UN Yearbook*, 226–27), although there was extremely strong evidence to suggest this. See, eg, Report of the Security Council Commission of Inquiry established under resolution 496 1981, UN Doc S/15492/Rev.1 (2nd Report), esp 11. Indeed, the General Assembly explicitly attributed responsibility to South Africa and condemned the action (GA Res 36/172c).

111 See generally, UN Docs S/PV.2314, S/PV.2359, S/PV.2361, S/PV.2365 and S/PV.2367.

112 See, eg, UN Doc S/14769/Corr.1.

forces seized a US vessel, the SS *Mayaguez,* off the coast of the Poulo Wai Islands (which Cambodia claimed were within its territorial waters)[113] and attempted to move both vessel and crew to the Cambodian mainland.[114] The United States responded with force both against the Cambodian vessels transporting the *Mayaguez* and its crew[115] and against targets on the mainland, avowedly in self-defence.[116] It was repeatedly indicated by the United States that it had initiated negotiations with the Cambodian government over the release of both the crew and the vessel itself.[117] However, it is telling that the United States saw this as an indication of good faith; it did not appear to have the character of a legal argument.

More recent examples include the action taken by the United States against avowed terrorist targets in Afghanistan and Sudan in 1998. Here, the United States argued that '[t]hese attacks were carried out only after repeated efforts to convince the government of Sudan and the Taliban regime in Afghanistan to shut these terrorist activities down.'[118] Similarly, South Korea stressed that its naval clash with North Korea in June 2002[119] was necessary, as it had provided ample warning and time for the crew of the North Korean vessel to respond before commencing its attack[120] and had thus attempted to resolve the situation without the use of force.[121]

[113] JJ Paust, 'The Seizure and Recovery of the *Mayaguez*' (1975–76) 85 *Yale Law Journal* 774, 775.

[114] *New York Times*, 16 May 1975, 14.

[115] AM, Weisburd, *Use of Force: The Practice of States Since World War II* (University Park, Pennsylvania State University Press, 1997) 275; and Paust (n 113) 779.

[116] Paust (n 113) 781.

[117] Two official letters of protest were lodged by the United States with the Cambodian government seeking the release of the vessel and its crew. See Weisburd (n 115) 274. The United States held that forcible action was taken '[i]n the absence of a positive response to our appeals through diplomatic channels'. It also made a point of requesting the Secretary General of the UN to take any steps he could to alleviate the situation: letter dated 14 May 1975 from the US Representative to the UN to the Secretary General of the UN, reproduced in (1975) 74 *Department of State Bulletin* 720.

[118] UN Doc S/1998/780.

[119] Which both states argued constituted an action taken in self-defence. For the claim of the South, see 'The Naval Clash on the Yellow Sea on 29 June between South and North Korea: The Situation and ROK's Position' 1 July 2002, press release of the Ministry of National Defence of the Republic of Korea, www.globalsecurity.org/wmd/library/news/rok/2002/0020704-naval.htm. For the corresponding claim of the North, see *New York Times*, 30 June 2002, 12.

[120] BBC news online, 'Koreas Clash in Sea Battle', 29 June 2002.

[121] It is worth noting that the same pattern appears in the context of collective self-defence. The best example of this is the Gulf conflict of 1991, during which attempts at negotiating an Iraqi withdrawal from Kuwait were undertaken prior to military intervention. Dinstein, 'Implementing Limitations on the Use of Force' (n 99) 57. Of course, it is contestable as to whether the legal basis for the coalition action in the Gulf was 'collective security' (ie, a measure authorised by the Security Council) or collective self-defence. Dinstein takes the latter view, on the basis that SC Res 660 and SC Res 678 act as 'blessings' of the use of forcible action in collective self-defence not as action under Chapter VII of the Charter (see 56). Certainly, the United States was explicit that the action was taken under Art 51, UN Doc S/21537. This is supported by the facts that the coalition forces were not permitted to use to UN flag during combat (unlike in Korea in 1950) and that SC Res 661 conspicuously reaffirms the right of individual and collective self-defence.

The above are examples of responses taken against attacks that occurred extraterritorially. However, there does not appear to be a *legal* distinction between this type of situation and a response to a traditional territorial attack: it is not suggested that a failed attempt at peaceful resolution is required in cases in which the initial attack occurred extraterritorially and not required with regard to territorial attacks. Rather, it is the case that when a state suffers an attack against its territory—particularly if the attack is of the nature of an invasion or threatens the institutions or structure of the state—the intervention itself acts as extremely persuasive evidence demonstrating the necessity of the response. In many cases, this in itself is viewed as *proving* necessity.[122]

Thus it would seem that there is no absolute requirement that states first attempt negotiation before responses in self-defence may be lawfully 'necessary'. Indeed, such a requirement of peaceful negotiation seems unrealistic in the reality of international disputes involving force. There may not be the time for negotiation or even complaint on the part of a defending state before force in defensive response is necessary.[123]

In the case of responses to extraterritorial attacks, it is much more likely that the responding state will indicate that it has attempted to negotiate prior to using force. This is because necessity in such situations is harder to establish, and therefore the additional evidential weight of having attempted negotiation or having exhausted the possibility of peaceful means of resolution generally, strengthens the claim that an action taken extraterritorially was necessary self-defence. State practice is not concrete on this distinction, however, and existing *opinio juris* is far from legally constituting in this regard. Thus, the distinction between territorial and non-territorial responses offers a useful guide as to whether a state should seek to exhaust peaceful measures, but the exhaustion of peaceful measures in either case still constitutes *evidence* that a legal requirement has been met, not a legal requirement in itself.

As such, it can be seen that the failure to exhaust all peaceful measures is not legally determinative as to whether a response was necessary. It is not a requirement that a state attempt negotiation prior to launching a forcible response or wait for the Security Council to conclude a debate on

[122] Indeed, Schachter concludes that in cases in which the territory of a state is attacked in this manner, necessity will *always* be established per se: Schachter, *International Law in Theory and Practice* (n 35) 152. This author takes the more cautious position adopted by Kenny: an attack on the territory of a state creates the 'strong presumption' that a forcible response will be necessary. KC Kenny, 'Self-Defence' in R Wolfrum and C Philipp (eds), *United Nations: Law, Policies and Practice, Vol II* (Dordrecht, Martinus Nijhoff, 1995) 1162, 1168. See also Dinstein, *War, Aggression and Self-Defence* (n 41) 237.

[123] Schachter, 'The Right of States to Use Armed Force' (n 27) 1635.

an issue before acting.[124] These factors are merely evidence, albeit good evidence, of necessity.

C. A 'Reasonableness' Test for Assessing Last Resort

We now turn to the second interpretation of whether an action was taken as a 'last resort': a state must show *either* that it resorted to peaceful measures before using force or that *it was not reasonable for it to do so*. It may be that in the case of a large-scale attack or an invasion of the defending state's territory, this is proved per se.[125] A good example of a situation of this kind would be the Seychellois response to mercenary aggression in 1981 discussed above.[126] The requirement of 'last resort' will be met so long as it may be established that it would have been unreasonable to expect the defending state to attempt to employ means other than force to resolve the situation.

Thus, the statement from the *Caroline* exchange arguing that there must be 'no choice of means' should be interpreted to mean that the criterion of necessity requires that the defending state has 'no *reasonable* choice of means'.[127] If an attack is of such a character that it would not be reasonable to expect a state to seek alternative non-forcible means of defensive response, then it would appear that the responding state does not need to do so. As this was phrased in the 'Principles of International Law on the Use of Force by States in Self-Defence' document prepared by the Chatham House International Law Programme in 2005, 'There must be no *practical* alternative to the proposed use of force that is likely to be effective in ending or averting the attack' (emphasis added).[128] It should be noted that this is not an alteration of the famous phrase from the *Caroline* as such.[129] By looking more closely at Webster's formula, we see that he envisaged the possibility of it not being reasonable for a state to resort first to peaceful measures: 'It must be shown that admonition or remonstrance

[124] Indeed, Art 51 provides that self-defence can be taken 'until the Security Council has taken measures necessary to maintain international peace and security', implying that there is no need to wait in the hope that the Security Council may resolve the matter peacefully.

[125] See above, n 122.

[126] Above, section IV-B.

[127] Here 'means' is used to refer to military force, as opposed to, eg, the specific type of weapon employed.

[128] 'The Chatham House Principles' (n 32) 966. Other scholars have taken similar positions. See, eg, K Chainoglou, 'Reconceptualising Self-Defence in International Law' (2007) 18 *King's Law Journal* 61, 88.

[129] Although it has been argued that the 'leaving no choice of means' aspect of the *Caroline* formula could be interpreted as requiring a state to exhaust all peaceful means (such as referring the matter to the Security Council) before using any force, even while a state *is being attacked*. See Kearley (n 2) 326.

to the persons on board the *Caroline* was impracticable, or would have been unavailing.'[130]

However, having examined the way necessity has been applied in the UN era, it is perhaps too stringent to hold that the need to respond must be 'overwhelming' (to use Webster's terminology), unless 'overwhelming' is taken to be a bland synonym for 'necessary'. Interpreting 'overwhelming' to mean 'fundamental' or 'total' we see that this aspect of the *Caroline* formula may paint an inaccurate picture of the contemporary necessity criterion, at least in relation to self-defence taken in response to an actual attack. Instead, it is more accurate to conclude that there must be a 'reasonable' need to respond with force based upon a balancing of the rights and interests of states against the general prohibition of the use of force.

Unfortunately for international lawyers, these standards are not as easy to apply in any given case as a test based upon state survival and objectively identifiable resort to negotiation. Nevertheless, it appears to be the way states apply and respond to the application of the necessity requirement. Thus, whether any given instance of self-defence can be considered to be 'necessary' is extremely difficult to assess.

V. PROPORTIONALITY

As with the principle of necessity, questions of proportionality with regard to self-defence are raised consistently in the practice of States. It was noted at the start of this chapter that the ICJ has referred to the proportionality criterion in cases in which it has dealt with self-defence, albeit in a somewhat limited manner. Yet when the Court has applied a proportionality requirement, it has done little more than confuse this already complex issue still further. A good example is the Court's application of the proportionality criterion to the avowedly defensive US response in *Oil Platforms*. As regards the two separate attacks of 19 October 1987 and 18 April 1988, the application of the proportionality test appears somewhat inconsistent. At paragraph 77, the Court stated:

> As to the requirement of proportionality, the attack of 19 October 1987 might, had the Court found that it was necessary in response to the *Sea Isle City* incident as an armed attack committed by Iran, have been considered proportionate. In the case of the attacks of 18 April 1988, however, they were conceived and executed as part of a more extensive operation entitled 'Operation Praying Mantis'. . . The question of the lawfulness of other aspects of that operation is not before the Court, since it is solely the action against the Salman and Nasr complexes that is presented as a breach of the 1955 Treaty; but the Court cannot assess in isolation the proportionality of that action to the attack to which it was said to be a response; it

[130] Letter of 27 July 1842 (n 21) 1138.

> cannot close its eyes to the scale of the whole operation, which involved, inter alia, the destruction of two Iranian frigates and a number of other naval vessels and aircraft. As a response to the mining, by an unidentified agency, of a single United States warship, which was severely damaged but not sunk, and without loss of life, neither 'Operation Praying Mantis' as a whole, nor even that part of it that destroyed the Salman and Nasr platforms, can be regarded, in the circumstances of this case, as a proportionate use of force in self-defence.[131]

The majority thus concluded that the first US attack might 'have been considered proportionate', if the other requirements for invoking self-defence had been met. Yet within the same paragraph, it finds that Operation Praying Mantis could not be considered a proportionate action, nor could 'even that part of it that destroyed the Salman and Nasr platforms.'[132]

Prima facie, then, the US attack of 19 October 1987 (the destruction of two oil platforms in response to a missile attack on a single merchant vessel) was considered proportionate—or at least the Court took the view that this action may have been proportionate. In contrast, the second US attack (the destruction of two oil platforms in response to the mining of a single military vessel) was viewed as being disproportionate. The reason for the Court's distinction between the two instances in respect of proportionality is not clear. Given that both actions of the United States were of essentially the same character and that both were responses to an attack on a single vessel, it is difficult to see why the Court saw the first response as potentially proportional and the second as clearly disproportional.

Of course, it might be argued that the fact that the attack of 18 April 1988 was part of a wider operation influenced the Court's conclusion regarding proportionality. This may well have been the case, but as noted, the Court was explicit that 'even that part of [Operation Preying Mantis] that destroyed the Salman and Nasr platforms' was disproportional in itself.[133] As such, in the alternative, Andreas Laursen assumes that the Court's distinction is based on the *means* of the original attacks (a missile or a mining). He concludes that finding one response proportional and the other not so on this basis is inconsistent.[134] It is possible that this was the position of the Court.

Perhaps a better reading of the decision, though, is that the nature of the target attacked (military or merchant) has a bearing on what constitutes a proportional response. It is arguable that the implications of an attack on the military means that what is proportional in terms of a response will be different from an attack of a similar scale on a merchant vessel. Yet this analysis would surely suggest that it would be the response to the attack

131 *Oil Platforms* merits (n 6) para 77.

132 *Ibid.*

133 *Ibid.*

134 A Laursen, 'The Judgment by the International Court of Justice in the *Oil Platforms* Case' (2004) 73 *Nordic Journal of International Law* 135, 152–53.

on the *Sea Isle City* that the Court would have viewed as inherently disproportionate, not the response to that on the USS *Samuel B Roberts.* As we have seen, the Court appeared to view the *latter* attack as being the more grave use of force (and thus being capable of constituting an armed attack).[135] In any event, this is but one possible reading of the jurisprudence, and whilst it is self-evident that what is proportional varies in each particular case, whether such a distinction is justified is arguable. Crucially, the Court may be criticised for not outlining what distinguishes the *Sea Isle City* instance from that of the USS *Samuel B Roberts* in the context of the application of the proportionality requirement.

Irrespective of the jurisprudence of the Court, it is clear that proportionality is an aspect of customary international law.[136] However, stating that a criterion of proportionality exists is of little use if it is not known what this in fact means. The major difficulty in this regard is in establishing in reference to what the military response taken in self-defence must be proportional. There are two distinct but related possibilities. Is the use of force taken in response to be commensurate with 1) the scale and means of the attack being responded to (in terms of destruction of life and property)?[137] Or is it to be commensurate with 2) the defensive requirements of the defending state (meaning that the measures taken are proportional to the ultimate goal of abating the attack suffered)? These methods of assessing proportionality cannot be neatly separated, and in reality both of them affect whether a use of force in self-defence will be considered 'proportional' to some degree.

The *Caroline* correspondence offers little guidance as to how proportionality is to be assessed, with the key term being 'excessive'; whether this means excessive in the context of the nature of the attack or the goal of ending the attack is hard to determine. Closer analysis of Webster's formulation suggests that the proportionality question is related to the right of the victim state to defend itself, rather than to the specifics of the particular attack that it is defending itself against: 'the act justified by the necessity of self-defence must be limited *by that necessity,* and kept clearly within it' (emphasis added).[138] Yet this interpretation of the *Caroline* formula is not conclusive.

An analysis of UN-era practice, however, does offer some guidance as to how the proportionality criterion is to be applied today. In the majority of cases, states appear to refer to proportionality as requiring equivalence between the response and the level of force required to abate the attack being responded to, not as an equivalence of scale or means between the

[135] See ch 1, section III-B.

[136] See above, n 3.

[137] This method of assessing proportionality has also been referred to as a determination based upon 'a strictly symmetric reaction'. Gazzini (n 46) 148.

[138] Letter of 27 July 1842 (n 21) 1138.

response and the attack being responded to. In other words, a response in self-defence must be both necessary and *proportional to that necessity*. This calculation inexorably links the criteria of necessity and proportionality, in that an examination of the necessity of an action in self-defence must be made before one can assess whether that action may be seen as being proportional (to the necessity of the action).

To better understand the nature of proportionality in contemporary customary international law, it is useful to examine a few examples. In the Indo-Pakistani conflict over Kashmir in 1947–48,[139] Pakistan made it clear that it was responding with a degree of force necessary to protect its security and saw itself as limited to not going beyond this level.[140] Pakistan seemingly took the view that this may go beyond an equivalence of scale or means with regard to the deployment of Indian forces. It should be noted, however, that Pakistan's action was not accepted as lawful by all third-party states.[141] In the same conflict, India's initial response was taken to combat irregular Pathan tribesmen, apparently directed by Pakistan.[142] In combating this with a full-scale regular armed response (which itself was similarly responded to by Pakistan), India appeared to take action that was disproportionate in terms of scale and means, given the comparatively limited number of Pathan tribesmen located in Kashmir. However, this action may be viewed as being commensurate to the goal of abating the tribal forces, in that the sporadic and targeted attacks of the tribesmen would have been difficult to respond to with a force of an equivalent size.[143] India's action was implicitly accepted by the members of the Security Council.[144]

Mr Blanco, the Cuban representative to the Security Council in 1950, stressed in the context of the Korean conflict that the forces deployed in Korea were empowered to do all that was necessary to 'repel the armed attack' of the North Korean forces against the South.[145] It has been further argued in the context of the Korean conflict that the actions of the US forces in pursuing the North Korean army above the dividing 38th parallel was

[139] In regard to which both parties claimed to be acting in self-defence. See UN Docs S/PV.464 and S/PV.285, 16 for the claims of Pakistan and India respectively.

[140] It should be noted that this position was not put forward in a clearly legal context; thus it should be treated with care. UN Doc S/PV.464, 29.

[141] See, eg, the statements of China in the Security Council, UN Doc S/PV.471, 13.

[142] R Indurthy, 'Kashmir between India and Pakistan: An Intractable Conflict, 1947 to Present' (unpublished) 2–3.

[143] Most notably because of the difficult terrain in the area.

[144] As shown by SC Res 47, which allowed India to maintain its presence in Kashmir, while demanding a Pakistani withdrawal.

[145] UN Doc S/PV.496, 5. It is contestable as to whether the legal basis of the action taken in Korea was UN-authorised collective security or a self-defence action on the part of the United States and its allies. Some scholars certainly take the latter view. See, eg, J Stone, *Aggression and World Order* (University of California Press, Berkley, 1958) 189; and TH Yoo, *The Korean War and the United Nations: A Legal and Diplomatic Historical Study* (Louvain, Librairie Desbarax, 1965) 104–5.

accepted, despite seeming disproportionate in terms of scale, because it was required to ensure the security of South Korea.[146]

It was in general accepted that the British action in the Falklands conflict was proportional to the incursion of its territory by Argentina.[147] Here the Security Council passed resolutions demanding that Argentina withdraw from the islands.[148] It has been argued that the action taken by the United Kingdom was designed to be proportional to securing this goal, given the Security Council's implicit acceptance of its position.[149]

The conclusion that proportionality is to be calculated by reference to the necessity of defence may be seen from the fact that customary international law will not tolerate forcible responses that continue beyond the end of the attack to which they are responding. Once an attack has been abated, any military response will no longer be proportional. This can be seen from the reaction to the US action in Grenada in 1983, so far as this was justified as an action in self-defence to protect nationals.[150] Here, the fact that the forces of the United States remained long after the removal of their nationals was viewed as being disproportionate. This is shown by the statement made by the representative of Zimbabwe in the Security Council, who questioned the factual basis for the claim that US citizens were in danger in Grenada and argued that, in any event, such a threat to its nationals could not provide the United States with a right to remain in the territory or 'choose a government for Grenada'.[151]

Another example evidencing the nature of the proportionality criterion is the Gulf conflict of 1991, following Security Council Resolutions 660 and 661.[152] In this case the action of the coalition can be seen to be an attempt to achieve compliance with these Resolutions, and the Security Council

[146] JA Meyer, 'Collective Security and Regional Security: Necessary Exceptions to a Globalist Doctrine' (1993) 11 *Boston University International Law Journal* 391, 403. However, whilst this conclusion is arguable, it should be treated with some care, given the dissent of the Soviet Union. See inter alia UN Doc S/PV.489, 3; for the People's Republic of China, see UN Doc S/1902; and for Egypt, see *The Times*, 1 July 1950, 4. Similarly, whether the silence of other states in this instance reflects so clearly on the proportionality criterion is open to debate.

[147] See above, n 84.

[148] SC Res 501 and SC Res 502.

[149] Gardam (n 3) 159.

[150] The United States presented three separate legal grounds for the intervention. It claimed self-defence to protect its nationals in Grenada; contended that it acted following an invitation to do so from the Governor-General of Grenada; and argued that it intervened under the invitation of the Organisation of Eastern Caribbean States (OECS). See Statement presented to the US House Committee on Foreign Affairs by Deputy Secretary of State KW Dam, 2 November 1983, reproduced in MN Leich (ed), 'Contemporary Practice of the United States Relating to International Law' (1984) 78 *American Journal of International Law* 200, esp 203–4.

[151] UN Doc S/PV.2491, 5. However, it should be noted that even the scale of the *initial* operation can be seen as disproportionate to the aim of protecting US nationals in Grenada. Additionally, certain objectives of the operation, such as the securing of the Richmond Hill prison, were clearly not necessary to ensure the safety of US citizens. See Levitin (n 84) 650.

[152] Gardam (n 3) 159.

accepted that 'all necessary means' could be employed in self-defence to secure an Iraqi withdrawal from Kuwait.[153] Thus the representative of the United Kingdom to the Security Council during the Gulf conflict of 1991 stated that 'the nature and scope of military action is dictated not by some abstract set of criteria but by the military capacity of the aggressor, who has refused all attempts to remove him from Kuwait.'[154] This indicates that the question was seen as being an assessment of what was necessary to liberate Kuwait, given the capacity of Iraq.

Finally, the Israeli action directed at the militant group Hezbollah in Lebanese territory in 2006 offers a useful example, not least because this action was far from universally accepted as a proportional one taken in self-defence. Indeed, it may be said that the main basis for legal criticism of that action was the disproportionate nature of the response taken.[155] Interestingly, when the Russian Federation argued that the Israeli action did not meet the test for proportionality in self-defence, it implicitly indicated how it perceived that test should be calculated. The Russian representative in the Security Council argued that the 'scale of the use of force' went well beyond that necessary for 'achieving this purpose . . . [of] a counter-terrorist operation'.[156] For its part, Israel stated in an official release of its Ministry of Foreign Affairs:

> One important principle established by international law . . . is that the proportionality of a response to an attack is to be measured not in regard to the specific attack suffered by a state but in regard to what is necessary to remove the overall threat.[157]

As such, Russia and Israel took the same position as to the method by which the proportionality aspect of self-defence is to be calculated, despite reaching different conclusions based on the facts as to whether the criteria had been fulfilled in the case of the Lebanon intervention.

It has been argued that the way in which the Court applied the proportionality principle in both *Nicaragua* and *Nuclear Weapons* reflects a similar

[153] This language is used in SC Res 678.

[154] UN Doc S/PV.2977 (Part II) 73.

[155] Eg, see the positions taken in the Security Council by Denmark, Brazil, Algeria, Norway, Jordan, Indonesia, Turkey, Iran, Djibouti, India and Venezuela (UN Doc S/PV.5493, 7, 19, 22, 23, 24, 25, 28, 30, 32, 34 and 36 respectively). Similarly, in a speech to the Security Council, the UN Secretary-General affirmed Israel's right to use force in self-defence given the attacks upon it and its nationals by Hezbollah but argued that the Israeli response was 'excessive', echoing the terminology of the *Caroline* exchange. UN Doc S/PV.5492, 3.

[156] UN Doc S/PV.5493 (Resumption 1) 2.

[157] *Responding to Hezbollah Attacks from Lebanon: Issues of Proportionality*, 25 July 2006, Israel Ministry of Foreign Affairs, www.mfa.gov.il/MFA/Government/Law/Legal+Issues+and+Rulings/Responding+to+Hizbullah+attacks+from+Lebanon-+Issues+of+proportionality+July+2006.htm. Further, in its letter invoking self-defence sent jointly to the Secretary-General and the President of the Security Council, Israel was careful to set out the 'goals' of its action in Lebanon, although it did not explicitly link these to the issue of proportionality. UN Doc A/60/937-S/2006/515.

position to that displayed in the above examples of state practice.[158] In *Nuclear Weapons*, the Court concluded: 'The proportionality principle [does] not in itself exclude the use of nuclear weapons in self-defence in all circumstances.'[159]

This finding has been cited as an indication that the Court in *Nuclear Weapons* was applying the proportionality test with regard to the goal of responding to the initial attack, rather than to the scale or means of the initial action.[160] This is supported by two passages from *Nicaragua*. In the first, the Court concluded:

> Whatever uncertainty may exist as to the exact scale of the aid received by the Salvadorian armed opposition from Nicaragua, it is clear that these latter United States activities could not have been proportional to that aid.[161]

The point here is that the Court focused not upon equivalence of scale between the aid to Salvadorian rebels and the actions taken by the United States, but rather on whether the actions of the United States were commensurate to the goal of stopping that aid.[162]

In another paragraph, the Court indicated that the actions of the United States could not be seen as proportional because too much time had elapsed between the alleged attack by Nicaragua and the US response:

> Finally on this point [regarding the proportionality of the US actions], the Court must also observe that the reaction of the United States in the context of what it regarded as self-defence was continued long after the period in which any presumed armed attack by Nicaragua could reasonably be contemplated.[163]

This would indicate that the Court felt that any defensive necessity had elapsed in this case, and therefore the actions of the United States could no longer be viewed as being proportional to that necessity.

In her dissent to *Nuclear Weapons*, Judge Higgins certainly interpreted the Court's treatment of proportionality in both that opinion and *Nicaragua* as indicating that the requirement is to be applied by reference to the necessity of restoring the defending state's security, not to the force used by the attacking state:

> [T]he concept of proportionality in self-defence limits a response to what is needed to reply to an attack. . . [The principle refers to] that which was propor-

[158] C Greenwood, '*Jus ad Bellum* and *Jus in Bello* in the *Nuclear Weapons* Advisory Opinion' in L Boisson de Charzournes and P Sands (eds), *International Law, the International Court of Justice and Nuclear Weapons* (Cambridge, Cambridge University Press, 1999) 247, 259; and Gardam (n 3) 158.

[159] *Nuclear Weapons* advisory opinion (n 8) para 42. Although the Court admittedly stressed (para 43) that the unique nature of nuclear weapons must be held in mind in any such application of self-defence.

[160] Greenwood, '*Jus ad Bellum* and *Jus in Bello* in the *Nuclear Weapons* Advisory Opinion' (n 158) 259.

[161] *Nicaragua* merits (n 1) para 237.

[162] Gardam (n 3) 158.

[163] *Nicaragua* merits (n 1) para 237.

tionate to repelling the attack, and not a requirement of symmetry between the mode of the initial attack and the mode of response.[164]

In his dissent to *Nicaragua*, Judge Schwebel took a similar position:

> It would be mistaken to think that there must be proportionality between the conduct constituting the armed attack and the opposing conduct. The action needed to halt and repulse the attack may well have to assume dimensions disproportionate to those of the attack suffered.[165]

This method of calculating proportionality was also implicitly employed by Judge Kooijmans is his separate opinion attached to *DRC v Uganda*,[166] although it should be borne in mind that the majority did not apply the criteria in this way.[167]

It is certainly arguable that the majority in both *Nuclear Weapons* and *Nicaragua* applied the proportionality criterion with regard to the aim of abating the attack being responded to, rather than with regard to an equivalence of scale or intensity, although in neither case was this explicit. For example, despite contentions to the contrary,[168] there is nothing inherent in the *Nuclear Weapons* decision to indicate that the Court was not simply indicating that the use of nuclear weapons is proportional *only* to an attack involving the use of nuclear weapons; it could be here that the majority did in fact employ an 'equivalence of scale' based approach.[169]

As with so much else in the jurisprudence, it is unclear whether the Court actually applied the proportionality criterion as requiring a balance between the goal to be achieved by the self-defence action and the force used in that action.[170] Yet, if this has been the case, the state practice

[164] *Nuclear Weapons* advisory opinion (n 8) dissenting opinion of Judge Higgins, para 5.

[165] *Nicaragua* merits (n 1) separate opinion of Judge Schwebel, para 212. However, it should be noted that unlike Judge Higgins, Judge Schwebel did not conclude that this was the way that the proportionality test was in fact applied by the majority in *Nicaragua*.

[166] *DRC v Uganda* merits (n 7) separate opinion of Judge Kooijmans, paras 33–34.

[167] The application of the proportionality criterion in the case was virtually non-existent, and there was nothing to suggest which method of calculating proportionality the Court here viewed as preferable. *DRC v Uganda* merits (n 7) para 147.

[168] Gardam (n 3) 159.

[169] Indeed, this was the interpretation of the majority's application of proportionality taken by Judge Weeramantry, who saw a 'nuclear-in-response-to-nuclear' scenario as being what was envisaged by the Court. *Nuclear Weapons* advisory opinion (n 8) dissenting opinion of Judge Weeramantry, paras 514–16. However, Judge Weeramantry did acknowledge that the Court may instead have been applying a proportionality test based upon the goal or end to be achieved. In any event, he found neither interpretation acceptable, taking the view that the use of nuclear weapons could *never* constitute a proportionate action in self-defence.

[170] Eg, Kirgis has interpreted the decisions of the Court regarding proportionality as being focused upon a calculation over proportionality of scale or intensity, not the requirements of defence. FL Kirgis, 'Some Proportionality Issues Raised by Israel's Use of Armed Force in Lebanon' (2006) 10 *American Society of International Insight*, available at www.asil.org/insights060817.cfm.

http://www.asil.org/insights/2006/08/insights060817.html. This interpretation is here disputed but cannot be refuted.

discussed above would suggest that the Court may be seen in this respect as applying the requirement in conformity with its scope in customary international law.

Having said this, it should also be noted that there is state practice that would seem to run contrary to this idea. In the context of the East Pakistan conflict of 1971, Pakistan clearly viewed India's action[171] as disproportionate given the scale of its activity. The Pakistani objection was based upon the fact that India's action was disproportionate to the attacks it claimed Pakistan had instigated against it in terms of the scale of those attacks, not in relation to what was required to abate them.[172] In relation to the Israeli incursions into Lebanon in February 1972,[173] Argentina argued that this conduct was disproportionate 'in terms of the scale of the action'.[174] Similar points were made by the representatives of France[175] and Sudan.[176] In relation to the 2002 Korean naval clash, North Korea argued that it had acted in self-defence.[177] It felt that this claim was evidenced by the fact that it had responded in kind to an attack by the South, in terms of *means* and *scale*.[178]

On analysing practice, it is clear that, in the main, states refer to equivalence between the response taken and the goal of restoring security, rather than the scale employed. Thus Ruth Wedgwood has pointed out that 'in the exercise of self-defence, a country is not limited to a predetermined ratio or exact relation between the acts of provocation and the force used in response.'[179] This is the position taken by several other scholars.[180] However, in many cases states do also refer to the scale or means of the response as being relevant to proportionality. This makes sense, as the two methods of assessing proportionality are usually linked. A response that

[171] Action that India claimed was taken in lawful self-defence: UN Doc S/PV. 1606, 3 and 17.

[172] See UN Doc S/PV.1606, 9; and especially UN Doc S/PV.1607, 13.

[173] Which were taken in response to various terrorist attacks that originated from Lebanese territory and which were explicitly justified by Israel as actions of self-defence: UN Doc S/10550.

[174] UN Doc S/PV.1644, 3.

[175] UN Doc S/PV.1650, 2.

[176] *Ibid*, 19.

[177] See above, n 119.

[178] BBC news online, 'North and South Korea Trade Accusations', 29 June 2002.

[179] R Wedgwood, 'Proportionality and Necessity in American National Security Decision Making' (1992) 86 *American Society of International Law Proceedings* 58, 59.

[180] Ago (n 85) 69; R Higgins, *Problems and Process: International Law and How We Use It* (Oxford, Oxford University Press, 1994) 232; MS McDougal and FP Feliciano, *Law and Minimum World Public Order: The Legal Regulation of International Coercion* (New Haven, Yale University Press, 1961) 242; O'Connell (n 76) 64; E Miller, 'Self-Defence, International Law and the Six Day War' (1985) 20 *Israeli Law Review* 49, 71; Gazzini (n 46) 147–48; Gardam (n 3) 142 and 161; and C Greenwood, 'New World Order or Old: The Invasion of Kuwait and the Rule of Law' (1992) 55 *Modern Law Review* 153, 164 (though this is implicit, in that Greenwood argues that an armed attack continues until it is repulsed, indicating that abatement is what is to be considered in relation to the proportionality requirement). This is also the view taken in the 'The Chatham House Principles' (n 32) 968–69.

is disproportionate in scale to the initial attack is also likely to be disproportional to the goal of abating that attack.

For example, with regard to Russia's intervention in August 2008 into the South Ossetia region of Georgia and beyond, Russia's primary claim was that it was acting in self-defence to protect its citizens in the region (including Russian peacekeepers and ethnic Ossetians who had Russian passports).[181] This claim of self-defence was criticised by many states on the basis that the Russian intervention was disproportionate.[182] Most States making this criticism appeared to view Russia's action as disproportionate in terms of what was required to secure its nationals.[183] However, both Russia and Georgia appeared themselves to be more concerned with the means and scale of force used by the Russian Federation when compared directly with the actions of Georgia in the region.[184]

Therefore, the question is not merely one of balancing the response with the legitimate defensive aims of responding: it would seem that there is also a need for states to ensure a level of equivalence in terms of the scale of their activity to that of the initial attack. Yoram Dinstein appears to argue that both methods of assessing proportionality are employed, but in different contexts. For him, there is a distinction between single or 'on-the-spot' uses of force in self-defence on the one hand—what he terms 'defensive armed reprisals'—and a 'full-scale war of self-defence' on the other hand.[185] In the former case, the question is simply one of scale: there must be a direct equation of attack to response. However, in the case of a 'full-scale war of self-defence', proportionality is to be assessed with regard to the general goal of responding to the defensive necessity created by the initial attack.[186] In fact, such a distinction is hard to support in practice. Instead, states employ a combination of the two methods in assessing proportionality, whether their self-defence actions constitute solitary responses or the entrance into full-blown conflict.[187] However, from our study above it would appear that the *primary* equation is based upon the defensive goal to be achieved.

[181] UN Doc S/2008/545.

[182] See, the position of the United States, in particular the televised statement of President George W Bush on 11 August 2008 (available at news.bbc.co.uk/2/hi/europe/7554507.stm); and statements made by German Chancellor Angela Merkel (www.dw-world.de/dw/article/0,2144,3567243,00.html).

[183] Eg, see the position of Panama (UN Doc S/PV.5953, 15) and that of Canada (http://news.gc.ca/web/article-eng.do?crtr.sj1D=10&mthd=advSrch&crtr.mnthndVl=11&nid=414319&crtr.dpt1D=&crtr.tp1D=&crtr.lc1D=&crtr.yrStrtVl=2008&crtr.kw=georgia&crtr.dyStrtVl=9&crtr.aud1D=&crtr.mnthStrtVl=8&crtr.yrndVl=2008&crtr.dyndVl=1).

[184] See UN Docs S/2008/545 and A/62/972 respectively.

[185] Dinstein, 'Implementing Limitations on the Use of Force' (n 99) 57 and c.2.137, 237–42.

[186] *Ibid*, using Pearl Harbour as an illustration.

[187] Kirgis (n 170).

This combination of methods 1 and 2 above provides a dual aspect to the proportionality criterion.[188] It is under this complex construction of proportionality that the goal of securing against future attacks may be acceptable, even if the action taken to ensure this is in some measure disproportionate in scale to the initial attack (thus allowing states to cross the border into the territory of invading states to repel them beyond the frontier).[189] However, some equivalence of scale must be taken into account, meaning that attacks that are wholly disproportionate in terms of scale (such as regime change) are unlikely to be legally proportional.[190]

Therefore, the ICJ's application of the proportionality criterion in *Nicaragua* and *Nuclear Weapons* was not, as such, 'incorrect': it linked proportionality to the necessity of abating an attack. Having said this, the Court's position on proportionality criterion is far from clear, and certainly the complex relationship between the scale of an initial attack, the scale of the response and the goal of abating the attack is not explored in the jurisprudence. Moreover, the application of the criterion in *Oil Platforms* appears inconsistent, and this merely adds to the confusion regarding the proportionality requirement as identified by the ICJ.

VI. TEMPORAL ASPECTS OF SELF-DEFENCE

It is convenient for a number of reasons to examine two temporal elements of the customary international law regarding self-defence under a separate heading from either 'necessity' or 'proportionality'. However, these elements are not 'separate' as such from the criteria already discussed.

A. Imminence

Returning to Webster's formula, it will be recalled that he held that self-defence can only be exercised in situations in which the need to respond is 'instant', 'leaving . . . no moment for deliberation'.[191] This phrase obviously indicates that temporality was viewed by Webster as being relevant

188 This idea of a dual method of calculating proportionality by reference to both scale *and* the goal of the self-defence action appears to have been advanced by the Attorney General of the United Kingdom, at least in relation to anticipatory self-defence. *Hansard* HL vol DCLX col 370 (21 April 2004).

189 A possible example being the crossing of the 38th Parallel into North Korea by US-led forces during the 1950 Korean conflict. See above, section V.

190 This is well evidenced by the international reaction to the US action in Grenada (1983) and the US action in Panama (1989), both of which were condemned as disproportional. (For examples of the kind of condemnation these actions faced, see UN Docs S/PV.2491, 5 and S/PV.2899, 3–17 respectively.) However, there is contrary practice, eg, the acceptance of the coalition intervention in Afghanistan (2001). See above, n 108.

191 Letter of 27 July 1842 (n 21) 1138.

to the question of self-defence in the *Caroline* episode. It is also here worth noting Andrew Stevenson's letter to Lord Palmerston, in which he stated that for self-defence, 'the necessity must be *imminent* and extreme' (emphasis added).[192] These correspondences concerned a claim of what would today be classed as 'anticipatory' self-defence.[193] The *Caroline* was supplying rebels who had yet to attack Canadian territory. Therefore, the terms employed by Webster and Stevenson indicate a need for a temporal connection between the *threat* of attack and the response to it: a threat must be 'imminent'.

As has already been noted, this work does not in general take a position as to the lawfulness of preventative action.[194] However, at this juncture, it is necessary briefly to refer to the idea of 'imminence' with regard to such self-defence claims. This is partly because the concept stems from the *Caroline* formula and forms an aspect of the criteria of necessity and proportionality that should not be ignored in the current analysis, and also because imminence naturally links to the temporal requirement of 'immediacy', which, unlike imminence, has appeared in the jurisprudence of the Court and is relevant to claims of self-defence in the context of responses to actual attacks.

It will be recalled that a distinction may be made between claims of 'anticipatory self-defence' (in which a threat is claimed to be imminent) and 'pre-emptive self-defence' (in which the perceived threat is more temporally remote), with 'preventative self-defence' being employed to cover both of the other terms.[195] By looking at state practice since 1945, it is apparent that neither type of claim is made often.[196] Nonetheless, in cases in which self-defence has been argued in relation to a threat, states generally refer to a threat that was *imminently* apparent, much as Webster outlined.

The classic example is the Israeli attack upon the Iraqi Osiraq nuclear reactor in June 1981. Here, Israel explicitly justified its action as self-defence in response to a threat.[197] In doing so, it stressed that the danger posed by the Iraqi reactor was imminent: if it had not been destroyed at that time, it would have been impossible to destroy it at all.[198] States

[192] Letter of 22 May 1838 (n 17). Of course, Stevenson's letter is not referred to by either states or scholars as representing contemporary customary international law in the way that Webster's has been, but it is a useful corroboration of the US legal position regarding the *Caroline* and the importance of an idea of temporality in relation to self-defence.

[193] Although the idea that the *Caroline* incident was an instance of anticipatory self-defence has been questioned. See above, n 36.

[194] See chapter one, section II-B.

[195] *Ibid.*

[196] Indeed, a number of the incidents that have been cited by writers as amounting to examples of preventative self-defence were not in fact justified as such by the states involved. See Gray, *International Law and the Use of Force* (n 3) 160–65.

[197] See inter alia UN Doc S/PV.2288, 32.

[198] UN Doc S/PV.2280, 44–48. Therefore Israel apparently argued that even though an actual nuclear strike against it was not imminent, a state of affairs whereby Israel would not be able to stop such an attack *was* imminent.

almost universally condemned the action.[199] It is notable that a number of states did so on the basis that the threat to Israel was not imminent.[200] Of course, a number of other states argued that the action was unlawful because self-defence against a threat was unlawful per se.[201]

Moreover, well before the often cited Osiraq incident, there existed examples of state reference to an 'imminence' criterion in the context of claims of preventative self-defence. So far as Pakistani action in Kashmir in 1947–48 was justified as a preventative action,[202] that state made it clear that this was in response to 'imminent danger that threatened the security of Pakistan'.[203] Ten years later, the United Kingdom justified its military operation in Jordan with what amounted to a fairly unique claim of collective anticipatory self-defence, arguing that it was there to protect Jordan against an attack that was yet to manifest itself.[204] In support of this claim, Jordan was very clear to stress that the threat against it was an imminent one.[205] The United Kingdom itself made a similar point, though less explicitly.[206]

Therefore, whilst preventative self-defence is far from being universally accepted as lawful, those states that do support the doctrine in general employ the concept of imminence as a vital part of any attempt to establish the lawfulness of such action.[207] Thus it may be said that anticipatory self-defence is now arguably lawful. Moreover, following the atrocities of 11 September 2001, the concept of self-defence against a *non-imminent* threat (or to use the terminology previously employed, 'pre-emptive self-

[199] As was pointed out by the representative of Bulgaria during the course of its own condemnation of Israel in the Security Council, UN Doc S/PV.2281, 36. Twenty-five individual states addressed letters of condemnation regarding the attack to the President of the Security Council. These documents can be found within the symbol range UN Doc S/14531–S/14560.

[200] Eg, Ireland (UN Doc S/PV.2283, 8–11) ; Niger (UN Doc S/PV.2284, 5) ; Sierra Leone (UN Doc S/PV.2283, 53–56); and China (UN Doc S/PV.2282, 32). See also A D'Amato, 'Israel's Air Strike against the Osiraq Reactor: A Retrospective' (1996) 10 *Temple International and Comparative Law Journal* 259, 261, who points out that the Osiraq attack could never qualify as an action meeting the *Caroline* formula's temporal restriction.

[201] See, eg, the statements made in the Security Council by the representatives of Brazil (UN Doc S/PV.2281, 21); the Soviet Union, which referred to such actions as 'the law of the jungle' (UN Doc S/PV.2283, 22); and Pakistan (UN Doc S/PV.2281, 32).

[202] Pakistan presented a dual argument to justify the sending of regular troops into Kashmir in May 1948. It firstly argued that in stationing its own troops in Kashmir, India had committed an 'act of aggression' against *Kashmir*, and therefore Pakistan was responding to this (UN Doc S/PV.464, 31) (though it was clear that the Kashmiri government had not requested such aid). Its second argument, however, was preventative: Pakistan claimed that it was acting to protect itself from the *threat* of attack from Kashmir (UN Doc S/PV.464, 1–26, esp 25).

[203] UN Doc S/PV.464, 30.

[204] UN Doc S/PV.831, 12–15.

[205] *Ibid*, 12.

[206] Whilst Jordan actually used the term 'imminent foreign armed aggression', the United Kingdom merely stated that the situation was one of 'extreme urgency'. *Ibid*, 16.

[207] Thus, whilst Gazzini does not conclude upon the lawfulness of preventative self-defence one way or another, he does hold that such action may be lawful once the point is reached where there is a 'concrete and immediate threat'. Gazzini (n 46) 199.

defence') has also been put forward, particularly by the United States. The infamous National Security Strategy of 2002 made the questionable claim that '[f]or centuries, international law recognised that nations need not suffer an attack before they can lawfully take action themselves against forces that present an imminent danger of attack.'[208] However, the document went further, arguing that:

> We must adapt the concept of imminent threat to the capabilities and objectives of today's adversaries. . . The greater the threat, the greater is the risk of inaction—and the more compelling the case for taking anticipatory action to defend ourselves, even if uncertainty remains as to the time and place of the enemy's attack.[209]

The notion of pre-emptive self-defence (being self-defence not merely against a demonstrably imminent threat but against *any* threat) was restated, essentially unmodified, in the US National Defence Strategy of 2005[210] and again in its National Security Strategy of 2006.[211]

This so-called 'Bush Doctrine' of pre-emptive self-defence is rather novel.[212] It could be said without straying into controversy that the 'doctrine' has not in general met with acceptance.[213] A rather stark example of this is the categorical rejection of the notion of pre-emptive self-defence by the Non-Aligned Movement (NAM) in the declaration that emerged from that organisation's fourteenth summit in Havana in September 2006.[214]

[208] The National Security Strategy of the United States of America, September 2002, http://www.state.gov/documents/organization/15538.pdf, 15.

[209] *Ibid.*

[210] The National Defence Strategy of the United States of America, March 2005, www.defenselink.mil/news/Apr2005/d20050408strategy.pdf, esp 9–12.

[211] The National Security Strategy of the United States of America, March 2006, http://www.iwar.org.uk/military/resources/nss-2006/nss2006.pdf, 18 and 23. The 2006 National Security Strategy does nothing to elucidate upon its 2002 counterpart. At page 23, it is stated: 'The place of pre-emption in our national security strategy remains the same.'

[212] It has been argued that the message on the use of force that is contained in the National Security Strategy of 2002 'is stark and revolutionary': C Gray, 'The US National Security Strategy and the New "Bush Doctrine" on Pre-emptive Self-Defence' (2002) 1 *Chinese Journal of International Law* 437, 437. However, it has also been argued that it is not entirely novel: Gazzini (n 46) 200.

[213] In the context of negative *academic* responses to the 'doctrine' see, eg, Gazzini (n 46) 221; N Shah, 'Self-Defence, Anticipatory Self-Defence and Pre-emption: International Law's Response to Terrorism' (2007) 12 *Journal of Conflict and Security Law* 95, 115–19; and Greenwood, 'International Law and the Pre-emptive Use of Force' (n 65) esp 12–16. Though of course some scholars have taken the view that Operation Iraqi Freedom was a lawful action of preventative self-defence (or, more accurately, that it could have been argued as such), based upon the Bush Doctrine. See J Yoo, 'International Law and the War in Iraq' (2003) 97 *American Journal of International Law* 563, esp 571–74. Yoo makes the claim (at 572) that imminence *is* required for preventative action to be lawful, but 'imminence' does not in customary international law refer to 'temporal proximity'. See also AD Sofaer, 'On the Necessity of Pre-emption' (2003) 14 *European Journal of International Law* 209.

[214] 14th Summit of Heads of State or Government of the Non-Aligned Movement, Final Document, Havana, 11–16 September, 2006, NAM 2006/Doc.1/Rev.3, www.cubanoal.cu/ingles/index.html.

The Heads of State for the NAM's one hundred plus members undertook in the Havana Declaration to:

> Oppose and condemn . . . the adoption of the doctrine of pre-emptive attack, including attack by nuclear weapons by certain states, which is inconsistent with international law . . . and further oppose and condemn all unilateral military actions, or use of force or threat of use of force against the sovereignty, territorial integrity and independence of Non-Aligned Countries, which constitute acts of aggression and blatant violations of the principles of the UN Charter, including non-interference in the internal affairs of states.[215]

Similarly, although Operation Iraqi Freedom was ultimately justified on the basis of Security Council authorisation,[216] pre-intervention indications that the United States may attempt to justify the action as self-defence[217] were met with negative responses from states. One of the main objections to this was that Iraq posed no *imminent* threat. For example, Iran stated in March 2003:

> The unilateral war against Iraq does not meet any standard of international legitimacy. It is not waged in self-defence against any prior armed attack. Nor, even by any stretch of the imagination, could Iraq, after 12 years of comprehensive sanctions, be considered an imminent threat against the national security of the belligerent Powers.[218]

[215] 14th Summit of Heads of State or Government of the Non-Aligned Movement, Final Document, Havana, 11–16 September, 2006, NAM 2006/Doc.1/Rev.3, www.cubanoal.cu/ingles/index.html, para 22.5.

[216] The US formal legal justification for Operation Iraqi Freedom was contained in a letter dated 20 March 2003 addressed to the President of the Security Council, UN Doc S/2003/351. (The arguments made to the Security Council by the United Kingdom (UN Doc S/2003/350) and Australia (UN Doc S/2003/352) mirror this argumentation.) The US letter to the Security Council did also allude to the notion of self-defence in addition to the claim of Security Council authorisation. Nonetheless, it is here argued that in *legal* terms, the United States offered a justification of Security Council authorisation, though it additionally employed self-defence arguments in the political arena, as well as reserving the right to act in self-defence in international law. See D Kritsiotis, 'Arguments of Mass Confusion' (2004) 15 *European Journal of International Law* 233, esp 241.

[217] See, eg, the *Authorisation for the Use of Military Force against Iraq* (Resolution of US Congress), esp 1498, 1499 and 1501, www.c-span.org/resources/pdf/hjres114.pdf. Prior to the intervention in March 2003, Gray argued that the 2002 National Security Strategy seemed 'to have been designed with Iraq in mind'. Gray, 'The New "Bush Doctrine"' (n 212) 443.

[218] UN Doc S/PV.4726, 33. See also statements made on the issue by Yemen (UN Doc S/PV.4625, 14); Malaysia (UN Doc S/PV.4726, 8); and Vietnam (UN Doc S/PV.4726, 32). In addition to state rejection of this legal claim, it is worth noting that the notion of pre-emptive self-defence was seen as unlawful by the UN High-Level Panel on Threats Challenges and Change, which was created by the UN Secretary-General in 2003 (Report of the Panel, UN Doc A/59/565, esp paras 188–92), and by the Secretary-General himself in his response to the Panel's Report in 2005 (*In Larger Freedom: Towards Development, Security and Human Rights for All*, UN Doc A/59/2005, paras 122–26, esp para 125, though note that this rejection was less explicit than that contained in the Report of the Panel). On the treatment of self-defence in these documents, see C Gray, 'A Crisis of Legitimacy for the UN Collective Security System?' (2007) 56 *International and Comparative Law Quarterly* 157, 160–64.

Such statements echo the concerns raised by States regarding a lack of imminence with regard to Israel's action against the Osiraq reactor in 1981.

Indeed, the terminology employed in the 2002 National Security Strategy itself indicates that the United States at that time perceived a customary international law requirement that responses against threats could only be taken if such threats were 'imminent'. The United States was arguing in that document that imminence was a requirement that should be revised[219] (and would, if the United States felt it necessary, be ignored),[220] *not that it did not exist*.

Therefore, leaving aside the arguable lawfulness of preventative self-defence generally, it is apparent that when such claims are put forward, accepted or not, they are generally accompanied by assertions that the threat being responded to is of an imminent nature. In contrast, recent claims regarding self-defence against a non-imminent threat have not in fact been advanced with regard to any actual state practice[221] but have *nonetheless* been criticised by other states. In other words, it would seem that anticipatory self-defence is controversial but *arguably* lawful, whereas pre-emptive self-defence is in general regarded by states and scholars as unlawful. It is the issue of temporal connection, or imminence, which distinguishes these two claims.

B. Immediacy

Having briefly set out the relevance of imminence with regard to controversial claims of self-defence in response to a threat, we now turn to temporal restrictions in relation to the uncontroversial situation of an action in self-defence taken in response to an actual attack.[222] In the *Nicaragua* case, the ICJ reached the conclusion that the actions of the United States could not be seen as necessary based upon the facts. One reason given by the Court for this brief finding was that the measures taken vis-à-vis the contras were instigated months after the armed opposition in El Salvador had been repulsed.[223] The Court thereby linked the necessity criterion to the speed of the response taken following an actual attack. If this is accepted, it means that the idea of temporal connection is relevant not only to claims

[219] Or as it was put in the document, 'adapted'. The National Security Strategy of the United States, 2002 (n 208).

[220] *Ibid*, 6, where it was stated that 'we will not hesitate to act alone, if necessary, to exercise our right of self-defence by acting pre-emptively.'

[221] A fact highlighted by the decision of the United States to justify the 2003 intervention in Iraq based upon Security Council authorisation rather than the Bush Doctrine.

[222] The relationship between the notion of 'immediacy' outlined in this section and the *Caroline* formula is not here discussed, but this author has examined it elsewhere: Green (n 67) 469–73.

[223] *Nicaragua* merits (n 1) para 237.

made regarding anticipatory self-defence but also to responses to actual attacks: the response must 'immediately' follow the attack being responded to.

In the UN era, many scholars refer to the criteria of necessity and proportionality in regard to the customary international law of self-defence in response to an actual attack yet fail to identify or discuss a temporal requirement.[224] In contrast, other writers refer to an 'immediacy' criterion that is itself a third requirement of customary international law, separate from the concepts of necessity and proportionality.[225] For example, it has been argued that customary international law requires that 'action in self-defence must immediately follow upon the start of an attack.'[226]

Reference to contemporary state practice indicates that there should be some temporal link between the response taken to an actual attack (as opposed to a threatened attack) and the attack itself. Further, it is important here to note that when the idea of 'immediacy' does form part of state practice, this is often done in the context of the requirement of necessity. For example, the South African attacks of 1986 against alleged ANC bases were criticised as being *unnecessary* because there had been no attacks by the ANC in or against South Africa in the weeks immediately preceding the action.[227] Therefore, as in *Nicaragua*, the idea of temporal connection is seen by states as part of a more general requirement that the action taken be 'necessary'. As such, it is perhaps preferable for the concept of immediacy to be seen as an aspect of the necessity requirement, rather than as a separate criterion.

Identifying the notion of the need for a response in self-defence to be temporally linked to the attack it is responding to, as an aspect of the necessity criterion, is fairly straightforward. However, the application of this idea is highly fact-specific and could be influenced by a number of possible factors. In the case of the Falklands, a period of twenty-three days was seen as an acceptable delay following the Argentine invasion.[228] This acceptance may have simply been due to the fact that following the initial Argentine attack there was a continued occupation of the islands, which, on one assessment, could be perceived as an ongoing attack. As such, one may take the view that the British need to respond remained compelling.[229] It may also have

[224] See eg, Brierly (n 27) 406; Rogoff and Collins (n 29); D Kretzmer, 'Targeted Killing of Suspected Terrorists: Extra Judicial Executions or Legitimate Means of Defence?' (2005) 16 *European Journal of International Law* 171, 187; O'Connell (n 76) 64; and Alexandrov (n 3) 19–20.

[225] See Dinstein, *War, Aggression and Self-Defence* (n 41) 237–44; Dinstein, 'Implementing Limitations on the Use of Force' (n 99) 57; Kenny (n 122) 1167–68; Gazzini (n 46) 143–46; and A Constantinou, *The Right of Self-Defence under Customary International Law and Article 51 of the UN Charter* (Brussels, Bruylant, 2000) 157.

[226] GM Badr, 'The Exculpatory Effect of Self-Defence in State Responsibility' (1980) 10 *Georgia Journal of International and Comparative Law* 1, 25.

[227] *New York Times*, 20 May 1986, A1.

[228] Levitin (n 84) 638.

[229] Myjer and White (n 108) 8.

been the case that the acceptability of such a delay was due in part to the scale of the necessary response. Time was needed to mobilise a force of a size suitable to meet the necessity of response required by the Argentine attack.

Another possible factor in the delay may have been the geographical location of the islands. As Rosalyn Higgins has rightly pointed out, geographical location will necessarily affect how quickly a state responds in self-defence.[230] In this context, it is worth noting that in *DRC v Uganda*, the ICJ stated, albeit rather equivocally, that 'the taking of airports and towns *many hundreds of kilometres from Uganda's border* would not seem proportionate to the series of transborder attacks it claimed had given rise to the right of self-defence, nor to be necessary to that end' (emphasis added).[231] Therefore, it would seem that the Court has similarly linked the locality of the response to the criteria of necessity and proportionality in some measure.[232]

Assuming that Operation Desert Storm was an action taken in collective self-defence,[233] a period of five months elapsed between the initial attack against Kuwait and the response in self-defence.[234] Again, though, there was continued occupation of Kuwait during this period.[235] In the context of the coalition intervention in Afghanistan in 2001, so far as this may be seen as a response to the 11 September atrocities and not as an action of preventative self-defence,[236] a delay of slightly under a month appears to have been acceptable,[237] in spite of the fact that the attack had abated.[238] This may have been due to the difficulties over intelligence gathering with regard to the perpetrators and the attempt to engage the Taliban diplomatically prior to the use of force.[239]

It therefore seems that some measure of temporal connection is required between an attack and the response to it. Identifying a general principle as to what that connection should be, however, is more difficult. The need for

[230] Higgins, *Problems and Process* (n 180) 241.

[231] *DRC v Uganda* merits (n 7) para 147.

[232] Supporting this is the fact that Judge Kooijmans made this point more strongly in his separate opinion. See *DRC v Uganda* merits (n 7) separate opinion of Judge Kooijmans, para 34.

[233] A contestable proposition. See above, n 121.

[234] Kenny (n 122) 1167.

[235] This is noted as a contributing factor to the acceptance of the operation by Kenny (n 122).

[236] The United States put forward a dual claim with regard to its action in Afghanistan; it argued that the intervention was a 'response to these attacks [of 11 September 2001]' and also was 'designed to prevent and deter further attacks on the United States' (UN Doc S/2001/946).

[237] On the general acceptance by other states to the response taken, see above, n 108.

[238] This has been contrasted with the Falklands situation, and thus Operation Enduring Freedom can arguably be viewed as amounting to a reprisal. See Myjer and White (n 108) 8.

[239] As noted, in 2001 the United States made a number of demands of the Afghani Taliban regime, which were rejected. See above, n 106.

an 'immediate' response appears to be extremely flexible, perhaps even more so than the general criteria of necessity and proportionality. Certainly it may be said that the requirement to act promptly is not absolute and will depend on the context of the situation.

Indeed, given that an attempt to negotiate goes a long way to establishing necessity[240] (not to mention the fact that such action is a desirable alternative to force on a moral level), if a state first tries to negotiate and then finds that it must resort to force following the failure of those negotiations, the delay will not mean that the state falls foul of the temporal element of the necessity requirement:

> If serious attempts are made to resolve the conflict through amicable means, surely the state that has pursued these alternative avenues cannot be faulted for having lost time unduly before it unleashes its armed forces.[241]

Thus it is argued that there must be an immediate *need* to respond but not that there must necessarily be an immediate *response*.[242] The response must be taken within reasonable temporal proximity, taking into account all the circumstances of the particular case: the difficulty of gathering evidence, the delay incurred though the mobilisation of the responding state's own forces, the time taken in attempts at negotiation and so on.

C. Temporal Aspects of Self-Defence in the Modern World

It has been argued that ideas of both immediacy and imminence in relation to self-defence are illogical in the context of the modern world.[243] This argument is not exactly new: it has been stressed in relation to the unique nature of nuclear weapons since the inception of such armaments.[244] Recently, however, this claim regarding the temporal aspects of the customary international law on self-defence has been restated in the context of twenty-first-century terrorism. This is on the basis that an inability to detect imminent terrorist threats, the need to gather information with regard to terrorist activities and the difficulties of mounting an instant response to

240 Above, section IV.

241 Dinstein, 'Implementing Limitations on the Use of Force' (n 99) 57.

242 *Ibid.*

243 See, eg, GM Travalio, 'Terrorism, International Law, and the Use of Military Force' (2000) 18 *Wisconsin International Law Journal* 145, 164–66. Travalio does not distinguish between ideas of immediacy or imminence here, but his arguments clearly refer to both concepts.

244 Israel stressed this point before the Security Council with regard to its action against the Osiraq reactor: UN Doc S/PV.2280, 53–55. As Higgins has phrased this, with specific reference to the *Caroline* formula, 'in a nuclear age, common sense cannot require one to interpret an ambiguous provision in a text in a way that requires a State to passively accept its fate before it can defend itself.' Higgins, *Problems and Process* (n 180) 242. See also Bowett (n 46) 191–92.

such attacks mean that such temporal elements should no longer be requirements for lawful self-defence. This argument has been taken further: the suggestion has been made that a concept of 'immediacy' is no longer an aspect of the customary international law on self-defence.[245]

State practice clearly runs counter to this conclusion: states still acknowledge the need for some kind of temporal link between a response in self-defence and the attack being responded to. It may be arguable, however, that these restrictions upon self-defence have become more flexible. Since the advent of nuclear weapons, some level of flexibility with regard to the temporal proximity required is the only logical way that self-defence can be understood. This 'flexibility' has arguably increased still further since 11 September 2001, in terms of what states will deem to be legally acceptable. It is true that the idea of temporal connection is referred to less often by states than the more general concepts of necessity or proportionality, even implicitly. However, it is not the case that such temporal safeguards have disappeared from customary international law altogether.

As such, it would seem that the ICJ was in principle correct in *Nicaragua* in implicitly holding that a delay in responding to an attack may mean that the response taken does not meet the necessity requirement. Of course, *how much* of a delay is required for this to be the case appears to be an extremely difficult thing to quantify in any given case.

VII. THE MARGINALISATION OF NECESSITY AND PROPORTIONALITY BY THE ICJ

From this chapter it is evident that, in broad terms, the jurisprudence of the ICJ can be seen to represent accurately the state practice and *opinio juris* in regard to the criteria of necessity and proportionality. The Court's treatment of the criteria of necessity and proportionality in self-defence cannot in general be criticised based upon what the Court has stated on the issue (although the manner in which the Court has *presented* its conclusions can be raised as a matter of concern). The Court has been clear and consistent over the need for a use of force in self-defence to be necessary and proportional, and when it has provided guidance as to the content and scope of these criteria its conclusions have largely been an accurate reflection of the manner the criteria appear to be applied in customary international law.

However, such guidance has been minimal: the Court has treated the criteria of necessity and proportionality as 'marginal considerations'.[246]

245 Occelli (n 25) 483–88.

246 Gray, *International Law and the Use of Force* (n 3) 151. Although Gray only makes this point with regard to the treatment of the criteria in *Nicaragua*, it may be seen as true for all the relevant decisions of the Court. This is perhaps with the exception of *Nuclear Weapons*, where the ICJ did place greater emphasis upon the criteria of necessity and proportionality. See

For example, in *Nicaragua*, the conclusions of the Court regarding both the necessity and the proportionality of the actions of the United States were stated in a single paragraph.[247] Similarly, in *DRC v Uganda*, the Court made almost no reference to the criteria of necessity and proportionality—in a case in which *both parties claimed to be acting in self-defence*.[248] When one compares the detailed nature of necessity and proportionality evident in the practice of states with the ICJ's statements, the Court's treatment of the criteria appears far too limited. In other words, for the most part, it is not what the Court has said on necessity and proportionality that is the problem, it is what it has not said.[249]

Of course, the inherent flexibility of the requirements of necessity and proportionality must be kept in mind. This flexibility may go some way towards explaining the lack of detail put forward by the ICJ on the criteria. The very nature of necessity and proportionality makes it difficult for the Court to put forward an objective standard for the requirements. Having said this, the criteria do have demonstrable content apparent in the customary international law, and it is arguable that, given that the criteria are complex and that their content is difficult to identify, there is an increased need for the Court to contribute to an understanding of them.

Additionally, it is important to recall that in all three of the contentious cases relating to self-defence, the Court held that an armed attack had not been established. As the Court concluded that this was the condition *sine qua non* for self-defence, necessity and proportionality were not determinative for the decisions in each case, given the Court's conception of self-defence. As the Court stated in *DRC v Uganda*,

> [S]ince the preconditions for the exercise of self-defence do not exist in the circumstances of the present case, the Court has no need to enquire whether such an entitlement to self-defence was in fact exercised in circumstances of necessity and in a manner that was proportionate.[250]

Therefore the marginal treatment of the criteria of necessity and proportionality by the ICJ may be seen as a natural consequence of the Court's conception of self-defence as a whole: in each case the fact that an armed

Nuclear Weapons advisory opinion (n 8) paras 38 and 41. See J Gardam, 'Necessity and Proportionality in *Jus ad Bellum* and *Jus in Bello*' in L Boisson de Charzournes and P Sands (eds), *International Law, the International Court of Justice and Nuclear Weapons* (Cambridge, Cambridge University Press, 1999) 275, 284.

[247] *Nicaragua* merits (n 1) para 237.

[248] For Court's brief references to the criteria, see *DRC v Uganda* merits (n 7) paras 147 and 304.

[249] SM Young, 'Destruction of Property (on an International Scale): The Recent *Oil Platforms* Case and the International Court of Justice's Inconsistent Commentary on the Use of Force by the United States' (2004–05) 30 *North Carolina Journal of International Law and Commercial Regulation* 335, 374–75 (esp focusing upon *Oil Platforms*).

[250] *DRC v Uganda* merits (n 7) para 147.

attack was not established[251] meant that the nature of necessity and proportionality was irrelevant to the dispute before the Court. Thus, the fact that the ICJ has not interacted with the criteria of necessity and proportionality to any significant degree may stem in part from its conception of armed attack as the fundamental requirement for self-defence in customary international law.

VIII. CONCLUSION

The analysis in this chapter produces a complex picture of interrelated criteria and demonstrates that necessity and proportionality in the context of self-defence are fluctuating and flexible requirements. On this basis, the representative of Cuba argued during state discussion concerning what ultimately became the Declaration on the Principle of the Prohibition of the Threat or Use of Force, which was adopted by the General Assembly in 1987,[252] that the crucial customary international law concepts of necessity, proportionality (and imminence) were still not adequately defined.[253] Indeed, Cuba was critical of the draft Declaration for not remedying this.[254]

Whilst this criticism of the law has some basis, in that the criteria of necessity and proportionality are extremely flexible, it is argued here that it is incorrect to view the content of these criteria as being unclear. In fact, the criteria are extremely detailed and can be, to a certain degree, determined through reference to state practice.

In general, the criterion of necessity refers to the action being the last resort of a state, meaning that the victim state has a reasonable need to respond with force based upon the circumstances of the incident. This assessment of reasonableness involves a balancing of the right of states to security with the prohibition contained in Article 2(4) of the UN Charter. Proportionality as a criterion for assessing the lawfulness of self-defence has two aspects. The most important of these is that the force used is proportional to the necessity of a response: the action must not be more than is required to meet the defensive necessity of the initial attack. Thus, necessity and proportionality are inherently linked. Additional to this is the fact that whilst there need not be an exact equivalence of scale between attack and response, some kind of relationship must exist

[251] Either because the Court's criteria for an 'armed attack' were not met, as in Nicaragua (n 1, esp para 230) or, more simply, because the available evidence did not establish that the accused party actually perpetrated the attack claimed by the applicant, as in *Oil Platforms* (n 6, paras 61 and 71) or *DRC v Uganda* (n 7, esp para 146).

[252] Declaration on the Enhancement of the Effectiveness of the Principle of Refraining from the Threat or Use of Force in International Relations 1987, GA Res 42/22.

[253] UN Doc A/C.6/42/SR.21, 3.

[254] *Ibid.*

between the two—responses that are particularly disproportionate in scale will be unlawful.

A further aspect of both necessity and proportionality is the need for temporal connection. In the context of preventative self-defence—so far as this may be considered lawful in itself—'temporal connection' refers to the need for a demonstrable imminent threat against the state taking the preventative action. In the case of an attack that has already occurred, a responding state must show that the response taken was reasonably immediate. In other words, taking into account all relevant factors specific to the case, the state must respond as soon as is practically possible.

The ICJ has correctly and consistently reaffirmed the applicability of necessity and proportionality to self-defence. However, having identified that these criteria exist, the Court has provided little guidance as to what they are. Although the Court has not misrepresented these criteria, it has failed to indicate the complexity and nuanced nature of necessity and proportionality—something that would be of great practical use to future applications of the law.

Crucially, state practice suggests that the view of an armed attack criterion as the condition *sine qua non* for self-defence may be a misconception. The position that actions taken in self-defence are limited by customary international law requirements of necessity and proportionality is uncontroversial.[255] This is affirmed when an examination of state practice is undertaken: the above analysis indicates that states in the vast majority of instances perceive necessity and proportionality as being lawful requirements for self-defence. Indeed, in the study of a cross-section of practice, *every* state that has claimed self-defence has invoked the criteria of necessity and proportionality to a greater or lesser degree (although this has sometimes been implicit in their arguments). State reference to necessity and proportionality in invoking self-defence is near universal, and states responding to such invocations in general similarly refer to these requirements.

This near universal reference to necessity and proportionality in relation to self-defence claims indicates that, in terms of the actual practice of states, *these criteria represent the fundamental aspect in the determination of the lawfulness of state claims.* It is argued here that the conception of self-defence as set out in the *Caroline* remains, albeit in a contemporary form, the essential test for the lawfulness of an action of self-defence in customary international law.

This is not to say that states never refer to the concept of an 'armed attack' in their self-defence claims or that such a concept is necessarily irrelevant to the determination of a self-defence action.[256] Indeed, the

[255] See above, n 3.

[256] As we will see in chapter three.

greater focus on necessity and proportionality in state practice may stem in part from the fact that in certain circumstances states hold that the existence of an armed attack is self-evident: in such cases, the focus of states would inevitably turn immediately to necessity and proportionality. However, whilst this may be true to an extent, as we saw in the previous chapter, it is often unclear if an armed attack—as the ICJ has defined it—has occurred. In the view of the current author, the idea of an 'armed attack' as conceived by the ICJ is simply not the primary aspect of any legal determination made by states regarding whether another state has acted in lawful self-defence. Therefore, it is argued here that the criteria of necessity and proportionality remain the primary aspect of the legal claims of states regarding self-defence:

> In state practice generally these factors of necessity and proportionality are often the *only factors relied on* in deciding the legality of particular actions. They constitute *a minimum test* by which to determine that a use of force does not constitute self-defence (emphasis added).[257]

Given this conclusion, the Court's focus upon armed attack can be seen as creating an inaccurate picture of the law on self-defence. The primary importance of necessity and proportionality in determining the lawfulness of self-defence actions in practice undermines the minimal treatment of those criteria by the ICJ.

This failing derives from the Court's reliance upon the armed attack criterion and its wider conception of the international law concerning self-defence. Subsequent chapters investigate the underlying reasons for this conception and thus for the Court's inadequate jurisprudence on the law of self-defence.

[257] Gray, *International Law and the Use of Force* (n 3) 154.

3

The Trouble with Armed Attack and the Merged Conceptions of Self-Defence

IT WAS ARGUED in chapter one that the ICJ has produced a 'conception' of self-defence in international law that focuses upon a primary criterion of an armed attack. However, this conception is difficult to penetrate from the relevant decisions and must be pieced together before any degree of coherence can be found. Moreover, the application by the Court of its own vision of the international law regarding self-defence may in some instances be seen as rather inconsistent. In chapter two, it was argued that in customary international law, the primary means of assessing the lawfulness of an avowed self-defence claim are the criteria of necessity and proportionality, not the question of an occurrence of an armed attack. An examination of practice highlights that these criteria are definable, albeit complex and flexible. Whilst the ICJ has consistently identified the need for action taken in self-defence to be both necessary and proportional, it has offered very little in the way of guidance as to the practical content of these concepts. This is compounded by the fact that when the Court has applied these criteria in relation to self-defence claims, this has again occurred in something of an inconsistent manner.

The preceding chapters therefore indicate that the jurisprudence of the ICJ regarding self-defence is problematic in a number of respects. In this and subsequent chapters, these problems will be further explored and the underlying reasons for much of the Court's inadequate treatment of the international law regarding self-defence will be examined. An understanding of why there exist such problems in the ICJ's jurisprudence regarding self-defence is essential before any possible improvement may be considered. This analysis has two main points of focus. The first is the inherent difficulties in the law, which will be examined in this chapter. A proposal for improving the current law governing self-defence will then be set out in chapter four. The second point of focus is the problems associated with the Court itself.[1] We will turn to these in chapter five.

[1] Interestingly, Judge Schwebel noted in 1986 that two of the primary reasons that states do not refer disputes (of any kind) to the ICJ are because a) 'The content of international law is uncertain, that is to say, the law to be applied by the Court is uncertain'; and b) 'the Court is unpredictable in its application of the law.' SM Schwebel, 'Reflections on the Role of the International Court of Justice' (1986) 61 *Washington Law Review* 1061, 1068.

I. 'ARMED ATTACK AS A GRAVE USE OF FORCE': AN ACCURATE REFLECTION OF THE LAW?

One must proceed with care when laying the blame for the apparent confusion in the jurisprudence of the Court solely at the feet of the ICJ. This is because, at least in the context of the law on self-defence, the law is itself problematic. The primary role of the ICJ is, it is submitted, to apply *existing* international law to resolve specific disputes. This is something that will be discussed in more detail in chapter five.[2] For present purposes, it is simply enough to note that when the Court is producing a judgment, its role should be to pronounce upon the dispute before it through the application of international law as it perceives it to be, not as it would wish it to be. The Court is not charged with making or developing international law; it is, as one may expect, a judicial and not a legislative body.[3]

As such, we must ask not just 'how the Court left that body of law [governing self-defence] . . . but how it found it'.[4] Assuming one accepts that the Court is in general obliged to produce its decisions based upon international law as it stands when those decisions are made, it is self-evident that the quality of the ICJ's jurisprudence relies greatly upon a level of coherence amongst the existing law:

> If the essential function of the Court is to apply international law, for it to be able to do so, the appropriate norm must exist in that law, and must be clear and not difficult to apply.[5]

The law governing self-defence, as it stands, is far from being a clear or coherent basis upon which to make a judgment in any particular dispute. As Peter Rowe put it with some delicacy, a year after the *Nicaragua* decision, the law governing self-defence is 'obscure'.[6] Little has changed since then.

Yet, so far as the existing *lex lata* of self-defence may be ascertained, by examining in detail what the Court has pronounced with regard to self-defence, it can be seen that a good deal of the ICJ's jurisprudence *does* in fact reflect conventional and customary international law.[7] Much of the

[2] See ch 5, section II.

[3] For a more detailed discussion, see *ibid*.

[4] JL Hargrove, 'The *Nicaragua* Judgment and the Future of the Law of Force and Self-Defence' (1987) 81 *American Journal of International Law* 135, 135.

[5] M Bedjaoui, 'Expediency in the Decisions of the International Court of Justice' (2000) 71 *British Yearbook of International Law* 1, 10. In relation to decisions of the Court relating to areas of law other than the use of force, see K Tanaka, 'The Character of World Law in the International Court of Justice' (1971) 15 *Japanese Annual of International Law* 1, 4.

[6] P Rowe, *Defence: The Legal Implications (Military Law and the Laws of War)* (London, Brassey's Defence, 1987) 102.

[7] Eg, it was concluded in ch 2 that, whilst the marginalisation of the criteria of necessity and proportionality in the jurisprudence of the ICJ can be seen as highly problematic, the *actual content* of what it has said can be seen as broadly corresponding to the way that states apply and respond to these criteria in a legal context in practice.

confusion inherent in the jurisprudence of the Court already exists in the law as it stands. Whether merely reflecting inadequate law to produce inadequate jurisprudence is acceptable—given that the ICJ is the primary judicial organ of the UN—is of course a separate issue and is something that will be examined in more detail subsequently.[8] However, a study of state application of the crucial criterion of armed attack produces some interesting results.

The most fundamental criticism that has been raised throughout preceding chapters with regard to the ICJ's self-defence jurisprudence has been its conception of the standard of an armed attack. Whilst the ICJ's conception of self-defence is in many respects undesirable, this is not the same as holding it to be a fundamentally *inaccurate* conception of existing international law. When one begins to examine state practice, the customary international law on self-defence *does* appear to include the concept of armed attack as constituting a use of force of a special 'quality' beyond a use of force *simpliciter* (what we have been referring to as 'armed attack as a grave use of force').

A majority of writers identify an 'armed attack as a grave use of force' criterion as an aspect of the legal regulation of self-defence.[9] In general, Article 51 of the UN Charter is referred to as the authority for this proposition. For example, Avra Constantinou has written: 'The provision in Article 51 in conjunction with Article 2(4) connotes that there is a difference in the level of a use of force *simpliciter* and a use of force that amounts to an armed attack.'[10] It will be recalled that Article 51 provides that '[n]othing in the present Charter shall impair the inherent right of individual or collective self-defence if an armed attack occurs.' Therefore, the idea of an armed attack is unavoidably and starkly present in Article 51. That Article appears clear, in itself, as to the *requirement* of an armed attack.

[8] See ch 5, esp section II.

[9] In 1980, in the context of its work on state responsibility, the ILC concluded that the majority of scholars took this view. *Yearbook of the International Law Commission*, 1980, vol II, Part Two, *Report of the Commission to the General Assembly on the Work of its Thirty-Second Session* (New York, United Nations Press, 1981) UN Doc A/35/10, 58. A few examples to support this include: TM Franck, 'Who Killed Article 2(4)? or Changing the Norms Governing the Use of Force by States' (1970) 64 *American Journal of International Law* 809, esp 812; L Henkin, 'The Use of Force: Law and US Policy' in *Right v Might* (New York, Council on Foreign Relations Press, 1991) 37, 45; I Brownlie, *International Law and the Use of Force by States* (Oxford, Oxford University Press, 1963) esp 278–79; ME O'Connell, 'Taking *Opinio Juris* Seriously' in E Cannizzaro and P Palchetti (eds), *Customary International Law on the Use of Force: A Methodological Approach* (Leiden, Martinus Nijhoff, 2005) 9, 26–27; C Gray, *International Law and the Use of Force*, 3rd edn (Oxford, Oxford University Press, 2008) esp 128–48 and 173–83; E Jiménez de Aréchaga, 'International Law in the Past Third of a Century' (1978) 159 *Recueil Des Cours* 13, 95–98; and A Constantinou, *The Right of Self-Defence under Customary International Law and Article 51 of the UN Charter* (Brussels, Bruylant, 2000) esp 56–110.

[10] Constantinou, *ibid*, 57.

Some scholars have—somewhat understandably—taken the view that the concept of an armed attack was a novel one in 1945, introduced into the international law governing self-defence by Article 51 of the UN Charter.[11] In fact, on rare occasions in the immediate pre-Charter period, the phrase 'armed attack' was employed by states in the context of self-defence, although 'attack', 'aggression' and 'force' were more common terms.[12] It is therefore perhaps incorrect to hold that this concept was *introduced* into international law by Article 51 of the UN Charter. Equally, it is important to note that Article 51 firmly placed the phrase 'armed attack' in the international legal vernacular, to an extent that was not apparent prior to 1945.

Irrespective of this, Article 51 alone does not make it clear whether the term 'armed attack' is used therein as a term of art to indicate a use of force *beyond* a breach of Article 2(4). This cannot be presumed: there is no guidance in Article 51 as to what an 'armed attack' constitutes.[13] The same can equally be said of the debates of the 1945 San Francisco Conference.[14] Indeed, an examination of the drafting of the Charter at San Francisco suggests that the majority of states did not view the phrase 'armed attack' as having a particular character as a legal term of art.[15] This perception—that armed attack was not employed during the drafting of the Charter as a term of art—is strengthened when it is considered that whilst the English version of Article 51 refers to an 'armed attack' (with the Spanish similarly requiring an '*ataque armado*'), the equally authoritative French version of the Charter employs the term '*agression armée*' and not '*attaque armée*', as would seem more logical. Partially based on this, writing in 1947, Kunz was clear that he saw the term as a strategic one, not a legal one.[16]

[11] See, eg, M Byers, 'Geopolitical Change and International Law' in D Armstrong, T Farrell and B Maiguashca (eds), *Force and Legitimacy in World Politics* (Cambridge, Cambridge University Press, 2005) 51, 52; and J Macdonald, 'The *Nicaragua* Case: New Answers to Old Questions' (1986) 24 *Canadian Yearbook of International Law* 127, 147 (though MacDonald actually ascribes this view to *the ICJ*, without making it clear whether he also takes this position himself).

[12] Thus Brownlie states, in reference to the pre-Charter practice: 'the state practice does not provide any precise definition of aggression, attack, resort to force, *et cetera*.' Brownlie (n 9) 232.

[13] Rowe (n 6) 99; KC Kenny, 'Self-Defence' in R Wolfrum and C Philipp (eds), *United Nations: Law, Policies and Practice, Vol II* (Dordrecht, Martinus Nijhoff, 1995) 1162, 1164; and J Combacau, 'The Exception of Self-Defence in UN Practice' in A Cassese (ed), *The Current Legal Regulation of the Use of Force* (Dordrecht, Martinus Nijhoff, 1986) 9, 22.

[14] Brownlie (n 9) 278; and SA Alexandrov, *Self-Defence Against the Use of Force in International Law* (The Hague, Kluwer Law International, 1996) 96.

[15] See *Documents of the United Nations Conference on International Organisation, Volume XII: Commission III*, Doc 576, III/4/9, 680–87. Eg, the delegation of Colombia stated that 'if at any time an armed attack should ensue, that is, *an aggression against a state* . . . self-defence whether individual or collective, exercised as an inherent right, shall operate automatically within the provisions of the Charter' (emphasis added) (687).

[16] JL Kunz, 'Individual and Collective Self-Defence Under Article 51 of the Charter of the United Nations' (1947) 41 *American Journal of International Law* 872, 877–78.

Moreover, as Judge Schwebel stated in his dissent to *Military and Paramilitary Activities in and against Nicaragua* (hereafter *Nicaragua*), Article 51 does not provide that self-defence is lawful 'if, and only if, an armed attack occurs'[17] (though it must be said that this is one possible interpretation of the text).[18] As such, the basis of the ICJ's conception of the armed attack criterion as a requirement beyond a mere breach of Article 2(4) cannot be derived from Article 51.[19] The question of what constitutes an armed attack therefore takes on the character of treaty interpretation through an assessment of practice: whilst 'Article 51 specifies that self-defence is permissible in response to an armed attack',[20] it is clear that 'the *definition* of armed attack is left to customary international law' (emphasis added).[21]

When one begins to examine state practice and *opinio juris* of states since the inception of the Charter with regard to the 'armed attack' criterion, it becomes apparent that the phrase does seem to have a level of normative value. In other words, the term 'armed attack' would seem to be a term of art possessed of specific legal meaning and not merely a pseudonym for the use of force. If it was arguable that in 1945 the term was merely 'strategic', it would appear that this does not hold true today.

It is certainly the case that when states invoke self-defence, they invariably claim that they are responding to a use of force.[22] This is to be expected: the entire theoretical basis for self-defence is that it is action taken as a *response*.[23] Only force (or arguably the threat of force)[24] may be met by force.[25] However, it is further arguable that, as the ICJ has repeatedly stressed, self-defence can be lawfully taken only when there exists

[17] *Military and Paramilitary Activities in and against Nicaragua* (*Nicaragua v United States of America*) merits (1986) ICJ Reports 14, dissenting opinion of Judge Schwebel, para 173.

[18] As Melzer succinctly put it, the debate is over whether 'if an armed attack occurs' means '*after* an armed attack occurs' or '*only if* an armed attack occurs' (emphasis added). Y Melzer, *Concepts of Just War* (Leiden, AW Sijthoff, 1975) 18.

[19] Combacau (n 13) esp 11.

[20] C Gray, 'The Use of Force and the International Legal Order' in MD Evans (ed), *International Law*, 2nd edn (Oxford, Oxford University Press, 2006) 589, 599.

[21] *Ibid*. See also T Gazzini, *The Changing Rules on the Use of Force in International Law* (Manchester, Manchester University Press, 2005) 119.

[22] A good example of this is the clash between Korean Naval vessels in 1999. Both North and South Korea claimed that their uses of force were lawful, and significantly, both repeatedly stressed that the other had opened fire first. *New York Times*, 16 June 1999, 7. Another example is the position taken by France with regard to the actions of its troops in Tunisia in 1958. France was keen to stress that its troops were instructed to remain passive until they were attacked themselves by Tunisian forces: UN Doc S/PV.819, 16.

[23] Combacau (n 13) 20–22; DJ Scheffer, 'The Use of Force After the Cold War' in *Right v Might* (New York, Council on Foreign Relations Press, 1991) 109, 137; and Y Dinstein, *War, Aggression and Self-Defence*, 4th edn (Cambridge, Cambridge University Press, 2005) 178.

[24] Obviously, in instances in which states have made a controversial claim of preventative self-defence, they are not arguing that they are responding to a use of force. Even here though, states generally ensure that they invoke a *specific* threat that is being responded to, as the classic case of Israel's Osiraq operation in 1981 demonstrates. See UN Doc S/PV. 2287, 32.

[25] Brownlie (n 9) 254.

something *more* than a mere breach of Article 2(4). The notion of a particularly grave attack is something that is often required by states when assessing the lawfulness of self-defence claims. Practice in this regard is erratic and certainly not as apparent as state reference to the criteria of necessity and proportionality. Nonetheless, the application of a 'gravity' requirement has occurred throughout the UN era. Some examples of practice prior to the Court's decision in *Nicaragua* will help to elucidate this further.

In 1947–48 during debates over the first Kashmiri conflict, both India and Pakistan claimed to be acting in self-defence.[26] Throughout the majority of the diplomatic discussion, neither party claimed to have been the victim of an armed attack. However, both states continually argued that they were the victims of 'aggression', entitling them to exercise the right to self-defence.[27] The legal content ascribed to that term during these debates is difficult to ascertain, and the dispute was argued in the main by reference to the requirements of necessity and proportionality. Yet, in 1950 (once the intervention by regular Indian forces could not be denied), India suddenly stressed that due to the lack of an 'armed attack'—clearly in reference to a use of force of a more grave kind than that which they could no longer deny had occurred—Pakistan could not claim self-defence.[28] China made a similar point,[29] whilst the representative of Argentina's assessment of the conflict back in 1948 referred to the terms of aggression and armed attack interchangeably.[30]

Another particularly useful example from early UN practice is the crisis in Lebanon in 1958,[31] which led to the intervention of US troops, avowedly in collective self-defence.[32] The arguments of various states relating to this intervention are particularly useful because they demonstrate the inconsistency of the *opinio juris* regarding an armed attack criterion. Initially, in May 1958 Lebanon claimed a right of self-defence based upon

[26] See ch 2, n 139.

[27] See, eg, the claim of India (UN Doc S/PV.463, 5) and the identical claim made the next day by Pakistan (UN Doc S/PV.464, 31).

[28] UN Doc S/PV.466, 4.

[29] Claiming that India had not even breached Art 2(4), *let alone* committed an armed attack—clearly viewing them as different things. UN Doc S/PV.471, 13.

[30] Apparently to indicate that the actions of both parties gave rise to a right of self-defence (UN Doc S/PV.229, 124), though this surely cannot be possible; opposing states in a conflict cannot both be acting in lawful self-defence. Dinstein (n 23) 178.

[31] For a useful examination of the role of 'armed attack' in the legal argumentation employed during the Lebanon conflict of 1958, see Franck, 'Who Killed Article 2(4)?' (n 9) 814–18.

[32] There is evidence to suggest that the interventions of the United States and the United Kingdom in Lebanon and Jordan respectively in 1958 were aimed at supporting unpopular pro-Western governments against internal opposition movements, rather than responding to a dubious external attack. FA Gerges, 'The Lebanese Crisis of 1958: The Risks of Inflated Self-Importance' (1993) 5 *Beirut Review* 83, www.lcps-lebanon.org/pub/breview/br5/gergesbr5pt1.html.

the 'intervention' of armed bands in Lebanon from the United Arab Republic (UAR).[33] This phrase was clearly not used to indicate any particularly grave type of forcible intervention. Indeed, even if it had been, there was no evidence of any grave attack against Lebanon. By June, this claim was elucidated, until the basis for what ultimately became an instance of avowed collective self-defence on the part of the United States was said by Lebanon to be the supply of arms and the training of irregulars in the UAR.[34] Neither of these activities would meet the ICJ's *Nicaragua* definition for armed attack. Five days later, Lebanon altered its claim to that of a lawful need to respond with force to 'aggression'.[35] Apparently, this was not merely a change in terminology, for Lebanon stressed that aggression (in its indirect form) gave rise to a right of self-defence, rather than something below the level of aggression, which it implied could only be lawfully responded to with force by the UN.[36]

In response to the intervention of the United States in Lebanon in July 1958, the Soviet Union referenced Article 51 and argued that the action could not constitute lawful self-defence because no armed attack had occurred.[37] Interestingly, the Soviet Union did not in general dispute the facts as presented by Lebanon (or by the United States), only whether these facts demonstrated the occurrence of an armed attack.[38] To confuse things still further, the UAR argued that Article 51 'demands *armed aggression* as a condition' for lawful self-defence (emphasis added).[39] Of the non-aligned states to speak on the issue, Sweden referred to the need for an 'armed attack', which it did not feel had occurred in this case.[40] Based upon this, China took the view that Sweden had advocated the need for 'direct aggression', which it disputed.[41] The United States, when *it* referred to the actions of the UAR, labelled this as 'aggression'.[42] However, there is no evidence that the United States used the phrase 'aggression' as a term of art in this context. All of which demonstrates that, in relation to the Lebanon situation of 1958, certain states took the view that some level of force beyond a mere breach of Article 2(4) was needed for lawful self-defence. Equally, this view was not shared by all states: some held that simply a use of force against the state was enough to trigger self-defence. Furthermore, the terminology employed in this regard was unhelpfully mixed.

[33] UN Doc S/4007.
[34] UN Doc S/PV.822, 4.
[35] UN Doc S/PV.824, 14.
[36] *Ibid.*
[37] UN Doc S/PV.827, 56.
[38] *Ibid.*
[39] UN Doc S/PV.828, 17. The UAR repeated this argument almost verbatim again at UN Doc S/PV.830, 3.
[40] UN Doc S/PV.830, 22–25.
[41] UN Doc S/PV.831, 53.
[42] See, eg, UN Doc S/PV.838, 96–97.

A further useful example is Israel's extraction of its nationals from Entebbe airport, Uganda, in 1976, which was largely condemned by third-party states.[43] It is notable that in some instances, this was on the basis that the taking of Israeli hostages on the part of Baader-Meinhof and the Popular Front for the Liberation of Palestine did not reach the level of gravity required to constitute an armed attack against Israel.[44] Similarly, other states saw the response of Israel as constituting a grave use of force and thus interpreted this in itself as an armed attack against Uganda.[45] Though, again, the terminology employed with regard to this was mixed, with some states using the phrase 'aggression' rather than 'armed attack', seemingly to mean the same thing.[46] Nonetheless, it would seem that with regard to the raid by Israeli forces, a number of states saw a need in law for an armed attack to have occurred and viewed the gravity of force as being relevant to the application of this criterion. Interestingly, though, whilst Israel itself was explicit in claiming self-defence, in no way did it claim to have been the victim of an armed attack.[47]

Varied approaches to the notion of armed attack can also be seen in the context of more abstract debates concerning the legal prohibition on the use of force. A good example of this is the protracted discussion over what ultimately became the Declaration on Friendly Relations,[48] adopted by the UN General Assembly in 1970. In both the Special Committee (set up to draft the Declaration)[49] and the Sixth Committee of the General Assembly, states touched upon the concept of armed attack, although again the implications of such references are difficult to assess, as certain states used the term 'aggression' when seemingly referring to the trigger necessary for self-defence (armed attack).[50] Even more confusingly, whilst some states were clear that they did not view the notions of 'armed attack' and 'use of force' as being synonymous and that an armed attack constituted a use of force of a specific gravity,[51] other states appeared to perceive an armed

[43] The vast majority of the Security Council condemned the action. See generally UN Docs S/PV.1939–43.

[44] See, eg, the views taken by Panama (UN Doc S/PV.1942, 4) and India (UN Doc S/PV.1942, 17).

[45] Eg, see the statements made by Pakistan (UN Doc S/PV.1941, 14) and the Soviet Union (UN Doc S/PV.1942, 21).

[46] See, eg, the position of Algeria (UN Doc S/12132) and, indeed, that of Uganda itself (UN Doc S/PV.1943, 13).

[47] UN Doc S/12123.

[48] Declaration on Principles of International Law Concerning Friendly Relations and Cooperation among States in Accordance with the Charter of the United Nations 1970, GA Res. 2625.

[49] Special Committee on Principles of International Law Concerning Friendly Relations and Cooperation among States.

[50] See, eg, the view expressed by Romania (UN Doc A/8018, 81).

[51] See, eg, the positions of Mexico and the United Arab Republic (UN Doc A/8018, at 107 and 117 respectively).

attack as constituting *any* use of military force.[52] An examination of these debates therefore suggests that states were divided over the question of armed attack (although admittedly this was not a particularly controversial question in this context).

This brief examination of pre-1986 state practice and supporting *opinio juris* indicates that it is difficult to conclude upon the customary international law status of the 'armed attack as a grave use of force' criterion as it existed when the *Nicaragua* merits decision was delivered by the ICJ. First, when states referred to a grave 'type' of use of force as being required to trigger self-defence, in many instances they employed the term 'aggression' and not the term 'armed attack' at all. States invoking self-defence often referred to the fact that they had been the victim of 'aggression'. This is similarly true of the states responding to such claims. Such a mixture of terminology only further confuses the state of the customary international law.[53] This terminology must also be treated with care because in some cases, states claim to have been the victim of 'aggression' or an 'armed attack' and yet seemingly ascribe no legal meaning to these terms as such. Equally, on occasion, states employ these terms simply to indicate that there has been a breach of Article 2(4).[54] It is important to note that 'aggression' is generally thought of as having a separate meaning in international law from 'intervention', 'use of force' or 'armed attack'.[55]

[52] Again, see the statement by Romania (UN Doc A/8018, 81) and also those of Pakistan and India (UN Doc A/C.6/25/SR.1179, at 13 and 36 respectively).

[53] A general point about the elastic terminology of international legal discourse is made by M Koskenniemi, *From Apology to Utopia: The Structure of International Legal Argument* (Cambridge, Cambridge University Press, 2005) esp 61.

[54] Indeed, scholars also may be seen as falling into this trap of terminological confusion on occasion. A notable example is a 2002 article by Ian Brownlie. Professor Brownlie is famously one of the most ardent advocates of the distinct normative content of the 'armed attack' criterion, holding that it represents something more than a use of force *simpliciter* (arguing that an 'armed attack' should be viewed as a use of force of distinct gravity, in a broadly similar manner to the ICJ). See Brownlie (n 9) esp 278–79. However, in the 2002 article, Brownlie states: 'There can be little doubt that "use of force" is commonly understood to imply a military attack, an "armed attack" . . . organised by a state.' See I Brownlie, '*International Law and the Use of Force by States* Revisited' (2002) 1 *Chinese Journal of International Law* 1, 8. In this passage, Brownlie appears to view the terms of 'use of force' and 'armed attack' as being synonymous. This presumably accidental lapse in terminological certainty highlights the difficulties inherent in clearly defining the concept of an armed attack.

[55] The legal concept of 'aggression' is particularly difficult to pin down. This is evidenced by the debate over the *crime* of aggression as enshrined (but not defined) in the Statute of the International Criminal Court, Art 5(2). See J Trahan, 'Defining Aggression: Why the Preparatory Commission for the International Criminal Court Has Faced Such a Conundrum' (2002) 24 *Loyola of Los Angeles International and Comparative Law Review* 448. It is evidenced as well by the forty-year period it took for the Definition of Aggression annexed to GA Res. 3314, Art 3(d) to be adopted by the General Assembly. The general academic view is that the concepts of 'armed attack' and 'aggression' are not synonymous. See Kenny (n 13) 1164; Alexandrov (n 14) 250; Combacau (n 13) 22; and NM Feder, 'Reading the UN Charter Connotatively: Towards a New Definition of Armed Attack' (1987) 19 *New York University Journal of International Law and Politics* 395, 408. However, for a contrary view, see Macdonald (n 11) 148.

Second, whatever terminology states employ, state invocation of a 'gravity' requirement is somewhat sporadic. Indeed, in contrast to the majority,[56] it should be noted that certain scholars have taken the view that there is no support in state practice for an armed attack criterion as amounting to anything other than a breach of Article 2(4). For example, Tarcisio Gazzini has stated, 'State practice is entirely inconsistent with the existence of a threshold of gravity or intensity below which the right of self-defence cannot be exercised.'[57] Similarly, Christopher Greenwood has claimed that the ICJ's distinction between armed attacks and other 'less grave' uses of force had 'no basis in state practice' and that 'there is nothing in the practice of states between 1945 and 1986 to suggest that any such line had hitherto been regarded as important.'[58] Most recently, in 2007 Constantine Antonopoulos argued, 'State practice does not make a distinction between armed attack and a use of force short of an armed attack.'[59]

The erratic nature and ambiguity of the state practice and *opinio juris* surrounding the criteria of armed attack and what it constitutes means that such claims are certainly understandable. However, it is argued here that there is enough practice to indicate that the ICJ did have a genuine basis in *Nicaragua* to hold that the concept of an armed attack has some relation to the *gravity* of the attack suffered and is therefore something more than a use of force *simpliciter*. Whilst the 'armed attack as a grave use of force' criterion is not referenced in the legal claims and responses of states anywhere near as regularly as necessity or proportionality, it is arguably a feature of contemporary customary international law: certainly practice in this regard cannot be discounted.

Given the non-uniform practice regarding armed attack, the ICJ was overly emphatic when it claimed in *Nicaragua* that there 'appears to be general agreement' as to the nature of the armed attack criterion.[60] Yet, equally, it is suggested that scholars arguing that there is *no* basis in practice for the ICJ's conception of self-defence are incorrect. Even Judge Schwebel, in his impassioned attack on the majority judgment in *Nicaragua*, acknowledged that whilst he disagreed with the Court's legal conclusions, he recognised 'that there is room for the Court's construction of the legal meaning of an armed attack'.[61]

[56] See above, n 9.

[57] Gazzini (n 21) 3–4, 133, 138 and quoted at 237.

[58] C Greenwood, 'The International Court of Justice and the Use of Force' in Lowe V and Fitzmaurice M (eds), *Fifty Years of the International Court of Justice: Essays in Honour of Sir Robert Jennings* (Cambridge, Cambridge University Press, 1996) 373, 380–81.

[59] C Antonopoulos, 'Force by Armed Groups as Armed Attack and the Broadening of Self-Defence' (2008) 55 *Netherlands International Law Review* 159, 166.

[60] *Nicaragua* merits (n 17) para 195.

[61] *Ibid*, dissenting opinion of Judge Schwebel, para 15. See also RA Falk, 'The World Court's Achievement' (1987) 81 *American Journal of International Law* 106, 111.

In identifying the armed attack criterion, then, the ICJ has in general terms performed its 'application of existing law' role more commendably than it may have initially appeared from our discussions in previous chapters. The problems inherent in the jurisprudence, seen this way, are of *emphasis* and *clarity*, not necessarily of *form*.

II. ARMED ATTACK AS A SELF-FULFILLING PROPHESY?

Having said this, the ICJ did not merely identify the 'armed attack as a grave use of force' criterion, which would arguably have been *jus dicere*, it raised the importance of this criterion to the level of a fundamental requirement. The Court defined armed attack in a way that simply had not been done before.[62]

Essentially, in *Nicaragua*, the Court made a concerted effort to clarify and develop the law governing self-defence.[63] It may be argued that in so doing, the Court reinforced the problems apparent in the existing law governing self-defence, which—as will be discussed in subsequent sections—was already highly confused due to the coexistence of 'armed attack as a grave use of force' with necessity and proportionality.[64] More than this, though, it can be argued that it altered the existing law by elevating the importance of the 'armed attack as a grave use of force' criterion.[65]

It is possible that this change has moved from the pages of the judgments of the ICJ into the practice of states. One may argue, although admittedly not with any certainty, that the Court's pronouncements in *Nicaragua* and subsequent cases have impacted directly upon customary international law.[66] Certainly, some scholars have taken this position. For example, as has been pointed out with regard to the advisory opinion in *Legal Consequences of the Construction of a Wall in the Occupied Palestinian*

[62] G Palmisano, 'Determining the Law on the Use of Force: the ICJ and Customary Rules on the Use of Force' in E Cannizzaro and P Palchetti (eds), *Customary International Law on the Use of Force: A Methodological Approach* (Leiden, Martinus Nijhoff, 2005) 197, 210–11.

[63] As Kritsiotis has put it, to 'assist us' in understanding the complex legal regime governing self-defence, 'the Court *attempted to articulate* an objective meaning to the term "armed attack"' (emphasis added). D Kritsiotis, 'When States Use Armed Force' in C Reus-Smit (ed), *The Politics of International Law* (Cambridge, Cambridge University Press, 2004) 45, 64.

[64] See below, sections III–VII.

[65] It has been argued that the *Nicaragua* case was an active attempt by the Court to develop international law and in so doing to increase the prestige and political relevance of the ICJ. RA Friedlander, 'Confusing Victims and Victimizers: *Nicaragua* and the Reinterpretation of International Law' (1985–86) 14 *Denver Journal of International Law and Policy* 87, 95. This is perhaps going too far. A better position is: 'The Court's actions [in *Nicaragua*] are characterised by an unusual display of judicial activism. . . That activism, applauded by some and bitterly criticised by others, has raised acute controversy.' TD Gill, *Rosenne's The World Court: What It is and How It Works*, 6th edn (Leiden, Martinus Nijhoff, 2003) 93.

[66] The issue of the impact the pronouncements of the ICJ upon the development of customary international law will be examined in more general terms in ch 5, section II.

Territory (hereafter *Israeli Wall*),[67] the Court's treatment of the issue of self-defence as it appears in that case has 'a two-fold nature.'[68] In one respect the Court's conclusions regarding self-defence impacted upon the question of whether the apparent wrongfulness of Israel's action may have been precluded (affecting the overall legal conclusion of the Court in response to the question asked of it by the General Assembly).

To put this in another way, the key consequence of the Court's conclusions regarding self-defence in *Israeli Wall* was the finding that the separation barrier could not be viewed as a manifestation of self-defence in international law. Additionally, however, in another 'much more significant' respect, the references to self-defence in the *Israeli Wall* opinion inevitably will have an impact upon 'the legal framework governing the conduct of Israel': the entire legal regime of self-defence.[69] In other words, the Court's pronouncements with regard to self-defence in that opinion have resonance far beyond the context of the opinion itself. Similarly, it was said in relation to the *Case Concerning Oil Platforms* (hereafter *Oil Platforms*)[70] that the ICJ judgments' 'impact and influence in state practice and judicial and arbitral decision are well-known, so any statement made by the Court could become a landmark in the current debate on self-defence'.[71]

If this is accepted, one could reasonably argue that the case most likely to have exerted this kind of influence upon state practice would be *Nicaragua*, both because of the fact that it was the first ICJ judgment to deal substantively with self-defence and because it has been the most extensive case of this character to date. Interestingly, some scholars around the time of the *Nicaragua* case asserted that the ICJ no longer had any real influence upon international law, and the relevance of a decision of the Court, if any, was only to the parties before it.[72] However, in contrast, the majority of scholars have taken a totally opposite view.[73] Louis Henkin, for example, described the *Nicaragua* case as being the '[a]uthoritative construction of

[67] *Legal Consequences of the Construction of a Wall in the Occupied Palestinian Territory* advisory opinion (2004) ICJ Reports 135.

[68] I Scobbie, 'Smoke, Mirrors and Killer Whales: the International Court of Justice's Opinion on the Israeli Barrier Wall' (2004) 5 *German Law Journal* 1107, 1125.

[69] *Ibid.* A very similar point is made by R Wedgwood, 'The ICJ Advisory Opinion on the Israeli Security Fence and the Limits of Self-Defence' (2005) 99 *American Journal of International Law* 52, 57.

[70] *Case Concerning Oil Platforms* (*Islamic Republic of Iran v United States of America*) merits (2003) ICJ Reports 161.

[71] N Ochoa-Ruiz and E Salamanca-Aguado, 'Exploring the Limits of International Law Relating to the Use of Force in Self-Defence' (2005) 16 *European Journal of International Law* 499, 501. See also M Lachs, 'Some Reflections on the Contribution of the International Court of Justice to the Development of International Law' (1983) 10 *Syracuse Journal of International Law and Commerce* 239.

[72] Friedlander (n 65) 95.

[73] See above, n 9.

the law [governing self-defence]'.[74] Whilst the aspects of the decision that we have identified in previous chapters mean this statement is contested by the current author, from at least one perspective Henkin is correct. It would seem that scholars, at least, have in many instances viewed *Nicaragua* as the *benchmark* for understanding the law of self-defence.[75]

It also may be contended that states have taken a similar view. As such, it is certainly arguable that the *Nicaragua* case itself has had a significant impact upon the development of customary international law in this area.[76] However, such a position must be speculative. The counterfactual claim that had the *Nicaragua* decision not been delivered, the 'armed attack as a grave use of force' criterion would be far more marginalised in current customary international law (or even non-existent) cannot be made with any certainty: it is impossible to ascertain what factors have influenced state conduct and therefore why general *opinio juris* has altered. Nonetheless, there is certainly an amount of what may be seen as 'circumstantial evidence' supporting a claim regarding the influential nature of the ICJ upon state practice with regard to self-defence, in terms of changes to the nature of the legal claims of states following the *Nicaragua* decision.

To illustrate this, it is useful to again examine some examples from state practice. It is argued here that an increase in the application of the 'armed attack as a grave use of force' criterion can be seen in post-*Nicaragua* practice. However, it must be made clear that identifying this trend is far from an exact science. There remains a degree of contrary practice, and as noted, even if such a trend can be identified, it is impossible to say for sure whether this was caused by the decisions of the Court. Nonetheless, it is worth referring to instances of post-1986 practice.

One useful example of the application of armed attack post-*Nicaragua* is the intervention by the United States in Panama in December 1989, through what was termed Operation Just Cause. One of the 'just causes' claimed by the United States was self-defence, in the guise of the protection of its nationals abroad.[77] The incidents cited by the United States as giving rise to self-defence certainly did not fit within the ICJ's definition of an armed attack.[78] Nonetheless, the United States framed its claim in this way:

[74] Henkin (n 9) 47. See also R Müllerson, 'Self-Defence in the Contemporary World' in LF Damrosch and DJ Scheffer (eds), *Law and Force in the New International Order* (Boulder, Westview Press, 1991) 13, 16; Palmisano (n 62) 208–11; and Gray (n 9) 192.

[75] Palmisano (n 62).

[76] This view is put forward by Gowlland-Debbas, who also takes this position with regard to the impact of *Corfu Channel* on the law on the use of force. V Gowlland-Debbas, 'Judicial Insights into Fundamental Values and Interests of the International Community' in AS Muller, D Raic and JM Thuranszky (eds), *The International Court of Justice: Its Future Role After Fifty Years* (The Hague, Martinus Nijhoff, 1997) 327, 336.

[77] UN Doc S/PV.2899, 31–37; and letter dated 21 December 1989 from President Bush to Congress, extract in R Wedgwood, 'The Use of Armed Force in International Affairs: Self-Defence and the Panama Invasion' (1991) 29 *Columbia Journal of Transnational Law* 609, 609.

[78] Wedgwood (*ibid*) 619–21.

> In accordance with Article 51 of the United Nations Charter, United States forces have exercised their inherent right of self-defence under international law by taking action in Panama in response to armed attacks by forces under the direction of Manuel Noriega. The action was designed to protect American lives.[79]

The reaction of other states was in general negative to the intervention.[80] This was, for the most part, due to issues of proportionality.[81] However, it is worth noting that some states argued the action of the United States was unlawful because no armed attack had occurred.[82] Significantly, the threat to the nationals of the United States in Panama was not seen as being grave enough to constitute an armed attack.

In justifying its missile attacks against Afghanistan and Sudan in 1998, the United States pointedly claimed that these were in response to armed attacks as prescribed by Article 51. It appeared to view 'armed attacks' as *significant* attacks upon it, suggesting the application of an 'armed attack as a grave use of force' criterion. Interestingly, it employed convoluted argumentation to support this claim rather than turning to a more controversial claim of preventative self-defence.[83]

Another useful example is the US formal legal position with regard to Operation Enduring Freedom in Afghanistan in 2001, as was presented to the Security Council in a letter dated 7 October 2001.[84] The primary focus of this document was upon the terrorist attack of 11 September 2001.[85] The United States explicitly identified the atrocities of 11 September as 'armed attacks' and, importantly, stressed the *scale* or *gravity* of those attacks.[86] Conversely, in relation to this particular self-defence claim, references to the legal requirements of necessity and proportionality by the United States were much more limited than the focus upon 11 September as an 'armed attack'.[87] We have already noted that 11 September was seen by many as a clear example of an armed attack, despite it not easily fitting into the 'classic' ICJ model for such an attack.[88]

In regard to its intervention in Lebanon in 2006, Israel claimed that it was acting in self-defence and, importantly, argued that this action was in

[79] UN Doc S/PV.2899, 31.

[80] See, inter alia, the statements of Nicaragua (UN Doc S/PV.2899, 3–17) and Peru (UN Doc S/PV.2900, 34–37).

[81] See, eg, the statement of Finland in the Security Council (UN Doc S/PV.2900, 14–15).

[82] See the claims of the Soviet Union (UN Doc S/PV.2899, 17–21), Cuba (UN Doc S/PV.2900, 28) and Libya (UN Doc S/PV.2900, 41).

[83] J Lobel, 'The Use of Force to Respond to Terrorist Attacks: The Bombing of Sudan and Afghanistan' (1999) 24 *Yale Journal of International Law* 537, esp 543–47.

[84] UN Doc S/2001/946.

[85] *Ibid*, although it will be recalled that this argument was combined with the threat of future attacks. See ch 2, n 236.

[86] UN Doc S/2001/946.

[87] Indeed, these criteria were not explicitly referred to in the document (although they are implicitly apparent in phrases such as 'The United States is committed to minimising civilian casualties'). *Ibid*.

[88] See ch 1, n 82.

response to an 'armed attack . . . launched against a Member of the United Nations'.[89] As we saw in the previous chapter, most states rejected Israel's claim of self-defence on the basis that its intervention into Lebanon could not be viewed as being proportional.[90] However, it is worth noting that a number of states framed the discussion as to the lawfulness of the intervention in the context of whether Israel had suffered an armed attack (singly or collectively) through the actions of Hezbollah. The issue for these states was whether the actions of Hezbollah could be seen as reaching a sufficient level of gravity.[91] Of course, Israel itself did not explicitly invest the phrase 'armed attack' with any connotation of gravity, but this is not to say that it did not view the criterion in that manner. In any event, although most states saw the key issue as being the disproportional nature of the response, it is clear that at least some states instead focussed on 'armed attack' in respect of the 2006 conflict.

Most recently, when making its controversial claim of self-defence with regard to its 2008 intervention in Georgia, Russia was careful to employ the term 'armed attack' when reporting to the Security Council.[92] Moreover, it explicitly referred to the 'scale of the attack'.[93] This indicates that the Russian Federation took the view not only that 'armed attack' must form a point of reference for the right of self-defence but also that the 'armed attack as a grave use of force' criterion should be employed.

The application of the 'armed attack as a grave use of force' criterion appears to have increased post-*Nicaragua*: states employ this criterion more regularly and with more consistent terminology than was the case prior to 1986. Having said this, such practice still remains somewhat sporadic; there is less consistency here than with regard to the application of necessity and proportionality. For example, in the naval clash of June 2002 between North and South Korea, it will be recalled that both states claimed to be acting in self-defence.[94] However, there was no suggestion that the comparatively small-scale nature of the incident had any effect on the parties' ability to so argue. Neither state referred to an armed attack or anything akin to this.[95] The question of lawfulness for other states appeared

[89] UN Doc A/60/937-S/2006/515.

[90] See ch 2, n 155.

[91] Thus the statements of Qatar (UN Doc S/PV.5489, 11) and Egypt (UN Doc S/PV.5493, 22)—both of which felt that such a gravity threshold had not been reached—can be contrasted with the position of Norway (UN Doc S/PV.5493, 23), which felt that the actions of Hezbollah did constitute an armed attack.

[92] UN Doc S/2008/545.

[93] *Ibid.*

[94] See ch 2, n 119.

[95] See 'The Naval Clash on the Yellow Sea on 29 June between South and North Korea: The Situation and ROK's Position' 1 July 2002, press release of the Ministry of National Defence of the Republic of Korea, www.globalsecurity.org/wmd/library/news/rok/2002/0020704-naval.htm for South Korea's official legal position; and *New York Times*, 30 June 2002, 12 for the claim of North Korea, being that 'provocation' was enough to trigger the right of self-defence.

to turn on a) who attacked first and b) issues of necessity and proportionality—and thus, by implication, not 'armed attack'.[96]

Moreover, in many instances of post-*Nicaragua* practice, states have refrained from setting out any position at all as to the nature of an armed attack. This may be because they view the meaning of the term as being self-evident, or it may be that states wish to retain an inherent flexibility in the concept. Thus, during the debates over what ultimately became the Declaration on the Principle of the Prohibition of the Threat or Use of Force, which was adopted by the General Assembly in 1987,[97] a number of states made it clear that self-defence could only be exercised in response to the occurrence of an armed attack.[98] However, none of these states in any way articulated what they perceived an armed attack to actually constitute, despite the obvious relevance of this question to the draft Declaration.

Although the application of an armed attack requirement remains somewhat sporadic, it is nonetheless argued here that practice post-1986 is at least suggestive of a degree of influence of the *Nicaragua* decision on the manner that states present their self-defence claims outside of the forum of the ICJ. Interestingly, this impression is also seemingly supported by an examination of the development of legal argumentation employed before the ICJ itself.

If one starts by examining the 1949 case of *Corfu Channel* (*United Kingdom v Albania*) (hereafter *Corfu Channel*),[99] a legal justification advanced by the United Kingdom for its intervention into Albanian waters of November 1946 was that it was acting in lawful 'self-help'.[100] For the United Kingdom, the lawful exercise of this right required it to comply with the criteria of necessity[101] and of proportionality.[102] However, despite the incident occurring after the inception of the UN Charter (and therefore Article 51), no reference was made by the United Kingdom to an 'armed attack' or indeed to a use of force of any particular gravity.[103]

The *Nicaragua* case shows a progression in terms of this type of argument. During the course of its oral arguments, Nicaragua claimed that it had been the victim of 'armed attacks' for which the United States was responsible and referred specifically to the 'scope and scale of the armed

[96] BBC news online, 'Koreas Trade Blame for Naval Clash', 30 June 2002.

[97] Declaration on the Enhancement of the Effectiveness of the Principle of Refraining from the Threat or Use of Force in International Relations 1987, GA Res. 42/22.

[98] See, eg, the views of Mexico (UN Doc A/C.6/42/SR.17, 4), Chile (UN Doc A/C.6/42/SR.18, 7) and Iran (UN Doc A/C.6/42/SR.21, 16).

[99] *Corfu Channel* (*United Kingdom v Albania*) merits (1949) ICJ Reports 4.

[100] *Corfu Channel* reply of the United Kingdom (1948) ICJ Pleadings vol II 241, 282–86.

[101] The United Kingdom stated that 'this right of self-help . . . can only be exercised when there is an immediate necessity.' *Ibid*, 284.

[102] The United Kingdom argued that lawful self-help required 'a minimum interference with the sovereignty of the State concerned.' *Ibid*.

[103] See *ibid*.

intervention'.[104] Yet, in its application, Nicaragua in general referred to 'uses of force'. When it did claim 'armed attacks against Nicaragua by air, land and sea' there is no evidence to suggest it used the phrase as a term of art.[105] For its part, the United States claimed—prior to removing itself from proceedings—that 'Nicaragua has engaged in armed attacks against its neighbours'.[106] However, the United States did not stress what an 'armed attack' entailed as a legal concept, and as with Nicaragua's use of the term, this may just have been employed to mean a breach of Article 2(4). Indeed, elsewhere, whilst invoking Article 51 and referencing the inherent right of self-defence, the United States avoided reference to 'armed attack' at all.[107]

Notably, by the time of *Armed Activities on the Territory of the Congo* (*Democratic Republic of the Congo v Uganda*) (hereafter *DRC v Uganda*),[108] a further shift in argumentation may be detected. In relation to that dispute, both parties argued self-defence[109] and, in doing so, were extremely clear in claiming to have been the victim of an armed attack. Far more importantly, both parties clearly set out what they saw an armed attack as pertaining to. In both instances, this essentially constituted a 'higher-level' or 'grave' use of force.[110]

Of course, how far this change in argumentation with regard to the armed attack criterion relates to the pronouncements of the ICJ in the *Nicaragua* case is impossible to know. Moreover, the post-*Nicaragua* practice regarding the armed attack criterion is still far from being universal and, while increased, still cannot be seen as attaining the consistency of legal claims involving necessity and proportionality. As such, reference to an armed attack (or lack of) in relation to a self-defence claim may merely amount to the invocation of what today is perceived by states to be the correct linguistic formula. It is as difficult today to assess the *content* of the claim that an armed attack has occurred as it was prior to *Nicaragua*.

[104] *Nicaragua* oral arguments on provisional measures submitted by Nicaragua (1984) ICJ Pleadings, vol I, 50.

[105] *Ibid.*

[106] *Nicaragua* counter-memorial of the United States (1984) ICJ Pleadings, Part II, 57.

[107] *Ibid*, Part IV, 164–65.

[108] *Armed Activities on the Territory of the Congo* (*Democratic Republic of the Congo v Uganda*) merits (2005) www.icj-cij.org/docket/files/116/10455.pdf.

[109] See Introduction, section II-C.

[110] For the DRC's claim see *DRC v Uganda* CR 2005/11, www.icj-cij.org/docket/files/116/4321.pdf, 24–30; and particularly in relation to gravity, *DRC v Uganda* CR 2005/2, www.icj-cij.org/docket/files/116/4275.pdf, 34. For Uganda's position, see *DRC v Uganda* rejoinder submitted by Uganda (2002) www.icj-cij.org/docket/files/116/8314.pdf, paras 268–76. It is interesting that Uganda saw the definition of an armed attack as more flexible than the Court articulated in *Nicaragua*—a point it made explicitly—although Uganda still viewed an armed attack as being something more than a use of force *simpliciter*.

For whatever reason, states have referred to the criterion of an armed attack more often since 1986.[111] As such, it is possible to argue from the practice of states—both inside and outside of the courtroom—that the 'armed attack as a grave use of force' criterion has become a more crucial aspect of the law of self-defence than it was prior to that decision. Under such an interpretation of the state practice, the Court's detailed examination of armed attack constitutes, in some measure, a self-fulfilling prophecy. One may take the view that the decision influenced state practice in a way that has strengthened the role of an armed attack criterion in the determination of the lawfulness of self-defence actions.[112] It is possible, then, that the practice of states in this regard may, post-*Nicaragua*, be somewhat illusory: states may refer to an armed attack only because this conforms to the *Nicaragua* judgment (the 'authoritative standard'), not necessarily because it conforms to previous customary international law or even the UN Charter.

The 'armed attack as a grave use of force' criterion existed both in Article 51 and indeed in state practice, prior to the *Nicaragua* decision. Therefore it is incorrect to claim that the ICJ 'introduced' this concept into international law. Instead, it developed and compounded it. However, in trying to reconcile the admittedly confused *lex lata*, the ICJ opted to focus upon the wrong criterion. This reasoning reinforced the armed attack requirement. In subsequent sections it will be argued that this criterion and its relationship with the key customary international law criteria are at the root of many of the problems with the contemporary law governing self-defence.

[111] As Gray has put it, 'especially since the *Nicaragua* case, states have taken care to invoke Article 51 to justify their uses of force.' See Gray (n 9) 118.

[112] The possible influence of *Nicaragua* upon the law of self-defence may also arguably be seen with regard to the requirement that states report self-defence actions to the Security Council. It will be recalled that Article 51 of the UN Charter provides that 'measures taken by members in the exercise of this right of self-defence shall be immediately reported to the Security Council.' Since *Nicaragua*, practice has undoubtedly increased significantly in the context of states reporting their self-defence actions. A study by Bailey and Daws indicates both that the level of reporting has increased since *Nicaragua*, though the study also indicates that this practice is still not universal. See SD Bailey and S Daws, *The Procedure of the UN Security Council*, 3rd edn (Oxford, Clarendon Press, 1998) 103–5. See also C Gray, 'The Eritrea / Ethiopia Claims Commission Oversteps its Boundaries: A Partial Award?' (2006) 17 *European Journal of International Law* 699, 719. In fact, in the post-*Nicaragua* period, many states have adopted a policy of repeated reporting, meaning that every incident of a conflict is reported to the Security Council. The best example of this phenomenon is the repeated reporting of the United States, through formal letters submitted to the President of the Security Council with regard to incidents occurring in the Persian Gulf during the 1980–88 Iran–Iraq conflict. See UN Docs S/19149, S/19194, S/19219, S/19791 and S/19989. On this and other examples, see Gray (n 9) 121–24. At least prima facie, then, *Nicaragua* has had an effect on the practice with regard to reporting. However, once again, this cannot be said with certainty, given that a variety of other factors may have influenced this change in practice. For example, it is possible that the end of the Cold War signalled an increase in reporting due to a renewed confidence in the Security Council.

III. THE MERGED CONCEPTIONS OF SELF-DEFENCE

Throughout the previous two chapters, a somewhat artificial distinction has been drawn between two 'conceptions' of the law of self-defence: one based upon the 'armed attack as a grave use of force' criterion and one based upon necessity and proportionality. It has been implicit in the analysis in chapters one and two that the former conception stems from conventional international law, in that the notion of armed attack is present in Article 51 (with that term being defined as 'the most grave form of the use of force' by the ICJ, with some support in state practice), whilst the latter derives purely from customary international law. Does the law governing self-defence therefore stem from two distinct 'conceptions', with their roots in two different formal sources of international law?

In the *Nicaragua* case, the question of where the rules of self-defence derive from took on a particular significance given the multilateral treaty reservation of the United States, which the Court was by its own assertion bound to apply in the case. This meant that the Court was unable to apply the UN Charter or any other multilateral conventional international law relevant to the dispute.[113] The question, then, was whether the international law on self-defence existed in custom, convention or both. The ICJ took the view:

> There can be no doubt that the issues of the use of force and collective self-defence raised in the present proceedings are issues which are regulated both by customary international law and by treaties, in particular by the United Nations Charter.[114]

In itself, the fact that the law governing self-defence is sourced from both treaty and custom is largely uncontroversial. However, a difficulty arises when an attempt is made to ascertain the relationship between the two formal sources of self-defence. Is the substantive content of self-defence the same irrespective of its source? If so, the distinction over the source of the law is largely an issue of semantic categorisation and would only become relevant when questions of *applicability* arise, as in *Nicaragua*. In contrast, if the law stemming from treaty law is different from that which can be found in custom, then this creates questions as to the content of the two 'conceptions' of self-defence and how they relate.

The ICJ, for its part, viewed the rules governing self-defence as having a different content in conventional international law and customary international law, at least in part.[115] Thus the Court held that 'on a number of

[113] See Introduction, section II.

[114] *Nicaragua* merits (n 17) para 34.

[115] Not all scholars have interpreted the Court's judgment in *Nicaragua* in this way. Eg, MacDonald incorrectly takes the view that the Court treated the content of the rules of the UN Charter on the use of force as being 'interchangeable' with customary international law,

points, the areas governed by the two sources of law do not exactly overlap, and the substantive rules in which they are framed are not identical in content.'[116] It went on to say that even when the substance of the law in treaty and custom does overlap, this does not mean that they are conceptually the same; as such, rules contained in customary international law that had the same content as the UN Charter could still be applied to the dispute regardless of the US reservation.[117]

It would seem, then, that the Court has perceived two distinct 'conceptions' of the law on self-defence—derived from different sources—that in some instances coincide and at others diverge. This would seem to indicate two separate areas of the law: 'self-defence A' and 'self-defence B'. However, this analysis of what the Court has held is overly simplistic. Whilst these differently sourced 'conceptions' of self-defence are distinct, the way the Court interpreted the customary international law in *Nicaragua*—and indeed in the other relevant cases—suggests that it did not view the two sources of self-defence as being wholly separate. Rather, the Court indicated that they are conjoined or merged, meaning that one cannot function without the other.[118]

This is further supported by the decision in *Legality of the Threat or Use of Nuclear Weapons* (hereafter *Nuclear Weapons*), in which the Court stated that some of the constraints upon the resort to self-defence 'are inherent in the very concept of self-defence. Other requirements are specified in Article 51.'[119] This suggests that both conventional and customary international law are required to understand the right. An analysis of the substantive picture the Court paints of the law on self-defence appears to indicate that there is, at least in the view of the ICJ, a fundamental relationship between customary rules and conventional ones.

The Court's treatment of the relationship between the customary rules on self-defence and Article 51 has been heavily criticised. For example, it has been argued that the conclusions of the ICJ are incorrect because the provisions of the UN Charter in fact 'subsumed' the pre-existing customary international law rules.[120] This position was in fact adopted by the United States itself in its claims before the Court at the jurisdictional phase of the *Nicaragua* decision. The United States held that 'the provisions of the United Nations Charter relevant here subsume and supervene related

although he later concedes that the Court was not explicit in this regard. Macdonald (n 11) 136 and 147 respectively. In fact, the ICJ was explicit that the two 'sources' of law were possessed of differing content, at least to some extent.

[116] *Nicaragua* merits (n 17) para 175.

[117] *Ibid.*

[118] *Ibid*, para 176.

[119] *Legality of the Threat or Use of Nuclear Weapons* advisory opinion (1996) ICJ Reports 226, para 40.

[120] See WB Briggs, 'The International Court of Justice Lives Up to Its Name' (1987) 81 *American Journal of International Law* 78, 82–83.

principles of customary and general international law.'[121] The argument made here is that the UN Charter—particularly given its quasi-constitutional character—had the effect of superseding any previous customary law, and as such, any subsequent development of the law governing self-defence must be done interpretively within the Charter framework (albeit including the practice of states as one method of interpretation). In a similar vein, it has been claimed that if custom can develop separately from treaty law, then any constraints imposed by the treaty can be eroded all too easily.[122] This would allow for the circumvention of the restrictions inherent in the UN Charter.

However, there are a number of difficulties with such arguments. First, the UN Charter is formally a treaty like any other. As such, however 'constitutional' the Charter may be, it can influence the development of customary international law—that is, if its content is adopted into state practice and is supported by requisite *opinio juris*.[123] The rules contained in Articles 2(4) and 51 are certainly capable of forming part of customary international law, with the proviso that the usual requirements for identifying custom are met. It matters not that these rules may have their origins in treaty law. Similarly, customary international law is dynamic, and it is quite possible that rules that had their roots in a treaty can subsequently develop in state practice separate from the originating treaty,[124] even a treaty of such significance as the UN Charter. Article 2(4) did not 'freeze' the development of customary international law in 1945.[125]

Of course, as Judge Jennings indicated in his dissenting opinion to *Nicaragua*, because virtually all states are party to the UN Charter, subsequent practice with regard to Article 2(4) and 51 may simply be seen as a result of states fulfilling their obligations under the Charter.[126] It has already been argued that the requirement of an armed attack is not merely present in Article 51 but also forms an aspect of state practice. However, importantly, it is the view of the present author that the 'armed attack as a grave use of force' interpretation of the term 'armed attack' has some basis

[121] *Nicaragua* counter-memorial of the United States (n 106) Part III, 94–96, quoted at 94.

[122] GA Christenson, 'The World Court and *Jus Cogens*' (1987) 81 *American Journal of International Law* 93, 99.

[123] W Czapliński, 'Sources of International Law in the *Nicaragua* Case' (1989) 38 *International and Comparative Law Quarterly* 151, 157–58; and A Boyle and C Chinkin, *The Making of International Law* (Oxford, Oxford University Press, 2007) 234–38.

[124] A D'Amato, 'Trashing Customary International Law' (1987) 81 *American Journal of International Law* 101, 104; and M Byers, *Custom, Power and the Power of Rules: International Relations and Customary International Law* (Cambridge, Cambridge University Press, 1999) 171–72.

[125] D'Amato, *ibid*.

[126] *Nicaragua* merits (n 17) dissenting opinion of Judge Jennings, para 532. This point was also made by the United States in its pleadings: *Nicaragua* counter-memorial of the United States (n 106) Part III, 96. See also M Akehurst, 'Custom as a Source of International Law' (1974–75) 47 *British Yearbook of International Law* 1, 43–44.

in customary international law, given the state practice and *opinio juris* supporting this, particularly since the adoption of the Charter. This interpretation of 'armed attack' cannot be derived from Article 51 itself, and as such, the state practice on this question represents the interpretation of a treaty provision *through the development of customary international law*. Even if one holds that the 'armed attack as a grave use of force' criterion is used more sporadically than those of necessity and proportionality, and that the Court itself had a major role in strengthening its application by states, it is inaccurate to suggest that the criterion exists only in treaty law (or in the pronouncements of the Court). It also has a customary basis.

Second, if the provisions of a treaty do not *explicitly* supersede, subsume or codify existing customary international law, then the content of the pre-existing customary law remains untouched by the treaty, albeit only to the extent that such provisions are compatible with those of the treaty in question.[127] When we look at Article 51, then, not only does that provision not explicitly subsume the prior customary international law rules on self-defence, it clearly affirms the 'inherent' nature of the right. This may not be conclusive as to the continuing existence of the customary regime, but the inclusion of the term 'inherent' in Article 51 is certainly indicative of this.

Equally, it is not the case that treaty obligations will be eroded by an alternative customary law development. The process of customary international law development of a treaty provision can produce (or maintain) rules in addition to those set out in the treaty and can act as an interpretive matrix for the treaty provisions themselves. Indeed, it could even create customary norms, derived from treaty provisions, which possess a modified content from such conventional provisions.[128] However, the treaty would remain as much in force as before. It is simply that there would exist a parallel, and potentially somewhat different, customary rule on the same subject matter.[129] As Michael Byers has pointed out, in instances of conflict, the question would then be which provision can be seen as possessing more legitimacy, based upon state acceptance.[130] Given that the UN Charter has been almost universally ratified,[131] it would be difficult to see an alternate customary regime concerning the use of force as *overriding*

[127] On the basis of the general rule that the most recent legal provision supersedes contrary preceding ones—the rule of *lex posterior*—but does not remove preceding compatible provisions unless it does so explicitly. See Czapliński (n 123) 164–65; and Boyle and Chinkin (n 123) 248–52 (although their discussion refers specifically to the relationship between two treaties and not to treaty and custom).

[128] Czapliński (n 123) 163.

[129] Byers (n 124) 172–80.

[130] *Ibid*, 178–79.

[131] As well as the fact that even non-parties are expected to observe the principles of the UN under Article 2(6) of the Charter, 'so far as may be necessary for the maintenance of international peace and security' (a category that the exercise of self-defence is likely to fall into).

the Charter provisions, though it may help to interpret them or augment them with provisions not provided for in the document (such as the requirements of necessity and proportionality).

Perhaps most crucially, as we have already seen, it is uncontroversial that the criteria of necessity and proportionality still apply today, irrespective of the fact that they are nowhere to be found in the Charter.[132] Indeed, it has been argued throughout this book that they represent the most fundamental criteria for any legal assessment of self-defence. Necessity and proportionality predate the concept of armed attack, originating as they do in the *Caroline* incident of 1837.[133] If Article 51 subsumed the pre-existing customary international law, then the criteria of necessity and proportionality would no longer apply—something that has clearly not occurred.

Given all of this, the ICJ must be seen as being correct in holding that the law governing self-defence is capable of existing—in potentially different forms—in both custom and convention. However, this is not to say that the Court's treatment of customary international law and its relationship with treaty law, particularly in *Nicaragua*, is unproblematic. The ICJ has been correctly criticised for the superficial manner in which it ascertained the content of the customary international law relating to self-defence. When attempting to determine the scope of the relevant customary international law, the Court did not make any reference to the manner in which states actually behave.[134] It may be said that the Court's reliance instead on declarations adopted by the General Assembly and upon indicative treaties (that were not themselves applicable in the case) 'suggests the strained nature of its analysis'.[135]

The Court can also be criticised for in fact applying only the customary rules governing self-defence to the *Nicaragua* dispute. This is because, in the case of self-defence, conventional law cannot be adequately applied to a dispute without the concurrent application of customary international law (necessity and proportionality), and vice versa. Whilst it is possible to identify two separate sources of law, it is difficult to apply an armed attack criterion without reference to the criteria of necessity and proportionality. Any distinction between two different 'conceptions' of self-defence is therefore highly artificial. Indeed, this is a point that the Court itself

[132] Interestingly, self-defence can be seen as one of the few areas of international law in which a customary rule is more detailed than the corresponding treaty provisions on the question. Customary international law encompasses, to an extent, the concept of an armed attack, as well as the criteria of necessity and proportionality, with the latter being absent from Article 51. See Czapliński (n 123) 161.

[133] See ch 2.

[134] FL Kirgis, 'Custom on a Sliding Scale' (1987) 81 *American Journal of International Law* 146, 147.

[135] HCM Charlesworth, 'Customary International Law and the *Nicaragua* Case' (1984–87) 11 *Australian Yearbook of International Law* 1, 26. See also Czapliński (n 123) 160–61.

made.[136] The President of the Court set the position out well in his separate opinion to *Nicaragua*:

> In any search to determine whether these concepts belong to customary or conventional international law it would appear to be a fallacy to try to split any concept to ascertain what part or percentage of it belongs to customary law and what fraction belongs to conventional law.[137]

Therefore it may be argued that whilst the Court was correct that customary international law can develop independently of treaty law on the same matters of substance, in the case of self-defence, there is a clear overlap between the two 'conceptions', which makes any true distinction difficult. Thus applying one conception but not the other is highly undesirable.[138] Of course, in *Nicaragua*, given the multilateral treaty reservation of the United States, the Court had no choice but to do so, other than refusing to pronounce upon the merits at all.

None of the above invalidates the conceptual conclusion of the Court that self-defence derives from two distinct—and, in places, *different*—sources of international law. Equally, the Court was correct in taking the view that these sources are merged. In the UN era the 'armed attack as a grave use of force' criterion coexists with the criteria that preceded it: necessity and proportionality. In reality, these two conceptions regulate, *together*, claims of self-defence. As such, self-defence today belongs 'simultaneously to the planes of UN and customary law'.[139]

Crucially, it is argued here that this 'merging' of necessity and proportionality with an 'armed attack as a grave use of force' criterion (whether this stems from treaty law, customary international law or both) is a major reason for the problems faced by the Court—or by anyone—when dealing with the law of self-defence. The increase in state practice in the latter half of the twentieth century in employing the 'armed attack as a grave use of force' criterion as an aspect of the legal regulation of force employed in self-defence did not eradicate the pre-existing customary international law criteria of necessity and proportionality. Together, the two merged conceptions of self-defence create a complex regime that comprises conceptions that possess both overlapping and different functions.

[136] *Nicaragua* merits (n 17) para 176. The inconsistency between this conclusion of the Court and the manner in which it in fact applied the law in *Nicargua* was noted by Judge Ago: *Nicaragua* merits (n 17) separate opinion of Judge Ago, para 6.

[137] *Nicaragua* merits (n 17) separate opinion of President Nagendra Singh, para 152.

[138] Christenson (n 122) 96.

[139] E Cannizzaro and P Palchetti, 'Introduction' in E Cannizzaro and P Palchetti (eds), *Customary International Law on the Use of Force: A Methodological Approach* (Leiden, Martinus Nijhoff, 2005) 4.

IV. THE OVERLAPPING FUNCTIONS OF THE MERGED CONCEPTIONS

This merging of 'armed attack' with '*Caroline*' means that the *lex lata* of self-defence is actually an amalgam of two different systems, and as such, the criterion of armed attack, coupled with necessity and proportionality, does not constitute a seamless and coherent whole on the law of self-defence. This is because the *Caroline* criteria have overlapping functions with the 'armed attack as a grave use of force' criterion, particularly in the case of necessity. In one sense, '*Caroline*' and 'armed attack as a grave use of force' are different methods ('taken' from different sources of international law) for achieving the same basic aim.

That aim is to limit forcible state action wherever possible, whilst acknowledging the fact that states must and will protect themselves through an inherent right of self-defence. If an 'armed attack as a grave use of force' criterion is applied, force can be used only in extreme cases in which there has been a particularly 'grave' attack (an attempt to control any potential escalation of violence, through the exclusion of 'minor' incidents as a trigger for a forcible response).[140] Equally, the necessity criterion aims to limit forcible responses to extreme cases in which military action in self-defence is a last resort.[141] In the vast majority of situations, these two criteria are likely to cover the same extreme cases. The concepts of 'armed attack as a grave use of force' and necessity possess a very similar function, which goes some way to explain the confusion inherent in the *lex lata*. It seems illogical to employ two different methods of reaching the same conclusion. To put all this more simply: if an armed attack is established, does this not automatically prove necessity? A particularly grave attack is surely—in virtually all cases—going to give rise to a defensive necessity.[142]

Given this overlap, could it be concluded that the Court has in fact applied 'necessity' and 'armed attack as a grave use of force' as interchangeable terms for the same criterion? For example, it has been argued that the conclusion reached by the ICJ in *Nicaragua* was that a response in self-defence will be necessary in the case of an armed attack and

[140] WM Reisman, 'Old Wine in New Bottles: The Reagan and Brezhnev Doctrines in Contemporary International Law and Practice' (1988) 13 *Yale Journal of International Law* 171, 194–96.

[141] See ch 2, section IV.

[142] Higgins has similarly identified a degree of 'overlap' between the armed attack criterion and proportionality, though this is admittedly less pronounced than as with necessity. She has stated: 'Is the question of level of violence by regular forces not really an issue of proportionality, rather than a question of determining what is an armed attack?' R Higgins, *Problems and Process: International Law and How We Use It* (Oxford, Oxford University Press, 1994) 251.

conversely will be unnecessary when there has been no armed attack.[143] This is attractive in its simplicity and would remove much of the confusion of requiring two different criteria for the same basic purpose[144] (although of course it would not deal with the proportionality issue).

However, this is not what the ICJ has held: it seems that the criteria of necessity and proportionality are needed *in addition* to the requirement of the victim state having suffered an armed attack.[145] Very early in the *Nicaragua* merits decision, a clear distinction was made between two aspects of a valid self-defence claim. The first of these is an armed attack (or, plausibly, a threatened armed attack). The second aspect is 'whether the measures allegedly taken in self-defence were a legally appropriate reaction',[146] meaning that the response meets the criteria of necessity and proportionality. For the Court, these two aspects combined constitute a self-defence action:[147]

Armed attack	+	Criteria derived from *Caroline* (necessity and proportionality)	=	Self-defence

As such, the ICJ has identified two separate assessments that must be made for lawful self-defence to be established. Thus, in *Oil Platforms*, the Court held that the United States was required to show that it had been a victim of an armed attack as set out in *Nicaragua* and that it 'must also show that its actions were necessary and proportional.'[148] This implies that there may be situations in which an armed attack has occurred, but the response taken nevertheless fails to meet either the necessity or the proportionality requirements.[149] In general, state practice does not support such a clear distinction between 'armed attack' and 'necessity and proportionality'. There does not seem to be a two-stage evaluation of lawfulness: whilst states do at times refer to both, the two concepts are usually presented as part of the same legal claim (if armed attack is referenced at all).[150]

143 Constantinou (n 9) 158.

144 Although it must be said that even if the issue is merely one of terminology, for reasons of clarity, applying a mixture of the terms 'necessity' and 'armed attack' in reference to the same thing is not desirable.

145 *Nicaragua* merits (n 17) para 194.

146 *Ibid*, para 35.

147 The following formulation is adapted from one employed by D Kritsiotis, 'Rules on Self-Defence in International Law' Memorandum for the Royal Institute of International Affairs, London Chatham House International Law Programme, 8 December 2004 (unpublished) 6.

148 *Oil Platforms* merits (n 70) para 51.

149 J Gardam, 'Necessity and Proportionality in *Jus ad Bellum* and *Jus in Bello*' in L Boisson de Charzournes and P Sands (eds), *International Law, the International Court of Justice and Nuclear Weapons* (Cambridge, Cambridge University Press, 1999) 275, 278.

150 A good example of this amalgam of argument is the Ugandan reaction to the Osiraq raid of 1981. Uganda claimed, unsurprisingly, that Israel had not acted lawfully. Yet Uganda saw this as being because there was no armed attack, and therefore the action was unnecessary: UN Doc S/PV.2282, 6–7.

In general, the fact that the law seems to require an assessment of whether an armed attack has occurred and a *separate* assessment of whether this necessitates a response (and whether that response is proportionate) amounts, in many respects, to a dual requirement that attempts to achieve the same thing: the restriction of responses in self-defence to extreme cases whenever possible. It is this overlap that causes so much of the confusion regarding self-defence and permeates the Court's jurisprudence.

V. THE DIFFERENT FUNCTIONS OF THE MERGED CONCEPTIONS

The above section suggests that there are significant overlaps between the two 'conceptions' that, together, form the *lex lata* on self-defence. However, '*Caroline*' and 'armed attack as a grave use of force' are not achieving entirely the same thing: there are evident differences in the consequences of employing one system over the other.

Perhaps the most important distinction between the results achieved by employing the armed attack conception and that of the *Caroline* is the function of the proportionality requirement. The armed attack criterion (if it were to be taken as the sole criterion for lawful self-defence) restricts states from using force in relation to comparatively 'minor' incidents, which therefore limits forcible responses to 'exceptional' circumstances only. However, this in itself in no way restricts the nature of the response that may be taken *once an armed attack is established*. This would clearly allow for lawful escalation of forcible actions, with ever increasing responses. Once an armed attack is established (which could be an attack on a single vessel, following *Oil Platforms*), the responding state would be entitled to ensure the total destruction of the attacking state. The legal criterion that restricts states from responding in such a way is that of proportionality.

As such, the proportionality requirement has been identified by some scholars as the most important means of restraining force in self-defence.[151] Whether the attack being responded to is large or small, the requirement of proportionality ensures that states are restrained in the exercise of their inherent defensive right. However much the Court may have stressed the primacy of an armed attack, it could not abandon the criterion of proportionality. Such a criterion is essential: without it the occurrence of an armed attack would, in itself, allow a state to respond in any manner and to any degree that it wished. Therefore, even leaving aside the regular invocation and application of proportionality in state practice (and thus its position in customary international law), it must be seen—practically and politically—as a fundamental element of any legal framework for the exercise of self-defence.

[151] See Kenny (n 13) 1168; and Brownlie (n 9) 261.

In addition to the different function of the proportionality requirement as opposed to armed attack, it is also the case that the overlap between necessity and armed attack is not total. Whilst they perform a similar function, they should not be seen as the same criterion. As we saw in the previous section, the ICJ has certainly viewed armed attack and necessity as separate.[152] Although this is problematic in terms of practical application, it makes conceptual sense.

First, it is perhaps conceivable that an armed attack could occur and yet there still be no necessity for response to that grave use of force, given alternative non-forcible options. However, while this is conceptually possible, it seems unlikely that a state would determine (or could be expected to determine) that a *grave* use of force occurring against it did not necessitate a forcible response. In the vast majority of cases the 'most grave' manifestation of the use of force will necessitate a forcible response: establishing an armed attack is in practice tantamount to establishing necessity.

Second, and more easily conceived of, are situations in which a defensive necessity requiring a forcible response exists, and yet the attack being responded to does not amount to an armed attack as the ICJ has defined it. Here necessity and armed attack do not overlap, and it is to such instances that we now turn.

VI. THE GAP BETWEEN A USE OF FORCE *SIMPLICITER* AND AN ARMED ATTACK

Whilst establishing an armed attack is likely to be tantamount to establishing necessity, establishing the necessity of a forcible response may not be tantamount to establishing an armed attack. It is possible that a 'minor' violation of Article 2(4) (a 'less grave' use of force) may still create a defensive necessity (requiring a proportional defensive response involving the use of force). Under the 'armed attack as a grave use of force' criterion, to respond in a forcible manner to a 'minor' attack of this kind would constitute an unlawful action. The 'armed attack as a grave use of force' criterion represents a 'rigid barrier'[153] to responses from states faced with relatively minor attacks, 'no matter how reasonably necessary and proportionate the [response] may be'.[154] It is argued here that it seems illogical that if a state is faced with a defensive necessity, it is not lawfully entitled to respond.[155] As Barry Levenfeld has put this, 'there is no logic to the limitation of the

[152] Above, section IV.

[153] To use the term employed by TM Franck, 'Some Observations on the ICJ's Procedural and Substantive Innovations' (1987) 81 *American Journal of International Law* 116, 120.

[154] Hargrove (n 4) 138.

[155] JN Moore, 'The *Nicaragua* Case and the Deterioration of World Order' (1987) 81 *American Journal of International Law* 151, 152; and K Chainoglou, 'Reconceptualising Self-Defence in International Law' (2007) 18 *King's Law Journal* 61, 71 (in the context of potential WMD attacks).

right of self-defence to armed attacks. . . [T]he necessity of defending a state may arise without the occurrence of an armed attack.'[156]

To put this another way, a requirement of an armed attack as interpreted by the ICJ (admittedly, with some evident support in state practice) means there is necessarily a 'gap' between a 'minor' violation of Article 2(4) of the UN Charter against a state and the requirement that any violation must amount to an 'armed attack' before the victim state can lawfully defend itself under Article 51.[157] Under the position that has been taken by the ICJ, states that are victims of an unlawful use of force not amounting to an armed attack are without recourse to defend themselves. In the view of Michael Reisman, it is therefore the case that 'the ICJ issues one of the parties round after round of blanks.'[158] Figure 3.1 demonstrates the problem.[159]

The value of 'y' today is reasonably well understood. It is in general fairly straightforward to identify when a use of force in breach of Article 2(4) has occurred.[160] The biggest problem facing the legal regulation of

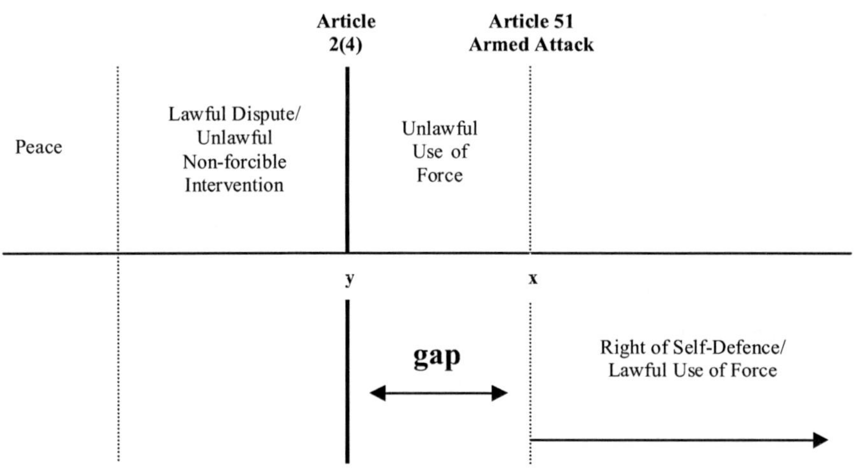

Figure 3.1 The Gap between a Use of Force *Simpliciter* and an Armed Attack

[156] B Levenfeld, 'Israel's Counter-*Fedayeen* Tactics in Lebanon: Self-Defence and Reprisal under Modern International Law' (1982–83) 21 *Columbia Journal of Transnational Law* 1, 20.

[157] A Randelzhofer, 'Article 51' in B Simma (ed), *The Charter of the United Nations: A Commentary, Vol I*, 2nd edn (Oxford, Oxford University Press, 2002) 788, 790–92 and 796; E Miller, 'Self-Defence, International Law and the Six Day War' (1985) 20 *Israeli Law Review* 49, 52–56; Gazzini (n 21) 138; WH Taft IV, 'Self-Defence and the *Oil Platforms* Decision' (2004) 29 *Yale Journal of International Law* 295, 300; Higgins (n 142) 251; Franck, 'Who Killed Article 2(4)?' (n 9) 812–13; Ochoa-Ruiz and Salamanca-Aguado (n 71) 511; Hargrove (n 4) 139; and Dinstein (n 23) 193–96.

[158] Reisman, 'Old Wine in New Bottles' (n 140) 196.

[159] This diagram has been adapted from one used by Miller (n 157) 54.

[160] Eg, it is fairly clear that economic measures are not regulated by Art 2(4). TJ Farer, 'Political and Economic Coercion in Contemporary International Law' (1985) 79 *American Journal of International Law* 405, 408–13; and Randelzhofer (n 157) 118.

force between states is that the value of 'x' is unknown and is potentially even unknowable.

Notably, in a world where 'traditional' uses of force by way of engagement between large-scale regular armed forces has become infrequent, this problem has particular consequences for states faced with attacks from terrorist groups. Modern terrorist attacks tend to be comparatively small-scale in themselves,[161] but this is not to say that they fail to create a defensive necessity, particularly if they form part of a wider pattern of attacks intended to have a much greater cumulative impact on the attacked state. If minor attacks cannot be responded to as they do not constitute armed attacks, this may leave a state suffering terrorist aggression with no adequate means of responding.

A useful example would be the bombings of US embassies in Kenya and Tanzania in 1998.[162] It is uncontroversial to hold that these attacks constituted uses of force against the United States. However, whether these attacks could be viewed (individually or taken together) as *armed attack* is difficult to ascertain.[163] This is particularly true if the 'armed attack as a grave use of force' criterion is applied, given the comparatively small scale of the incidents.[164]

The ICJ has tried to define 'x'. However, as is evident from our preceding analysis, the nature and scope of the armed attack criterion remains far from clear. As Judge Kateka stated in his *DRC v Uganda* dissent, 'The dictum [in *Nicaragua*] left open the definition of "armed attack" as applied in the Charter of the United Nations and under customary international law.'[165] It will further be recalled that, based upon the ICJ's conception, 'x' is a value that can be reached through a combination of less grave uses of force (the accumulation of events theory).[166] Thus two or more actions that fall between 'y' and 'x' could be added together to equal 'x'. This, of course, makes the calculation even more indefinite.

Attempts by the Court to define its central criterion of armed attack have meant that the gap between 'x' and 'y' has, if anything, grown. It will be recalled that the ICJ appeared to respond to this problem through the introduction of an idea of 'proportionate countermeasures'.[167] However, its acceptance of such measures was at best tentative. The concept of

161 CS Gray, 'Combating Terrorism' (1993) 23 *Parameters: US Army War College Quarterly* 17, 23.

162 See http://www.globalsecurity.org/security/ops/98emb.htm.

163 MN Shaw, *International Law*, 5th edn (Cambridge, Cambridge University Press, 2003) 1027. However, it was certainly the position of the United States that the embassy bombings constituted armed attacks. The United States responded to these attacks by striking against alleged terrorist bases in Afghanistan and Sudan, and it argued that these responses were lawful instances of self-defence: UN Doc S/1998/780.

164 When viewed in contrast to 'traditional' notions of cross-border military incursions.

165 *DRC v Uganda* merits (n 108) dissenting opinion of Judge Kateka, para 12.

166 See ch 1, section IV.

167 *Ibid*, section VII.

forcible individual countermeasures is not supported by state practice. Further, as noted in chapter one, there are a number of problems with the notion. It is a concept that has little or no legal definition or boundaries. Also, it can be seen as amounting to a semantic exercise of 'low-grade' self-defence by another name and thus ultimately confuses the law concerning self-defence still further. Finally, even if one accepts forcible countermeasures as being lawful in the context of individual responses, the ICJ was clear that any *collective* forcible response has to take the form of self-defence. This means that the Court took the view that collective action *must* be taken in response to an armed attack. Therefore, the problematic 'gap' between Articles 2(4) and 51 would continue to exist for states in need of military support from a third party. As has already been discussed, this leaves weak states (those most likely to request other states to aid them in collective self-defence) with no lawful response to comparatively less grave forcible intervention.[168]

In addition to these concerns, some scholars have argued that despite the fact that the ICJ's expression of the 'armed attack as a grave use of force' criterion was clearly intended by the Court to limit or restrict the escalation of military force, the requirement of a 'gravity threshold' for armed attack—and thus the gap between the concepts of 'use of force' and 'armed attack'—in fact makes the use of force more, as opposed to less, likely. There are two versions of this argument.

First, it has been argued by some scholars that the 'armed attack as a grave use of force' criterion encourages states to initiate small-scale uses of force against other states. This is on the basis that a victim state will not be lawfully entitled to respond with force in response to such attacks (or certainly no other state will be entitled to respond collectively). Therefore, the state initiating such minor attacks can operate with a degree of impunity, making states more willing to instigate small-scale attacks.[169] The Court has thus been accused of being tolerant of low-level conflict to an extent that this may increase the aggregate use of force in international relations.[170] Equally, it has been argued that if a responding state is forced to wait until attacks against it can be considered 'grave', it is likely that the response will ultimately itself be much greater, 'making it more difficult to prevent disputes from escalating into full-scale conflicts'.[171]

A second version of this claim argues that because the Court has taken a somewhat 'progressive' view with regard to identifying the 'armed attack as a grave use of force' criterion as an aspect of customary international

[168] *Ibid*.

[169] WM Reisman, 'Allocating Competences to Use Coercion in the Post-Cold War World: Practices, Conditions and Prospects' in LF Damrosch and DJ Scheffer (eds), *Law and Force in the New International Order* (Boulder, Westview Press, 1991) 26, 40; and Taft (n 157) 300–1.

[170] Reisman, 'Allocating Competences to Use Coercion' (*ibid*) 39.

[171] Taft (n 157) 301.

law—through rather vague reference to certain declarations of the General Assembly as representing state practice in *Nicaragua*, for example—this will lead governments to be equally creative when making self-defence claims. Instead of referencing Article 51, states will be likely to assert poorly defined customary doctrines, most notably preventative self-defence. As such, force will be employed more often under the guise of debatable self-defence claims.[172]

However, although an increase in the use of military force could be seen as resulting from the 'armed attack as a grave use of force' criterion, because of the ICJ's 'tolerance' of small-scale attacks, there is in fact little in state practice to suggest that this has been the case.[173] Similarly, as we saw in chapter two, whilst some states do invoke a doctrine of preventative self-defence in one form or another, this represents minority practice.[174] As was noted earlier in this chapter, post-*Nicaragua*, state invocation of the 'armed attack as a grave use of force' criterion appears to have increased.[175] It is notable that this has been coupled with reference to Article 51. Therefore, the Court's position has, if anything, limited wide-ranging claims regarding self-defence in customary international law and has increased focus on Article 51 (although necessity and proportionality remain the key criteria for an assessment of self-defence in practice).

As such, criticism of the gravity requirement on the basis that it will lead to the increased use of military force may be somewhat unfounded. Equally, though, the counter argument—that uses of force would increase were it not for the gravity requirement for armed attack, as inter-state conflict would escalate from minor incidents[176]—is similarly difficult to demonstrate through an examination of practice. Irrespective of the gravity threshold, responses to minor uses of force would be limited in scope to proportional responses, and even then, a proportional response could only be taken as a last resort. The proposition that the gravity threshold *limits* state uses of force is as questionable as the claim that it increases them.

Whilst it is difficult to argue that the 'armed attack as a grave use of force' criterion will increase state resort to force, it is clear that the gap between a use of force under Article 2(4) and an armed attack under Article 51 restricts states from responding in certain circumstances, even when there is a defensive necessity to respond. In the view of the present author, this gap is an undesirable aspect of the law on the use of force. Taking the same view, John Lawrence Hargrove has dramatically stated:

[172] Hargrove (n 4) 142.
[173] Gray (n 9) 148.
[174] See ch 2, section VI-A.
[175] Above, section II.
[176] Put forward by Gray (n 9) 148; Müllerson (n 74) 18; and TJ Farer, 'Drawing the Right Line' (1987) 81 *American Journal of International Law* 112, 113–14.

> Any suggestion that there are any acts of unlawful force between states that international law forbids a state from defending against by proportionate force, by the means and to the extent necessary to protect itself *degrades the concept of international law* (emphasis added).[177]

This may be going too far. Nonetheless, it is argued here the concept of 'armed attack as a grave use of force' is highly problematic, and its existence and relationship with the customary international law criteria of necessity and proportionality are at the root of much of the difficulty inherent in the jurisprudence of the ICJ on self-defence.

VII. THE OVERALL INDETERMINACY OF SELF-DEFENCE

Upon examination, then, the law governing actions taken in self-defence can be seen to be somewhat confused. The indeterminacy inherent in the law, stems from the fact that two (partially overlapping) 'conceptions' together regulate self-defence actions.[178] Moreover, it has been argued herein that the content of each criterion is, in itself, indeterminate. In particular, the content of the criterion of an armed attack is unclear, as is how that criterion should be applied. To the extent that the nature and scope of the criterion can be identified (for example, as a 'grave' use of force that must have in fact occurred), this can potentially lead to undesirable results, such as victim states being left with no recourse to defend themselves in comparatively 'minor' cases.

It is worth noting that the indeterminacy within the law governing self-defence has fundamental consequences for the prohibition on the use of force. This is because of the fact that indeterminate rules directly impact upon what Thomas Franck has termed the 'legitimacy' of the legal regime in question.[179] The legitimacy of a rule, in the manner used by Franck, is one of the primary factors that will affect its compliance-pull. Rules that possess a high degree of legitimacy are likely to be applied more uniformly by states than rules with a low degree of legitimacy. This is obviously something that is particularly important in the non-coercive international system. One major factor contributing to the legitimacy of a

[177] Hargrove (n 4) 139.

[178] One could take a further step back and argue that the indeterminate nature of legal rule creation in the international legal system and the non-hierarchical nature of the two 'formal' sources of international law underlie this problem. Eg, Allott sees these factors as causing confusion in many areas of international law, including self-determination, the recognition of states and, notably, self-defence. P Allott, 'The ICJ and the Voice of Justice' in V Lowe and M Fitzmaurice (eds), *Fifty Years of the International Court of Justice: Essays in Honour of Sir Robert Jennings* (Cambridge, Cambridge University Press, 1996) 17, esp 35–36. However, such discussions run beyond the scope of this work.

[179] See generally TM Franck, *The Power of Legitimacy among Nations* (Oxford, Oxford University Press, 1990).

norm is its determinacy. By this it is meant that in a legal framework with no systematic enforcement, the determinacy (in most cases meaning the clarity but also the transparency and practical applicability) of a rule or collection of rules will have a great bearing upon whether states comply with the law.[180]

Despite the best efforts of the ICJ, the law governing self-defence remains indeterminate; certainly, Franck has argued that the legitimacy of Article 51 is extremely weakened by its low degree of determinacy.[181] Indeed, it is arguable that the ICJ has contributed to this indeterminacy. Interestingly, the absence of determinacy behind Article 51 may be starkly contrasted with the high degree of determinacy attached to Article 2(4), which—in simplified terms—dictates: *do not use force*.[182] Yet the only unilateral exception to this norm—the law governing self-defence—is anything but clear. This lack of determinacy in the context of self-defence has the effect of negating the apparent determinacy of Article 2(4). Whilst the rule itself is clear, the exception to the rule is not: the scope of the legal justification to the use of force is unclear and therefore open to abuse, and thus the compliance-pull of the prohibition against the use of force is greatly undermined.[183]

To temper this point slightly, it is important to be aware that absolute definitional clarity of a norm is not necessarily desirable. In some cases a lack of flexibility and context-specificity in relation to a norm can lead to absurd results. Some rules simply *need* to have a level of flexibility.[184] It should be noted that the practical realities of self-defence mean that the rules governing such action certainly require a degree of flexibility. For example, there is of course a level of flexibility inherent in the notions of necessity and proportionality. Moreover, to an extent, flexibility is *desirable* in the context of self-defence.[185] However, as we have also seen, this is not to say that these criteria are in themselves indeterminate. When necessity and proportionality are coupled with the 'armed attack as a grave use of force' criterion, though, the law governing self-defence as a whole has a low aggregate degree of determinacy.

The law governing self-defence must contain a degree of flexibility; it must, due to the very nature of defensive uses of force, comprise a system of flexible rules. However, as the law stands, it is not merely flexible; it is unclear. There is a need to make it more determinate.

[180] See generally TM Franck, *The Power of Legitimacy among Nations* (Oxford, Oxford University Press, 1990), esp 52–66.

[181] *Ibid*, 75–77.

[182] *Ibid*, 62; and Kritsiotis, 'When States Use Armed Force' (n 63) 57–61.

[183] Franck, *The Power of Legitimacy among Nations* (n 179) 70–71. Franck does not make this point specifically with regard to the *jus ad bellum*.

[184] *Ibid*, esp 67–83.

[185] Koskenniemi (n 53) 594.

VIII. CONCLUSION

The view is taken in this book that the primacy given to the armed attack criterion by the ICJ in the *Nicaragua* case was an inaccurate representation of the existing state practice and *opinio juris*. However, today this inaccuracy would seem to be less evident than it was in 1986. The discrepancy between the jurisprudence of the Court and customary international law as evident in the practice of states would appear to have narrowed. This may be in part due to the influence of the *Nicaragua* judgment (as since reinforced by *Oil Platforms, DRC v Uganda, Nuclear Weapons* and *Israeli Wall*) upon customary international law, though how far this is true is impossible to say. Certainly the jurisprudence represents an undesirable strengthening of a needless and ultimately confusing criterion. Having said this, it must be concluded that the ICJ has faced an impossible task in reconciling the two conceptions of self-defence as they appear—merged—in the law governing actions taken in self-defence. As has been argued by Dino Kritsiotis, the Court is operating 'in an age when [necessity and proportionality] are now juxtaposed to a (customary) requirement of an armed attack'.[186] It would have been very difficult for the Court simply to have discarded the need for an armed attack in self-defence cases; Article 51 appears clear that an armed attack is required, and it is arguable that customary international law requires a higher level or 'quality' of force against a responding state before the right of self-defence is triggered.[187] As such, the law in itself may be seen as being incoherent and confused, irrespective of what the ICJ has held on the issue. The concept of 'armed attack as a grave use of force' certainly predated the *Nicaragua* case, although it appeared in state practice somewhat sporadically. In some respects, then, the Court has been the innocent victim of circumstance: as a former trial judge of the International Criminal Tribunal for the Former Yugoslavia has pointed out, 'the murkiness of much of international law [and] its multiple sources . . . make the international judge's task more difficult [than that of the domestic judge].'[188] This phenomenon is particularly notable in the context of self-defence and the ICJ.

The armed attack criterion is apparent in Article 51, and it has appeared in the legal practice of states as a criterion beyond a mere breach of Article 2(4). It is here argued that the criterion is unnecessary and unhelpful—but that is not to say that it is not evident in customary international law. Nonetheless, this should be seen as mitigation, not exoneration, in relation

186 Kritsiotis, 'Rules on Self-Defence in International Law' (n 147) 19.

187 Above, section I.

188 Though this point was made in a very different context—that of the administrative support needed for international adjudication. See PM Wald, 'Running the Trial of the Century: The Nuremberg Legacy' (2005–06) 27 *Cardozo Law Review* 1559, 1567.

to the flaws in the Court's jurisprudence. The primacy given by the Court to the unhelpful 'armed attack as a grave use of force' criterion and its reinforcement of a customary international law on self-defence based upon two conceptions that do not form a cohesive whole has reinforced existing difficulties inherent in the international law governing self-defence. The 'armed attack as a grave use of force' criterion creates a concerning gap between Article 2(4) and Article 51, and the partial (but not complete) overlap of this criterion with the pre-existing customary rules lowers the aggregate determinacy of self-defence, and thus the prohibition on the use of force.

Ultimately, the development of international law governing self-defence (most notably through the merged conceptions discussed in this chapter) has led to 'a very complex calculus for determining lawfulness in particular cases',[189] as can be observed from an examination of incidents in state practice. The ICJ has endorsed this complex conception of the law and then presented this conception in a confusing manner. In chapter four a proposal for dealing with the problem of the merged conceptions of self-defence, and thus improving the current law, will be advanced.

[189] Reisman, 'Allocating Competences to Use Coercion' (n 169) 28.

4

A Proposal for Redefining Armed Attack

IN CHAPTER THREE it was argued that a major reason for the problems that may be identified in the jurisprudence of the ICJ regarding self-defence is the confused nature of the law itself in this area, and ultimately because self-defence stems from two partially overlapping, merged conceptions of law. In this chapter, a proposal to clarify the law and thus improve upon the jurisprudence of the Court will be advanced.

I. DEFINING ARMED ATTACK DIFFERENTLY: PROPOSALS OLD AND NEW

One possible means of resolving the problem of the merged conceptions of self-defence would be to abandon the criterion of necessity and rely upon the dual criteria of armed attack and proportionality. However, there are a number of problems with this. First, reliance upon 'armed attack as a grave use of force' leaves open the possibility that a state may be unable to respond in self-defence even when faced with a defensive necessity. This is the issue of the 'gap' that the 'armed attack as a grave use of force' criterion creates between Article 2(4) and Article 51 of the UN Charter.[1]

More importantly, because of the historical development of necessity and proportionality from the *Caroline* incident, and the similar content of these criteria, the division between 'necessity' and 'proportionality' is difficult to define. In particular, it was noted in chapter two that as the proportionality requirement is measured against the necessity of response (and not, at least primarily, against the scale of the attack being responded to), the criteria of necessity and proportionality are inherently linked.[2] Thus Christine Gray has indicated that it is hard to see 'how far the two concepts [of necessity and proportionality] can operate separately. If a use of force is not necessary, it cannot be proportionate and, if it is not

[1] See ch 3, section VI.
[2] See ch 2, section V.

proportionate, it is difficult to see how it can be necessary.'[3] It has also already been argued that proportionality simply *must* form an aspect of the modern regulation of self-defence.[4] It follows from this that it would be extremely difficult to 'remove' the necessity criterion from the same legal framework.

Therefore, it is proposed here that the best method of improving the current law is to redefine the notion of an armed attack. The criterion as defined by the ICJ, so far as such a requirement may be identified in state practice, should be abandoned in the regulation of self-defence. Instead, reliance should be placed on the traditional customary international law criteria of necessity and proportionality.

Importantly, it should be stressed that what is suggested here is not that the term 'armed attack' should be abandoned entirely in the context of self-defence. Such a step would amount to a direct attack on the UN Charter, as the phrase is clearly and undeniably present in Article 51 and thus must be seen as an aspect of the law.[5] To remove totally the term from discourse on self-defence would be to disregard a provision of the Charter and thus weaken the entire Charter regime for the regulation of force, a wholly retrograde step. It is certainly not desirable to 'introduce a process of deconstructing the edifice of the *jus ad bellum*'.[6]

Instead, what is suggested here is a reinterpretation of the phrase as it appears in Article 51: it is desirable for the *meaning* attached to the phrase 'armed attack' to be reassessed. As was discussed in chapter three, the notion of 'armed attack as a grave use of force' may be seen as an aspect of contemporary customary international law.[7] Interpreting armed attack to mean something other than this would therefore arguably amount to a reform of the customary international law position; certainly, it would go against the jurisprudence of the ICJ. However, as we have seen, there is nothing in the Charter or its drafting history that necessitates a particular reading of armed attack,[8] and there is certainly not anything therein to suggest that the term should be interpreted as meaning a particularly

[3] C Gray, *International Law and the Use of Force*, 3rd edn (Oxford, Oxford University Press, 2008) 150.

[4] See ch 3, section V. As has been stated, 'there simply must be a limit to how far a state acting in self-defence . . . may go.' ME O'Connell, 'Review: *Necessity, Proportionality and the Use of Force by States* by Judith Gardam' (2006) 100 *American Journal of International Law* 973, 975.

[5] E Jiménez de Aréchaga, 'International Law in the Past Third of a Century' (1978) 159 *Recueil Des Cours* 13, 95–98.

[6] C Antonopoulos, 'Force by Armed Groups as Armed Attack and the Broadening of Self-Defence' (2008) 55 *Netherlands International Law Review* 159, 180, who uses this phrase with respect to controversial applications of the law of self-defence by states and the possible implications of these claims for the future development of international law.

[7] See ch 3, section I.

[8] *Ibid.*

grave use of force.[9] Therefore, the essential question concerning the law governing self-defence is:

> [H]ow do we define 'armed attack' in a way relevant to the modern conditions of indirect limited warfare, without broadening it to the point at which disproportionate armed force can be used against imagined or slight provocation[?][10]

It is here suggested that the answer is to define 'armed attack' as meaning, simply, a 'use of force'. After all, the proportionality requirement guards against excessive forcible responses, and necessity acts to assess the need to respond against small-scale violations of Article 2(4).[11] Under such a conception, the gravity of an attack would still be important, in that it would be relevant to the necessity and proportionality of the response. However, *all* uses of force could be responded to—it would simply mean that 'minor' uses of force could only be responded to if a forcible response was necessary to defend a state against such an attack and, even then, that forcible response could be undertaken only to the extent necessary to curtail that attack. In other words, the suggestion here is to 'permit real force to be resisted by force, but scrupulously require that the defence fit the conduct defended against'.[12]

This is not to say that self-defence could be taken against something other than a use of force (or arguably a threat of force). There are, of course, examples of self-defence being claimed in response to something other than a forcible attack (actual or threatened). For example, when making its dubious claim that its intervention in East Pakistan in 1971 was an action taken in self-defence, India indicated that it had been the victim of what may be termed 'refugee aggression'. Due to the brutal treatment of Awami League separatists (and the civilian population in general) in East Pakistan by the Pakistani government, there was an exodus of as many as ten million refugees into India.[13] It was initially claimed by India that this in itself was enough to give rise to the right of self-defence.[14] However, this legal

[9] JL Hargrove, 'The *Nicaragua* Judgment and the Future of the Law of Force and Self-Defence' (1987) 81 *American Journal of International Law* 135, 139; and WH Taft IV, 'Self-Defence and the *Oil Platforms* Decision' (2004) 29 *Yale Journal of International Law* 295, 300.

[10] TM Franck, 'Who Killed Article 2(4)? or Changing the Norms Governing the Use of Force by States' (1970) 64 *American Journal of International Law* 809, 816.

[11] T Gazzini, *The Changing Rules on the Use of Force in International Law* (Manchester, Manchester University Press, 2005) 138.

[12] Hargrove (n 9) 139. It should be noted that Hargrove felt that this was the legal position prior to *Nicaragua* anyway and that the Court implanted the requirement for gravity into international law with that decision. It has already been argued, however, that the criterion did have a basis in state practice prior to 1986. See ch 3, section I.

[13] This was the figure claimed by India (UN Doc S/PV.1606, 15), though it may have been fewer than this. In any event, the refugees who sought sanctuary in India still numbered millions. See the Report of the International Commission of Jurists, 'The Events in East Pakistan' (Geneva, International Commission of Jurists, 1972) 24–45.

[14] UN Doc S/PV.1606, 15.

justification was not accepted by other states.[15] As such, India quickly reverted to the claim that Pakistan had on a number of occasions dispatched troops into India itself.[16]

Non-forcible triggers of the kind initially claimed by India in 1971 cannot be seen as falling within the concept of 'armed attack'. The ordinary meaning of that term simply cannot be stretched to allow for a forcible response against something that does not involve an 'attack' that is 'armed'. Indeed, it would be undesirable even if it could be stretched in this way: force should be restricted to situations in which it constitutes a response to force. The trigger for self-defence must be a use of force, to which the victim state (or other states acting in collective self-defence) respond with force. However, the phrase 'armed attack' can certainly be seen as referring to any use of force, be it grave or less grave. Importantly, it will be argued in this chapter that there are a number of benefits in prima facie allowing responses to all uses of force, not just to especially grave ones.

Interestingly, the proposal advanced here—the notion of removing the conception of 'armed attack as a grave use of force' from the law governing self-defence and redefining the armed attack criterion—has much in common with three separate proposals made during the debates over the issue of defining the legal concept of 'aggression' during the 1950s. It is therefore useful for us to refer to them here. By far the most notable of these was a proposal made in the context of the 1956 incarnation of the Special Committee on the Question of Defining Aggression, by the Committee's Rapporteur, BVA Röling, acting in his capacity as the representative of the Netherlands.

At the start of the debates over the issue in 1956, the Netherlands argued that, in the alternative to defining aggression, it would be useful for the Committee to produce a draft definition of *armed attack* as employed in Article 51.[17] Over the course of subsequent debates in the Special Committee the Netherlands set out a fairly detailed conception of an armed attack, which it argued should form the basis of such a definition.

Upon initial inspection, this 1956 Dutch conception of armed attack appears to be similar in content to that later outlined by the ICJ. Röling argued that to prove an armed attack, it was not enough to simply prove a use of force.[18] In addition, 'qualitative and quantitative considerations'

[15] The negative reaction of other states to the claim of force deployed in response to an influx of refugees can be seen from the responses in both the General Assembly and the Security Council. Eg, see the statements of Ghana (UN Doc A/PV.2002, 6), Iran (UN Doc A/PV.2003, 5), Sweden (UN Doc A/PV.2003, 27), the United States (UN Doc S/PV.1606, 18), the People's Republic of China (UN Doc S/PV.1606, 22) and Saudi Arabia (UN Doc S/PV.1607, 23).

[16] UN Doc S/PV.1606, 17.

[17] See, eg, UN Doc A/AC.77/SR.3, 8.

[18] UN Doc A/AC.77/SR.8, 8.

needed to be taken into account, including the 'nature and magnitude' of the attack.[19] Similarly, the Dutch proposal apparently excluded 'frontier incidents' from the definition of armed attack.[20] Thus, prima facie, the proposal amounted to a call for a definition based upon the 'gravity' of the incident. Such a conception of armed attack would seem much like that espoused by the ICJ and the arguable content of the armed attack criteria in customary international law as it stands today.

In fact, the Netherlands proposal had a very different character: it was not fundamentally based upon the gravity of the attack suffered but instead upon the defensive necessity created by that attack.[21] The development of a conception of armed attack culminated in a proposed definition:

> Armed attack as the term is used in Article 51 is the use of armed force *which leaves the state against which it is directed no means other than military means* to preserve its territorial integrity or political independence; it being understood that the definition may never be construed to comprise acts of legitimate individual or collective self-defence or any act in pursuance of a decision or recommendation of a competent organ of the United Nations (emphasis added).[22]

It should be noted that this definition was prefaced by the statement that the term 'the use of armed force' should be taken to include an attack that had commenced but not yet reached the frontier of the defending state. Therefore, with this qualification, the definition allowed for a limited form of preventative self-defence in response to an imminent threat (what we have been referring to as 'anticipatory self-defence').[23] The Netherlands representative similarly stated that an armed attack should be defined as 'such acts of military force as leave the state attacked *no room to wait* for United Nations action in defending its territorial integrity or political independence' (emphasis added).[24] When asked by the representatives of Mexico[25] and the United Kingdom[26] to clarify the phrase 'no room to wait for United Nations action', Röling pointed out that what was really intended was to express the notion that forcible action in self-defence must be 'the only

[19] *Ibid*, 8–9.

[20] UN Doc A/AC.77/SR.12, 5.

[21] It should be noted that a contrary interpretation of the proposal has been put forward: N Feinberg, *Studies in International Law with Special Reference to the Arab–Israeli Conflict* (Jerusalem, Magnes Press, 1979) 60.

[22] UN Doc A/AC.77/SR.13, 17.

[23] The Netherlands also stressed elsewhere that its proposal intentionally allows for preventative self-defence but only under the restrictive criteria of imminence: UN Doc A/AC.77/SR.13, 16. Further, during an earlier debate of 1953, the Netherlands argued that aggression (not, admittedly, *armed attack*) should be defined as 'the *threat* or use of force by a state or government against the territorial integrity or political independence of another state' (emphasis added): *UN Yearbook* (1954) 428.

[24] UN Doc A/AC.77/SR.8, 9.

[25] UN Doc A/AC.77/SR.12, 3.

[26] *Ibid*, 4.

remaining remedy' available to a state.[27] Such a calculation would be made on a case-by-case basis, with the need for an immediate response being only one possible contributing factor to this determination.[28]

Such phrases clearly reflect the nomenclature of *Caroline*[29] and the contemporary notion of last resort. In examining these definitions, it becomes clear that an armed attack, in the view of the Netherlands in 1956, amounted to *a use of force giving rise to a necessity of self-defence.* A qualitative and quantitative assessment of the nature and magnitude of an attack was seen as simply one possible way to assess the necessity of response. Similarly, whilst the Netherlands prima facie appeared to exclude frontier incidents from the definition of armed attack, in actuality, it allowed for force to be employed *when necessary* in response to such incidents (and seemingly only when the response was also proportional).[30]

Thus, the Dutch proposal held that an armed attack should be defined as a use of force *simpliciter* that created a necessity of self-defence. It was not alone in doing so. Independently of the Dutch proposal, in 1957, when debate on the question of defining aggression was referred to the Sixth Committee of the General Assembly, two other states, Belgium and Venezuela, set out definitions of armed attack as employed in Article 51. Neither of these conceptions of self-defence was as detailed as the earlier Dutch proposal, but they were substantively the same. Thus, Belgium proposed:

> Any use of weapons or armed forces against another state, or against its territory, or any use of such forces which penetrated that territory without the permission of the government concerned, should be regarded as an armed attack within the meaning of Article 51 of the UN Charter [unless such action constituted an action in self-defence or a lawful use of force under Chapter VII].[31]

Whereas Venezuela used the following formulation:

> An armed attack within the meaning of Article 51 of the Charter of the United Nations is the consequence of direct or indirect use by a state, or group of states, of armed force against the territorial integrity or independence of any state, or group of states [unless such action constitutes an action in self-defence or a lawful use of force under Chapter VII].[32]

[27] UN Doc A/AC.77/SR.12, 3.

[28] *Ibid.*

[29] Indeed, at another point in the debate, the Netherlands representative explicitly referenced the *Caroline* formula: UN Doc A/AC.77/SR.13, 16. Having argued that the Dutch proposal was based essentially upon a 'gravity' conception of armed attack, Feinberg then correctly (though somewhat nonsensically, given his earlier conclusion) has argued that Röling's articulation of armed attack was in general based upon the *Caroline* incident: Feinberg (n 21) 60–63.

[30] UN Doc A/AC.77/SR.12, 5. The requirement for a proportional response was only implicit in the statements of the Netherlands.

[31] UN Doc A/C.6/SR.514, 30.

[32] UN Doc A/C.6/SR.517, 39.

Neither definition alludes to a required level of gravity. Indeed, unlike the Netherlands proposal, neither contains clear reference to the creation of a defensive necessity either. These definitions essentially identify an armed attack as a use of armed force.

It is unclear from the debates of the Special Committee on the Question of Defining Aggression or the Sixth Committee of the General Assembly whether the definitions set out by the Netherlands, Belgium or Venezuela were intended as statements of what the states concerned viewed the law to be at the time (declaratory *de lege lata*) or what they felt the law *should* be (aspirational *de lege ferenda*).[33] In either case, the proposals offer useful models for improving the contemporary law.[34] What is important is that the essential restrictive tool for lawful self-defence is the necessity of the response. When this is coupled with the requirement of proportionality, the 'armed attack as a grave use of force' criterion becomes unnecessary.

Having said this, what is suggested here is somewhat different from the Dutch proposal, in that it is not argued that 'armed attack' should be defined as *a use of force giving rise to a defensive necessity*. Instead, a clearer position would be for armed attack to be defined, simply, as a use of force. Therefore any use of force against a state would give rise to the right of self-defence. However, that right would still be subject to the customary international law principles of necessity and proportionality, and as such, not all uses of force would give rise to the lawful exercise of self-defence.

II. THE GENERAL SUITABILITY OF NECESSITY AND PROPORTIONALITY

The major doctrinal controversy regarding self-defence since the adoption of the UN Charter has involved the meaning of the phrase 'if an armed attack occurs' in Article 51.[35] This debate has polarised writers and yet has done little to clarify the law. This is because there is no guidance in Article

[33] Feinberg (n 21) 71–72.

[34] At the time, however, these proposals met with very little state support. See Feinberg (n 21) 67–69. Indeed, the general response that greeted the Dutch proposal meant that the proposal was never even set it out in a formal draft; the Netherlands made it clear that it would produce a formal written draft only if there was enough support to make this worthwhile: UN Doc A/AC.77/SR.12, 5. States refused to support the Dutch proposal for a number of reasons. See the various arguments raised by Czechoslovakia (UN Doc A/AC.77/SR.10, 7), China (UN Doc A/C.6/SR.517, 41), Uruguay (UN Doc A/C.6/SR.519, 46), Pakistan (UN Doc A/C.6/SR.530, 95) and Iraq (UN Doc A/AC.77/SR.14, 7). However, by far the most significant objection to the proposal was that, as has been noted, the Dutch proposal allowed for anticipatory self-defence. For more, see below, n 60.

[35] This debate is well known and is, eg, set out by Gray (n 3) 117–19; NM Feder, 'Reading the UN Charter Connotatively: Towards a New Definition of Armed Attack' (1987) 19 *New York University Journal of International Law and Politics* 395, 404; Y Melzer, *Concepts of Just War* (Leiden, AW Sijthoff, 1975) 18–20; and P Rowe, *Defence: The Legal Implications (Military Law and the Laws of War)* (London, Brassey's Defence, 1987) 100.

51 as to the content of the concept of 'armed attack' and only sporadic guidance in practice. The results of the ICJ's attempt in *Military and Paramilitary Activities in and against Nicaragua* (hereafter *Nicaragua*)[36] to define the criterion demonstrate the difficulties inherent in attempting to define the scope and content of the criterion.

In contrast, the criterion of necessity has no such controversy attached to it.[37] Admittedly, 'necessity' as a concept is far from being an easily definable one (as may be seen from chapter two).[38] However, there is more guidance from customary international law regarding 'necessity' than 'armed attack': practice has been more uniform and has occurred over a longer period. It is not here claimed that the abandonment of 'armed attack as a grave use of force' and a reliance on necessity would remove the definitional controversy over self-defence. Nevertheless, a doctrinal change of this kind would increase the clarity of the law governing self-defence, as the necessity criterion is better defined than that of an armed attack and, in the view of the present writer, is more suited to the regulation of self-defence.

The necessity criterion limits self-defence actions to extreme cases just like the 'armed attack as a grave use of force' criterion, and yet it is more logical in this context because it fits more comfortably within the conceptual understanding of self-defence as being about the right of a victim of an attack to defend itself. With a reliance on necessity, the focus is shifted from the gravity of the attack to the need of the victim state to defend itself. Of course, these two factors are likely to be linked. Indeed, it must be made clear that necessity and proportionality are criteria that must be tested *against* something: the basis for any application of these criteria must be by way of reference to an actual or imminent attack. However, this is not to say that that attack must in itself be particularly grave, only that when an initial attack is 'minor' in nature, it is less likely that a response will be necessary, and even if it is, any response must itself be 'minor' to fall within the boundaries of proportionality. Ultimately, it is argued here that if the crux of the matter is the defensive requirements of states, this—far better than the *type* of attack suffered—represents the theoretical basis of the right of self-defence.[39] Moreover, it reflects the reality of *justifiable* inter-state force.

[36] *Military and Paramilitary Activities in and against Nicaragua* (*Nicaragua v United States of America*) merits (1986) ICJ Reports 14.

[37] It has been pointed out that the lack of controversy surrounding both necessity and proportionality has allowed many states to avoid the doctrinal debates surrounding Art 51 and refer to a better defined legal system for evaluating claims of self-defence. See C Gray, 'The Use of Force and the International Legal Order' in MD Evans (ed), *International Law*, 2nd edn (Oxford, Oxford University Press, 2006) 589, 599.

[38] See ch 2, section IV.

[39] As Combacau states: 'If . . . self-defence cannot legally have any aim other than to repulse the assailant [a combination of last resort and proportional response to that defensive necessity], this must be considered as the *only* criterion for judging the lawfulness of

A useful example from state practice is the mercenary intervention in the Seychelles in 1981, which was apparently controlled and directed by the government of South Africa. This attack on the Seychelles involved a relatively small number of mercenary soldiers.[40] As such, it is contestable as to whether the attack would have met the gravity threshold for armed attack as set out by the ICJ. However, despite its small scale, this attack totally disrupted the infrastructure of the Seychelles.[41] It is therefore difficult to deny that the attack created a defensive necessity, something that is supported by the unanimous condonation the Seychelles received for its forcible response.[42]

So long as the defensive need is genuine and not illusory, it surely matters not how small the initial attack was. This is only true, of course, when the necessity criterion is coupled with that of proportionality, which effectively limits the response that may be taken to avoid escalation even in minor cases: in such instances a 'less grave use of force' can be responded to with a 'less grave' (that is to say, proportional) forcible response in self-defence. As we have seen, an analysis of state practice and *opinio juris* shows that it is possible to define the nature of the criteria of necessity and proportionality: there is demonstrable content to these requirements, and guidance may be provided as to how they should be applied in practice.[43] Yet equally, these criteria are flexible enough to adapt to the genuine complexities of the contemporary defensive needs of states. Moreover, a reliance on necessity and proportionality alone would alleviate a number of the difficulties associated with the concepts of 'armed attack' and 'countermeasures'. First and most importantly, as we have already noted in this section, the redefinition of 'armed attack' to mean 'use of force' would allow states facing 'minor' attacks that create a defensive necessity to respond with force, bridging the gap between unlawful uses of force and lawful responses in self-defence. There are, however, additional benefits to this approach.

III. IMPLICATIONS FOR THE 'ACCUMULATION OF EVENTS' PROBLEM

The confusion over whether an accumulation of events is acceptable for reaching the required armed attack standard (and how to calculate this) would, it is here argued, be removed if armed attack were to be redefined

measures which claim to be performed in self-defence.' J Combacau, 'The Exception of Self-Defence in UN Practice' in A Cassese (ed), *The Current Legal Regulation of the Use of Force* (Dordrecht, Martinus Nijhoff, 1986) 9, 25.

[40] UN Doc S/PV.2314, 4–5.

[41] UN Doc S/14905/Rev.1 (1st Report) esp 44.

[42] See generally UN Docs S/PV.2314, S/PV.2359, S/PV.2361, S/PV.2365 and S/PV.2367.

[43] See ch 2 generally.

in this way. However, repeated and connected attacks could still be factored into the determinations of necessity and proportionality.[44] States that face sporadic attacks would not therefore be prejudiced in terms of the responses that could be taken, as long as these are necessary and proportional to the overall need to respond to the cumulative attack.

If the controversy over whether a number of smaller attacks could constitute an armed attack cumulatively were removed (because the requirement that a grave use of force is needed to trigger self-defence were itself removed) this would clearly have important implications for states that face attacks from modern terrorist groups. Such attacks tend to be comparatively small-scale in themselves but often form part of a pattern of forcible action intended to have a large cumulative effect.[45] Under the proposed definition of armed attack, a state facing terrorist attacks of this nature would be entitled to respond with force, provided that the cumulative attacks against it create a genuine defensive necessity and that the response taken is proportional to the attacks being suffered.

IV. IMPLICATIONS FOR THE 'LEVEL OF STATE INVOLVEMENT' PROBLEM

The abandonment of 'armed attack as a grave use of force' and an increased reliance on the criteria of necessity and proportionality would also clarify and improve the law with regard to forcible responses taken extraterritorially against non-state actors (where the 'host' state has little or no control over the actors in question). Again, this is particularly important in the context of responses to terrorist activity. It will be recalled that under the ICJ's armed attack formulation, an (undefined) level of state collaboration is required before a genuine armed attack can be said to have occurred.[46] As noted in chapter one, it may be asked: what 'level' of state involvement is (or should) be required before a response may be taken? The requirement that a state must have a degree of involvement in an attack before self-defence may be seen as lawful has the potential to leave a state that has suffered a terrorist perpetrated use of force (even one grave enough to constitute an armed attack under the 'armed attack as a grave use of force' criterion) with no recourse to defend itself.[47]

In assessing the lawfulness of an avowed self-defence action based upon criteria of necessity and proportionality—and not 'armed attack as a grave use of force'—the issue in each case would not be an illusory standard of

[44] Gazzini (n 11) 143–44 and 192.

[45] CS Gray, 'Combating Terrorism' (1993) 23 *Parameters: US Army War College Quarterly* 17, 23.

[46] See ch 1, section V.

[47] *Ibid.*

culpability or collaboration, but rather would concord more to the practical requirements of defence. There would be no absolute criterion of state culpability, or even responsibility. This would correspond to the Dutch proposal of 1956, which took the view that in certain circumstances an attack giving rise to a necessity of self-defence can originate from a non-state actor.[48]

More importantly, this would correspond to growing trends in contemporary state practice.[49] The most obvious example to support this is the 2001 intervention in Afghanistan, Operation Enduring Freedom. As we have already seen, this intervention was in general viewed by states as a lawful action in self-defence.[50] This was irrespective of the fact that the action was taken against a state (Afghanistan) in response to an attack (which had abated) perpetrated by a non-state terrorist group (al Qaeda), which could hardly be described as being under the 'effective control' of that state.[51]

Similarly, Israel claimed a right of self-defence in 2006 against Hezbollah,[52] a non-state actor, though the response taken by Israel was also against the state of Lebanon, which again could not be said to control the terrorist group. Admittedly, the Israeli intervention was in general viewed as being unlawful, but this was on the basis that it was a disproportional response[53] and not because there was an insufficient link between Lebanon and Hezbollah. It would seem that it was accepted in principle that such a response, had it been proportionate, may have been legally acceptable. These two examples are probably not enough in themselves to constitute a change in customary international law with regard to extraterritorial responses to non-state orchestrated attacks, but they certainly indicate the beginning of a paradigm shift in that direction.[54]

[48] This notion was also supported by Iraq and China. See UN Doc A/3574, 25. In contrast, though, the Venezuelan proposal of 1957 *did* articulate a requirement that the author of the attack being responded to was a state: UN Doc A/C.6/SR.517, 39.

[49] For academic support of this view, see ch 1, n 96. Notably, Murphy goes on to argue the *travaux préparatoires* of the UN Charter also supports this position. See SD Murphy, 'Self-Defence and the *Israeli Wall* Advisory Opinion: An *Ipse Dixit* from the ICJ?' (2005) 99 *American Journal of International Law* 62, 67–70.

[50] See ch 2, n 108.

[51] Having said this, the United States was careful in presenting its legal claims in 2001 to argue that the Taliban was at least in some manner linked to al Qaeda, to the extent that it proved unwilling to attempt to stop the activities of that group within its territory: UN Doc S/2001/946. Similarly, in 2006 Israel pointed out that whilst Lebanon was not controlling Hezbollah, it was allowing that group to use its territory when it could take steps to stop this: UN Doc S/PV.5488. This suggests that states still believe that some degree of complicity on the part of a 'host' state may still be required.

[52] UN Doc S/2006/515.

[53] See ch 2, n 155.

[54] M Byers, 'Terrorism, the Use of Force and International Law After 11 September' (2002) 51 *International and Comparative Law Quarterly* 401, 407–9, although this appears to be contrary to what he states elsewhere. See M Byers, 'Geopolitical Change and International Law' in D Armstrong, T Farrell and B Maiguashca (eds), *Force and Legitimacy in World Politics*

It has been argued that military intervention against non-state actors 'residing' in another state should be viewed as being lawful when the 'host' state is genuinely unwilling or unable to take steps to prevent the group or groups operating upon their territory from using force against the victim state.[55] This would amount to a widening of the parameters of lawful responses in self-defence beyond the ICJ's collaboration requirement. However, in cases in which the activity of non-state actors creates a defensive necessity, the victim state has little choice.[56] Moreover, application of the necessity criterion would temper the widening of self-defence from the ICJ's conception by still attempting to find a balance between the essential need for defence and the inviolability of a state's territorial sovereignty: the 'innocent' host state must be allowed to deal with the situation itself, if this is at all possible. Indeed, responses taken when the 'host' state is not at 'fault' for the attack would need to meet high standards before they could be seen as necessary or proportional. In other words:

> [T]he condition of necessity . . . requires that, before resorting to self-defence, a state must satisfy itself that the state in which the non-state actor is located is unwilling or unable to take steps necessary to remove the threat caused by the non-state actor. . . [T]he necessity of defending cannot be established if a possibility remains that another state could terminate the threat. . . [U]nder such a position, the focus is less on whether a prior armed attack can be imputed to a state, than on whether that state is capable of preventing further attacks and is willing to do so.[57]

Thus, for a response to be a *last resort* in this context, the victim state *must* have explored all non-forcible methods of cooperation and coordination with the 'host' state to stop the attackers.

Equally, application of the proportionality requirement would allow for a more nuanced, context-specific response to terrorist attacks. In instances when the 'host' state is not in any way at 'fault' (meaning that it is willing but unable to stop attacks from emanating from their territory) it would seem logical that the proportionality requirement would place a particularly heavy burden upon the responding state. Not only must there be a

(Cambridge, Cambridge University Press, 2005) 51, 58, where he holds that Operation Enduring Freedom has in fact altered the law in this respect.

[55] Murphy (n 49) 63–67.

[56] KN Trapp, 'Back to Basics: Necessity, Proportionality and the Right of Self-Defence Against Non-state Terrorist Actors' (2007) 56 *International and Comparative Law Quarterly* 141, 147; and JA Green, 'Legality of Attacks Inside Pakistan: US Needs to First Satisfy Itself that Pakistan is Unable to Suppress the Militants' (2008) *Pakistan Institute for Peace Studies*, san-pips.com/PIPS-SAN-Files/SAN-Pakistan/SAN-PAK-Article68/San-Pak-Main-A68-D.asp.

[57] Murphy (n 49) 66. It should be noted that the author has taken this quote somewhat out of context in that was made with specific reference to the *Israeli Wall* opinion and was intended as a possible interpretation of parts of that opinion, not, as it is employed here, as a proposal for improving the state of the law governing self-defence. See also Trapp (*ibid*) esp 142, 145–47 and 155–56.

balance between the necessity of a response and the implications of using force against an attacking state (the usual calculation), but there must be a balance between the necessity of the response and the implications of using force *against a state that is not even responsible for the attack*. As such, that 'necessity' must be extremely high for an action to be found to be proportional. In such a case, the only way an action could possibly meet the proportionality criterion would be for any action to involve only attacks on known terrorist bases or other sources of the terrorist attack.[58] Any response at all against the population or infrastructure of an innocent 'host' state would mean the response would not meet the requirement of proportionality.[59]

In contrast, when a military response could be said to be necessary because the state is able but unwilling to act, then what is required by the proportionality criterion in terms of a response against the territory of the 'host' state is likely to be less onerous, particularly if the state in question is in direct control of the terrorist group. In other words, what will be proportional to the goal of meeting the defensive necessity created by terrorist attacks is directly linked to the degree of support for such attacks from the state in which the group is based.

Ultimately, without the confusion of the 'armed attack as a grave use of force' criterion, responses taken extraterritorially against terrorist groups or other non-state actors would not be per se unlawful, even when the 'host' state is not legally responsible or otherwise culpable for the attacks. Having said this, in situations involving non-state actors, the lower the level of 'host' state involvement in the actions of the terrorist group, the greater would be the burden on the responding state to ensure that a response is limited and directed in a proportional manner. The reinterpretation of armed attack therefore provides a clearer and more practical (but not overly permissive) framework for dealing with the problem of terrorist attacks.

V. PRE-EMPTING THE ISSUE OF PREVENTATIVE SELF-DEFENCE

It is important here to pre-empt, as it were, a potential criticism that may be levelled at the proposal outlined in this chapter. One of the primary reasons why states rejected the broadly equivalent Dutch Proposal of 1956 was the fact that they perceived the proposal to be an endorsement of preventative self-defence.[60] As we have seen, the Dutch proposal explicitly

[58] N Shah, 'Self-Defence, Anticipatory Self-Defence and Pre-emption: International Law's Response to Terrorism' (2007) 12 *Journal of Conflict and Security Law* 95, 110.

[59] Antonopoulos (n 6) 167.

[60] This concern was raised repeatedly by the Soviet Union (UN Docs A/AC.77/SR.3, 10; A/AC.77/SR.10, 6; and A/C.6/SR.525, 76) and various other Eastern block states, such as

allowed for anticipatory self-defence,[61] and the vast majority of states in 1956 were unwilling to accept anticipatory self-defence as being lawful.

This concern may well be raised with regard to what is proposed here. The argument would presumably run thus: a preventative action may be seen to be necessary and proportional (certainly if the threat can be seen to be imminent). This is evidenced by the facts of the *Caroline* itself. Therefore, a reliance on criteria of necessity and proportionality and the abandonment of 'armed attack as a grave use of force' are together a green light for anticipatory self-defence. Thus, as a criterion for restricting inter-state force in self-defence, the armed attack requirement is preferable to a *Caroline*-based restriction because it restricts self-defence as a preventative measure.[62]

However, it is extremely important to note that, unlike the Dutch proposal, it is not necessarily the case that the proposal herein endorses any form of preventative self-defence. It will be recalled that a position is not taken herein on the controversial debate over the lawfulness of self-defence in response to the threat of force,[63] and the proposed redefinition of armed attack advanced here does not affect the question of preventative self-defence at all. The issue of whether an armed attack (meaning a use of force) must have occurred before a military response can be taken would remain.

As was argued in chapter two, reliance upon the criteria of necessity and proportionality would mean, as customary international law currently stands, that a response to a threat that cannot be shown to be imminent would certainly constitute an unlawful action.[64] Thus, what has been herein termed anticipatory self-defence (self-defence against a demonstrably imminent threat) could conceivably be lawful, though this would remain controversial. The Dutch proposal of 1956 was explicit on the issue of anticipatory self-defence; this work leaves the question open. Thus, the reform proposed here would not widen the scope of self-defence with regard to threats. It will be recalled that what is proposed is not the abandonment of Article 51: thus ink could continue to be spilt in the debate over the meaning of 'if . . . occurs'. What is important is that the phrase from Article 51 should be read as: 'if an armed attack [meaning *any* use of force] occurs'.

Czechoslovakia (UN Doc A/AC.77/SR.6, 5), Poland (UN Doc A/AC.77/SR.7, 3) and the Belorussian SSR (UN Doc A/C.6/SR.528, 88). Yet it was also a concern of the United States (UN Docs A/AC.77/SR.5, 6; and A/AC.77/SR.13, 4–5) and to a degree, China (UN Doc A/AC.77/SR.3, 5).

[61] Above, n 23 and accompanying text.

[62] See, eg, I Brownlie, *International Law and the Use of Force by States* (Oxford, Oxford University Press, 1963) 275–78.

[63] See ch 1, section II-B.

[64] See ch 2, section VI-A.

VI. ADDITIONAL SUPPORT FOR A DIFFERENT INTERPRETATION OF ARMED ATTACK

Significantly, the reinterpretation of armed attack advocated here is not merely to be found in a number of forgotten proposals from the 1950s; it has re-emerged more recently. For example, whilst principle 'B' of the Chatham House Principles on the Use of Force by States in Self-Defence of 2005[65] uncontroversially holds that an armed attack is required for lawful self-defence,[66] it is then argued:

> An armed attack means *any use of armed force*, and does not need to cross some threshold of intensity. Any requirement that a use of force must attain a certain gravity and that frontier incidents, for example, are excluded is relevant only in so far as the minor nature of an attack is prima facie evidence of absence of intention to attack or honest mistake. It may also be relevant to issues of necessity and proportionality (emphasis added).[67]

This may go slightly too far at the current time, given the practice of states that was noted in chapter three.[68] A more conservative claim would be: 'An armed attack *should mean* any use of armed force'. From our assessment of state practice and accompanying *opinio juris*, it would seem that, so far as a meaning can be ascertained for armed attack in customary international law, this is more closely related to the Court's definition than to the above Chatham House formula. As such, the Chatham House position, along with the 1956 Dutch proposal, should be seen as aspirational.

The same may be said of the position taken by Tarcisio Gazzini, who argues that the armed attack criterion as defined by the ICJ is undesirable, given the gap it creates between Articles 2(4) and 51 (amongst other reasons).[69] He then goes on to conclude that state practice indicates that an 'armed attack' constitutes a use of force *simpliciter*, yet he offers little evidence to support this.[70] In other words, Gazzini argues that an 'armed

[65] 'The Chatham House Principles of International Law on the Use of Force by States in Self-Defence'(2006) 55 *International and Comparative Law Quarterly* 963 (originally published on the internet: Chatham House International Law Programme, *Principles of International Law on the Use of Force by States in Self-Defence*, Royal Institute of International Affairs, October 2005, ILP WP 05/01, http://www.chathamhouse.org.uk/files/3278_ilpforce.doc). This document was prepared following the consultation of a number of eminent international legal scholars. The fact that thirteen notable scholars took part in the preparation of the document inevitably instils in it a weight of authority beyond that associated with the position taken by a single author. Having said this, the document obviously possesses no legally constituting value in itself. Moreover, it should be treated with care, as the final document did not necessarily represent the views of all of the jurisconsults who took part in the study (as was admitted in the document itself at 964).

[66] *Ibid*, 965.

[67] *Ibid*, 966.

[68] See ch 3, section I.

[69] Gazzini (n 11) esp 138–39.

[70] *Ibid*.

attack as a grave use of force' criterion would be problematical *if it existed*, but the *actual* problem is that the ICJ and numerous writers have identified and developed what is in practice a nonexistent criterion.[71] It is argued here that this again confuses the *desirable* status of the law governing self-defence with the actual position. The 'armed attack as a grave use of force' criterion is, in the view of the present writer, undesirable and confusing. As such, given the erratic nature of the state practice and *opinio juris* concerning it, the argument that the criterion has little basis in international law is understandable. Nonetheless, there is a weight of practice to support the Court's concept of a 'grave' use of force criterion: as such, to some degree, the 'armed attack as a grave use of force' requirement should be seen as an aspect of contemporary customary international law.

VII. CONCLUSION

It has been argued in this chapter that reform of the notion of armed attack and reliance upon the criteria of necessity and proportionality in regulating self-defence would greatly improve the state of the law. The view is taken that the 'armed attack as a grave use of force' criterion as set out by the ICJ is unhelpful. In response to this, a proposal has been advanced: the phrase 'armed attack' as present in Article 51 should be redefined to mean 'use of force'. This reinterpretation would have huge benefits in terms of the clarity and practical application of the law governing self-defence. Moreover, this would correspond to the fact that the criteria of necessity and proportionality remain the most important and frequent legal criteria employed by states.

However, the question remains as to how such an alteration of the current law in self-defence could be achieved in practice. It goes beyond the scope of a book focused upon the ICJ and self-defence to delve into practical means of reforming self-defence. The manner in which the law might be reformed to redefine the concept of an armed attack is something that must be examined elsewhere. However, the negative responses of states to the equivalent proposals of the 1950s[72] suggests that, as a practical matter, the proposed reforms would be difficult to implement.

It is interesting that Belgium recognised this fact in 1957 when advancing its own proposal for a definition of armed attack in the Sixth Committee of the General Assembly.[73] Unlike either the Netherlands or Venezuela, Belgium argued that if there was no agreement between states on the issue, the best course of action would be *to refer the matter to the ICJ*

[71] Gazzini (n 11) esp, 3–4.
[72] Above, n 15.
[73] UN Doc A/C.6/SR.514, 29.

for an advisory opinion.[74] Presumably the rationale for this suggestion was that the Court could provide an authoritative conception of armed attack by way of an advisory opinion, which would then essentially amount to a soft law instrument on the issue.

Given the fact that reform by states in this area seems unlikely, is it desirable today that we follow this course and rely on the ICJ to help clarify and reform the law governing self-defence? Based upon the analysis throughout this work so far, it would seem that ICJ has proven itself to be unsuited to the goal of regulating, clarifying and developing self-defence.[75] The reasons for this stem in part from the nature of the law that it has attempted to apply in the cases before it. However, the Court is also restricted by its own nature and the nature of the UN system. Such restrictions have gravely limited the Court in its dealings with self-defence and help to explain its problematic contribution to the development of the law. They also further underscore the undesirability of utilising the Court as a means of clarifying self-defence, by way of an advisory opinion or otherwise. It is to these additional problems that we now turn.

[74] *Ibid.*

[75] This was certainly the position taken by Christopher Greenwood at a lecture delivered at University College London, 10 November 2004.

5

The ICJ: Roles and Restrictions

IN CHAPTER THREE, problematic aspects of the law governing self-defence were discussed in order to elucidate upon the jurisprudence of the ICJ that emerged in chapters one and two. To complement that analysis, this chapter examines the problematic aspects, or potentially problematic aspects, of the Court's interaction with the law, rather than the law itself. Thus, the focus is upon the restrictions the Court has faced with regard to self-defence. Indeed, given such restrictions, various arguments have been raised over whether the ICJ is a suitable institution to deal with issues governing the use of force at all, and these claims will be examined in due course.

There exist numerous restraints upon the Court, jurisdictional and otherwise, that relate to its fundamental nature as a consent-based dispute settlement body. These restraints make any attempt of the Court to provide a clear and holistic appraisal of the law that will be useful in future instances extremely difficult. It is apparent that in general this is not caused by the practices and procedures of the Court or its members but rather in the very nature of its composition.[1] The ICJ is often hamstrung by its own institutional history as an organ created for the settlement of disputes between states, the lawmakers of the international system. Indeed, it is limited by the very nature of international law: 'A court epitomizes the *social* reality of the society of which it is an institution.'[2] These inherent problems of composition, coupled with the Court's attempts to push beyond such limitations, will be examined here to see how they have contributed to the substantive jurisprudential picture of the law of self-defence as provided by the Court.

It is worth noting here that a number of the points made in this chapter apply to the ICJ in general. For example, many of the jurisdictional issues discussed are not necessarily restricted to disputes involving claims of self-defence. However, as will be seen, in some instances these problems are more pronounced in cases involving the use of force, whilst others are

[1] GG Fitzmaurice, 'Enlargement of the Contentious Jurisdiction of the Court' in L Gross (ed), *The Future of the International Court of Justice, Vol II* (New York, Oceana, 1976) 461, 462.

[2] P Allott, 'The ICJ and the Voice of Justice' in V Lowe and M Fitzmaurice (eds), *Fifty Years of the International Court of Justice: Essays in Honour of Sir Robert Jennings* (Cambridge, Cambridge University Press, 1996) 17, quoted at 27; but on this point, see 26–36.

specific to such disputes. Similarly, certain issues may relate not simply to the ICJ or to international adjudication but to courts and adjudication more generally. In any event, the wider implications of the issues raised are for the most part not examined here, for the obvious reason that the focus of this work is on the ICJ and the international law regarding self-defence.

I. NON-APPEARANCE

A. Non-appearance In *Nicaragua*

The first issue to be noted at this juncture is the fact that in the case of *Military and Paramilitary Activities in and against Nicaragua* (hereafter *Nicaragua*),[3] the respondent party, the United States, was not present at the merits phase. This is not the place to discuss in general terms the complicated issue of state non-appearance before the ICJ.[4] However, given the fact that the *Nicaragua* case still represents the Court's most comprehensive decision on self-defence, the impact of the non-appearance of the United States in terms of its effect upon the quality of that specific decision (and thus the direct substantive impact upon this area of law) must briefly be discussed.

For the most part, academic appraisal of the non-appearance issue has focused upon the procedural disadvantages of such action upon the non-appearing state.[5] However, non-appearance is also highly problematic for the Court.[6] Article 53 of the Court's Statute provides:

1. Whenever one of the parties does not appear before the Court, or fails to defend its case, the other party may call upon the Court to decide in favour of its claim.
2. The Court must, before doing so, satisfy itself, not only that it has jurisdiction in accordance with Articles 36 and 37, but also that the claim must be well founded in fact and law.

[3] *Military and Paramilitary Activities in and against Nicaragua* (*Nicaragua v United States of America*) merits (1986) ICJ Reports 14.

[4] On this general problem, see JB Elkind, *Non-appearance Before the International Court of Justice: Functional and Comparative Analysis* (Dordrecht, Martinus Nijhoff, 1984) esp 31–78 and 171–206; TO Elias, *The International Court of Justice and Some Contemporary Problems* (The Hague, Martinus Nijhoff, 1983) 33–66; H Thirlway, *Non-appearance Before the International Court of Justice* (Cambridge, Cambridge University Press, 1985); and JI Charney, 'Disputes Implicating the Institutional Credibility of the Court: Problems of Non-appearance, Non-participation and Non-performance' in LF Damrosch (ed), *The International Court of Justice at a Crossroads* (New York, Transnational, 1987) 288.

[5] See, eg, PJIM De Waart, 'Non-appearance Does Not Make Sense' in A Bloed and P Van Dijk (eds), *Forty Years International Court of Justice: Jurisdiction, Equity and Equality* (Utrecht, Europa Institute, 1988) 73; and Elkind (*ibid*) esp 171.

[6] Both in terms of its ability to decide the specific case at hand and in terms of its general credibility and stature. The former is what will be discussed here, in relation to the *Nicaragua* case. On the latter, see Charney (n 4) esp 302–4.

The ICJ was well aware of the non-appearance issue in the *Nicaragua* case, explicitly acknowledging the problem.[7] Crucially, the Court made every effort to ensure that it fulfilled its obligations under Article 53.[8] Without criticising the Court's efforts in this regard,[9] it must be acknowledged that the fact that the United States abandoned the process inevitably made it more difficult for the Court to produce a clear legal judgment on the facts. For example, it may be asked how the ICJ can be expected to evaluate arguments *that have not even been made* by a non-appearing state.[10] After all, as the Court itself noted in *Nicaragua*, it does not possess 'authority to ascribe to states legal views which they do not themselves advance'.[11]

Of course, the United States *was* present in *Nicaragua*, albeit only for the early stages of the case. As such, the Court was able to rely on substantive arguments made by the United States at the jurisdictional phase. Based upon this, it was noted in the merits decision that the United States had formally relied upon a justification of collective self-defence before the Court, despite the fact that this claim was made in the US counter-memorial on questions of jurisdiction and admissibility.[12] The Court therefore had at least *some* legal argumentation concerning the issue of self-defence from the United States with which to work, and it understandably saw the fact that claims were made at the jurisdictional phase as preferable to a position where there existed no argumentation at all.[13] Moreover, there was nothing to suggest that the United States would have altered its substantive legal case at the merits phase had it chosen to appear.

However, the substantive legal arguments previously advanced by the United States were, at the time when they were made, of a distinctly secondary nature. As one might expect, the focus of such claims was on jurisdictional issues. The claims made that were relevant to the ultimate merits decision were thus cursory and undeveloped: for example, the fundamental justification of the United States that it was acting in collective self-defence of El Salvador, Honduras and Costa Rica was primarily

[7] *Nicaragua* merits (n 3) para 27.

[8] *Ibid*, esp paras 26–31.

[9] Unlike Judge Schwebel, who indicated that he felt that in finding that the US claim of collective self-defence could not be maintained, the Court had not met its obligations under Art 53. *Nicaragua* merits (n 3) dissenting opinion of Judge Schwebel, paras 114–27. In contrast, Falk takes a position that goes too far in the other direction, holding that the non-appearance of the United States essentially had no effect on the judgment. RA Falk, 'The World Court's Achievement' (1987) 81 *American Journal of International Law* 106, 107.

[10] This question is adapted from one posed by K Highet, 'You Can Run but You Can't Hide: Reflections on the US Position in the *Nicaragua* Case' (1986–87) 27 *Virginia Journal of International Law* 551, 555–56.

[11] *Nicaragua* merits (n 3) para 207.

[12] *Ibid*, inter alia, para 24.

[13] See *ibid*, paras 28 and 29.

presented to the Court in just a few paragraphs of its counter-memorial on jurisdiction, without scope for detailed examination of the substance of such a legal claim.[14] As such, the result of the US decision to remove itself from proceedings in the *Nicaragua* case was that the judgment that emerged was reached based upon legal arguments that were underdeveloped substantively (at least with regard to one of the parties). This fact must inevitably have inhibited the Court's ability to reason the decision thoroughly.[15]

At one point in the *Nicaragua* merits decision, the Court referred to collective self-defence as amounting to 'the *principal justification* announced by the United States for its conduct' (emphasis added).[16] Elsewhere, however, it stated that to 'justify certain activities involving the use of force, the United States *relied solely* on the exercise of its right of collective self-defence' (emphasis added).[17] This amounts to yet another entry on the list of confused aspects of the ICJ's self-defence jurisprudence.[18] Having said this, one could conclude that this apparent inconsistency (amongst others) was in part due to the absence of detailed legal argumentation on the part of the United States. Indeed, this factor may go some way towards explaining some of the confusion in *Nicaragua*, for the very reason that the ICJ could not know for sure what the exact legal claims of the United States actually were.

The failure of the United States to appear on the merits did not only mean that the ICJ had to decide the case based upon comparatively limited legal argumentation, it also had implications for the factual aspects of the dispute. Non-appearance had the effect of limiting the ICJ's access to evidence and obviously meant that the presentation of any evidence that the Court *did* have available to it was somewhat one-sided.[19] Moreover, conversely, due to the wording of Article 53 and the political implications of the US withdrawal, there existed the danger that the Court could overcompensate for the absence of the United States. There is little to suggest

[14] See *Nicaragua* counter-memorial of the United States (1984) ICJ Pleadings, Part II, 57–61. This claim was made elsewhere by the United States, though in a similarly cursory manner. See, eg, 'Statement on the US Withdrawal from the Proceedings Initiated by Nicaragua in the International Court of Justice', US Department of State Statement, 18 January 1985, reproduced in (1985) *International Legal Materials* 246, 246. Judge Schwebel argued in his dissenting opinion that the United States submitted extensive pleadings at the jurisdictional phase that had a bearing upon the merits. However, the examples he cites to support this are in general instances of the submission of factual evidence, not legal claims. See *Nicaragua* merits (n 3) dissenting opinion of Judge Schwebel, para 120.

[15] As the Court noted, whilst it is not bound to confine its consideration to 'formal' material submitted to it by the parties, the lack of such material inevitably places the Court at a disadvantage. *Nicaragua* merits (n 3) para 10.

[16] *Ibid*, para 131.

[17] *Ibid*, para 201.

[18] This apparent inconsistency was noted by D Kritsiotis, 'Arguments of Mass Confusion' (2004) 15 *European Journal of International Law* 233, 236.

[19] It has been argued on this basis that 'The United States did not in any meaningful way controvert or deny most of the factual charges.' Highet (n 10) 555.

that this was the case: the Court explicitly noted this risk and indicated that a non-appearing party 'cannot be permitted to profit from its absence'.[20] The ultimate finding of the Court that the United States had breached its international obligations in relation to the use of force and the principle of non-intervention would certainly indicate that the United States did not 'profit' in this way. Nonetheless, this concern must have acted as a further restriction upon the Court's ability to decide the case.

Whilst such problems associated with non-appearance are not unique to *Nicaragua*, in this context they are placed in perspective when it is recalled just how important that case has been in shaping academic and, to a degree, state opinion of the law on self-defence. The fact that a decision many view as the benchmark for self-defence was decided with the respondent party wholly absent from the merits phase is concerning. The non-appearance of the United States surely must be viewed as a factor contributing to the confused quality of much of the *Nicaragua* decision, as it inevitably made deciding that case far more difficult for the Court than it otherwise would have been, particularly as the Court had to walk a political tightrope in trying to ensure—so far as possible—that neither party benefited from the absence of the United States.

B. Non-appearance in Use of Force Disputes Generally

An additional point relevant to our discussion is that it is possible to argue that the US decision to withdraw in *Nicaragua* was part of a wider pattern of state practice in the context of forcible disputes. In cases involving the use of force, given their contentious and fundamental nature, state non-appearance or withdrawal is perhaps more likely than in other cases before the Court. There have been a number of ICJ cases in which states have either withdrawn from the proceedings at some stage or failed to appear at all.[21] These cases relate to a range of disputes. It is perhaps notable, however, that in addition to *Nicaragua*, *Corfu Channel* (*United Kingdom v Albania*) (hereafter *Corfu Channel*)[22] and *United States Diplomatic and Consular Staff in*

[20] *Nicaragua* merits (n 3) para 31.

[21] Charney (n 4) esp 293–99 and 310–19. See *Corfu Channel* (*United Kingdom v Albania*) merits (1949) ICJ Reports 4; *Anglo–Iranian Oil Co Case* (*United Kingdom v Iran*) preliminary objection (1952) ICJ Reports 93; *Nottebohm* (*Liechtenstein v Guatemala*) merits (1955) ICJ Reports 4; *Case Concerning Trial of Pakistani Prisoners of War* (*Pakistan v India*) order (1973) ICJ Reports 347; *Fisheries Jurisdiction Case* (*United Kingdom v Iceland*) merits (1974) ICJ Reports 3; *Fisheries Jurisdiction Case* (*Federal Republic of Germany v Iceland*) merits (1974) ICJ Reports 175; *Nuclear Tests Case* (*Australia v France*) questions of jurisdiction and admissibility (1974) ICJ Reports 253; *Nuclear Tests Case* (*New Zealand v France*) questions of jurisdiction and admissibility (1974) ICJ Reports 457; *Aegean Sea Continental Shelf Case* (*Greece v Turkey*) jurisdiction of the court (1978) ICJ Reports 3; *United States Diplomatic and Consular Staff in Tehran* (*United States v Iran*) merits (1980) ICJ Reports 3; and *Nicaragua* merits (n 3).

[22] *Corfu Channel* merits (*ibid*).

Tehran (*United States v* Iran) (hereafter *Iranian Hostages*),[23] both of which touched upon use of force issues, are amongst them.

As we will see, states may view fundamental issues concerning the use of force as solely 'political' and thus exclusively within their decision-making competence.[24] Whether this is the case or not, when the vital interests or survival of states are at stake, it would appear that they are less likely to be willing to subject themselves to judicial examination of their actions, even if jurisdiction has been established by the Court. Therefore, the issue of non-appearance in this context may not merely be problematic in regard to its impact upon the quality of the *Nicaragua* decision but also may be a recurrent problem in future cases involving the use of force.

II. THE UNDERLYING ROLES OF THE ICJ

A major theme underpinning the discussion in this chapter is the role (or more accurately, the *roles*) of the ICJ within the UN system and the potential tensions that exist between two related but distinct roles that the Court performs. It is important to note that the term 'roles of the Court' is not employed here in reference to that institution's functions as provided for by its statute. These formal functions are: 1) the contentious jurisdiction of the Court (aimed at the settlement of international disputes between states); 2) the Court's incidental jurisdiction (allowing it to prescribe interim measures of protection); and 3) the advisory competence of the Court (under which the ICJ can render an opinion on an issue of international law at the request of competent bodies).[25] Broadly linked to but distinct from these functions are what are here termed the *roles* of the Court. By this it is meant that underpinning the functions of the ICJ are the more generic conceptual roles of the Court within the UN system: 1) the settlement of international disputes; and 2) the development of international law. In evaluating the 'success' of the Court's work regarding self-defence (or indeed any other area of international law) one must ascertain what may be expected from the ICJ as an institution.

A. The Settlement of Disputes through the Application of Existing Law

In an advisory opinion of 1954, the ICJ defined the role of a judicial organ thus: 'considering the arguments of the parties, appraising the evidence

[23] *Iranian Hostages* merits (n 21).
[24] See below, section IV.
[25] On these functions of the ICJ, see H Thirlway, 'The International Court of Justice' in MD Evans (ed), *International Law*, 2nd edn (Oxford, Oxford University Press, 2006) 561; JG Merrills, *International Dispute Settlement*, 4th edn (Cambridge, Cambridge University Press, 2005) 127–47; and A Cassese, *International Law*, 2nd edn (Oxford, Oxford University Press, 2005) 322.

produced by them, establishing the facts and *declaring the law* applicable to them' (emphasis added).[26] This can be applied to the ICJ itself without straying into controversy. The ICJ, like its predecessor, the Permanent Court of International Justice (PCIJ), was created for the primary purpose of settling individual international disputes through the application of existing international law to the facts of the case before it.[27] Looked at from this perspective, in terms of the Court's interaction with international law, its role is essentially declaratory: the Court identifies and then applies.

This is supported when one turns to the Statute of the Court, which clearly holds, 'The Court, whose function is to decide in accordance with international law such disputes as are submitted to it, shall apply [existing international law from various sources].'[28] Further, the decisions of the Court apply only to the parties before it[29] and are binding only with respect to the dispute considered.[30] Similarly, the ICJ can examine only law relevant to the submissions of the parties in the dispute before it[31] and has no formal system of precedent, or *stare decisis*, regarding its own decisions or those of other international courts and tribunals.[32] All of these factors indicate a court designed to act as a dispute settlement mechanism and not to contribute to the development of wider international law:

> The task, or rather the function, of the Court is to *ius dicere*: 'to say the law'. The Court is nothing but an instrument created by states in order to provide the most exact and impartial determination of existing international law.[33]

[26] *Effects of Awards of Compensation Made by the United Nations Administrative Tribunal* advisory opinion (1954) ICJ Reports 47, 56.

[27] As the delegation of Venezuela stated at the San Francisco conference of 1945, the role of the new Court would be to settle 'legal controversies' between individual state parties. *Documents of the United Nations Conference on International Organisation, San Francisco, 1945*, 'Volume III: Dumbarton Oaks Proposals: Comments and Proposal Amendments' (London, United Nations Information Organisations, 1945) Doc 2 G/7(d) (1) 205–06.

[28] Statute of the International Court of Justice, Art 38(1).

[29] *Ibid*, Art 59.

[30] *Ibid.*

[31] This is the '*non ultra petita* rule'. See ch 1, n 4.

[32] Having said this, the Court does in general try to be *consistent* with earlier decisions. See M Shahabuddeen, *Precedent in the World Court* (Cambridge, Grotius/Cambridge University Press, 1997) esp 23–31 and 97–109; B Kelly, 'The International Court of Justice: Its Role in a New World Legal Order' (1992) 3 *Touro Journal of Transnational Law* 223, 226; G Schwarzenberger, *International Law as Applied by International Courts and Tribunals, Vol I*, 3rd edn (London, Stevens & Sons, 1957) 31; D Terris, CPR Romano and L Swigart, *The International Judge: An Introduction to the Men and Women who Decide the World's Cases* (Oxford, Oxford University Press, 2007) 118; and I Brownlie, *Principles of Public International Law*, 6th edn (Oxford, Oxford University Press, 2003) 21–22.

[33] G Palmisano, 'Determining the Law on the Use of Force: the ICJ and Customary Rules on the Use of Force' in E Cannizzaro and P Palchetti (eds), *Customary International Law on the Use of Force: A Methodological Approach* (Leiden, Martinus Nijhoff, 2005) 197, 208. See also TD Gill, *Rosenne's The World Court: What It is and How It Works*, 6th edn (Leiden, Martinus Nijhoff, 2003) 31; Thirlway, 'The International Court of Justice' (n 25) 581; E Dumbauld, 'Dissenting Opinions in International Adjudication' (1941-1942) 90 *University of Pennsylvania Law Review* 929, 934; Terris, Romano and Swigart (*ibid*) 102; and Kelly (*ibid*) 225–26.

This is certainly the *primary* role of the Court.[34] The main responsibility of the Court is to identify and apply existing law to the individual dispute before it. As such, it may be unfair to criticise the Court for failing to 'improve' the law regarding self-defence. This is worth keeping in mind when considering our analysis in previous chapters.

B. The Development of International Law

Whilst it must be correct to view the primary role of the ICJ as the settlement of disputes between states through the identification and application of international law, there is another role that the ICJ performs. This is to clarify, develop and 'improve' the law in a manner that impacts beyond the case before it.[35] A role of this kind is not provided for, as such, by the Court's Statute.[36] Nonetheless, this is an extremely important role that the Court performs, even if it was not one it was explicitly designed to perform.[37]

The idea that the World Court has a role to play in the development of international law is not a new one. The ICJ's predecessor, the PCIJ, clearly contributed to the development of international law during the inter-war period.[38] This tradition has continued with regard to the ICJ:

[34] RY Jennings, 'The Judicial Function and the Rule of Law in International Relations' in *International Law at the Time of its Codification: Essays in Honour of Roberto Ago, Vol III* (Milan, Giuffre, 1987) 139, esp 140–41; and H Thirlway, 'The Drafting of ICJ Decisions: Some Personal Reflections and Observations' (2006) 5 *Chinese Journal of International Law* 15, 23–24, though Thirlway uses the term 'function' to mean what is here termed 'role'.

[35] RP Anand, *Studies in International Adjudication* (Delhi, Vikas, 1969) esp 167–80; LV Prott, *The Latent Power of Culture and the International Judge* (Abingdon, Professional Books, 1979) 86–109; Terris, Romano and Swigart (n 32) 115; J Fernando, 'The International Court of Justice: A Critique of its Role' (1992) 4 *Sri Lanka Journal of International Law* 27, 52; M Lachs, 'Some Reflections on the Contribution of the International Court of Justice to the Development of International Law' (1983) 10 *Syracuse Journal of International Law and Commerce* 239, esp 245; HN Meyer, *The World Court in Action: Judging Among the Nations* (Oxford, Rowman and Littlefield, 2002) 67–68; and B Chipp, *Going to Court Not War*, 7th edn (London, Institute for Law and Peace, 2002) 10.

[36] Although some element of judicial decision-making beyond existing objective international law does exist in the Statute, as is evidenced by Art 38(2): 'This provision [Art 38(1), see above, n 28 and accompanying text] shall not prejudice the power of the Court to decide a case *ex aequo et bono*, if the parties agree thereto.' Similarly, some of the debates at the San Francisco Conference suggest that something more than mere dispute settlement was envisaged by at least some of the drafters. See, eg, the statement of C Parra-Pérez (President of Commission IV at San Francisco), *Documents of the United Nations Conference on International Organisation, Volume XIII: Commission IV, Judicial Organisation*, Doc 430 IU/5, 31.

[37] Compare the International Law Commission (ILC), which was explicitly set up with the mandate to promote the progressive development of international law and its codification: Statute of the International Law Commission, Art 1(1).

[38] In general, see H Lauterpacht, *The Development of International Law by the International Court*, revised edn (London, Stevens & Sons, 1958); and SM Schwebel, 'Reflections on the Role of the International Court of Justice' (1986) 61 *Washington Law Review* 1061, 1063.

> [Its role] is to settle disputes between states and to provide advice to authorised organs. It is not to develop international law in the abstract. But, of course, the very determination of specific disputes, and the provision of specific advice does develop international law.'[39]

It is therefore important that the ICJ should not be seen as an international legislature. As the Court has itself pointed out, it 'is not a legislative body. Its duty is to apply the law as it finds it, not to make it.'[40] Equally, it is indisputable that the decisions of the ICJ[41] have huge influence upon the development of international law, for good or ill. The fact that the Court is a greatly respected institution (both in terms of its individual members[42] and collectively as the primary judicial organ of the UN) means that its decisions have, perhaps inevitably, had an effect on state practice and *opinio juris*,[43] as well as upon the writings of scholars.[44] When a judicial body is accepted as representing an authoritative source of law, then its judgments are themselves likely to be seen as having an authoritative character, even if they technically bind only the parties to the case with respect to the dispute at hand.[45] Given this influence, the ICJ must be seen

[39] R Higgins, *Problems and Process: International Law and How We Use It* (Oxford, Oxford University Press, 1994) 202. See also P Kooijmans, 'The ICJ in the 21st Century: Judicial Restraint, Judicial Activism, or Proactive Judicial Policy' (2007) 53 *International and Comparative Law Quarterly* 741, esp 742.

[40] *South West Africa Cases* (*Ethiopia v South Africa, Liberia v South Africa*) second phase (1966) ICJ Reports 4, para 89. The Court also made similar statements in the *Legality of the Threat or Use of Nuclear Weapons* advisory opinion (1996) ICJ Reports 226, para 18.

[41] Including its advisory opinions. GG Fitzmaurice, 'The Law and Procedure of the International Court of Justice: Part III, International Organisations and Tribunals' (1952) 29 *British Yearbook International Law* 1, 54–55.

[42] Art 2 of the ICJ's Statute provides: 'The Court shall be composed of a body of independent judges, elected regardless of their nationality from among persons of high moral character, who possess the qualifications required in their respective countries for appointment to the highest judicial offices, or are jurisconsults of recognized competence in international law.' See Merrills (n 25) 148; and O Schachter, *International Law in Theory and Practice* (Dordrecht, Martinus Nijhoff, 1991) 40.

[43] JJ Paust, 'Domestic Influence of the International Court of Justice' (1997–98) 26 *Denver Journal of International Law and Policy* 787, 788; GG Fitzmaurice, 'Some Problems Regarding the Formal Sources of International Law' in *Symbolae Verzijl* (The Hague, Martinus Nijhoff, 1958) 153, 169; Palmisano (n 33) 208–11; and M Koskenniemi, *The Gentle Civilizer of Nations: The Rise and Fall of International Law 1870–1960* (Cambridge, Cambridge University Press, 2001) 403, as part of an assessment of the work of Hersch Lauterpacht. See also *Asylum* case (*Colombia/Peru*) merits (1950) ICJ Reports 266, dissenting opinion of Judge Azevedo, 332.

[44] Paust notes this phenomenon also and provides examples (*ibid*, 787). See also MW Janis, 'The International Court' in MW Janis (ed), *International Courts for the Twenty-First Century* (Dordrecht, Martinus Nijhoff, 1992) 19; and Schachter, *International Law in Theory and Practice* (n 42) 40–41. Having said this, Koskenniemi has claimed that traditionally, international lawyers have taken a more oppositional stance against any kind of judicial development of international law than their municipal counterparts (although he also suggests this opposition has begun to soften). M Koskenniemi, *From Apology to Utopia: The Structure of International Legal Argument*, reissue with epilogue (Cambridge, Cambridge University Press, 2005) 30–35, esp 30.

[45] HG Maier, 'Appraisals of the ICJ's Decision: *Nicaragua v Unites States* (Merits): Introduction' (1987) 81 *American Journal of International Law* 77, 77; and Higgins, *Problems and Process: International Law and How We Use It* (n 39) 202–4.

as having a responsibility, at the very least, to ensure clarity and coherence in its decisions so far as possible, as it must surely be aware that its judgments take on a significant life beyond the specific dispute at issue. It is argued in this book that, at least so far as the law governing self-defence goes, the ICJ has not adequately discharged this responsibility.

C. Is the Development of the Law Desirable?

Although the above separation of the two roles of the ICJ is conceptually useful, it must be kept in mind that there is in fact no neat distinction between the Court's 'identification and application' role and its 'development' role: one in some measure flows from the other.[46] Certainly, in many instances the ICJ must attempt to impose clarity upon existing international law simply *to be able* to apply it to any given dispute.[47] Where 'clarification' ends and 'augmentation' or 'development' of the law begins is something that cannot be contended with any certainty. Choice and a level of legal 'creativity' are apparent in all forms of adjudication, and as such, clarification and development of the law is intrinsic in a dispute settlement role.[48]

Having said this, the *degree* of development that the Court takes upon itself to perform may vary greatly. Whilst some developmental influence is an inevitable ancillary consequence of the Court's primary settlement of disputes role, to some extent the Court, or perhaps more accurately the members of the Court, have a level of influence as to how progressive a decision is to be. This is at times undoubtedly 'subconscious', whilst at other times, the Court may be seen to be actively pushing legal boundaries of existing international law in its decisions.

Some scholars have argued that a comparatively progressive developmental role for the Court is a desirable one.[49] Thus it has been stated that the need for judicial creativity is 'more conspicuous and troublesome in international law. One reason obviously is the large area of uncertainty in international law.'[50] From this perspective, the development of inter-

[46] Thus, whilst Prott identifies the two roles of the Court here discussed, she takes the view that they are two aspects of the same judicial role: the role of the ICJ has a 'dual nature'. Prott (n 35) 86–109, and esp 92.

[47] The common law 'fiction' of a wholly comprehensive, knowable legal regime is not accepted in international adjudication. Gill (n 33) 30; and Anand (n 35) 167.

[48] Schachter, *International Law in Theory and Practice* (n 42) 40–43; M Bedjaoui, 'Expediency in the Decisions of the International Court of Justice' (2000) 71 *British Yearbook of International Law* 1, esp 5; and Thirlway, 'The Drafting of ICJ Decisions' (n 34) 23–24.

[49] This desirability of a developmental or 'creative' role for international courts (heightened by the lack of authoritative sovereign in international law) was implicit in much of the work of Hersch Lauterpacht, as discussed in Koskenniemi, *The Gentle Civilizer of Nations* (n 43) 402–6.

[50] Schachter, *International Law in Theory and Practice* (n 42) 40–41.

national law in judicial decisions appears desirable. Indeed, it could even be suggested that the ICJ has a *responsibility* to develop progressively international law, especially in relation to fundamental principles such as the prohibition on the use of force.[51]

In contrast, it may equally be argued that the desire of some members of the Court that its decisions have as positive an impact as possible for wider international law, and active attempts from within the Peace Palace to influence legal development, potentially run counter to the main role of the Court as a dispute settlement organ between consenting parties on the issue before it. One may therefore take the view that progressive development in the Court in fact has a negative impact upon the quality, clarity and effectiveness of its decisions. The tension in international arbitration between settlement of disputes and progressive development of the law was identified in 1958 by Hersch Lauterpacht, who noted that the Court will inevitably desire 'to supplement and remedy the deficiencies and inconsistencies of an imperfect system of law' whilst equally continually facing 'the requirement of caution and restraint called for by sovereign states and . . . the voluntary and therefore precarious nature of the jurisdiction of international tribunals'.[52] More recently, in 1991, Oscar Schachter similarly described the need for judges of the ICJ to avoid both 'excess of valour and excess of caution'.[53]

Like Schachter, the view is taken here that the most desirable path is one of balance between caution and valour. This, of course, is easier to say than to do.[54] Specific to our analysis, there exists a conflict between the inclination of the ICJ to attempt to improve the law of self-defence and reaffirm the prohibition on the use of force on the one hand and, on the other hand, the need for constraint given the jurisdictional straitjacket forced upon the Court (due, primarily, to the fact that State consent to adjudication in this area is either nonexistent or only partial).[55] It is argued that this conflict between the two roles of the Court has had a fundamental impact upon the substantive law on self-defence. As such, it is an issue that will be returned to throughout the remainder of this chapter.

[51] Some members of the Court have recently taken such a position (though not always explicitly). See, eg, *Legal Consequences of the Construction of a Wall in the Occupied Palestinian Territory* advisory opinion (2004) ICJ Reports 135, separate opinion of Judge Higgins, para 23; and *Case Concerning Oil Platforms* (*Islamic Republic of Iran v United States of America*) merits (2003) ICJ Reports 161, separate opinion of Judge Simma, esp paras 3, 5 and 6. See also Kelly (n 32) 239–41.

[52] Lauterpacht (n 38) 155.

[53] Schachter, *International Law in Theory and Practice* (n 42) 42.

[54] Prott (n 35) 105.

[55] See below, sections V and VI.

III. POLITICISATION AND DECISION-MAKING

It should be noted at this juncture what is meant herein by terms such as 'political' or 'politicised' as employed in relation to judicial decision-making. As Joel Levin has noted, the label of politics or politicisation 'covers tremendous ground'.[56] Here, such terms are used with regard not merely to awareness on the part of judges of the political quality of the law, but rather to a policy-orientated approach on the part of any given judge (be this conscious or unconscious). 'Politicisation' is employed to mean an attempt to alter or improve the law based upon the policy goals of the individual judge, as opposed to a mere application of the law—in other words, we are talking about an active move towards the 'development role' set out in the previous section. However, as we will see, there is no neat distinction between the political factors inherent in the law and the political views (conscious or unconscious) inherent in judicial decision-makers. The term 'politicisation' is not intended to be used in a pejorative sense, nor is it necessarily intended to imply a particular value judgment as to its desirability: as has been noted already, it is certainly possible to argue that politicisation is a desirable aspect of international decision-making.

A. The Hive Mind Fallacy

The ICJ is not a living being. Like the entities we call 'states', the Court is an artificial construct, comprised of a collection of individuals. Its judgments are those of its members taken collectively. Moreover, those members, over the sixty plus years of the Court's existence, have quite obviously not always been the same individuals.[57] As such, one must be very careful when referring to the 'view' or 'position' of the ICJ. Members of the Court may not necessarily agree upon any given issue. Indeed, they often do not: 'to conceive any pronouncement of the International Court as monolithic is to commit the logical fallacy of composition.'[58] Judgments often involve a bargaining process between judges, with points of substance conceded and bartered.[59] This is the nature of judicial deliberation at the Peace Palace. The ICJ does not possess a single hive mind.

[56] J Levin, *How Judges Reason: The Logic of Adjudication* (New York, Peter Lang, 1992) 28, with regard to adjudicative decision-making in a municipal common law context.

[57] Elections to the ICJ occur every three years, with one third of its membership being elected. Judges serve for a period of nine years, though they may be re-elected: Art 13 of the Statute of the ICJ.

[58] I Scobbie, 'Smoke, Mirrors and Killer Whales: the International Court of Justice's Opinion on the Israeli Barrier Wall' (2004) 5 *German Law Journal* 1107, 1111.

[59] *Ibid*; Elias (n 4) 15–17; Prott (n 35) 60–63; Terris, Romano and Swigart (n 32) 58–59; RY Jennings, 'The Internal Judicial Practice of the International Court of Justice' (1988) 59 *British Yearbook of International Law* 31, 36–46; Gill (n 33) 108–11; and Schwarzenberger (n 32) 31.

When looking at the process of deliberation in the ICJ, a distinction may be drawn, from the wider context of adjudicative theory, between a *consensus* and a *convergence* of judicial opinion.[60] A consensus of judicial opinion indicates an agreement between the members of a court as to what rules of law must be applied in any given case. Moreover, it indicates an agreement as to the reasoning process itself: agreement as to *why* such rules of law should be applied. In contrast, convergence is a weaker notion. The agreement here relates only to the *result* of the judicial process: in the case of the ICJ, the *dispositif* of the decision. In cases of convergence this is reached not by consensus but by compromise.

In the main, it is the second type of process that is present in the workings of the ICJ. Indeed, even such a convergence of opinion is rarely unanimously accepted. This is a fact well demonstrated by the number of judgments reached without unanimous vote and by the plethora of separate and dissenting opinions that have been appended to the decisions of the Court.[61] Consequentially, under a convergence of judicial opinion model, controversial aspects of the decision must be softened or removed to ensure that a result of some kind can be achieved. The larger the number of members of a court, the more pronounced this problem becomes. It is has been argued that for the ICJ this has meant that 'it issues findings on both fact and law that often appear to be watered down or anodyne.'[62]

Disagreement between the judges is commonplace, particularly in the context of disputes involving contentious and politically charged issues, such as the use of force. For example, it has been argued in relation to *Nicaragua* that the strong differences of judicial opinion that apparently manifested during that case were unique to the subject matter of that case.[63] In other words, disputes involving the use of force may be seen as polarising the Court to a degree that other issues have not.[64] This is in part due to the controversial nature of the subject matter but also because the law concerning self-defence is unclear, increasing the scope for disagreement as to its content. As we will see later in this chapter, the members of the Court have been required, in self-defence cases, to resort (at least subconsciously) to a comparative assessment of the underlying legal 'principles' of the international system.[65] This further increases the scope

[60] This distinction is adapted from Levin (n 56) 60–64.

[61] Koskenniemi, *From Apology to Utopia* (n 44) 33.

[62] SD Murphy, 'Self-Defence and the *Israeli Wall* Advisory Opinion: An *Ipse Dixit* from the ICJ?' (2005) 99 *American Journal of International Law* 62, 75. See also E McWhinney, *The World Court and the Contemporary International Law-Making Process* (Alphen aan den Rijn, Sijthoff & Noordhoff, 1979) esp 67 and 107–9.

[63] E Brown Weiss, 'Judicial Independence and Impartiality: A Preliminary Inquiry' in LF Damrosch (ed), *The International Court of Justice at a Crossroads* (New York, Transnational, 1987) 123, 130, suggesting that *Nicaragua* represented a 'relatively unusual disagreement by the judges'.

[64] Murphy (n 62) 75.

[65] Below, section III-C.

for disagreement, as it posits decision-making at a fundamental 'value-based' level.

The claim that use of force cases are inherently more likely to give rise to disagreements in the ICJ must necessarily be speculative, as the inner workings of the judicial deliberations within the Peace Palace cannot be known with any certainty.[66] However, the decision in the *Case Concerning Oil Platforms* (hereafter *Oil Platforms*)[67] offers further suggestive evidence: out of the sixteen judges who sat on that case (including Judge ad hoc Rigaux), eleven appended individual opinions to the merits decision. The majority of the judges in that case therefore felt that there were one or more elements of the majority judgment that were disputable, or at least needed clarification. Similarly, the advisory opinion in *Legality of the Threat or Use of Nuclear Weapons* (hereafter *Nuclear Weapons*)[68] had fourteen individual opinions appended to it.

Whilst differences of judicial opinion are symptomatic of all forms of arbitration and in themselves are not always necessarily undesirable, such divisions are more problematic for international adjudicative bodies like the ICJ, because such institutions are in general comprised of many more members than equivalent domestic courts of last resort.[69] Bartering and dissent of the kind apparent in cases like *Oil Platforms* somewhat undermines the perception that ICJ decisions are authoritative statements of international law. Of course, there is little question that the judges of the Court are individually expert in the field. Collectively, however, ICJ judgments are often compromises between differing legal and political views. In the context of the law governing self-defence, such compromises between the various judges, past and present, have been an important factor in the formation of the Court's jurisprudence on the issue.

B. Judicial Bias and Politicisation

Despite the fact that the Statute of the ICJ provides that its members are 'independent' and 'of high moral character',[70] it has been argued, particu-

[66] To some extent, though, they can be inferred from judgments, individual opinions and voting records, as well as from extrajudicial publications and speeches.

[67] *Oil Platforms* merits (n 51).

[68] *Nuclear Weapons* advisory opinion (n 40).

[69] Compare the European Court of Human Rights, which consists of as many members as there are state parties to the European Convention on Human Rights (Convention for the Protection of Human Rights and Fundamental Freedoms, as amended, Art 20). Currently this constitutes an unwieldy forty-seven judges. The ICJ has a membership of fifteen permanent judges (ICJ Statute, Art 3), though in practice the Court is usually comprised of sixteen, or even seventeen, members, due to the regular appearance of judges ad hoc, as proscribed for by Art 31 of the Court's Statute. Moreover, it would seem that all members of the Court take an active role in each case: Jennings, 'The Internal Judicial Practice of the International Court of Justice' (n 59) 37.

[70] Art 2 of the Statute of the ICJ.

larly by scholars from the United States since the *Nicaragua* decision,[71] that the judges of the ICJ are inherently biased.[72] For example, it has been claimed that there is evidence to support the idea that they are biased towards their states of origin or more generally towards their 'regions' of origin.[73] It is possible to interpret the voting records of ICJ judges to indicate that they are less likely to take a stance opposed to a state party of which they are a national than to find in favour of that state.[74] Moreover, the provision for judges ad hoc in the Statute of the Court has been seen as an implicit acknowledgement of the likelihood of such partisanship on the part of the drafters of the ICJ's Statute,[75] however much Article 2 of that instrument provides for the independence of the members of the Court. If the permanent judges were genuinely independent—so the argument goes—there would be no need for judges ad hoc at all.[76] Even more than with permanent members of the Court, the voting records of judges ad hoc indicate that they vote in favour of the states that nominated them.[77]

The realities of international dispute settlement mean that the charge that ICJ judges are to some degree biased or 'politicised' is undoubtedly true.[78] It is impossible for fifteen individuals of different legal, cultural and political backgrounds to reach a unanimous single legal vision of any

[71] Though not exclusively by American scholars. See Brown Weiss (n 63) 123.

[72] See, eg, M Leigh and SD Ramsey, 'Confidence in the Court: It Need not be a Hollow Chamber' in LF Damrosch (ed), *The International Court of Justice at a Crossroads* (New York, Transnational, 1987) 106, esp 108; WM Reisman, 'Termination of the United States Declaration Under Article 36(2) of the Statute of the International Court' in AC Arend (ed), *The United States and the Compulsory Jurisdiction of the International Court of Justice* (Lanham, University Press of America, 1986) 71, esp 86–89; EA Posner, 'The International Court of Justice: Voting and Usage Statistics' (2005) 99 *American Society of International Law Proceedings* 130; RA Friedlander, 'Confusing Victims and Victimizers: *Nicaragua* and the Reinterpretation of International Law' (1985–86) 14 *Denver Journal of International Law and Policy* 87, 94; JR Stevenson, 'The World Court: Remarks' (1986) 80 *American Society of International Law Proceedings* 201, 202; A Chayes, 'Nicaragua, the United States, and the World Court' (1985) 85 *Columbia Law Review* 1445, 1447–48; and TM Franck, *Judging the World Court* (New York, Priority Press, 1986) 35–38. It should be noted that Stevenson, Chayes and Franck all highlight this view without necessarily subscribing to it.

[73] Eg, Friedlander cites *Iranian Hostages* merits (n 21) as a clear example of this, claiming that the Soviet and Islamic judges voted 'as one would expect.' Friedlander (*ibid*) 94–95. See similarly Posner (*ibid*) esp 131.

[74] This interpretation of the voting records has been taken by TR Hensley, 'National Bias and the International Court of Justice' (1968) 12 *Midwest Journal of Political Science* 568; and IR Suh, 'Voting Behaviour of National Judges in International Courts' (1969) 63 *American Journal of International Law* 224, esp 228. However, more recent studies are far less conclusive upon this point. See, eg, the 1987 study of Brown Weiss (n 63) 128–33; or more recently still, a study of 2004, AM Smith, 'Judicial Nationalism in International Law: National Identity and Judicial Autonomy at the ICJ' (2004–05) 40 *Texas International Law Journal* 197.

[75] Schachter, *International Law in Theory and Practice* (n 42) 43.

[76] DD Nsereko, 'The International Court, Impartiality and Judges Ad Hoc' (1973) 13 *Indian Journal of International Law* 207, 217–22.

[77] Hensley (n 74) 574–75; and Thirlway, 'The International Court of Justice' (n 25) 564.

[78] Franck (n 72) 36.

given dispute.[79] ICJ judges are people, and they reason and vote with the fallibility of people.[80] Therefore, whilst the functions of the ICJ are clearly 'legal', it is necessarily on some level a political animal.[81]

However, whilst the voting and the content of the various individual opinions of the Court indicate some level of predilection towards the states from which the judges originate (particularly in the context of judges ad hoc), there is not enough evidence to suggest a pervading judicial 'bias' of this kind in the ICJ.[82] As Judge Higgins has so eloquently argued, the notion of national or regional bias in the ICJ is a rather fallacious one.[83] Whilst it is true that in the majority of cases in which a judge has been faced with a dispute involving his or her state of origin, he or she has voted in favour of that state, it is also true that in the greater number of such decisions, the judge in question has also voted *with the majority of the Court*.[84] Viewed thus, voting statistics cannot be seen as evidence of any kind of national bias on the part of members of the ICJ.

Indeed, even if some degree of regional bias could be detected in the Court, the regional distribution of is members would presumably act to balance this concern.[85] In the context of use of force disputes, initial claims of a degree of 'Western bias'[86] have since been replaced by post-*Nicaragua* claims of 'anti-Western bias'.[87] Yet, ultimately, neither can be genuinely

[79] As Bedjaoui points out, 'Considering that there are fifteen judges from different backgrounds, it is out of the question that they could simultaneously be biased *in the same direction*' (emphasis added). Bedjaoui (n 48) 4.

[80] TM Franck, 'Some Psychological Factors in International Third-Party Decision-Making' (1966–67) 19 *Stanford Law Review* 1217, 1220–22.

[81] A useful example of this fact is the election of the judges to the Court. This tri-annual event is highly politically charged, with the nomination process more reminiscent of a campaign for political office than the process of appointment to a judicial organ. See S Rosenne, *The Law and Practice of the International Court of Justice, 1920–2005, Vol I: The Court and the United Nations*, 4th edn (Leiden, Martinus Nijhoff, 2006) 364–78). Moreover, an increasing number of the appointees to the ICJ come from a 'governmental' rather than a purely 'legal' background—a fact that could arguably influence the 'political' nature of the Court. Schachter, *International Law in Theory and Practice* (n 42) 44.

[82] Chayes (n 72) 1447–48; and Brown Weiss (n 63) 128–33.

[83] R Higgins, 'Alternative Perspectives on the Independence of International Courts: Remarks' (2005) 99 *American Society of International Law Proceedings* 135.

[84] *Ibid*, esp 137.

[85] Posner himself notes this (n 72) 131. The disparate cultural and political background of ICJ judges in some respects may inhibit the work of the Court. However, as Jennings points out, the Court's composition is certainly appropriate for a 'world' court. It gives the body a level of political credibility and a useful diversity of opinion. Jennings, 'The Internal Judicial Practice of the International Court of Justice' (n 59) 33 and 35–36. Obviously, such diversity is specifically required by Art 9 of the ICJ's Statute.

[86] Eg, as made by BVA Röling, *International Law in an Expanded World* (Amsterdam, Djambatan, 1960) 76.

[87] Noted by C Gray, 'The Use and Abuse of the International Court of Justice: Cases Concerning the Use of Force Since *Nicaragua*' (2003) 14 *European Journal of International Law* 867, 885.

detected in the work of the Court.[88] In general, the judges must be seen as fulfilling their duty by acting in high moral character and, so far as possible, independently of the views or wishes of their states of origin.[89] International judges and international courts (including the ICJ) should not be viewed as 'agents'.[90] In other words, even the most hardnosed 'realist' political scientist will have difficulty in concluding that the ICJ is *controlled* by states, irrespective of the fact that it is a *creation* of states.[91]

As such, there is no 'first-order' disagreement within the Court.[92] In the vast majority of cases, judges do not select or apply the law because it suits their political ends or those of their states of origin.[93] They do so because, at least as far as they perceive, *it is the law*.[94] To put this differently, a decision made by any judge is reached through the application of legal rules, or at least by *reference* to such rules.[95] Judicial discretion is therefore highly restricted in the 'first order'. In the specific case of the ICJ, it is argued above that the judges act as impartially as possible. A naked realist vision of judges using the veil of 'the law' as a mask for political decision-making simply does not fit the reality of the decisions of the ICJ. As such, the charge that the ICJ is an institution that is 'too political' to be able to deal with disputes involving the use of force seems unsustainable.

[88] M Shahabuddeen, 'The World Court at the Turn of the Century' in AS Muller, D Raic and JM Thuranszky (eds), *The International Court of Justice: Its Future Role after Fifty Years* (The Hague, Martinus Nijhoff, 1997) 3, 7 and 11; and Schwarzenberger (n 32) 30.

[89] Thus it has been argued that so far as any such bias can be said to exist, this is almost always subconscious: AD Renteln, 'Cultural Bias in International Law' (1998) 92 *American Society of International Law Proceedings* 232, 236; Reisman (n 72) 87; and K Tanaka, 'The Character of World Law in the International Court of Justice' (1971) 15 *Japanese Annual of International Law* 1, 11–14.

[90] KJ Alter, 'International Courts are Not Agents! The Perils of the Principal–Agent Approach to Thinking about the Independence of International Courts' (2005) 99 *American Society of International Law Proceedings* 138.

[91] Having said this, Alter goes on to argue that whilst there is no *direct* control of international courts and tribunals on the part of states, such bodies remain to a degree 'handmaidens' of the political interests of states, in that they apply law created by states for political purposes. *Ibid*, 141.

[92] Levin (n 56) 18–19 and 111–18.

[93] Terris, Romano and Swigart (n 32) 66.

[94] HLA Hart, *The Concept of Law*, 2nd edn (Oxford, Oxford University Press, 1994) 141–47. A related point is that judges are restricted in applying their 'beliefs' (meaning political motivations) to decisions *by the very fact that they are judges*. They are expected *and expect themselves* to conduct their decision-making in a certain way: so far as possible in an 'objective' legal manner. The social and cultural creation of 'the judge' thus has a significant effect on the nature of a court's jurisprudence. See generally Terris, Romano and Swigart (n 32), 25–26 and 54–55; and W Lucy, 'The Possibility of Impartiality' (2005) 25 *Oxford Journal of Legal Studies* 3, 12–13 and 16–17. This idea is extended to international adjudication in Allott (n 2) 23–26; and Prott (n 35) 27 and 33–34.

[95] This is touched upon in KC Davis, *Discretionary Justice: A Preliminary Inquiry* (Baton Rouge, Louisiana State University Press, 1969) esp 15–21.

C. Dworkinian 'Principles' and Decision-Making

The conclusion reached in the previous section must be accompanied by a caveat. When the legal rules applicable to a dispute are clear, judges will generally apply them whether they agree with those rules or not. However, when the rules applicable to a dispute cannot be clearly determined (or, conceivably, do not exist at all) the situation is more complex. Disputes of this kind are what Ronald Dworkin would term 'hard cases'.[96]

There are a number of possible reasons why a case may be seen as being juridically 'hard'. These may be seen as problems inherent in the relevant legal system: 1) there is no proposition of law applicable to the dispute, or the relevant proposition cannot be identified; 2) the applicable norm is poorly defined; or 3) there exists a range of apparently applicable legal propositions from which the judge must choose but which may directly or partially conflict.[97] These issues can manifest individually or in combination.

As we have seen throughout this work, self-defence in international law is far from well defined. It is an area of the law that, to return to the terminology employed by Thomas Franck, has a low degree of determinacy.[98] As we have seen in previous chapters, this is both because of a lack of clarity and due to the fact that the rules as articulated do not form a coherent whole. Thus, when deciding disputes involving self-defence, judges of the ICJ are faced with both problem 2 and problem 3 as described above. In other words: *self-defence cases are hard cases*. On this basis, it has been argued that the ICJ's conception of self-defence must to a significant degree be seen as an 'ideological exercise' because that area of the law 'lacks substance'.[99]

The notion that the exercise of the ICJ in (hard) self-defence cases is 'ideological' suggests that members of the Court have made, in the cases we have examined, pure policy decisions (for example, by taking a restrictive view of self-defence in interpreting armed attack narrowly). In fact, it is argued here that whilst there is certainly some discretionary element to

[96] R Dworkin, *Law's Empire* (London, Fontana Press, 1986) esp 128–29 and 255–56.

[97] These three causes of hard cases are adapted from an alternative conception employed by Lucy (who in turn adapted his conception from analysis by Neil MacCormick). W Lucy, 'Adjudication' in J Coleman and S Shapiro (eds), *The Oxford Handbook of Jurisprudence and Philosophy of Law* (Oxford, Oxford University Press, 2002) 206, 213.

[98] TM Franck, *The Power of Legitimacy among Nations* (Oxford, Oxford University Press, 1990) esp 52–66. See *Ibid*.

[99] N Tsagourias, 'The *Nicaragua* Case and the Use of Force: The Theoretical Construction of the Decision and its Deconstruction' (1996) 1 *Journal of Conflict and Security Law* 81, 90. See also Schachter, who has stated: 'The rules of self-defence fall far short of a code of conduct that would prove precise "hard law" for many cases likely to arise. . . General formulas accepted as law are subject to continuing interpretation and, therefore, to fresh arguments as to what the law should be.' O Schachter, 'Self-Defence and the Rule of Law' (1989) 83 *American Journal of International Law* 259, 267.

the decisions made by the ICJ in these cases, the practice of the ICJ is not simply one of filling the legal gaps with the putty of policy.

To help us to understand this, it is useful briefly to refer to Dworkin's conception of legal reasoning and adjudication.[100] Dworkin takes the view that in hard cases a judge must look beyond 'policy' (mere political choice) to the principles underlying the law.[101] These represent the political morality upon which the law is based and must be appealed to when the law is found wanting.[102] A decision made by a judge is not an unrestrained political one.[103] This is because there is a requirement to ensure, so far as is possible, that the decision is one of best 'fit' with the existing law of the community and, further, that it constitutes the best realisation of the political and social goals of the community through law.[104] A judge must order and then apply competing 'principles' based upon the importance of the values that they represent. This process goes well beyond mere dispute resolution through the application of law. Instead, judges must produce a 'discerning assessment of . . . [the] underpinning purposes or values' of the law.[105]

The interpretive concept of 'law as integrity' as articulated by Dworkin restrains judges beyond pure policy in hard cases. Ultimately, however, each judge has to determine what the principles of the community (in our context, of the international system) actually are. Further, there is the

[100] Dworkin's theory of judicial reasoning has been criticised on a number of grounds. Some of these criticisms are noted in the following discussion, whilst others run beyond its scope. For general criticism, see E Bodenheimer, 'Hart, Dworkin, and the Problem of Judicial Lawmaking Discretion' (1976–77) 11 *Georgia Law Review* 1143; N MacCormick, *Legal Reasoning and Legal Theory* (Oxford, Oxford University Press, 1978) esp 229–74; and the judgment of Lord Hoffman in the UK House of Lords case *Jones v Ministry of Interior of the Kingdom of Saudi Arabia and another* (*Secretary of State for Constitutional Affairs and Others Intervening*); *Mitchell and Others v Al-Dali and Others* (Conjoined Appeals) [2007] 1 All ER 113, 138, para 63 (specifically with regard to international law). Irrespective of these criticisms, a Dworkinian analysis is useful in the context of the ICJ's reasoning process, as has been demonstrated by Koskenniemi, *From Apology to Utopia* (n 44) esp 24–70 (although Koskenniemi ultimately takes a very different position). It is the view of the present author that Dworkin's theory best represents the realities of the Court's decision-making process (generally, and specifically in relation to self-defence). The detailed reasons for this assumption go beyond the scope of this work, but it is primarily because as an 'underdeveloped' legal system, international law is comparatively lacking in posited 'rules'. As such, it is hugely dependent upon underlying 'Dworkinian' principles. Moreover, it is especially notable that in a survey of judicial opinion conducted by way of interviews with thirty-seven international judges, Terris et al had the impression that the pervading view *of the judges themselves* was that they perceived their practice as being largely Dworkinian. See, Terris, Romano and Swigart (n 32) 210.

[101] Dworkin, *Law's Empire* (n 96) esp 225–75.

[102] *Ibid.*

[103] *Ibid*, esp 258–60. Dworkin famously took an opposite view to Hart on this issue (amongst others). For Hart, when legal rules run dry (or are unclear or opaque), judges are forced to resort to pure discretion: they simply must *make* the law as they see fit. Hart (n 94) 141–47 and 272–76. This is pure policy-orientated decision-making. However, for the reasons given above (n 100) it is assumed in the following discussion that Dworkin's analysis of judicial decision-making better represents the practice of the ICJ.

[104] Dworkin, *Law's Empire* (n 96) esp 225–28 and 254–58.

[105] Lucy, 'The Possibility of Impartiality' (n 94) 19.

secondary question of how such principles, once determined, are best applied in concrete cases,[106] especially when they conflict. Therefore a dual claim is made here: the judges of the ICJ are restricted to producing—and in fact do produce—judgments that are based upon legal principles. However, a level of discretion—and thus potential confusion—is inevitable in hard cases. Legal interpretation, particularly at the international level, is an art and not a science.[107]

Whilst Dworkin claims a theoretical 'single right answer' for any legal decision, he nonetheless admits that 'different judges will disagree about [how to compromise between competing political considerations] and will accordingly take different views of what the law of their community, properly understood, really is.'[108] The question of whether there is a theoretical single right answer in every case is irrelevant for our purposes.[109] This is because even if there is an objectively 'correct' legal decision for every case in theory, this single right answer will not always be empirically identifiable: it cannot necessarily be discerned by judges *in practice*.[110]

What is important in this context is, first, that Dworkin's theory indicates that the judges of the ICJ act based upon something more than political motivation; they act based upon legal rules and, if necessary, upon legal principles. This is particularly relevant when considering the problematic aspects of the legal rules governing self-defence as already discussed in previous chapters. Second, it can equally be seen that judges are likely, in hard cases such as self-defence, to have different views to each other as to which principles are to be applied and as to what 'applying' them in any given case entails. The less well defined an area of law, the more that political and ideological viewpoints of the judges *as to the principle(s) of law underlying the system* are likely to influence the legal position that is ultimately adopted by them. In applying Dworkin's analysis specifically to international law, Martii Koskenniemi thus states: 'the ascertainment of the "relative weights" of different principles would involve a degree of subjective discretion.'[111]

[106] For Dworkin, an important element of the distinction between principle and policy is that the former concept relates directly to the individuals—or here, states—before the court. In other words, community values must be employed with regard to the parties to the case (application of principle) and not for the wellbeing community or to further its goals generally (application of policy). R Dworkin, 'Hard Cases' (1974–75) 88 *Harvard Law Review* 1057, 1059.

[107] Terris, Romano and Swigart (n 32) 103.

[108] Dworkin, *Law's Empire* (n 96) 256.

[109] Though it must be said that this seems a dubious aspect of Dworkin's theory: the very nature of a hard case adjudication would suggest a plurality of potentially valid legal solutions. See Lucy, 'Adjudication' (n 97) esp 219; and MacCormick (n 100) 246–50.

[110] HLA Hart, 'American Jurisprudence through English Eyes: The Nightmare and the Noble Dream' (first published 1977) in HLA Hart, *Essays in Jurisprudence and Philosophy* (Oxford, Oxford University Press, 1983) 123, 137–40.

[111] Admittedly Koskenniemi then goes on to point out that such discretion nonetheless takes place within the framework of the legal system and thus the choice of principles used is restricted. Koskenniemi, *From Apology to Utopia* (n 44) 36–58, quoted at 38.

Dworkin's theory of principles conforms in part to a useful conception of decision-making in the ICJ put forward by Mohammed Bedjaoui, a former President of the ICJ. Bedjaoui has argued that in cases in which members of the Court must utilise their own discretion (due to the fact that legal rules are either not present or not clear), they will resort to a notion of what he terms 'expediency' in exercising that discretion to reach a legal decision.[112] This means that a judge appeals to 'feelings of appropriateness, wisdom or prudence'[113] that *underlie* the law. Such a process 'is neither opportunism nor arbitrariness'[114] but rather is an recognition that the 'best' legal solution in a hard case is one that appeals to the core values of the legal system. This analysis is somewhat different to that of Dworkin in that Bedjaoui sees a number of possible 'correct' legal decisions in any case. A judge must exercise his discretion to pick between them based upon criteria of expediency (meaning what the judge sees as the best possible *legal* decision based upon the principles of the international legal system as he identifies them). This takes us a step beyond Dworkin to a marriage of principle to discretion.

Another former member of the Court, Kotaro Tanaka, has pointed to the fact that any discretionary element in international judicial activity stems from a judge's personal inclinations with regard to the concept of international law itself (and particularly, the role of the ICJ within the international legal system) rather than any regional or cultural affiliations or political conceptions concerning specific disputes.[115] This position is interesting because it would support the conclusion that any disagreement in the ICJ regarding self-defence is not, in general terms, over the specific political implications of, for example, a dispute between the United States and Iran. Rather, differences within the ICJ have been (and continue to be) over how best to implement the *principles* underlying international law in the context of hard cases of self-defence.[116] As Judge Higgins has said, 'The alignments on the bench are not those of "national bias". They are about conservative or liberal approaches, strict constructionism or teleological perspectives.'[117] These constitute 'second-order' disagreements in the ICJ.[118]

112 Bedjaoui (n 48) 1–5 and 14–27.

113 *Ibid*, 3.

114 *Ibid*, 4.

115 Tanaka (n 89) 15. See also Chayes (n 72) 1447–48.

116 Compare the view taken by Meyer, who suggests that there is a long established tradition, dating back to the PCIJ, of 'judicial collegiality' in the ICJ with regard to the role and 'purposes' of the *Court* when fulfilling its functions. Meyer (n 34) 68–69. This point may be arguable in the context of the history of the Court, but it is suggested here that this does not reflect the more recent practice of the members of the ICJ—or at least not with regard to use of force issues.

117 Higgins, 'Alternative Perspectives on the Independence of International Courts' (n 83) esp 137. Compare the view taken by Kooijmans (n 39) 742.

118 Levin (n 56) 19–20 and 118–25.

So, what are the relevant principles underlying self-defence decisions? Koskenniemi has pointed out that in identifying Dwokinian principles in international law, a purposive approach has a stronger normative foundation than reliance upon general notions based upon natural justice.[119] In other words, an international judge should turn to the legislative 'object and purpose' of a treaty or the utility or equity of 'general principles of law'[120] rather than basing decisions upon principles of political or social morality. In this vein, it has been suggested that, as the primary judicial organ of the UN, the ICJ in fact has a duty to uphold the principles of that organisation wherever possible.[121] This would make sense, in that such principles are more objectively identifiable than other (more vague and subjective) conceptions of the values underpinning international law, as they are set out for all to see in Article 1 of the UN Charter. Thus, the suggestion is that in any hard case, the ICJ should turn to the principles of the UN to reach its legal decision.

Based upon this idea, Nicholas Tsagourias has suggested that in the context of the use of force, the ICJ's primary underlying policy consideration is to preserve peace. He supports this by referring to the formative principles of the UN.[122] Tsagourias thus argues that, at least in part, the restrictive definition of self-defence in *Nicaragua* has its roots in the second-order Dworkinian principles underlying the 'hard case' of the US self-defence claim concerning the contra forces.[123] The restrictive notion of an 'armed attack as a grave use of force' can therefore be seen as stemming from this underlying desire to restrict violence wherever possible. Interestingly, following their survey of international judicial opinion published in 2007, conducted by way of interviews with thirty-seven international judges, Daniel Terris et al also took the view that—in the opinion of judges themselves, across international courts and tribunals—the most crucial principle underpinning judicial decision-making was 'the prevention of violence and war'.[124]

Such a conclusion is necessarily somewhat speculative: for example, we cannot know for sure what factors influenced the Court's decision in *Nicaragua*.[125] Moreover, even if it is correct that the preservation of peace

[119] Koskenniemi, *From Apology to Utopia* (n 44) 44–58. It should be noted that ultimately Koskenniemi rejects this method of identifying international legal principles in hard cases also.

[120] A material source of law identified in Art 38(1)(c) of the Court's Statute.

[121] LC Green, 'The United Nations, South West Africa and the World Court' (1967) 7 *Indian Journal of International Law* 491, 512. See also Prott (n 35) 31–32.

[122] Tsagourias (n 99) 82. The idea that the preservation and restoration of peace is a fundamental legal principle applied in ICJ decisions is also seemingly advanced by Bedjaoui, who argues that this idea informs the 'expediency' of the Court's decisions, along with the notion of 'justice'. Bedjaoui (n 48) 3–4.

[123] It should be noted that Tsagourias does not employ this terminology.

[124] Terris, Romano and Swigart (n 32) 229–33, quoted at 229.

[125] Indeed, such an assessment also runs the risk of ascribing a political motivation to the Court as a whole, when, as we have seen, each member of the Court has his or her own legal and political conceptions. See above, section III-A.

is an underlying legal principle applied by the Court, the notion that the preservation of peace is in fact best served by a restricted right of self-defence based upon an 'armed attack as a grave use of force' criterion is, as can be seen from our analysis in previous chapters, controversial. It would be difficult to produce empirical support for such a claim. It may well be that a more expansive right of self-defence, encompassing necessary and proportional responses to more 'minor' breaches of Article 2(4), would act as a deterrent in such cases or would stop incidents escalating before they reach the level of an armed attack. Thus, we can see that even when principles can be identified, the manner in which they are interpreted and applied can lead to contrary legal results.[126] It is almost impossible to know what the best practical legal application of a 'principle of the preservation of peace' would entail.

The next essential issue in this analysis involves the issue of conflict between underlying principles (of the UN or otherwise).[127] Surely, just as legal rules conflict, so may the principles of the system? The 'preservation of peace' may well clash with a basic principle of justice in international law: the right of a state to defend itself when it has been unlawfully attacked. Clearly 'a policy conflict which deeply splits the international community is likely to split the Court also.'[128] As has already been stated, each member of the Court will have his or her own view as to the best means of identifying the relevant values and thus applying the principles underlying international law.[129] It is argued that this kind of internal conflict over principle manifests itself in the weak convergence in ICJ decisions (and the consequent anodyne jurisprudence) already discussed.[130]

With regard to the decisions of the ICJ concerning self-defence, there is another, particularly notable, conflict of principle. This clash goes beyond the values underlying the law concerning the use of force. On one hand, disputes involving military intervention require an assessment of the values of peace and non-use of force already discussed. However, on the other hand, principles of what Dworkin would term 'procedural due process'[131] require that the Court restrict itself to making decisions only when it has jurisdiction to do so. As we will see below, there is scope to argue that in its decisions concerning self-defence the ICJ has strayed beyond its jurisdictional restraints.[132] Here, the integrity of the UN value

126 HLA Hart, '1776–1976: Law in the Perspective of Philosophy' (first published 1976) in HLA Hart, *Essays in Jurisprudence and Philosophy* (Oxford, Oxford University Press, 1983) 145, 155–58.

127 This problem is tentatively acknowledged by Green, after he suggests that the members of the Court should try to uphold the purposes of the UN where possible. Green (n 121) 512.

128 Prott (n 35) 33.

129 Above, section III.

130 *Ibid.*

131 Dworkin, *Law's Empire* (n 96) esp 166–67.

132 Below, especially section VI.

system conflicts with the integrity of the ICJ's procedural and jurisdictional restrictions (primarily the sovereign concept of state consent to adjudication). This particular conflict of principle has, it is contended, had huge ramifications for self-defence.

In this section it has been argued that the ICJ is not politically biased in its decision-making. The members of the Court reason decisions in a constrained legal manner. Nonetheless, the function of the Court in hard cases such as self-defence is highly restricted by value pluralism (albeit value pluralism attached more to the international system than to the judge). Thus, some members of the Court have taken the view that it is essential that an institution such as the ICJ takes every opportunity to try to clarify and improve the law on self-defence, given its importance. Individual positions of this kind have contributed to the Court arguably straying beyond substantive and jurisdictional bounds in this context. In contrast, other members of the ICJ seem to have taken the more formalist position that the Court should not attempt to stretch its jurisdiction in any situation, especially in a controversial area such as the use of force. This type of stance has meant that the 'development' aspects of the Court's self-defence decisions have been half-hearted and thus ineffectual.

Given this, it has been said that the ICJ may be seen as being 'divided between conservatism and progressivism'.[133] This dichotomy perhaps paints a slightly unhelpful picture of what is occurring. It is not the case that the ICJ has formed two opposing 'camps' with regard to self-defence: progressive and conservative. Such a conception is too simplistic. Instead, what may be identified is a spectrum of thought with regard to the identification and application of the legal principles underlying the law governing self-defence on the part of the various judges who have been responsible for the ICJ's jurisprudence on the issue.[134] It nonetheless would appear that the Court has been pulled in various directions from within as to the course it should take regarding self-defence due to the scope of this spectrum. This may be seen as a contributing factor to many of the problems that we have identified in the jurisprudence.

IV. THE SUITABILITY OF THE ICJ FOR DEALING WITH USE OF FORCE ISSUES

In this section, the claim that the ICJ, as a legal organ, is not suited for dealing with use of force issues at all will be examined. The argument that the

[133] Brown Weiss (n 63) 128; and E McWhinney, 'The International Court of Justice and International Law-Making: The Judicial Activism/Self-Restraint Antinomy' (2006) 5 *Chinese Journal of International Law* 3, esp 6–13.

[134] This point is made (though not necessarily specifically with regard to self-defence or international law) by Dworkin, *Law's Empire* (n 96) 8 and 398–99; Terris, Romano and Swigart (n 32) 66 and 103; and Levin (n 56) 27–28.

Court and its members are 'too political', particularly in the context of the law on the use of force, was explored in the previous section. This section looks at the wholly inverse argument that as a purely legal body, the Court cannot validly pronounce upon disputes involving military intervention because such issues are of a wholly political nature. Essentially, then, this is the claim that the ICJ is not 'political' enough to deal with such issues.

A. The Justiciability of 'Political' Disputes and the Separation of Powers

Given the fundamental nature of self-defence for states and the individuals who inhabit them, it has been argued that disputes involving military intervention cannot be resolved by any international court or tribunal, including the ICJ. As the United States so categorically put it following the *Nicaragua* jurisdiction decision, 'The International Court of Justice was never intended to resolve issues of collective security and self-defence and is patently unsuited for such a role.'[135]

It has been claimed that issues involving the use of force are inherently 'non-justiciable'. This is because disputes of this kind have such a politically charged nature. In other words, they have such a fundamental impact upon the interests and, particularly, the *security* of states that they inevitably give rise to strongly held and maintained—and often wholly divergent—positions of policy on the part of states.[136] Those who make the argument that issues concerning the use of force are of a kind that should not give rise to legal scrutiny reinforce it by pointing to the role of the Security Council in this context. It is claimed that there is a need for separation of powers in the UN system, and as the Security Council is explicitly charged with ensuring the maintenance of peace and security, the ICJ is unable to examine this type of dispute.[137]

[135] 'Statement on the United States Withdrawal from the Proceedings Initiated by Nicaragua' (n 14) 246–47. Elsewhere in the same document, the United States argued that the decision represented, *due to its very subject matter*, 'an overreaching of the Court's limits, a departure from its tradition of judicial restraint, and a risk venture into treacherous political waters' (at 248). It is important to note that this argument has been made by states other than the United States: see, eg, the position taken by Uganda. See below, n 147 and accompanying text.

[136] See the famous statement made by former US Secretary of State Dean Acheson in relation to the Cuban Missile crisis. D Acheson, speaking as part of 'Law and Conflict: Changing Patterns and Contemporary Challenges, Panel on the Cuban Quarantine: Implications for the Future: Remarks' (1963) 57 *American Society of International Law Proceedings* 10–15, 14. Again, it is worth noting that this argument has not merely been made by American scholars. See, eg, RY Jennings, 'International Force and the International Court of Justice' in A Cassese (ed), *The Current Legal Regulation of the Use of Force* (Dordrecht, Martinus Nijhoff, 1986) 323, 327. Nor has it been restricted to forcible disputes: see *Certain Expenses of the United Nations* advisory opinion (1962) ICJ Reports 151, dissenting opinion of Judge Koretsky, 254.

[137] DE Acevedo, 'Disputes Under Consideration by the UN Security Council or Regional Bodies' in LF Damrosch (ed), *The International Court of Justice at a Crossroads* (New York, Transnational, 1987) 242, esp 252–62; Jennings, 'International Force and the International

Contentions of this kind go to the very heart of the relationship between the ICJ and the law governing self-defence. Is the poor quality of the Court's jurisprudence in this area caused by the fact that the ICJ is fundamentally unsuited to dealing with use of force issues? The *Nicaragua* case offered the Court an opportunity to respond to this kind of argument. In that case, the United States made a multitude of jurisdictional objections prior to the merits stage. Some of these objections derived from the proposition that the ICJ cannot validly examine issues of force at all.[138]

The United States argued before the Court that the UN Charter dictates that allegations over unlawful uses of force fall under the competence of other UN organs, particularly the Security Council. Article 24 of the Charter, which gives the Security Council 'primary responsibility for the maintenance of international peace and security', was specifically referred to by the United States. Therefore, it was argued, based on a requirement of 'separation of powers', the Court was debarred from examining such accusations.[139]

In a similar vein, the United States also argued that the Court could not exercise jurisdiction over an *ongoing* exercise of the inherent right of self-defence. This was because Article 51 provides that nothing within the Charter will impair the right of self-defence until the Security Council has taken measures to maintain international peace and security, and that exercises of the right must be reported to the Council. The United States argued that this clearly devolved authority to analyse the exercise of self-defence upon the Security Council. As with the above objection, the United States therefore indicated that the Security Council was the competent body to deal with uses of force, meaning, a priori, that the Court was not.[140]

These jurisdictional objections raised by the United States in the *Nicaragua* case were unsurprisingly rejected by the ICJ.[141] Referring to Article 24 of the Charter, the ICJ indicated that while *primary* responsibility for the maintenance of international peace and security was conferred upon the Security Council, this did not amount to *exclusive* responsibility. The Court further indicated that whilst the Security Council performed a

Court of Justice' (*ibid*) 327; T Sugihara, 'The Judicial Function of the International Court of Justice with Respect to Disputes Involving Highly Political Issues' in AS Muller, D Raic and JM Thuranszky (eds), *The International Court of Justice: Its Future Role after Fifty Years* (The Hague, Martinus Nijhoff, 1997) 117, 124–27; O Schachter, 'Disputes Involving the Use of Force' in LF Damrosch (ed), *The International Court of Justice at a Crossroads* (New York, Transnational, 1987) 223, 231–35; and C Greenwood, 'The International Court of Justice and the Use of Force' in Lowe V and Fitzmaurice M (eds), *Fifty Years of the International Court of Justice: Essays in Honour of Sir Robert Jennings* (Cambridge, Cambridge University Press, 1996) 373, 376–77.

[138] For an overview of the arguments of this kind made by the United States in *Nicaragua*, see Gray (n 87) 869–71; and Chayes (n 72) 1449–51.

[139] *Nicaragua* counter-memorial of the United States (n 14) 136–55.

[140] *Ibid*, 156–65.

[141] *Nicaragua* jurisdiction of the court and admissibility of the application (1984) ICJ Reports 392, para 113.

political function in relation to disputes, the Court's role was purely judicial and, as such, complimentary.[142] Additionally, the ICJ reaffirmed its position in the *Iranian Hostages* case, in which it stated:

> Whereas Article 12 of the Charter expressly forbids the General Assembly to make any recommendation with regard to a dispute or situation while the Security Council is exercising its functions in respect of that dispute or situation, no such restriction is placed on the functioning of the Court by any provision of either the Charter or the Statute of the Court.[143]

Therefore the Court concluded that nothing in the Charter or in customary international law required a distinct separation of powers between the Security Council and the ICJ. It was made clear that 'the use of force was a matter subject to international law and thus raised a legal question capable of objective determination by a judicial tribunal.'[144] More specifically, the Court was explicit in indicating that despite the role for the Security Council set out in Article 51 of the Charter, it did not consider that this precluded the ICJ from ruling upon arguments of self-defence.[145]

However, the contention that issues of military force are too politically fundamental to be examined by the ICJ has not disappeared following its wholesale rejection by the Court in *Nicaragua*.[146] For example, in response to the request of the Democratic Republic of the Congo (DRC) for provisional measures in relation to the Congo conflict, Uganda adopted an argument that mirrored one of those employed by the United States in *Nicaragua*. Uganda indicated that due to the requirement of separation of powers, the conflict within the DRC was a matter for the Security Council. It highlighted the Lusaka Agreement, endorsed by the Council, as evidence of that organ dealing with the matter and stressed that ICJ involvement may undermine this process.[147] The Court rejected the Ugandan claim, employing similar reasoning as it did in *Nicaragua*.[148]

B. The Need for a Legal Approach

Leaving aside the *quality* of the substantive jurisprudence of the ICJ on self-defence (something that has been brought into question throughout

[142] *Ibid*, para 95.

[143] *Ibid*, para 93, citing *Iranian Hostages* merits (n 21) 22.

[144] Greenwood (n 137) 375.

[145] *Nicaragua* jurisdiction of the court and admissibility of the application (n 141) para 98.

[146] Gray (n 87) 876–81. However, it is interesting that the United States itself has not returned to these arguments since *Nicaragua*, relying on alternative jurisdictional objections in subsequent ICJ cases involving use of force issues to which it has been party.

[147] *DRC v Uganda* CR 2000/23, www.icj-cij.org/docket/files/116/4265.pdf. Rwanda made a similar argument in its oral pleadings over preliminary measures in *DRC v Rwanda* (*New Application: 2002*) CR 2002/37, www.icj-cij.org/docket/files/126/4143.pdf.

[148] *DRC v Uganda* provisional measures order (2000) ICJ Reports 110, para 37.

this book), the Court's assertion that it is able to deal with disputes involving military intervention, *as a matter of principle*, must be seen as being correct.[149] All disputes, not merely those that relate to uses of force, have political elements.[150] The view that uses of force should be regulated by law, and specifically adjudication, has developed since the end of the Second World War.[151] It has been argued that this has to be the correct view if international law on the use of force is to have any meaning at all.[152]

Based on our analysis of the Court's jurisprudence on self-defence, it is questionable whether the Court has been a desirable forum for examining the use of force. However, it must be concluded that simply because a dispute involves politically contentious aspects does not mean that it is beyond the scope of legal rules. Indeed, no state would today claim that the use of force is not subject to a level of legal regulation. In principle, then, the ICJ should not be barred from applying those rules to specific disputes where it otherwise has jurisdiction to do so.

Although it is submitted that the Court should not in principle be precluded from examining a dispute that involves the use of force, it is not

[149] Schachter, 'Self-Defence and the Rule of Law' (n 99) 276.

[150] As Judge Lachs stated in his separate opinion to the *Nicaragua* case, 'Almost all disputes arising between states have both political and legal aspects; politics and law meet at almost every point on the road.' *Nicaragua* merits (n 3) separate opinion of Judge Lachs, para 168. See also Franck (n 72) 39; Sugihara (n 137) 118; E Gordon, 'Legal Disputes Under Article 36(2) of the Statute' in LF Damrosch (ed), *The International Court of Justice at a Crossroads* (New York, Transnational, 1987) 183, 185; Rosenne, *The Law and Practice of the International Court of Justice* (n 81) 2–4; and R Szafarz, *The Compulsory Jurisdiction of the International Court of Justice* (Dordrecht, Martinus Nijhoff, 1993) 93. Couvreur inverts this, claiming that all political disputes have at least some legal dimension, though whether this is similarly universally true is perhaps debatable. P Couvreur, 'The Effectiveness of the International Court of Justice in the Peaceful Settlement of Disputes' in AS Muller, D Raic and JM Thuranszky (eds), *The International Court of Justice: Its Future Role after Fifty Years* (The Hague, Martinus Nijhoff, 1997) 83, 93.

[151] Eg, the Nuremburg Tribunal stressed the desirability of judicial examination of arguments of self-defence,:'Judicial Decisions Involving Questions of International Law: *International Military Tribunal* (*Nuremburg*), judgment and sentences' (1947) 41 *American Journal of International Law* 172, 207.

[152] AW Rovine, 'Should the United States Reconsider Its Acceptance of World Court Jurisdiction? Remarks' (1985) 79 *American Society of International Law Proceedings* 101, 102–3. Indeed, it has been argued that the ICJ may in some cases represent a *preferable* mechanism for assessing uses of force than the Security Council, as it is comparatively 'depoliticised'. See Y Dinstein, *War, Aggression and Self-Defence*, 4th edn (Cambridge, Cambridge University Press, 2005) 319 (who categorically states that 'the Court, not being hampered by political constraints or by motivations of expediency, is fully qualified to bring legal yardsticks to bear upon armed conflict in a dispassionate fashion'); AW Rovine, 'The National Interest and the World Court' in L Gross (ed), *The Future of the International Court of Justice, Vol I* (New York, Oceana, 1976) 313–35; Schachter, 'Disputes Involving the Use of Force' (n 137) 228–41; BS Chimni, 'The International Court and the Maintenance of Peace and Security: The *Nicaragua* Decision and the United States Response' (1986) 35 *International and Comparative Law Quarterly* 960, 968–69; R Higgins, 'Policy Considerations and the International Judicial Process' (1968) 17 *International and Comparative Law Quarterly* 58, esp 81–84; and Sugihara (n 137) 127–29.

here claimed that the ICJ is capable of examining *all aspects* of all disputes. Whilst the ICJ has affirmed its role with regard to disputes involving uses of force, it has also made clear that it can examine only 'justiciable' aspects of disputes,[153] meaning aspects to which legal criteria may be applied.[154] In other words, the Court can examine only aspects of disputes to which it is possible to apply legal rules (or at least, legal principles).[155] As the Court itself has stated, disputes before it must be 'clothed in legal form'.[156]

Again, this is a general problem for the ICJ, but one which has particular resonance with regard to use of force disputes, given the politically charged nature of forcible intervention and armed conflict. The result of this inevitable restriction to the legal aspects of disputes 'is that the dispute which can be the subject of a ruling by the Court will often consist of an issue, or set of issues, considerably narrower than the overall dispute of which it is a part'.[157]

Having said this, any distinction between political and legal elements of a dispute is necessarily somewhat artificial, as all disputes contain both of these elements. To expect the Court to be able to operate in a political vacuum—in terms of either its decision-making or the implications of its judgments—is wholly unrealistic. Therefore, the real issue here is how the ICJ *approaches* disputes. The ICJ's approach to any dispute must, so far as possible, be limited to the logical application of the law.[158]

Such a focus on methodology with regard to judicial reasoning returns us to the notion of an application of legal principles, rather than a mere political choice. It also recalls the tension between the two roles of the ICJ and the differing views of its members (past and present) over how the Court should deal with issues of this kind. It has been argued that in areas where the law is unclear, as in the case of self-defence, a more policy-orientated approach to judicial activity may well be a desirable method of examining disputes, in the interests of future clarity and development.[159] Equally,

[153] See, eg, *Nicaragua* jurisdiction of the court and admissibility of the application (n 141) para 101. See also the comments made in the *South West Africa Cases* preliminary objections (1962) ICJ Reports 319, joint dissenting opinion of Judge Spencer and Judge Fitzmaurice, para 466. See generally Gordon (n 150).

[154] This definition of 'justiciability' is taken from Koskenniemi, *From Apology to Utopia* (n 44) 29 but is also in accord with general contemporary conceptions of that notion. See also Dumbauld (n 33) 935.

[155] CE Amerasinghe, 'Reflections on the Judicial Function in International Law' in TM Ndiaye and R Wolfrum (eds), *Law of the Sea, Environmental Law and Settlement of Disputes:* Liber Amicorum *Judge Thomas A Mensah* (Leiden, Martinus Nijhoff, 2007) 121, 125; Merrills (n 25) 169–71; Jennings, 'International Force and the International Court of Justice' (n 136) 324–27; and Szafarz (n 150) 93.

[156] *South West Africa Cases* second phase (n 40) para 51.

[157] Greenwood (n 137) 377. See also Schachter, 'Self-Defence and the Rule of Law' (n 99) 276–77; Couvreur (n 150) 93–95; Jennings, 'International Force and the International Court of Justice' (n 136) 324–27; and Merrills (n 25) 169–71.

[158] Higgins, 'Policy Considerations and the International Judicial Process' (n 152) 74.

[159] *Ibid*, 67–70.

however, it has been argued that explicit adoption of a normative course due to policy considerations is 'an option not open to the Court' on the basis that the ICJ must restrict itself to legal methodology and reasoning and the application of legal principles.[160] The question of how far the ICJ may incorporate policy considerations into legal decisions is not a phenomenon unique to use of force decisions, but it is clearly apparent in this context. Here lies the crux: self-defence surely must be regulated by law and thus by the ICJ as primary judicial organ of the UN, but it cannot adequately be regulated by reference to law alone, and as such, the ICJ is not suited to dealing with it. This evident paradox will come more into focus as we begin to examine some of the other restraints upon the Court's ability to deal comprehensively with disputes involving self-defence claims.

C. Evidence-Gathering

The ICJ has inherent problems in terms of the collation of reliable evidence in the context of any of the cases on its docket.[161] For example, it is often over-reliant upon the parties before it to provide the evidence upon which it bases its decisions.[162] As such, the Court found the collation of evidence particularly difficult in the *Nicaragua* case, due to the non-appearance of the United States, which did not provide any evidence, at least not formally, after its departure from the proceedings. More generally, given the nature of conflict situations, the problem of evidence-gathering is greater in relation to disputes concerning uses of force and self-defence.[163] Gathering evidence on the ground relating to forcible incidents or during the realities of conflict situations is obviously extremely problematic. Such difficulties are likely to be particularly pronounced in instances when hostilities are ongoing.[164] This is due both to the practical difficulties involved in ascertaining the facts of a chaotic current conflict and to the sensitive nature of such situations.[165]

160 Higgins, 'Policy Considerations and the International Judicial Process' (n 152) 70.

161 For an overview, see WF Foster, 'Fact Finding and the World Court' (1969) 7 *Canadian Yearbook of International Law* 150. See also RN Gardner, 'Commentary of the Law of Self-Defence' in LF Damrosch and DJ Scheffer (eds), *Law and Force in the New International Order* (Boulder, Westview Press, 1991) 49, 53.

162 K Highet, 'Evidence and Proof of Facts' in LF Damrosch (ed), *The International Court of Justice at a Crossroads* (New York, Transnational, 1987) 355, 357.

163 JA Green, 'Fluctuating Evidentiary Standards for Self-Defence in the International Court of Justice' (2009) 58 *International and Comparative Law Quarterly* 163, 164; Gray (n 87) 899; Schachter, 'Disputes Involving the Use of Force' (n 137) 235–36; and *Nicaragua* jurisdiction of the court and admissibility of the application (n 141) para 101.

164 Schachter, 'Disputes Involving the Use of Force' (n 137) 239–40.

165 Eg, an argument made by the United States with regard to *Nicaragua* was that much of the evidence that would support its claim was 'of a highly sensitive intelligence character'. Presenting this evidence in the public domain (especially to a Court including 'two judges from Warsaw Pact nations') would therefore be detrimental to national security. See

Thus it was argued by the United States in *Nicaragua* that ongoing conflicts create such extreme difficulties in terms of evidence-gathering that they cannot form the basis of claims before the ICJ *at all*, which necessarily require discernable factual material.[166] The counter-memorial of the United States held in connection with ongoing conflicts:

> The pattern of facts necessary to the achievement of a legal conclusion, and to an effective resolution of the conflict itself, is incapable of judicial ascertainment through the technical and formal procedures, and evidentiary standards applicable to proofs at law.[167]

In relation to this objection, the Court held that despite the undeniable difficulties in obtaining reliable evidence in conflict situations, use of force disputes were not the only example of cases that led to evidential difficulties. Ultimately, it was the state seeking to establish any given fact that would bear the burden of proving it, and therefore potential evidential difficulties did not make submissions inadmissible prima facie.[168]

More recently, in *Cameroon v Nigeria*, Nigeria responded to initial allegations of an unlawful use of force by contending that the Court should decline jurisdiction given the ongoing nature of the conflict and the consequent evidential difficulties involved.[169] It was claimed that the complexity of the situation meant that the assertions made by Cameroon in its application and memorial were 'vague and unsubstantiated' and that difficulties in evidence-gathering would mean that the Court would be unable to reach a valid decision.[170] The Court dismissed Nigeria's suggestion that the evidential difficulties of an ongoing conflict precluded the Court from examining the dispute by citing the *Nicaragua* jurisdictional judgment:[171] 'It is the applicant which must bear the consequences of an application that gives an inadequate rendering of the facts and grounds on which the claim is based.'[172]

It is clear, then, that the difficulty of evidence-gathering in use of force cases has not been viewed by the Court as barring it from dealing with use of force disputes in principle, any more than the political nature of such disputes or the role of the Security Council in disputes involving military force. Again, in principle at least, this would seem to be a correct conclusion: mere

'Statement on the US Withdrawal from the Proceedings Initiated by Nicaragua' (n 14) 248. This evidential problem is again likely to be more pronounced in the context of use of force disputes than in many other types of dispute before the ICJ.

166 *Nicaragua* counter-memorial of the United States (n 14) Part IV, 166–69.

167 *Ibid*, 166.

168 *Nicaragua* jurisdiction of the court and admissibility of the application (n 141) para 101.

169 *Cameroon v Nigeria* preliminary objections of Nigeria (1995) www.icj-cij.org/docket/files/94/8598.pdf.

170 *Ibid*, vol I, paras 6.1–6.18.

171 Specifically, *Nicaragua* jurisdiction of the court and admissibility of the application (n 141) para 101.

172 *Cameroon v Nigeria* preliminary objections (1998) ICJ Reports 296, para 101.

'difficulty' in evidence-gathering should not bar the Court from examining a dispute per se. Nonetheless, problems with evidence-gathering have, one may assume, impeded the work of the ICJ in this area.

V. CONSENT AND THE LIMITED NUMBER OF SELF-DEFENCE CASES

In spite of all the above, it is argued here that by far the biggest restriction upon the Court in terms of its ability to pronounce upon issues of international law and impact upon specific disputes in practice is the fact that it is dependent upon state consent to function. It has been stated by a former judge of the ICJ that 'the Court is handicapped by the principle of consent.'[173] Yet, for good or ill, consent is the fundamental basis of the Court's entire jurisdictional framework.[174] The result of this aspect of the Court's composition is that ultimately, very few cases are heard on the merits by the ICJ. The Court often has extreme difficulty in finding jurisdiction to hear cases when an application has been made to it. Even more tellingly, states in general do not lodge applications with the ICJ at all; they instead opt to resolve their disputes through alternative means. It has been suggested that this is because states in general prefer to settle disputes through political means that they understand—and more importantly can control—rather than through juridical ones.[175]

Again, this problem is one that is pronounced with regard to disputes involving the use of force.[176] This is due to the particularly controversial

[173] Kooijmans (n 39) 747.

[174] As Judge Oda put it, 'the Court's jurisdiction must rest upon the free will of sovereign states, clearly and categorically expressed, to grant the Court the competence to settle the dispute in question'. *Border and Transborder Armed Actions* (*Nicaragua v Honduras*) jurisdiction of the court and admissibility of the application (1988) ICJ Reports 69, separate opinion of Judge Oda, para 1. See also SA Alexandrov, 'The Compulsory Jurisdiction of the International Court of Justice: How Compulsory is it?' (2006) 5 *Chinese Journal of International Law* 29; Rosenne, *The Law and Practice of the International Court of Justice* (n 81) 175; Szafarz (n 150) 3–4; and Merrills (n 25) 127–28. The basis of the Court's consensual jurisdiction may be found in Art 36 of its Statute. The main methods by which jurisdiction may be conferred are: 1) by special agreement between the parties to take a dispute before the ICJ; 2) through a declaration accepting the Court's compulsory jurisdiction under Art 36(2) of the ICJ's Statute (what is known as 'the optional clause'); and 3) by way of a compromissory clause in a treaty, usually providing that disputes with regard to the interpretation or application of that treaty are to be referred to the Court. M Dixon and R McCorquodale, *Cases and Materials on International Law*, 4th edn (Oxford, Oxford University Press, 2003) 592.

[175] Fitzmaurice (n 1) 463. This is due to 'how far the international community accept[s] the need for judicial settlement' and not a failing of the ICJ as such. Shahabuddeen (n 88) 19. However, given this fact, it is incumbent upon the Court to be seen as a viable and impartial means of settling international disputes.

[176] Moreover, the reliance upon state consent and the general lack of it are arguably more concerning in regard to disputes involving 'fundamental' areas of international law, such as alleged breaches of human rights or humanitarian law, or in disputes involving the use of force. This has been expressed by members of the Court as recently as 2006: 'It is a matter of serious concern that at the beginning of the twenty-first century it is still for states to choose

nature of any relationship between forcible action and adjudication, as well as the view of some states that issues of force are inherently non-justiciable, as discussed above.[177] Such attitudes can be seen from the fact that a number of the states that have accepted the compulsory jurisdiction of the ICJ under Article 36(2) of the Statute of the Court have specifically reserved from that acceptance disputes involving the use of force.[178] Thus, Kenya, for example, has in general consented to the Court's assessment of its disputes, but not

> disputes concerning any question relating to or arising out of belligerent or military occupation or the discharge of any functions pursuant to any recommendation or decision of an organ of the United Nations, in accordance with which the Government of the Republic of Kenya have accepted obligations.[179]

As was noted in the Introduction to this book, there has been a great increase in applications to the Court regarding such issues in recent years.[180] However, with only one exception, every state that has faced allegations in an application to the ICJ concerning an unlawful use of force has raised preliminary objections over the Court's jurisdiction.[181]

In any event, the important result of such practice in this context is that the vast majority of disputes involving claims of self-defence do not reach the ICJ on the merits, despite the increase of substantive cases on the issue in recent years. The overwhelming majority of these disputes are simply not brought before the Court through application or special agreement. Moreover, even of the disputes that do appear on the ICJ's docket, very few make it to the merits phase due to jurisdictional restrictions.[182] For example, as a result of the major conflict in the DRC that followed the overthrow of President Mobutu Sese Seko,[183] four applications were

whether they consent to the Court adjudicating genocide.' *Armed Activities on the Territory of the Congo* (*New Application: 2002*) (*DRC v Rwanda*) jurisdiction of the court and admissibility of the application (2006) www.icj-cij.org/docket/files/126/7070.pdf, joint separate opinion of Judges Higgins, Kooijmans, Elaraby, Owada and Simma, para 25.

[177] Above, section IV.

[178] This is what Shabtai Rosenne calls the 'war exclusion clause'. S Rosenne, *The Law and Practice of the International Court of Justice, 1920–2005, Vol II: Jurisdiction*, 4th edn (Leiden, Martinus Nijhoff, 2006) 772–76. On the implications of 'war exclusion clauses', see Franck (n 72) 71. However, for a contrary view, see Gray (n 87) 885–88, who holds that the number of such reservations are still comparatively small, thus indicating that states in general accept the role of the Court in relation to disputes involving the use of force.

[179] Declaration of Kenya. See also the declarations of India, Malawi and Malta, reproduced in S Rosenne, *Documents on the International Court of Justice*, 2nd edn (Alphen aan den Rejn, Sijthoff & Noordhoof, 1979) 382–83, 375–79, 385–86 and 386–87 respectively.

[180] See Introduction, section I.

[181] Gray (n 87) 868. Uganda is the only state not to have done this: in *DRC v Uganda* it instead merely reserved the right to do so. *DRC v Uganda* rejoinder submitted by Uganda (2002) www.icj-cij.org/docket/files/116/8314.pdf, para 34. However, Uganda nonetheless questioned the suitability of the Court in the context of the award of provisional measures.

[182] Gray (n 87) 868.

[183] See introduction, section II-C for factual references.

ultimately filed with the ICJ's registry. Of these, only *DRC v Uganda* advanced to the merits phase. That case had an unusually strong jurisdictional basis,[184] but it is notable that the three other cases relating to the conflict failed to lead to a decision from the Court.[185] This is symptomatic: in one respect or another, the ICJ does not have jurisdiction to entertain disputes concerning self-defence in the vast majority of cases. This is due simply to a lack of state consent.

There is certainly no political will for the introduction of mandatory jurisdiction[186] before the ICJ.[187] Proposals have occasionally been advanced along these lines.[188] However, in general, such proposals have met with little support.[189] It must be accepted that any wholesale reform of the jurisdiction of the ICJ is unlikely. In terms of the Court's dispute settlement role, this is somewhat problematic: only a limited number of cases can be resolved through legal settlement at the ICJ. However, resort to the Court is only one means of international dispute settlement, and in terms of the use of force, it may not always even be the most desirable of these.[190] So long as disputes are resolved in some manner (a separate issue), the fact that use of the Court in this context is a small percentage of the total is not all that concerning in itself.

A greater problem emerges when one looks at the impact of ICJ decisions on the development of the law or focuses upon the wider significance of the jurisprudence. Of the numerous instances when states have made legal claims of self-defence, only three have reached the merits phase at the ICJ. Therefore, the jurisprudence of the Court derived from contentious cases—so relied upon to elucidate the international law

[184] Indeed, arguably the strongest of any of the ICJ's self-defence decisions. See below, n 197.

[185] *DRC v Rwanda* and *DRC v Burundi* were both discontinued in 2001 at the request of the DRC when it became evident that there was not sufficient basis in either case for the Court to find jurisdiction, and more recently, the Court found that it did not have jurisdiction to hear the DRC's second application instituting proceedings against Rwanda. See introduction, section II-C.

[186] The term 'mandatory jurisdiction' is here used to refer to a requirement that states refer their disputes to the ICJ irrespective of consent (other than in the form of acceptance of the instrument constituting such jurisdiction in the first place—which presumably would be an amended Statute of the ICJ). This is in contrast to 'compulsory jurisdiction', which is used to refer to instances in which the Court's jurisdiction is based upon a declaration made by the state in question under Art 36(2) of the Court's Statute (the 'optional clause').

[187] Jennings, 'International Force and the International Court of Justice' (n 136) 324; Alexandrov (n 174) 32; and G Hafner, K Boon, A Rübesame and J Huston, 'A Response to the American View as Presented by Ruth Wedgwood' (1999) *European Journal of International Law* 108, 122 in the context of a discussion of the International Criminal Court.

[188] A notable proposal of this kind in this context was one set out by the Soviet Union in 1988 (UN Doc A/43/629, 5–6).

[189] The Soviet proposal (*ibid*) essentially met with no support. In general, see Fitzmaurice (n 1) esp 470–78.

[190] As pointed out by Schachter, 'Self-Defence and the Rule of Law' (n 99) 276–78 and evidenced by the nature of the substantive jurisprudence discussed throughout this book.

governing self-defence—has necessarily been derived from only a tiny percentage of disputes. Drawing essential general principles from a limited number of specific applications cannot be desirable: it seems self-evident that the greater the number of cases in which the Court has pronounced on self-defence, the more reliable the picture that the aggregate jurisprudence produces. This point is particularly relevant in this context because of the specific factual, substantive and jurisdictional problems of the few self-defence merits cases, such as the non-appearance of the United States or the necessary reliance upon customary international law alone in *Nicaragua*. These problems thus not only have affected the decisions themselves but have had a significant impact upon the 'depth' of the wider jurisprudence that the Court has produced upon the issue.

Therefore, a lack of consent by states to submit such disputes to the Court has implications for both for the settlement of specific disputes concerning self-defence through the application of law and, importantly, for the development of that law more generally. In terms of the former, the vast majority of disputes are not resolved in this way, and thus the juridical option for resolving such disputes may be said to be underemployed. In terms of the latter, a pervasive lack of applications to the Court (or jurisdiction in cases in which applications have been made) in this area has meant that the jurisprudence of the Court on self-defence is notably 'thin', deriving as it does from only a handful of cases.

VI. CONSENT AND PARTIAL JURISDICTION

It is not simply the case that the Court either does or does not have jurisdiction to entertain a dispute. Instead, cases that reach the merits stage before the Court usually do so on the basis of *partial* jurisdiction. In other words, even when self-defence cases *do* make it through the jurisdictional fortress surrounding the Court,[191] the jurisdictional basis for cases is almost never total.[192] We have already seen that the ICJ is naturally

[191] To borrow a phrase from Kritsiotis (n 18) 243.

[192] This holds true irrespective of how jurisdiction has been conferred. If jurisdiction is conferred by a special agreement between the parties to take a dispute before the ICJ, this will naturally set out the parameters for the involvement of the ICJ. Eg, the jurisdictional basis for the *Land, Island and Maritime Frontier Dispute* (*El Salvador/Honduras: Nicaragua intervening*) merits (1992) ICJ Reports 351 was a special agreement between the parties. That instrument made it clear that the parties submitted the issues as set out in Art 2 (the delimitation of the boundary line under dispute and the legal status of the islands) *only* to the ICJ: see paras 1–5 of the decision. Alternatively, if jurisdiction has been conferred by way of a clause of a treaty, inevitably the Court is restricted to examining the legal questions relating to the subject matter of the constituting treaty. JI Charney, 'Compromissory Clauses and the Jurisdiction of the International Court of Justice' (1987) 81 *American Journal of International Law* 855, esp 859–60. Even when a state has set out a declaration under the optional clause, this almost always comprises reservations as to the scope of the jurisdiction conferred.

restricted to examining only the 'legal' aspects of a dispute.[193] However, due to the limited manner in which jurisdiction has been conferred upon the Court in the major self-defence cases, this is far from being the only jurisdictional restriction upon the ICJ: in the main it can examine only some of the legal aspects of a dispute. The issue of how much jurisdictional scope the Court has in any given dispute is the reason that it has been remarked:

> One of the most controversial issues in the judicial settlement of disputes before the ICJ is the relationship between the scope of the jurisdiction conferred on the Court and the law applicable to the dispute.[194]

The most obvious example of the kind of partial jurisdiction here discussed is the fact that in the *Nicaragua* case the Court was effectively able to examine only customary international law. It will be recalled that this was due to the multilateral treaty reservation that formed part of the US declaration under Article 36(2) of the ICJ's Statute.[195] Essentially the US declaration amounted to a partial consent to the compulsory jurisdiction of the ICJ.[196]

Indeed, both *Nicaragua* and *Oil Platforms* were decided based upon a fragmented picture of the law: the consent-based nature of the Court's jurisdiction meant that the Court had to approach both disputes in the manner of a judicial horse wearing legal blinkers.[197] Thus, not only does the self-defence jurisprudence derive from only a handful of disputes, it derives from a handful of disputes of partial or restricted jurisdiction. Again, this is particularly notable when it is considered that these cases are often viewed as authoritative statements of the law.

A judgment that is later referred to for guidance actually represents law that has, to utilise the metaphor of Judge Higgins, been squeezed through the eye of a jurisdictional needle.[198] Such a partial view of the disputes and legal issues before it is obviously detrimental in itself for the quality of the

[193] Above, section IV-B.

[194] E Cannizzaro and B Bonafé, 'Fragmenting International Law through Compromissory Clauses? Some Remarks on the Decision of the ICJ in the *Oil Platforms* Case' (2005) 16 *European Journal of International Law* 481, 481.

[195] See introduction, section II-A.

[196] Rosenne, *Documents on the International Court of Justice* (n 179) 415.

[197] It is important to note that this does not hold true for the *DRC v Uganda* decision. This case is therefore exceptional in the context of the law governing self-defence in that it is the first contentious case to have an uncontroversial or 'full' jurisdictional basis to examine self-defence issues. Both states explicitly invoked the law of self-defence (see Introduction, section II-C), and both had made declarations under Art 36(2). Neither declaration contained anything that precluded the Court from examining the law on the use of force in any way. See the declaration of the DRC (then Zaire), reproduced in *ICJ Yearbook* 43 (1988–89) 95; and the declaration of Uganda, reproduced in Rosenne, *Documents on the International Court of Justice* (n 179) 407. As such, it is even more regrettable that the Court said so little on this area of the law in the *DRC v Uganda* merits decision, as for the first time it truly had a secure jurisdictional basis from which to do so.

[198] *Oil Platforms* merits (n 51) separate opinion of Judge Higgins, para 26.

jurisprudence produced by the ICJ: 'In a matter as fundamental and as contested as self-defence, it is dysfunctional to build comprehensive exposition on the shaky foundations provided by essentially passing references.'[199] By pushing the law on self-defence through the eye of the metaphorical needle, the Court has, it is argued, ended up with an insufficient picture of that law on the other side.

Moreover, the manner that the Court has approached the apparent restrictions upon its jurisdiction has been controversial. The ICJ has on occasion taken an overtly policy-orientated, legally progressive stance with regard to its findings of jurisdiction in its use of force related decisions. Instances may be identified when the Court either has found jurisdiction in dubious circumstances or, perhaps more commonly, has widened the scope of a limited jurisdictional base to pronounce upon legal issues not necessarily covered by the clearly established jurisdictional base for the case. Thus, in the context of the use of force, the Court has at times stretched the partial jurisdiction that formed the basis of the cases, thus allowing it to deal with use of force questions that may otherwise have remained beyond its competence.

The best example of this is the *Oil Platforms* case.[200] Indeed, one may question whether the ICJ had jurisdiction to examine the law governing self-defence in *Oil Platforms* at all. The Court's sole jurisdictional base in that case was a 1955 treaty of navigation and commerce between the United States and Iran. Article XXI(2) of that treaty conferred jurisdiction on the Court regarding 'the interpretation or application *of the present treaty*' (emphasis added). However, when examining whether the United States could rely upon Article XX(1)(d), which offered the defence of measures 'necessary to protect [a state's] essential security interests', the Court turned to the law governing self-defence. The essential claim made by the majority here was that to determine whether the actions were necessary for the essential security interests of the United States, the Court had to determine whether such actions amounted to lawful instances of self-defence. Yet, Article XX(1)(d) of the 1955 treaty was clearly not synonymous with an assessment of the lawfulness of a given action under the *jus ad bellum*.[201]

By equating a provision in a bilateral freedom and navigation treaty with the law governing self-defence, the Court in *Oil Platforms* controversially stretched the principles of treaty interpretation to find jurisdiction to

[199] I Scobbie, 'Words My Mother Never Taught Me: In Defence of the International Court' (2005) 99 *American Journal of International Law* 76, 86–88, quoted at 88; and Jennings, 'The Judicial Function and the Rule of Law in International Relations' (n 34) 142–43.

[200] A decision that one judge referred to as representing 'an upsurge of misplaced activism'. Kooijmans (n 39) 752.

[201] JA Green, 'The *Oil Platforms* Case: An Error in Judgment?' (2004) 9 *Journal of Conflict and Security Law* 357, 373–77.

examine this area of the law.[202] The question submitted by the parties for determination by the Court was whether the actions of the United States amounted to measures 'necessary to protect its essential security interests', not whether the US attacks constituted lawful actions in self-defence. A ruling on the lawfulness of the actions of the United States under the law of self-defence was not requested by either of the parties at final submissions stage.[203] As such, the Court's examination of self-defence constituted a breach of the *non ultra petita* rule.[204] As Judge Higgins rightly pointed out, while it is arguably desirable for the Court to examine the law of the use of force, it cannot (or at least should not) when it does not have the competence to do so.[205]

In contrast to this somewhat elastic approach to jurisdiction, in some instances the Court has seemingly been quite reluctant to examine issues concerning the law on the use of force. In *Cameroon v Nigeria,* for example, the ICJ appeared to possess jurisdiction to examine whether the parties had breached obligations under the *jus ad bellum*. The jurisdictional basis for the dispute was based upon reciprocal declarations made by the parties under Article 36(2) of the Statute of the ICJ.[206] Neither of these declarations restricted the Court from examining use of force issues; indeed, they were both made without reservation. Importantly, both states argued that the other was in breach of the *jus ad bellum* as an aspect of the litigation.[207]

[202] *Ibid*; H Rishikof, 'When Naked Came the Doctrine of "Self-Defence": What is the Proper Role of the International Court of Justice in Use of Force Cases?' (2004) 29 *Yale Journal of International Law* 331, 339–40; and N Ochoa-Ruiz and E Salamanca-Aguado, 'Exploring the Limits of International Law Relating to the Use of Force in Self-Defence' (2005) 16 *European Journal of International Law* 499, 506–10. Moreover, it is evident that the Court need not have examined the issue of self-defence in *Oil Platforms* in any event, given that it ultimately found that the US actions did not interfere with Iran's freedom of commerce. The ICJ concluded that the United States did not breach Art X(1) of the 1955 Treaty at all. Thus, the discussion of Art XX(1)(d) (and as a result, of self-defence) in the case may be seen as wholly superfluous to the decision at hand. This can be viewed as one example of the Court attempting to 'stretch' the scope of its judgment to enable it to make pronouncements on the law of the use of force. See *ibid*, 370–73.

[203] Iran ultimately dropped the reference to 'international law' from its initial application. See *Oil Platforms* observations and submissions on the US preliminary objections submitted by the Iran (1994) www.icj-cij.org/docket/files/90/8626.pdf, Part III, para 2.11; and *Oil Platforms* CR 2003/16, www.icj-cij.org/docket/files/90/5173.pdf, 36. Admittedly, the United States did maintain that its actions were lawful instances of self-defence. See *Oil Platforms* counter-memorial and counterclaim submitted by the United States (1997) www.icj-cij.org/docket/files/90/8632.pdf, Part IV; and *Oil Platforms* CR 2003/11, www.icj-cij.org/docket/files/90/5153.pdf, 13. However, it also stated that the jurisdiction of the Court was confined to the issue of measures necessary to protect its essential security interests and did not extend to the legality of its actions under the law of self-defence. Again, see *Oil Platforms*, CR 2003/11, 13.

[204] *Oil Platforms* merits (n 51) separate opinion of Judge Buergenthal, esp para 19. On the *non ultra petita* rule, see ch 1, n 4.

[205] *Oil Platforms* merits (n 51) separate opinion of Judge Higgins, esp para 23.

[206] *Cameroon v Nigeria* preliminary objections (n 172) esp paras 21–47.

[207] Eg, Cameroon asked the Court to adjudge and declare, inter alia, 'that by using force against the Republic of Cameroon, the Federal Republic of Nigeria has violated and is

However, having rejected at the preliminary objections stage Nigeria's claim that the law on the use of force was not justiciable in the case due to evidential difficulties,[208] the ICJ merits judgment offered only a very cursory examination of the parties' claims concerning state responsibility[209] and offered no examination whatsoever of the law on the use of force or how it applied to the dispute.[210] The claim of self-defence that was explicitly (though, admittedly, briefly) made by Nigeria[211] was also not discussed.[212] The Court gave little reason for this.[213] Admittedly, it is clear that the use of force was not the primary focus of the submissions of the parties.[214] Yet, they both explicitly requested findings on this issue, and the Court had what appeared to be firm jurisdictional ground from which to make such findings. It has therefore been pointed out that the ICJ 'was clearly anxious to avoid a decision on the use of force at the merits stage'.[215]

Such caution seems somewhat anomalous when one considers the lengths to which the Court appeared to go to pronounce upon the law on the use of force elsewhere, for example in *Oil Platforms*. Moreover, it is not merely that the Court has appeared to act in a particularly restrictive manner with regard to finding jurisdiction to examine use of force issues in some cases whilst being wholly progressive in approach in others. This discrepancy in approach may at times be identified within a single decision.

For example, returning to *Oil Platforms*, the Court examined the law on the use of force when it did not have the jurisdictional basis to do so, as we have seen. However, having determined that the United States had used force in a manner that was not justified as self-defence, the Court then refused to take this a step further and condemn the United States for

violating its obligations under international treaty law and customary law'. *Cameroon v Nigeria* application instituting proceedings (1994) www.icj-cij.org/docket/files/94/7201.pdf, para 20. For the corresponding counterclaims of Nigeria, see *Cameroon v Nigeria* counter-memorial submitted by Nigeria (1999) www.icj-cij.org/docket/files/94/8602.pdf, Part VI.

208 See above, section IV-C.

209 *Land and Maritime Boundary between Cameroon and Nigeria* (*Cameroon v Nigeria: Equatorial Guinea intervening*) merits (2002) ICJ Reports 9, paras 308–24.

210 Instead, the Court merely observed that the parties were under obligations to remove any military forces from the territory of the other (as it had just defined such boundaries). *Ibid*, paras 314–15.

211 *Cameroon v Nigeria* counter-memorial of Nigeria (n 207) Part V, para 24.49; CR 2002/14, www.icj-cij.org/docket/files/94/5029.pdf, para 41; and CR 2002/18, www.icj-cij.org/docket/files/94/5045.pdf, para 68.

212 Though the Court did take note of it. *Cameroon v Nigeria* merits (n 209) para 311.

213 Gray (n 87) 881–83.

214 Thus Cameroon stated, 'The dispute relates *essentially* to the question of sovereignty over the Bakassi Peninsula' (emphasis added). *Cameroon v Nigeria* application instituting proceedings (n 207) para 1. There was also a similar focus upon the sovereignty of the Lake Chad region.

215 C Gray, 'The Eritrea/Ethiopia Claims Commission Oversteps its Boundaries: A Partial Award?' (2006) 17 *European Journal of International Law* 699, 713.

failing to breach Article 2(4) of the UN Charter. In other words, the United States was implicitly found to be in breach of Article 2(4) of the UN Charter, in that the Court held that its attacks on the oil platforms could not be justified as measures of self-defence. However, the ICJ did not explicitly condemn the United States for what by the Court's own reasoning must have been an unlawful action.[216]

Therefore, it would seem that having strayed beyond its jurisdictional boundaries, the ICJ quickly retreated back again. It is submitted that this was a result of the fact that some members of the Court wished to use the case as a means of clarifying the law on the use of force,[217] whilst others felt that due to jurisdictional restrictions, the dispute was patently unsuited for that purpose.[218] Thus, the Court pulled itself one way and then the other; it ultimately tried to go beyond the established boundaries of the partial jurisdiction it had in the case, whilst at the same time attempting to ensure that in doing so it did not stray too far.

This problem of the Court pulling itself one way and then the other—the tension between a restrictive approach and a more progressive one—can be seen in the ICJ's jurisprudence more widely. In 1979, Edward McWhinney produced a study of a number of ICJ judgments (both contentious decisions and advisory opinions) from the 1960s and 1970s.[219] In that study, he traced tendencies towards both strict formalism and comparatively policy-directed adjudication—across these cases and, perhaps more interestingly, *within* them.[220] McWhinney's assumption that some cases (or some aspects of some cases) represent instances of 'judicial activism' whilst others represent 'judicial restraint' is, it is argued here, too simplistic, and his claims as to the policy factors underlying the decisions examined are more speculative than he admitted. Nonetheless, his study provides an interesting expansion of the basic problem that has been identified herein with regards to the ICJ's use of force cases.

It is here that one of the greatest difficulties facing the Court with regard to the law governing self-defence is evident. The cases that have thus far reached the merits stage before the ICJ have been jurisdictionally unsuited to legal clarification of self-defence:

> The general problem of self-defence under international law is an extremely complex and even controversial subject both in terms of theory and practice . . . [W]hile it is of utmost importance for the Court to pronounce its authoritative position on this general problem in a proper context, it should do so in a context where it should be possible for the Court to deal with the problem squarely in a

[216] A fact lamented by Judge Simma. *Oil Platforms* merits (n 51) separate opinion of Judge Simma, esp paras 1–8.

[217] See, eg, *ibid*.

[218] *Ibid*, separate opinion of Judge Buergenthal, para 19.

[219] McWhinney (n 62) esp 17–109.

[220] *Ibid*, esp 17–109 and 163–64.

> full-fledged manner, with all its ramifications both in terms of the law and the facts involved.[221]

With the possible exception of *DRC v Uganda*, none of the cases that have reached the ICJ as yet have provided the Court with the opportunity to examine self-defence 'squarely in a full-fledged manner'. Moreover, the consent-based jurisdiction of the Court, coupled with the 'controversial' nature of self-defence, makes the chances of a case with such an open jurisdictional basis reaching the Peace Palace somewhat unlikely. In trying to examine the law on self-defence in cases unsuited to this purpose, the Court has produced a fragmented analysis of the law that, it may be argued, is in fact more damaging than no judicial picture of this area at all.

VII. CONCLUSION

Many of the issues discussed in this chapter highlight the fact that the ICJ is inhibited by its very nature when examining cases involving self-defence. These are not problems for which the members of the ICJ are to blame or which the Court as an institution can readily 'solve'. Problems of evidence-gathering, justiciability and, most importantly, jurisdictional restrictions due to a pervading lack of state consent to adjudication, are inherent in the Court as it was devised. Coupled with the problems inherent in the law of self-defence as discussed in previous chapters, these issues go a long way towards explaining the inadequate jurisprudence that the ICJ has produced on this area of international law. Such inherent problems cannot be changed through reform, at least not without a fundamental rethinking of the role and nature of the ICJ in the UN system.

The inherent limitations upon the ICJ are obviously concerning in themselves in terms of the impact they have had on the relevant jurisprudence. Yet the response to such limitations on the part of the various members of the ICJ has contributed still further to this, in that the position of the Court is unclear. Given the spectrum of thought in the Court with regard to these issues at the present time, it is impossible to know whether the ICJ will in the future as a collective organ be willing to stretch its role and jurisdiction as a necessary consequence of playing a significant role in the much needed clarification and development on the law of self-defence. In contrast, will the Court, in the next case to reach its docket on these issues, view its role more conservatively, accepting that in the majority of cases, its inherent limitations bar it from dealing with such issues at all? Both approaches have positive and negative implications. Therefore, Vera Gowlland-Debbas, amongst others, has suggested that the desired approach for the ICJ should be a compromise between active development

221 *Oil Platforms* merits (n 51) separate opinion of Judge Owada, para 38.

and more traditional judicial restraint.[222] Yet what this suggestion entails in practice is unclear: how is the Court to achieve such a balance?[223] Indeed, it would seem that this is exactly what the Court has attempted to do: to settle the disputes of the parties before it in a 'restrained' manner whilst equally attempting to use its cases to pronounce upon the law of self-defence more widely. In the context of self-defence, the ICJ may be seen to have attempted to walk a tightrope between two approaches. With the members of the Court pulling in different directions, rather than having found some kind of happy medium between dispute settlement and legal development, it has actually failed to follow either path adequately.

Around the time of the *Nicaragua* case, W Michael Reisman indicated that the ICJ might choose not to hear certain disputes because it would pitch them against powerful enemies.[224] In other words, he questioned whether political pressure would prevent the Court from examining controversial issues involving superpower states. Instead, in the context of self-defence, the decisions reached in *Nicaragua* and *Oil Platforms* indicate the opposite: the Court has perhaps been too eager to pronounce upon disputes involving superpower uses of force, doing so in cases in which its jurisdiction is dubious or partial (or in actuality, both). Yet, it has also been very aware of the restrictions it faces and thus has provided jurisprudence that is half-heartedly progressive with regard to self-defence, something which is perhaps more dangerous than full-blown activism. Ultimately, Sir Robert Jennings' conclusion in 1982 that '[t]he extent to which the Hague Court might properly be presented with questions of allegedly illegal force as such, is really an open one'[225] remains true.

[222] V Gowlland-Debbas, 'Judicial Insights into Fundamental Values and Interests of the International Community' in AS Muller, D Raic and JM Thuranszky (eds), *The International Court of Justice: Its Future Role after Fifty Years* (The Hague, Martinus Nijhoff, 1997) 327, 365–66.

[223] Koskenniemi, *From Apology to Utopia* (n 44) 35–36.

[224] WM Reisman, 'International Incidents: Introduction to a New Genre in the Study of International Law' (1984–85) 10 *Yale Journal of International* Law 1, 14.

[225] Jennings, 'International Force and the International Court of Justice' (n 136) 327–28.

Conclusion

THE *JUS AD BELLUM* is one of the most fundamental aspects of the international legal system. It relates to issues as elementary as the security of states (and of the people who populate them), international peace and security, the restraint of military power and the essence of statehood. The inherent right of self-defence forms an essential aspect of the *jus ad bellum*. Since 1945 it has constituted the only lawful means of unilateral forcible action. Following 2001, the law governing the use of force has faced a greatly increased level of scrutiny in the international media. Whether the events of 11 September 2001 have had an impact on the *jus ad bellum* is something, it is argued here, which is yet to be seen. However, what cannot be denied is that this area of the law has come startlingly to prominence as a result of the attacks and the subsequent 'war on terror'. As an aspect of the *jus ad bellum*, an understanding of the law governing self-defence is as essential today as it has ever been, if not more so. Moreover, in the relatively short period since the 11 September attacks, the ICJ has decided four cases that have related directly to self-defence, to a greater or lesser extent. Prior to 2001, there was but one solitary pronouncement by the primary judicial organ of the UN concerning this vital area. As such, not only is the time ripe for re-evaluation of self-defence in general; it is imperative that the jurisprudence of the ICJ on the issue be examined and the growing relationship between the Court and self-defence assessed. We have explored in detail the ICJ's contribution to the law of self-defence. This jurisprudence has then been set in a wider context: self-defence outside of the four walls of the Peace Palace.

The seminal *Nicaragua* case saw the ICJ attempt to tackle the vital issue of self-defence in some detail. Although the salient aspects of the judgment are initially somewhat difficult to establish, a demonstrable 'conception' of the law on self-defence can be ascertained from the case. In that judgment, the Court's main focus was upon a single criterion, that of an armed attack. This was defined as a particularly grave use of force, beyond a breach of Article 2(4) *simpliciter*, and it was held that an armed attack (thus defined) represented the condition *sine qua non* for the lawful exercise of self-defence. This position has clearly been reaffirmed by more recent cases such as *Oil Platforms* and *DRC v Uganda*.

Despite the fact that a particular conception of the law of self-defence may be identified throughout the Court's jurisprudence, when one begins to try to expand upon the Court's armed attack model for self-defence many unclear aspects of that model become apparent. The most important such issue is: how 'grave' must an attack be in practice to constitute an armed attack? Indeed, how does one grade 'gravity'? Other issues left unexplained by the Court include: 1) whether attacks on merchant vessels constitute armed attacks; 2) whether there must be a level of culpability (or at least involvement) on the part of a state for an armed attack to have taken place, and if so, what that level is; 3) whether anticipatory self-defence may in some circumstances be lawful, and if so, under what circumstances; and 4) whether forcible countermeasures in response to a use of force below the level of an armed attack may be lawful.

Even more fundamentally, it would appear that an armed attack is *not* the primary criterion for self-defence in customary international law at all. Whilst the phrase 'armed attack' is used in Article 51 and other multilateral conventions, it is not defined in such instruments. Certainly, there is nothing in the Charter or its drafting history that requires the phrase to be read as meaning a grave use of force. Therefore, for this conception of armed attack to have any legal validity, it must stem from the practice and *opinio juris* of states.

When one begins to examine in detail the practice of states, it becomes evident that the criteria of necessity and proportionality consistently form the fundamental basis of legal claims and responses concerning self-defence. By examining the roots of these criteria in the *Caroline* incident and then tracing their development through the UN era, one can see that they possess a demonstrable content. They are definable and applicable in practice, although admittedly they are complex and flexible requirements.

The criterion of necessity can be seen as being related to the notion of force used as a last resort of a state, meaning that the responding state has a reasonable need to respond with force based upon the circumstances of the incident. An assessment of proportionality requires that the force used is proportional to the necessity of a response, as well as requiring some degree of parity (in terms of scale) between the response taken and the initial attack.

In addition, necessity and proportionality have further aspects of a 'temporal' nature. For an action in self-defence to meet the criteria of necessity and proportionality there is a need for temporal connection between attack and response. This aspect of the criteria can be identified in two distinct but related forms, which may be described as requirements of immediacy and imminence.

Thus, prima facie, one may argue that the ICJ has erred in articulating an armed attack criterion as the basis for self-defence actions. In the legal evaluation of uses of force in practice, other detailed and applicable criteria are being used by states. However, whilst it is submitted herein that an armed attack criterion cannot, in customary international law, be viewed as the condition *sine qua non* for self-defence, further assessment of the claims and responses of states reveals that such a criterion *is* invoked and applied to a consistent degree in relation to state practice. Moreover, in numerous instances the phrase 'armed attack' is employed to refer to a *grave* use of force giving rise to the right of self-defence.

As such, the Court's conception of self-defence may be seen as having a basis in customary international law. The extent of the 'armed attack as a grave use of force' criterion as an aspect of customary international law is unclear. However, it is fair to say that such a criterion exists beyond the four walls of the Peace Palace and the writings of scholars and is today a significant fixture of practical legal applications of self-defence. Again, how far this fact has been influenced by the judgments of the ICJ in holding that such a criterion exists, and how far the Court has in its judgments simply been reflecting the development of this criterion in customary international law cannot be said with any certainty.

In any event, it has been argued here that the coexistence, as it were, of 'armed attack as a grave use of force' and the criteria of necessity and proportionality in the contemporary law on self-defence—requirements that share partially but not fully overlapping functions—has meant that the method for assessing self-defence is highly confused and is in need of reform. It is further argued that it is desirable that such reform should constitute the reinterpretation of the armed attack criterion as understood by the ICJ, so far as this may be identified as an aspect of the customary international law governing self-defence.

Reliance upon necessity and proportionality and the removal of an 'armed attack as a grave use of force' requirement would: 1) alleviate many of the problems and controversies inherent in the ICJ's conception of self-defence; 2) provide for a clearer framework for assessing the lawfulness of self-defence; 3) reflect more accurately the most salient feature of state *opinio juris* in this area; and 4) act as a more flexible means of regulating unilateral inter-state force, which could develop through the usual process of customary international law formation so as to be able to respond to types of attacks (or even, potentially, threatened attacks) not yet envisioned.

Unfortunately, the ICJ has not advocated this position and has done little to improve the confused law on self-defence more generally. Indeed, the ICJ has compounded the problems inherent in the armed attack criterion through its unmerited promotion of the fundamental self-defence requirement and the Court's confusing presentation of that requirement. Reform of this area of international law is thus required.

In mitigation, the ICJ's failings with regard to self-defence must be considered in the light of the extreme difficulty in attempting to reconcile the two interlinked 'conceptions' of self-defence as the law currently stands and, further, in light of the inherent limitations of the Court itself. Many of the problems apparent in the jurisprudence stem from the limitations the

Court faces due to the way the institution of the ICJ was devised. These include problems of evidence-gathering, justiciability and jurisdictional restrictions due to the requirement that states consent to international adjudication. Such limitations upon the ICJ necessarily have, in themselves, an impact upon the quality of the jurisprudence the Court is able to produce on self-defence.

It is here argued that the response to such limitations on the part of the ICJ and, more specifically, on the part of the individual *members* of the Court, has contributed still further to the inadequate treatment of self-defence by the ICJ. In the context of self-defence, the Court has been pulled in different directions from within. It is incorrect to argue that the judges of the ICJ reason decisions on a purely political basis. Nonetheless, judges are forced, in hard cases such as self-defence, to select and apply Dworkinian 'principles' to a given dispute. In a court with fifteen members, it is inevitable that there will be a variety of principles selected and that they will be applied in different ways. In the final analysis, the Court has perhaps been too eager to pronounce upon disputes involving self-defence, doing so in instances when its jurisdiction has been severely limited. Yet, equally, it has remained aware of the restrictions it faces and thus has provided jurisprudence that has been limited to only partial aspects of the legal regulation of self-defence.

Ultimately, this book makes the claim that the law on self-defence should be reformed and the 'armed attack as a grave use of force' criterion abandoned. It is the view of the present writer that the ICJ has significantly contributed to the need for reformation in this area. It is not claimed that the Court is 'too political' to deal with use of force issues per se or that it is inherently incapable of adequately dealing with the law governing self-defence. However, the restrictions upon the Court, particularly the fact that it relies entirely upon state consent, have made its task with regard to self-defence all the more difficult. More importantly, in the cases that have reached the Court, it has demonstrated itself to be unsuitable to deal with the crucial question of self-defence in international law.

Bibliography

BOOKS

Alexandrov, SA, *Self-Defence against the Use of Force in International Law* (The Hague, Kluwer Law International, 1996).

Anand, RP, *Studies in International Adjudication* (Delhi, Vikas, 1969).

Arend, AC (ed), *The United States and the Compulsory Jurisdiction of the International Court of Justice* (Lanham, University Press of America, 1986).

Armstrong, D, Farrell, T and Maiguashca, B (eds), *Force and Legitimacy in World Politics* (Cambridge, Cambridge University Press, 2005).

Bailey, SD and Daws, S, *The Procedure of the UN Security Council*, 3rd edn (Oxford, Clarendon Press, 1998).

Black, CE and Falk, RA (eds), *The Future of International Order, Vol III: Conflict Management* (Princeton, Princeton University Press, 1971).

Bloed, A and Van Dijk, P (eds), *Forty Years International Court of Justice: Jurisdiction, Equity and Equality* (Utrecht, Europa Institute, 1988).

Boisson de Charzournes, L and Sands, P (eds), *International Law, the International Court of Justice and Nuclear Weapons* (Cambridge, Cambridge University Press, 1999).

Bowett, DW, *Self-Defence in International Law* (Manchester, Manchester University Press, 1958).

Boyle, A and Chinkin, C, *The Making of International Law* (Oxford, Oxford University Press, 2007).

Brierly, JL, *The Law of Nations: An Introduction to the International Law of Peace*, 6th edn (Clarendon Press, Oxford, 1963).

Brownlie, I, *International Law and the Use of Force by States* (Oxford, Oxford University Press, 1963).

——, *Principles of Public International Law*, 6th edn (Oxford, Oxford University Press, 2003).

Byers, M, *Custom, Power and the Power of Rules: International Relations and Customary International Law* (Cambridge, Cambridge University Press, 1999).

Cannizzaro, E and Palchetti, P (eds), *Customary International Law on the Use of Force: A Methodological Approach* (Leiden, Martinus Nijhoff, 2005).

Cassese, A (ed), *The Current Legal Regulation of the Use of Force* (Dordrecht, Martinus Nijhoff, 1986).

Cassese, A, *International Law*, 2nd edn (Oxford, Oxford University Press, 2005).

Chipp, B, *Going to Court Not War*, 7th edn (London, Institute for Law and Peace, 2002).

Coleman, J and Shapiro, S (eds), *The Oxford Handbook of Jurisprudence and Philosophy of Law* (Oxford, Oxford University Press, 2002).

Constantinou, A, *The Right of Self-Defence under Customary International Law and Article 51 of the UN Charter* (Brussels, Bruylant, 2000).

Corey, AB, *The Crisis of 1830–1842 in Canadian–American Relations* (New Haven, Yale University Press, 1941).
Council on Foreign Relations, *Right v Might* (New York, Council on Foreign Relations Press, 1991).
Damrosch, LF (ed), *The International Court of Justice at a Crossroads* (New York, Transnational, 1987).
Damrosch, LF and Scheffer, DJ (eds), *Law and Force in the New International Order* (Boulder, Westview Press, 1991).
Davis, KC, *Discretionary Justice: A Preliminary Inquiry* (Baton Rouge, Louisiana State University Press, 1969).
Dekker, IF and Post, HHG (eds), *The Gulf War of 1980–1988: The Iran–Iraq War in International Legal Perspective* (Dordrecht, Martinus Nijhoff, 1992).
Dickey, C, *With the Contras: A Reporter in the Wilds of Nicaragua* (New York, Touchstone, 1987).
Dinstein, Y, *War, Aggression and Self-Defence*, 4th edn (Cambridge, Cambridge University Press, 2005).
Dinstein, Y and Tabory M (eds), *International Law at a Time of Perplexity: Essays in Honour of Shabtai Rosenne* (Dordrecht, Martinus Nijhoff, 1989).
Dixon, M and McCorquodale, R, *Cases and Materials on International Law*, 4th edn (Oxford, Oxford University Press, 2003).
Dworkin, R, *Law's Empire* (London, Fontana Press, 1986).
Elias, TO, *The International Court of Justice and Some Contemporary Problems* (The Hague, Martinus Nijhoff, 1983).
Elkind, JB, *Non-appearance before the International Court of Justice: Functional and Comparative Analysis* (Dordrecht, Martinus Nijhoff, 1984).
Erickson, RJ, *Legitimate Use of Military Force against State Sponsored International Terrorism* (Maxwell Air Force Base, Alabama, Air University Press, 1989).
Evans, MD (ed), *International Law*, 2nd, edn (Oxford, Oxford University Press, 2006).
Feinberg, N, *Studies in International Law with Special Reference to the Arab–Israeli Conflict* (Jerusalem, Magnes Press, 1979).
Franck, TM, *Judging the World Court* (New York, Priority Press, 1986).
——, *The Power of Legitimacy Among Nations* (Oxford, Oxford University Press, 1990).
——, *Recourse to Force: State Action against Threats and Armed Attacks* (Cambridge, Cambridge University Press, 2002).
Gardam, J, *Necessity, Proportionality and the Use of Force by States* (Cambridge, Cambridge University Press, 2004).
Gazzini, T, *The Changing Rules on the Use of Force in International Law* (Manchester, Manchester University Press, 2005).
Gill, TD, *Rosenne's The World Court: What It is and How It Works*, 6th edn (Leiden, Martinus Nijhoff, 2003).
Gray, C, *International Law and the Use of Force*, 3rd edn (Oxford, Oxford University Press, 2008).
Gross, L (ed), *The Future of the International Court of Justice, Vols I and II* (New York, Oceana, 1976).
Hart, HLA, *The Concept of Law*, 2nd edn (Oxford, Oxford University Press, 1994).
——, *Essays in Jurisprudence and Philosophy* (Oxford, Oxford University Press, 1983).

Henckaerts, J-M and Doswald Beck, L (eds), *Customary International Humanitarian Law, Vols I and II (Parts 1 and 2)*, ICRC Study (Cambridge, Cambridge University Press, 2005).
Higgins, R, *Problems and Process: International Law and How We Use It* (Oxford, Oxford University Press, 1994).
International Law at the Time of its Codification: Essays in Honour of Roberto Ago, Vol III [No ascribed editor] (Milan, Giuffre, 1987).
Janis, MW (ed), *International Courts for the Twenty-First Century* (Dordrecht, Martinus Nijhoff, 1992).
Jennings, RY and Watts, A (eds), *Oppenheim's International Law, Vol I*, 9th edn (Harlow, Longman, 1992).
Jones, H, *To the Webster-Ashburton Treaty: A Study in Anglo-American Relations, 1783–1843* (Chapel Hill, University of North Carolina Press, 1977).
Kagan, R, *A Twilight Struggle: American Power and Nicaragua, 1977–1990* (New York, Free Press, 1996).
Koskenniemi, M, *The Gentle Civilizer of Nations: The Rise and Fall of International Law 1870–1960* (Cambridge, Cambridge University Press, 2001).
——, *From Apology to Utopia: The Structure of International Legal Argument*, reissue with epilogue (Cambridge, Cambridge University Press, 2005).
Lauterpacht, H, *The Development of International Law by the International Court*, revised edn (London, Stevens & Sons, 1958).
Levin, J, *How Judges Reason: The Logic of Adjudication* (New York, Peter Lang, 1992)
Lowe, V and Fitzmaurice, M (eds), *Fifty Years of the International Court of Justice: Essays in Honour of Sir Robert Jennings* (Cambridge, Cambridge University Press, 1996).
MacCormick, N, *Legal Reasoning and Legal Theory* (Oxford, Oxford University Press, 1978).
Maogoto, JN, *Battling Terrorism: Legal Perspectives on the Use of Force and the War on Terror* (Aldershot, Ashgate, 2005).
McCoubrey, H and White, ND, *International Law and Armed Conflict* (Aldershot, Dartmouth Publishing, 1992).
McDougal, MS and Feliciano, FP, *Law and Minimum World Public Order: The Legal Regulation of International Coercion* (New Haven, Yale University Press, 1961).
McWhinney, E, *The World Court and the Contemporary International Law-Making Process* (Alphen aan den Rijn, Sijthoff & Noordhoff, 1979).
Melzer, Y, *Concepts of Just War* (Leiden, AW Sijthoff, 1975).
Merrills, JG, *International Dispute Settlement*, 4th edn (Cambridge, Cambridge University Press, 2005).
Meyer, HN, *The World Court in Action: Judging Among the Nations* (Oxford, Rowman and Littlefield, 2002).
Moore, JB, *A Digest of International Law, Vol II* (Washington, Government Printing Office, 1906).
Muller, AS, Raic, D and Thuranszky, JM (eds), *The International Court of Justice: Its Future Role after Fifty Years* (The Hague, Martinus Nijhoff, 1997).
Ndiaye, TM and Wolfrum, R (eds), *Law of the Sea, Environmental Law and Settlement of Disputes:* Liber Amicorum *Judge Thomas A Mensah* (Leiden, Martinus Nijhoff, 2007).
O'Connell, DP, *The Influence of Law on Sea Power* (Manchester, Manchester University Press, 1975).

Prott, LV, *The Latent Power of Culture and the International Judge* (Abingdon, Professional Books, 1979).
Reus-Smit, C (ed), *The Politics of International Law* (Cambridge, Cambridge University Press, 2004).
Röling, BVA, *International Law in an Expanded World* (Amsterdam, Djambatan, 1960).
Rosenne, S, *Documents on the International Court of Justice*, 2nd edn (Alphen aan den Rejn, Sijthoff & Noordhoof, 1979).
——, *The Law and Practice of the International Court of Justice, 1920–2005, Vol I: The Court and the United Nations*, 4th edn (Leiden, Martinus Nijhoff, 2006).
——, *The Law and Practice of the International Court of Justice, 1920–2005, Vol II: Jurisdiction*, 4th edn (Leiden, Martinus Nijhoff, 2006).
Rowe, P, *Defence: The Legal Implications (Military Law and the Laws of War)* (London, Brassey's Defence, 1987).
Schachter, O, *International Law in Theory and Practice* (Dordrecht, Martinus Nijhoff, 1991).
Schwarzenberger, G, *International Law as Applied by International Courts and Tribunals, Vol I*, 3rd edn (London, Stevens & Sons, 1957).
Schwarzenberger, G and Brown, ED, *A Manual of International Law*, 6th edn (Abingdon, Professional Books, 1976).
Shahabuddeen, M, *Precedent in the World Court* (Cambridge, Grotius/Cambridge University Press, 1997).
Shaw, MN, *International Law*, 5th edn (Cambridge, Cambridge University Press, 2003).
Shihata, IFI, *The Power of the International Court to Determine its Own Jurisdiction* (The Hague, Martinus Nijhoff, 1965).
Simma, B (ed), *The Charter of the United Nations: A Commentary, Vol I*, 2nd edn (Oxford, Oxford University Press, 2002).
Sorkin, M (ed), *Against the Wall* (New York, New Press, 2005).
Stevens, KR, *Border Diplomacy: The* Caroline *and McLeod Affairs in Anglo–American–Canadian Relations, 1837–1842* (Tuscaloosa, University of Alabama Press, 1989).
Stone, J, *Aggression and World Order* (University of California Press, Berkley, 1958).
Stürchler, N, *The Threat of Force in International Law* (Cambridge, Cambridge University Press, 2007).
Symbolae Verzijl [No ascribed editor] (The Hague, Martinus Nijhoff, 1958).
Szafarz, R, *The Compulsory Jurisdiction of the International Court of Justice* (Dordrecht, Martinus Nijhoff, 1993).
Terris, D, Romano, CPR and Swigart, L, *The International Judge: An Introduction to the Men and Women who Decide the World's Cases* (Oxford, Oxford University Press, 2007).
Thirlway, H, *Non-appearance before the International Court of Justice* (Cambridge, Cambridge University Press, 1985).
de Vattel, E, *Le Droit des Gens, ou Principes de la Loi Naturelle, appliqués a la Conduite et aux Affaires des Nations et des Souverains, Vol III*, Fenwick, CG (trans) in Scott, JB (ed), *The Classics of International Law* (Washington, Carnegie Institution of Washington, 1916).
Weisburd, AM, *Use of Force: The Practice of States since World War II* (University Park, Pennsylvania State University Press, 1997).

White, ND, *The United Nations System: Towards International Justice* (London, Lynne Rienner, 2002).
Wolfrum, R and Philipp, C (eds), *United Nations: Law, Policies and Practice, Vol II* (Dordrecht, Martinus Nijhoff, 1995).
Yoo, TH, *The Korean War and the United Nations: A Legal and Diplomatic Historical Study* (Louvain, Librairie Desbarax, 1965)

CHAPTERS FROM COLLECTIONS

Acevedo, DE, 'Disputes Under Consideration by the UN Security Council or Regional Bodies' in Damrosch, LF (ed), *The International Court of Justice at a Crossroads* (New York, Transnational, 1987) 242.
Allott, P, 'The ICJ and the Voice of Justice' in Lowe, V and Fitzmaurice, M (eds), *Fifty Years of the International Court of Justice: Essays in Honour of Sir Robert Jennings* (Cambridge, Cambridge University Press, 1996) 17.
Amerasinghe, CE, 'Reflections on the Judicial Function in International Law' in Ndiaye, TM and Wolfrum, R (eds), *Law of the Sea, Environmental Law and Settlement of Disputes:* Liber Amicorum *Judge Thomas A Mensah* (Leiden, Martinus Nijhoff, 2007) 121.
Brown Weiss, E, 'Judicial Independence and Impartiality: A Preliminary Inquiry' in Damrosch, LF (ed), *The International Court of Justice at a Crossroads* (New York, Transnational, 1987) 123.
Byers, M, 'Geopolitical Change and International Law' in Armstrong, D, Farrell, T and Maiguashca, B (eds), *Force and Legitimacy in World Politics* (Cambridge, Cambridge University Press, 2005) 51.
Charney, JI, 'Disputes Implicating the Institutional Credibility of the Court: Problems of Non-appearance, Non-participation and Non-performance' in Damrosch, LF (ed), *The International Court of Justice at a Crossroads* (New York, Transnational, 1987) 288.
Combacau, J, 'The Exception of Self-Defence in UN Practice' in Cassese, A (ed), *The Current Legal Regulation of the Use of Force* (Dordrecht, Martinus Nijhoff, 1986) 9.
Couvreur, P, 'The Effectiveness of the International Court of Justice in the Peaceful Settlement of Disputes' in Muller, AS, Raic, D and Thuranszky, JM (eds), *The International Court of Justice: Its Future Role after Fifty Years* (The Hague, Martinus Nijhoff, 1997) 83.
De Waart, PJIM, 'Non-appearance Does Not Make Sense' in Bloed, A and Van Dijk, P (eds), *Forty Years International Court of Justice: Jurisdiction, Equity and Equality* (Utrecht, Europa Institute, 1988) 73.
Farer, TJ, 'Law and War' in Black, CE and Falk, RA (eds), *The Future of International Order, Vol III: Conflict Management* (Princeton, Princeton University Press, 1971) 64.
Fitzmaurice, GG, 'Some Problems Regarding the Formal Sources of International Law' in *Symbolae Verzijl* (The Hague, Martinus Nijhoff, 1958) 153.
——, 'Enlargement of the Contentious Jurisdiction of the Court' in Gross, L (ed), *The Future of the International Court of Justice, Vol II* (New York, Oceana, 1976) 461.

Gardam, J, 'Necessity and Proportionality in *Jus ad Bellum* and *Jus in Bello*' in Boisson de Charzournes, L and Sands, P (eds), *International Law, the International Court of Justice and Nuclear Weapons* (Cambridge, Cambridge University Press, 1999) 275.

Gardner, RN, 'Commentary of the Law of Self-Defence' in Damrosch, LF and Scheffer, DJ (eds), *Law and Force in the New International Order* (Boulder, Westview Press, 1991) 49.

Gordon, E, 'Legal Disputes under Article 36(2) of the Statute' in Damrosch, LF (ed), *The International Court of Justice at a Crossroads* (New York, Transnational, 1987) 183.

Gowlland-Debbas, V, 'Judicial Insights into Fundamental Values and Interests of the International Community' in Muller, AS, Raic, D and Thuranszky, JM (eds), *The International Court of Justice: Its Future Role after Fifty Years* (The Hague, Martinus Nijhoff, 1997) 327.

Gray, C, 'The Use of Force and the International Legal Order' in Evans, MD (ed), *International Law*, 2nd edn (Oxford, Oxford University Press, 2006) 589.

Greenwood, C, 'The International Court of Justice and the Use of Force' in Lowe, V and Fitzmaurice, M (eds), *Fifty Years of the International Court of Justice: Essays in Honour of Sir Robert Jennings* (Cambridge, Cambridge University Press, 1996) 373.

——, '*Jus ad Bellum* and *Jus in Bello* in the *Nuclear Weapons* Advisory Opinion' in Boisson de Charzournes, L and Sands, P (eds), *International Law, the International Court of Justice and Nuclear Weapons* (Cambridge, Cambridge University Press, 1999) 247.

Hart, HLA, 'American Jurisprudence through English Eyes: The Nightmare and the Noble Dream' (first published 1977) in Hart, HLA, *Essays in Jurisprudence and Philosophy* (Oxford, Oxford University Press, 1983) 123.

——, '1776–1976: Law in the Perspective of Philosophy' (first published 1976) in Hart, HLA, *Essays in Jurisprudence and Philosophy* (Oxford, Oxford University Press, 1983) 145.

Henkin, L, 'The Use of Force: Law and US Policy' in *Right v Might* (New York, Council on Foreign Relations Press, 1991) 37.

Highet, K, 'Evidence and Proof of Facts' in Damrosch, LF (ed), *The International Court of Justice at a Crossroads* (New York, Transnational, 1987) 355.

Janis, MW, 'The International Court' in Janis, MW (ed), *International Courts for the Twenty-First Century* (Dordrecht, Martinus Nijhoff, 1992) 19.

Jennings, RY, 'International Force and the International Court of Justice' in Cassese, A (ed), *The Current Legal Regulation of the Use of Force* (Dordrecht, Martinus Nijhoff, 1986) 323.

——, 'The Judicial Function and the Rule of Law in International Relations' in *International Law at the Time of its Codification: Essays in Honour of Roberto Ago, Vol III* (Milan, Giuffre, 1987) 139.

Kenny, KC, 'Self-Defence' in Wolfrum, R and Philipp, C (eds), *United Nations: Law, Policies and Practice, Vol II* (Dordrecht, Martinus Nijhoff, 1995) 1162.

Koury, S, 'Why this Wall?' in Sorkin, M (ed), *Against the Wall* (New York, New Press, 2005) 48.

Kritsiotis, D, 'When States Use Armed Force' in Reus-Smit, C (ed), *The Politics of International Law* (Cambridge, Cambridge University Press, 2004) 45.

Leigh, M and Ramsey, SD, 'Confidence in the Court: It Need Not be a Hollow Chamber' in Damrosch, LF (ed) *The International Court of Justice at a Crossroads* (New York, Transnational, 1987) 106.

Lucy, W, 'Adjudication' in Coleman, J and Shapiro, S (eds), *The Oxford Handbook of Jurisprudence and Philosophy of Law* (Oxford, Oxford University Press, 2002) 206.

Meng, W, 'The *Caroline*' in Bernhardt, R (ed), *Encyclopaedia of Public International Law, Vol 3: Use of Force, War and Neutrality Peace Treaties (A–M)* (Amsterdam, North-Holland Publishing Company, 1982) 81.

Müllerson, R, 'Self-Defence in the Contemporary World' in Damrosch, LF and Scheffer, DJ (eds), *Law and Force in the New International Order* (Boulder, Westview Press, 1991) 13.

O'Connell, ME, 'Taking *Opinio Juris* Seriously' in Cannizzaro, E and Palchetti, P (eds), *Customary International Law on the Use of Force: A Methodological Approach* (Leiden, Martinus Nijhoff, 2005) 9.

Palmisano, G, 'Determining the Law on the Use of Force: The ICJ and Customary Rules on the Use of Force' in Cannizzaro, E and Palchetti, P (eds), *Customary International Law on the Use of Force: A Methodological Approach* (Leiden, Martinus Nijhoff, 2005) 197.

Post, HHG, 'Border Conflicts Between Iran and Iraq: Review and Legal Reflections' in Dekker, IF and Post, HHG (eds), *The Gulf War of 1980–1988: The Iran-Iraq War in International Legal Perspective* (Dordrecht, Martinus Nijhoff, 1992) 7.

Randelzhofer, A, 'Article 2(4)' in Simma, B (ed), *The Charter of the United Nations: A Commentary, Vol I*, 2nd edn (Oxford, Oxford University Press, 2002) 112.

——, 'Article 51' in Simma, B (ed), *The Charter of the United Nations: A Commentary, Vol I*, 2nd edn (Oxford, Oxford University Press, 2002) 788.

Reisman, WM, 'Termination of the United States Declaration under Article 36(2) of the Statute of the International Court' in Arend, AC (ed), *The United States and the Compulsory Jurisdiction of the International Court of Justice* (Lanham, University Press of America, 1986) 71.

——, 'Allocating Competences to Use Coercion in the Post-Cold War World: Practices, Conditions and Prospects' in Damrosch, LF and Scheffer, DJ (eds), *Law and Force in the New International Order* (Boulder, Westview Press, 1991) 26.

Rovine, AW, 'The National Interest and the World Court' in Gross, L (ed), *The Future of the International Court of Justice, Vol I* (New York, Oceana, 1976) 313.

Schachter, O, 'Disputes Involving the Use of Force' in Damrosch, LF (ed) *The International Court of Justice at a Crossroads* (New York, Transnational, 1987) 223.

Scheffer, DJ, 'The Use of Force after the Cold War' in *Right v Might* (New York, Council on Foreign Relations Press, 1991) 109.

Shahabuddeen, M, 'The World Court at the Turn of the Century' in Muller, AS, Raic, D and Thuranszky, JM (eds), *The International Court of Justice: Its Future Role after Fifty Years* (The Hague, Martinus Nijhoff, 1997) 3.

Sohn, LB, 'The International Court of Justice and the Scope of the Right of Self-Defence and the Duty of Non-intervention' in Dinstein, Y and Tabory, M (eds), *International Law at a Time of Perplexity: Essays in Honour of Shabtai Rosenne* (Dordrecht, Martinus Nijhoff, 1989) 869.

Sugihara, T, 'The Judicial Function of the International Court of Justice with Respect to Disputes Involving Highly Political Issues' in Muller, AS, Raic, D and Thuranszky, JM (eds), *The International Court of Justice: Its Future Role after Fifty Years* (The Hague, Martinus Nijhoff, 1997) 117.

Thirlway, H, 'The International Court of Justice' in Evans, MD (ed), *International Law*, 2nd edn (Oxford, Oxford University Press, 2006) 561.

ARTICLES

Acheson, D, 'Law and Conflict: Changing Patterns and Contemporary Challenges, Panel on the Cuban Quarantine: Implications for the Future: Remarks' (1963) 57 *American Society of International Law Proceedings* 10.

Akehurst, M, 'Custom as a Source of International Law' (1974–75) 47 *British Yearbook of International Law* 1.

Alexandrov, SA, 'The Compulsory Jurisdiction of the International Court of Justice: How Compulsory is it?' (2006) 5 *Chinese Journal of International Law* 29.

Allain, J, 'The True Challenge to the United Nations System of the Use of Force: The Failures of Kosovo and Iraq and the Emergence of the African Union' (2004) 8 *Max Planck Yearbook of United Nations Law* 237.

Allott, P, 'State Responsibility and the Unmaking of International Law' (1998) 29 *Harvard International Law Journal* 1.

Alter, KJ, 'International Courts are Not Agents! The Perils of the Principal-Agent Approach to Thinking about the Independence of International Courts' (2005) 99 *American Society of International Law Proceedings* 138.

Antonopoulos, C, 'Force by Armed Groups as Armed Attack and the Broadening of Self-Defence' (2008) 55 *Netherlands International Law Review* 159.

Badr, GM, 'The Exculpatory Effect of Self-Defence in State Responsibility' (1980) 10 *Georgia Journal of International and Comparative Law* 1.

Baxter, RR, 'Multilateral Treaties as Evidence of Customary International Law' (1965–66) 41 *British Yearbook of International Law* 275.

——, 'The Legal Consequences of the Unlawful Use of Force under the Charter' (1968) 62 *American Society of International Law Proceedings* 68.

Bedjaoui, M, 'Expediency in the Decisions of the International Court of Justice' (2000) 71 *British Yearbook of International Law* 1.

Bodansky, D and Crook, JR, 'Symposium: The ILC's State Responsibility Articles: Introduction and Overview' (2002) 96 *American Journal of International Law* 773.

Bodenheimer, E, 'Hart, Dworkin, and the Problem of Judicial Lawmaking Discretion' (1976–77) 11 *Georgia Law Review* 1143.

Bowett, DW, 'Reprisals Involving Recourse to Armed Force' (1972) 66 *American Journal of International Law* 1.

Briggs, WB, 'The International Court of Justice Lives up to Its Name' (1987) 81 *American Journal of International Law* 78.

Brown, D, 'Use of Force against Terrorism after September 11th: State Responsibility, Self-Defence and Other Responses' (2003–04) 11 *Cardozo Journal of International and Comparative Law* 1.

Brownlie, I, '*International Law and the Use of Force by States* Revisited' (2002) 1 *Chinese Journal of International Law* 1.

Byers, M, 'Terrorism, the Use of Force and International Law after 11 September' (2002) 51 *International and Comparative Law Quarterly* 401.

Cannizzaro, E and Bonafé, B, 'Fragmenting International Law through Compromissory Clauses? Some Remarks on the Decision of the ICJ in the *Oil Platforms* Case' (2005) 16 *European Journal of International Law* 481.

Chainoglou, K, 'Reconceptualising Self-Defence in International Law' (2007) 18 *King's Law Journal* 61.

Charlesworth, HCM, 'Customary International Law and the *Nicaragua* Case' (1984–87) 11 *Australian Yearbook of International Law* 1.

Charney, JI, 'Compromissory Clauses and the Jurisdiction of the International Court of Justice' (1987) 81 *American Journal of International Law* 855.

Chayes, A, 'Nicaragua, the United States, and the World Court' (1985) 85 *Columbia Law Review* 1445.

Chimni, BS, 'The International Court and the Maintenance of Peace and Security: The *Nicaragua* Decision and the United States Response' (1986) 35 *International and Comparative Law Quarterly* 960.

Clemmons, BQ and Brown, GD, 'Rethinking International Self-Defence: The United Nations' Emerging Role' (1998) 45 *Naval Law Review* 217.

Christenson, GA, 'The World Court and *Jus Cogens*' (1987) 81 *American Journal of International Law* 93.

Czaplifski, W, 'Sources of International Law in the *Nicaragua* Case' (1989) 38 *International and Comparative Law Quarterly* 151.

D'Amato, A, 'Trashing Customary International Law' (1987) 81 *American Journal of International Law* 101.

——, 'Israel's Air Strike against the Osiraq Reactor: A Retrospective' (1996) 10 *Temple International and Comparative Law Journal* 259.

Dinstein, Y, 'Implementing Limitations on the Use of Force: The Doctrine of Proportionality and Necessity: Remarks' (1992) 86 *American Society of International Law Proceedings* 54.

Dumbauld, E, 'Dissenting Opinions in International Adjudication' (1942–42) 90 *University of Pennsylvania Law Review* 929.

Dworkin, R, 'Hard Cases' (1974–75) 88 *Harvard Law Review* 1057.

Falk, RA, 'The World Court's Achievement' (1987) 81 *American Journal of International Law* 106.

Farer, TJ, 'Political and Economic Coercion in Contemporary International Law' (1985) 79 *American Journal of International Law* 405.

Farer, TJ, 'Drawing the Right Line' (1987) 81 *American Journal of International Law* 112.

Feder, NM, 'Reading the UN Charter Connotatively: Towards a New Definition of Armed Attack' (1987) 19 *New York University Journal of International Law and Politics* 395.

Fernando, J, 'The International Court of Justice: A Critique of its Role' (1992) 4 *Sri Lanka Journal of International Law* 27.

Fitzmaurice, GG, 'The Law and Procedure of the International Court of Justice: Part III, International Organisations and Tribunals' (1952) 29 *British Yearbook of International Law* 1.

——, 'Definition of Aggression (Speech)' (1952) 1 *International and Comparative Law Quarterly* 137.

Franck, TM, 'Some Psychological Factors in International Third-Party Decision-Making' (1966–67) 19 *Stanford Law Review* 1217.

——, 'Who Killed Article 2(4)? Or Changing the Norms Governing the Use of Force by States' (1970) 64 *American Journal of International Law* 809.

——, 'Some Observations on the ICJ's Procedural and Substantive Innovations' (1987) 81 *American Journal of International Law* 116.

——, 'Terrorism and the Right of Self-Defence' (2001) 95 *American Journal of International Law* 839.

Friedlander, RA, 'Confusing Victims and Victimizers: *Nicaragua* and the Reinterpretation of International Law' (1985–86) 14 *Denver Journal of International Law and Policy* 87.

Foster, WF, 'Fact Finding and the World Court' (1969) 7 *Canadian Yearbook of International Law* 150.

Gardner, RN, 'Neither Bush nor the Jurisprudes (Agora: Future implications of the Iraq Conflict)' (2003) 97 *American Journal of International Law* 585.

Garner, JW, 'Some Questions of International Law in the European War' (1915) 9 *American Journal of International Law* 72.

Gerges, FA, 'The Lebanese Crisis of 1958: The Risks of Inflated Self-Importance' (1993) 5 *Beirut Review* 83.

Gill, TD, 'The Law of Armed Attack in the Context of the *Nicaragua* Case' (1988) 1 *Hague Yearbook of International Law* 30.

Gray, C, 'The British Position in Regard to the Gulf Conflict' (1988) 37 *International and Comparative Law Quarterly* 420.

——, 'The US *National Security Strategy* and the New "Bush Doctrine" on Pre-emptive Self-Defence' (2002) 1 *Chinese Journal of International Law* 437.

——, 'The Use and Abuse of the International Court of Justice: Cases concerning the Use of Force Since *Nicaragua*' (2003) 14 *European Journal of International Law* 867.

——, 'The Eritrea/Ethiopia Claims Commission Oversteps its Boundaries: A Partial Award?' (2006) 17 *European Journal of International Law* 699.

——, 'A Crisis of Legitimacy for the UN Collective Security System?' (2007) 56 *International and Comparative Law Quarterly* 157.

Gray, CS, 'Combating Terrorism' (1993) 23 *Parameters: US Army War College Quarterly* 17.

Greig, DW, 'Self-Defence and the Security Council: What Does Article 51 Require?' (1991) 40 *International and Comparative Law Quarterly* 366.

Green, LC, 'The United Nations, South West Africa and the World Court' (1967) 7 *Indian Journal of International Law* 491.

Green, JA, 'Docking the *Caroline*: Understanding the Relevance of the Formula in Contemporary Customary International Law Concerning Self-Defence' (2006) 14 *Cardozo Journal of International and Comparative Law* 429.

——, 'The *Oil Platforms* Case: An Error in Judgment?' (2004) 9 *Journal of Conflict and Security Law* 357.

——, 'An Unusual Silence' (2007) 157 *New Law Journal* 1478.

——, 'Self-Defence: A State of Mind for States?' (2008) 55 *Netherlands International Law Review* 181.

——, 'Legality of Attacks Inside Pakistan: US Needs to First Satisfy Itself that Pakistan is Unable to Suppress the Militants', Pakistan Institute for Peace

Studies, 2008, available at san-pips.com/PIPS-SAN-Files/SAN-Pakistan/SAN-PAK-Article68/San-Pak-Main-A68-D.asp.
——, 'Fluctuating Evidentiary Standards for Self-Defence in the International Court of Justice' (2009) 58 *International and Comparative Law Quarterly* 163.
Greenwood, C, 'New World Order or Old: The Invasion of Kuwait and the Rule of Law' (1992) 55 *Modern Law Review* 153.
——, 'International Law and the Pre-emptive Use of Force: Afghanistan, Al-Qaida, and Iraq' (2003) 4 *San Diego International Law Journal* 7.
Hafner, G, Boon, K, Rübesame, A and Huston, J, 'A Response to the American View as Presented by Ruth Wedgwood' (1999) *European Journal of International Law* 108.
Hargrove, JL, 'The *Nicaragua* Judgment and the Future of the Law of Force and Self-Defence' (1987) 81 *American Journal of International Law* 135.
Hensley, TR, 'National Bias and the International Court of Justice' (1968) 12 *Midwest Journal of Political Science* 568.
Higgins, R, 'Alternative Perspectives on the Independence of International Courts: Remarks' (2005) 99 *American Society of International Law Proceedings* 135
——, 'The Legal Limits to the Use of Force by Sovereign States: United Nations Practice' (1961) 37 *British Yearbook of International Law* 269.
——, 'Policy Considerations and the International Judicial Process' (1968) 17 *International and Comparative Law Quarterly* 58.
Highet, K, 'You Can Run but You Can't Hide: Reflections on the US Position in the *Nicaragua* Case' (1986–87) 27 *Virginia Journal of International Law* 551.
Indurthy, R, 'Kashmir between India and Pakistan: An Intractable Conflict, 1947 to Present' (unpublished).
Jiménez de Aréchaga, E, 'International Law in the Past Third of a Century' (1978) 159 *Recueil Des Cours* 13.
Jennings, RY, 'The *Caroline* and McLeod Cases' (1938) 32 *American Journal of International Law* 82.
——, 'The Internal Judicial Practice of the International Court of Justice' (1988) 59 *British Yearbook of International Law* 31.
Kasaija, PA, 'International Law and Uganda's Involvement in the Democratic Republic of Congo' (2001–02) 10 *Miami International and Comparative Law Review* 75.
Kearley, T, 'Raising the *Caroline*' (1999) 17 *Wisconsin International Law Journal* 325.
Kelly, B, 'The International Court of Justice: Its Role in a New World Legal Order' (1992) 3 *Touro Journal of Transnational Law* 223.
Kelly, MJ, 'Understanding September 11th: An International Legal Perspective on the War in Afghanistan' (2001–02) 35 *Creighton Law Review* 283.
Kirgis, FL, 'Custom on a Sliding Scale' (1987) 81 *American Journal of International Law* 146.
——, 'Some Proportionality Issues Raised by Israel's Use of Armed Force in Lebanon' (2006) 10 *American Society of International Insight*, available at www.asil.org/?insights060817.cfm.
Kooijmans, P, 'The ICJ in the 21st Century: Judicial Restraint, Judicial Activism, or Proactive Judicial Policy' (2007) 53 *International and Comparative Law Quarterly* 741.

Kretzmer, D, 'Targeted Killing of Suspected Terrorists: Extra Judicial Executions or Legitimate Means of Defence?' (2005) 16 *European Journal of International Law* 171.
Kritsiotis, D, 'Arguments of Mass Confusion' (2004) 15 *European Journal of International Law* 233.
——, 'Armed Activities on the Territory of the Congo (*Democratic Republic of Congo v Uganda*): Provisional Measures' (2001) 50 *International and Comparative Law Quarterly* 662.
——, 'Rules on Self-Defence in International Law', Memorandum for the Royal Institute of International Affairs, Chatham House International Law Programme, London, 8 December 2004 (unpublished).
Kunz, JL, 'Individual and Collective Self-Defence under Article 51 of the Charter of the United Nations' (1947) 41 *American Journal of International Law* 872.
Kwakwa, E, 'South Africa's May 1986 Military Incursions into Neighbouring African States' (1987) 12 *Yale Journal of International Law* 421.
Lachs, M, 'Some Reflections on the Contribution of the International Court of Justice to the Development of International Law' (1983) 10 *Syracuse Journal of International Law and Commerce* 239.
Laursen, A, 'The Judgment by the International Court of Justice in the *Oil Platforms* Case' (2004) 73 *Nordic Journal of International Law* 135.
Leckow, R, 'The Iran-Iraq Conflict in the Gulf: The Law of War Zones' (1988) 37 *International and Comparative Law Quarterly* 629.
Leich, MN (ed), 'Contemporary Practice of the United States Relating to International Law' (1984) 78 *American Journal of International Law* 200.
Levenfeld, B, 'Israel's Counter-*Fedayeen* Tactics in Lebanon: Self-Defence and Reprisal Under Modern International Law' (1982–83) 21 *Columbia Journal of Transnational Law* 1.
Levitin, MJ, 'The Law of Force and the Force of Law: Grenada, the Falklands, and Humanitarian Intervention' (1986) 27 *Harvard International Law Journal* 621.
Lobel, J, 'The Use of Force to Respond to Terrorist Attacks: The Bombing of Sudan and Afghanistan' (1999) 24 *Yale Journal of International Law* 537.
Lucy, W, 'The Possibility of Impartiality' (2005) 25 *Oxford Journal of Legal Studies* 3.
Macdonald, J, 'The *Nicaragua* Case: New Answers to Old Questions' (1986) 24 *Canadian Yearbook of International Law* 127.
Maier, HG, 'Appraisals of the ICJ's Decision: *Nicaragua v Unites States* (Merits): Introduction' (1987) 81 *American Journal of International Law* 77.
McWhinney, 'The International Court of Justice and International Law-Making: The Judicial Activism/Self-Restraint Antinomy' (2006) 5 *Chinese Journal of International Law* 3.
Meyer, JA, 'Collective Security and Regional Security: Necessary Exceptions to a Globalist Doctrine' (1993) 11 *Boston University International Law Journal* 391.
Miller, E, 'Self-Defence, International Law and the Six Day War' (1985) 20 *Israeli Law Review* 49.
Modabbler, Z, 'Collective Self-Defence: *Nicaragua v United States*' (1988) 10 *Loyola of Los Angeles International & Comparative Law Review* 449.
Moore, JN, 'The *Nicaragua* Case and the Deterioration of World Order' (1987) 81 *American Journal of International Law* 151.
Murphy, SD (ed), 'Contemporary Practice of the United States Relating to International Law' (2002) 96 *American Journal of International Law* 237.

——, 'Terrorism and the Concept of Armed Attack in Article 51 of the UN Charter' (2002) 43 *Harvard International Law Journal* 41.

——, 'Self-Defence and the *Israeli Wall* Advisory Opinion: An *Ipse Dixit* from the ICJ?' (2005) 99 *American Journal of International Law* 62.

Myjer, EPJ and White, N, 'The Twin Towers Attack: An Unlimited Right to Self-Defence?' (2002) 7 *Journal of Conflict and Security Law* 5.

Nsereko, DD, 'The International Court, Impartiality and Judges *Ad Hoc*' (1973) 13 *Indian Journal of International Law* 207.

Occelli, MB, 'Sinking the *Caroline*: Why the *Caroline* Doctrine's Restrictions on Self-Defence Should not be Regarded as Customary International Law' (2003) 4 *San Diego International Law Journal* 467.

Ochoa-Ruiz, N and Salamanca-Aguado E, 'Exploring the Limits of International Law Relating to the Use of Force in Self-Defence' (2005) 16 *European Journal of International Law* 499.

O'Connell, ME, 'Review: *Necessity, Proportionality and the Use of Force by States* by Judith Gardam' (2006) 100 *American Journal of International Law* 973.

Paust, JJ, 'Domestic Influence of the International Court of Justice' (1997–98) 26 *Denver Journal of International Law and Policy* 87.

——, 'Post-9/11 Overreaction and Fallacies Regarding War and Defence, Guantanamo, the Status of Persons, Treatment, Judicial Review of Detention, and Due Process in Military Commissions' (2003–04) 79 *Notre Dame Law Review* 1335.

——, 'The Seizure and Recovery of the *Mayaguez*' (1975–76) 85 *Yale Law Journal* 774.

Posner, EA, 'The International Court of Justice: Voting and Usage Statistics' (2005) 99 *American Society of International Law Proceedings* 130.

Quigley, J, 'The Afghanistan War and Self-Defence' (2002–03) 37 *Valparaiso University Law Review* 541.

Reisman, WM, 'International Incidents: Introduction to a New Genre in the Study of International Law' (1984–85) 10 *Yale Journal of International Law* 1.

——, 'International Legal Responses to Terrorism' (1999) 22 *Houston Journal of International Law* 3.

——, 'Old Wine in New Bottles: The Reagan and Brezhnev Doctrines in Contemporary International Law and Practice' (1988) 13 *Yale Journal of International Law* 171.

Renteln, AD, 'Cultural Bias in International Law' (1998) 92 *American Society of International Law Proceedings* 232.

Rishikof, H, 'When Naked Came the Doctrine of "Self-Defence": What is the Proper Role of the International Court of Justice in Use of Force Cases?' (2004) 29 *Yale Journal of International Law* 331.

Rogers, APV, 'Terrorism and the Law of War: September 11 and Its Aftermath', Crimes of War Project, 2001, available at www.crimesofwar.org/expert/attack-apv.html.

Rogoff, MA and Collins, E, 'The *Caroline* Incident and the Development of International Law' (1990) 16 *Brooklyn Journal of International Law* 493.

Rosenstock, R, 'The ILC and State Responsibility' (2002) 96 *American Journal of International Law* 792.

Rovine, AW, 'Should the United States Reconsider Its Acceptance of World Court Jurisdiction: Remarks' (1985) 79 *American Society of International Law Proceedings* 101.

Ruda, JM, 'Some of the Contributions of the International Court of Justice to the Development of International Law' (1991–92) 24 *New York University Journal of International Law and Politics* 35.

Sadurska, R, 'Threats of Force' (1988) 82 *American Journal of International Law* 239.

Sapiro, M, 'Iraq: The Shifting Sands of Pre-emptive Self-Defence' (2003) 97 *American Journal of International Law* 599.

Schachter, O, 'Implementing Limitations on the Use of Force: The Doctrine of Proportionality and Necessity: Remarks' (1992) 86 *American Society of International Law Proceedings* 39.

——, 'The Right of States to Use Armed Force' (1983–84) 82 *Michigan Law Review* 1620.

——, 'Self-Defence and the Rule of Law' (1989) 83 *American Journal of International Law* 259.

Schwarzenberger, G, 'The Fundamental Principles of International Law' (1955) 87 *Recueil Des Cours* 9.

Schwebel, SM, 'Reflections on the Role of the International Court of Justice' (1986) 61 *Washington Law Review* 1061.

Scobbie, I, 'Smoke, Mirrors and Killer Whales: The International Court of Justice's Opinion on the Israeli Barrier Wall' (2004) 5 *German Law Journal* 1107.

Scobbie, I, 'Words My Mother Never Taught Me: In Defence of the International Court' (2005) 99 *American Journal of International Law* 76.

Shah, N, 'Self-Defence, Anticipatory Self-Defence and Pre-emption: International Law's Response to Terrorism' (2007) 12 *Journal of Conflict and Security Law* 95.

Smith, AM, 'Judicial Nationalism in International Law: National Identity and Judicial Autonomy at the ICJ' (2004–05) 40 *Texas International Law Journal* 197.

Sofaer, AD, 'On the Necessity of Pre-emption' (2003) 14 *European Journal of International Law* 209.

Stevenson, JR, 'The World Court: Remarks' (1986) 80 *American Society of International Law Proceedings* 201.

Suh, IR, 'Voting Behaviour of National Judges in International Courts' (1969) 63 *American Journal of International Law* 224.

Taft IV, WH, 'Self-Defence and the *Oil Platforms* Decision' (2004) 29 *Yale Journal of International Law* 295.

Tanaka, K, 'The Character of World Law in the International Court of Justice' (1971) 15 *Japanese Annual of International Law* 1.

Thirlway, H, 'The Drafting of ICJ Decisions: Some Personal Reflections and Observations' (2006) 5 *Chinese Journal of International Law* 15.

Trahan, J, 'Defining Aggression: Why the Preparatory Commission for the International Criminal Court Has Faced Such a Conundrum' (2002) 24 *Loyola of Los Angeles International & Comparative Law Review* 448.

Trapp, KN, 'Back to Basics: Necessity, Proportionality and the Right of Self-Defence against Non-state Terrorist Actors' (2007) 56 *International and Comparative Law Quarterly* 141.

Travalio, GM, 'Terrorism, International Law, and the Use of Military Force' (2000) 18 *Wisconsin International Law Journal* 145.

Tsagourias, N, 'The *Nicaragua* Case and the Use of Force: The Theoretical Construction of the Decision and its Deconstruction' (1996) 1 *Journal of Conflict and Security Law* 81.

Tucker, RW, 'Reprisals and Self-Defence: the Customary Law' (1972) 66 *American Journal of International Law* 586.

Wald, PM, 'Running the Trial of the Century: The Nuremberg Legacy' (2005–06) 27 *Cardozo Law Review* 1559.

Waldock, CHM, 'The Regulation of the Use of Force by Individual States in International Law' (1998) 81 *Recueil Des Cours* 455.

Wedgwood, R, 'The ICJ Advisory Opinion on the Israeli Security Fence and the Limits of Self-Defence' (2005) 99 *American Journal of International Law* 52.

——, 'Proportionality and Necessity in American National Security Decision Making' (1992) 86 *American Society of International Law Proceedings* 58.

——, 'Responding to Terrorism: Strikes against bin Laden' (1999) 24 *Yale Journal of International Law* 559.

——, 'The Use of Armed Force in International Affairs: Self-Defence and the Panama Invasion' (1991) 29 *Columbia Journal of Transnational Law* 609.

Wingfield, TC, 'Forcible Protection of Nationals Abroad' (1999–2000) 104 *Dickinson Law Review* 447.

Wigmore, JH, 'The Case of Italy v Greece under International Law and the Pact of Nations' (1923–24) 18 *Illinois Law Review* 131.

Willard, AR, 'Incidents: An Essay in Method' (1984–85) 10 *Yale Journal of International Law* 21.

Yoo, J, 'International Law and the War in Iraq' (2003) 97 *American Journal of International Law* 563.

Young, SM, 'Destruction of Property (on an International Scale): The Recent *Oil Platforms* Case and the International Court of Justice's Inconsistent Commentary on the Use of Force by the United States' (2004–05) 30 *North Carolina Journal of International Law and Commercial Regulation* 335.

Zedalis, RJ, 'Protection of Nationals Abroad: Is Consent the Basis of Legal Obligation?' (1990) 25 *Texas International Law Journal* 209.

Index